let a

SIMILE

be your

umbrella

Other Books by William Safire

let a
SIMILE
be your
umbrella

WILLIAM
SAFIRE

*Illustrations by
Terry Allen*

Crown Publishers
New York

Grateful acknowledgment is made to the *New York Times* for permission to reprint "On Language" columns by William Safire. Copyright © The New York Times Company. Reprinted by permission.

Published by Crown Publishers, New York, New York.
Member of the Crown Publishing Group.

Random House, Inc. New York, Toronto, London, Sydney, Auckland
www.randomhouse.com

CROWN is a trademark and the Crown colophon is a registered trademark of Random House, Inc.

Printed in the United States of America

Design by Elina D. Nudelman

Library of Congress Cataloging-in-Publication Data

Safire, William,
    Let a simile be your umbrella/by William Safire; illustrations by Terry Allen.—1st ed.
    Collection taken from the author's On Language column.
    1. English language—Usage.   2. English language—Style.
I. Title.
PE1421.S227 2001
428—dc21   2001042151

ISBN 0-609-60947-5

10 9 8 7 6 5 4 3 2 1

First Edition

For Karen Hirschfield Safire

"To me no cause is lost, no level the right level, no smooth ride as valuable as a rough ride, no like *interchangeable with* as, *and no ball game anything but chaotic if it lacks a mound, a box, bases, and foul lines. . . . And any attempt to tamper with this prickly design will get nobody nowhere fast."*

—E.B. White to his publisher

Introduction

The waiter asked, "Would you like a bibb lettuce salad?"

My lunch guest, Frederic Cassidy of the *Dictionary of American Regional English (DARE)*, nodded yes. Then the great lexicographer looked off into the distance and said, "I wonder who Bibb was."

We discussed the possibilities. Could it be a person named Bibb who sold a small, dark green lettuce with especially tender leaves? Or, not eponymous, the noun could be related to the piece of cloth tied under a child's chin to catch dripping food, which, when topped by lace and tucked under the chin of ladies, is enshrined in the phrase *best bib and tucker*. Was there some connection to the Latin *bibere*, "to drink," source of *imbibe*, "to absorb fluids," which would describe the use of a baby's *bib*—and *bibulous*, "tipsy," which might suggest an alcoholic beverage to wash down a salad? That reminded us to order a glass of wine, and we went on to fresh speculations.

Cassidy's mind was like that, delightedly examining the origins of words and phrases that most users of the language accept without thinking. He liked archaisms too: "Let me know if the next volume of *DARE* doesn't reach you next week, and I shall snib the publisher." Was *snib*, I asked, a variant of *snub*? "Sorry—a Chaucerian word slipped out," he replied. "Means 'to rebuke sharply,' I suppose related to *snub* in the Scandinavian. Don't you think a word like that deserves revival?"

The Jamaican-born Cassidy, who died on June 14, 2000, at 92 while still hard at work on the final volumes of his great dictionary, never snibbed anybody. Though an intensely purposeful scholar, he was a gentle soul whose love of the dialects and colorful metaphors of the American language was contagious. I have been an unabashed *shill* (slang origin in "gambler's decoy," now meaning "pitchman") for the University of Wisconsin's *DARE* for nearly two decades because Fred's organized wonderment made me a believer.

He was the master of the whatdyacallit question, asked by teams of interviewers in the furthest reaches of urban and rural America. This led to an understanding of patterns of usage by region. If you're hungry for a *hoagie*, you're probably in Pennsylvania or New Jersey; all along the Atlantic Coast, you ask for a *sub*; if you're in New England, you demand a *grinder*, in New York a *hero*, in Louisiana a *po'boy* and a *torpedo* all over.

(In New York City, this can be washed down with a *two cents plain*, which is straight soda water, also called *seltzer* and in expensive bars *sparkling water*; with chocolate syrup added, it becomes a *chawklit phosphate*, and with milk added to that, an *egg cream*. DARE is the only dictionary to report authoritatively, from the mouth of a delicatessen owner, that an *egg cream* contains neither egg nor cream.)

Whatdyacall those little accumulations of dust under the bed? In the Northeast, it's *kitten fur* and *pussy willows*; in the Midwest, it's *dust bunnies* and *dustballs*; up toward Illinois, it's *goose feathers*; and in Pennsylvania, *woolies*. There are scattered entries for *bunny tails, cussywops, fooskies, woozies, house moss* and *midnight fuzz*.

Cassidy sent his interviewers out to ask pedestrians: What is it you do to save steps by crossing a square diagonally?

The "national" answers were *cut across* and go *kitty-corner*. That last has nothing to do with felines; *catty-corner* and variants *catty-bias, catty-cue* and *catty-godlin* are rooted in the French *quatre*, part of "four corners." Americans in the South and West added the suffix *-wampus*, which led, said Fred, "to *catawampus* and its huge brood: *catty-wamp, kitty-wamp*, even *canky-wampus*."

In Minnesota, they *angle across*; Missourians *cut cabbages*; Texans *jayhawg*, Marylanders *walk bias acrost* and North Carolinians *take a nigh cut*. New Englanders are not likely to understand the Southern *antigogglin'*. "The older sense of *gogglin'* refers to eyes that squint; people who squint don't see things straight. They get things crooked, or *antigogglin'*."

When I looked *slaunchwise* at him, he looked back at me *skewhiffy* and allowed himself to philosophize: "Nobody wants to go straight all the time. To describe the unstraight, everyday things, we seem to feel a need for more lively language. As long as we're going to be crooked or diagonal, why not make it *keywampus*?"

The spoken voice was more valuable to him than the written citation. Example: In 1991, as President Bush was about to decide to end pursuit of Saddam Hussein's forces in Iraq, Gen. Colin Powell was asked to call Gen. Norman Schwarzkopf to see if he agreed. An eyewitness, Marlin Fitzwater, the White House press secretary, reported that Powell used the hotline to Riyadh and told the president, "Norm says he can handle it." Question to the dialect lexicographer: What does *I can handle it* mean?

"Print hides the voice," said Cassidy. "One meaning is 'I can control something that needs control.' A quite different meaning, indicated by inflection, is 'This hurts my pride, dignity, sense of what I deserve, but I can accept it and not let my feelings show.'" Or, as has been noted from the dawn of dialectology, it ain't what you say, it's the way that you say it.

What next for *DARE*? Cassidy's baton will be picked up by his longtime top editor, Joan Houston Hall, and philanthropists who want to preserve our cultural heritage should contribute to Cassidy *DARE* Fund, U. of Wisconsin, Madison, Wis., 53706. Volume IV, letters P to Sm, will be coming out in late 2002. Each volume has cost $75; if your local librarian doesn't have them, look *skewhiffy* at him.

And on the subject of lettuce, Fred Cassidy, following his wonderment, would inform you that a leading American horticulturist of the 19th century was Major John Bibb.

Adultery and Fraternization

Every scandal has its own lexicon. There stood Kelly Flinn, Air Force first lieutenant, pioneer female B-52 pilot, accused of *adultery* and its coverup.

"How can they accuse her of *adultery*?" asked a colleague. "She's single. The married guy was the *adulterer*."

Yes and no. The noun *adultery*, which appeared in Chaucer's *Canterbury Tales*, comes from the Latin verb *adulterare*, "to corrupt," from which we also get *adulterate*. (It's not the root of *adult*; that's from *adultus*, past participle of *adolescere*, "to grow up.")

The word is poetically defined by the *O.E.D.* as "violation of the marriage bed." Other dictionaries use variations of "voluntary sexual intercourse between a married person and someone not his or her spouse." In general speech, *adultery* is "an extramarital affair" or, more informally, "playin' around"; in politics, the candidate so playing is said to have "a zipper problem."

"Whosoever looketh on a woman to lust after her hath committed *adulterie*," reads a 1590 translation of Matthew 5:28. But the act lost its male identity and was dramatized by Nathaniel Hawthorne in his 1850 novel, *The Scarlet Letter*; the "A" for *adultery* was "embroidered and illuminated" on Hester Prynne's bosom as a punishment.

Under most religious law, the married participant is an *adulterer* and the single one merely a *fornicator*. Under the old common-law rule, however, "both participants commit *adultery* if the married participant is a woman," Bryan Garner, editor of *Black's Law Dictionary*, tells me. "But if the woman is the unmarried one, both participants are fornicators, not *adulterers*." Seems unfair; why? "This rule is premised on whether there is a possibility of *adulterating* the blood within a family. Offspring from *adulterous* unions were called *adulterism*."

What do courts say today? "Under modern statutory law," Garner says, "some courts hold that the unmarried participant is not guilty of *adultery* (that only the married participant is), but others hold that both participants are *adulterers*." *The Armed Services Manual for Courts-Martial*, Article 134, "*Adultery*," says that the act has occurred when sexual intercourse has taken place and "the accused person or the other person was married to someone else."

Both participants in an *adulterous* relationship have come to be understood as engaging in *adultery*, no matter which one is married. When *adulterer* or the less common *adulteress* is used, however, it usually identifies a married participant. Nobody calls the kids *adulterini* anymore.

All clear? To move on: Lieutenant Flinn was also charged with *fraternization*. Coined in 1611, the verb *fraternize* meant "to agree as brothers," from the

Latin *frater*, "brother." In Italy in 1851, the noun was pejorative: "a *fraterniza-tion* . . . with the dreaded foreign soldiery." But in 1897, George Bernard Shaw saw it as a verb of peace: "The whole army might . . . realize that they had no quarrel with the enemy and *fraternize* with them."

During the occupation of Germany after World War II, as the cold war with the Soviet Union began, the U.S. military and the diplomatic corps issued reg-ulations against *fraternization* with "locals" of the opposite sex. There was to be no "sleeping with the enemy."

In today's sexually integrated armed forces, *fraternize* has developed a new sense. Here's the Air Force regulation: "Unprofessional relationships, espe-cially *fraternization*, erode good order, discipline, respect for authority," etc.

The linguistic problem, long ignored, presses upon us: can women engage in *fraternization*, either with men or with each other? (We're not talking about brotherly love here.) Will the armed services have to amend their manuals to reflect *fraternization* or *sororization*? The gender-language police are letting down the side.

In that regard, what about the designation *Airman*? Lieutenant Flinn had an affair with a civilian soccer coach married to *Airman* Gayle Rigo. *Airman* is masculine, like *fireman* (now *firefighter*) or *policeman* (now *police officer*) or *garbageman* (now *waste disposal and recycling manager*).

Using *-person* to replace *-man* strained to affect equality and is on the wane; *chairperson*, for example, has given way to *chair* or the sex-specific *chairwoman*. Many female press aides, after a flirtation with *spokesperson*, have come around to *spokeswoman*, which has the advantage of linguistic clarity. I can see it now: "A *spokeswoman* for *Airwoman* Shirley Ujest today announced she would fight the charges of *sororization*. . . ."

Aha!

The problem facing the assembled editors of the *New York Times* in early 1979 was brow-furrowing: what kind of column could be created for the front of the magazine that would *seem* to be right on top of the news, as if written for the daily paper, but could be written a couple of weeks ahead to conform to the longer lead time of the color-paged magazine?

A. M. Rosenthal, then merely executive editor (before his elevation to columnist), suddenly remembered that the world's only political lexicogra-pher was on the payroll and snapped his fingers: *"Eureka!"* he cried, explaining to the others, "That's Greek for 'I've found it.' Safire will do a column about words. Could be sustained for a year, maybe."

That was 18 years ago. My introductory column was about the punctuation of "How do you do" (no question mark required when construed as a statement rather than a question), rather than the etymology of *Eureka!*, the exclamation attributed to the Greek scientist Archimedes when he discovered the way to determine the purity of gold.

Forget about *eureka!*; only classicist editors use it in everyday speech. Today, the word breathed when a lightbulb goes off in an inventor's head, or when some great insight flashes through a discoverer's mind, is *Aha!*

Aha!—an exclamation properly followed by an exclamation mark, that spelling now preferable to *A-hah!*—is one of the great, unappreciated and deliciously nuanced words in the English language.

Chaucer was the first to write it down. In *The Canterbury Tales* (1380s), he wrote: "They crieden, out! . . . *A ha* the fox! and after him they ran." Shakespeare in 1600 had Hamlet say to Horatio: "*Ah, ha!* Come, some music." By 1611, the translators of the King James Bible made one word of it in rendering Isaiah 44:16: "He warmeth himself, and saith, *Aha*, I am warm."

But what has the favorite exclamation of palindromists come to mean? A book by Jordan Ayan is titled *"Aha!"* its heuristic sense found in the subtitle "101 Ways to Free Your Creative Spirit and Find Your Great Ideas." But *aha!* does not always mean *eureka!* Robert Young, in his 1936 biblical concordance, found it three times in Ezekiel, transliterated from the Hebrew *heach*, and defined it with a nice twist: "malicious joy."

That's the "Gotcha!" sense, pulsing with savage glee through so many of my correspondents when finding me in error. Robert Clarke Brown of New York noted my use of "plunging meteorite" and explained that "a *meteoroid* leaves outer space, plunges through the earth's atmosphere leaving a *meteor* visible in the sky and strikes the earth, becoming a *meteorite.*" As he wrote this, catching the language maven in a blatant imprecision, undoubtedly the sly thrill of *aha!* surged through his mind. (*Aha!* yourself: Isn't *Earth* capitalized when referring to the planet? No, not usually; Mr. Brown is correct in using the lowercase. Ours is the only planet not capitalized, presumably because earthlings are modest. Withdraw my *aha!*)

That is not the only other sense of this rich exclamation. I can hear, in my mind's ear, the actor Lou Jacobi, in Neil Simon's first play, *Come Blow Your Horn* (1957), saying the word in a combination of triumph and derision. *Aha!* Why not ask Neil Simon himself for his definition? I did.

"*Aha!* So I've been asked to help contribute to your column," replies Mr. Simon. "In this case *aha!* meaning—A) I am surprised. B) So you finally asked me. C) Wait till I show this to my friends.

"*Aha!* is also stalling for time when someone makes a statement you don't understand but pretend to.

"*Aha!* is also said sarcastically to your daughter when she says she came home at 11:00 last night when you know it was 12:15.

"*Aha!* can be a response," continues the great playwright-synonymist, "when you know something but find it unnecessary to share, as for example, Sherlock Holmes picking up an object and exclaiming, '*Aha!*' to which Watson asks, 'What is it, Holmes?' 'I'll let you know when we get to Blenheim Castle. Quickly, Watson. To Victoria Station.'

"*Aha!* can also mean quite simply, when you finally think you know what life is about. And lastly," Simon concludes, "*Aha!* can be the first half of an incompleted sneeze."

How could you not mention the timeless tale (quoted below from *The Joys of Yinglish* by Leo Rosten, Plume Publishing, 1990, p. 22) that is the quintessential definition of Jewish humor?

For twenty years Mr. Rabinowitz had been eating at the same restaurant on Second Avenue. On this night, as on every other, Mr. Rabinowitz ordered chicken soup.

The waiter set it down and started off. Mr. Rabinowitz called, "Waiter! Eh-eh!"

"Yeah?"

"Taste this soup."

The waiter said, "*Hanh?* Twenty years you've been eating the chicken soup here, no? Have you ever had a bad plate—?"

"Waiter," said Rabinowitz firmly, "taste the soup."

"Listen, Mr. Rabinowitz, what's gotten into you?!"

"I said, 'Taste the soup!' *I'm* the customer, you're the waiter. You *are* supposed to please *me.* Taste the soup!"

"All right, all right," grimaced the waiter. "I'll taste—where's the spoon?"

"*Aha!*" cried Rabinowitz.

Alan A. Mazurek, M.D.
Great Neck, New York

And Above

In the extended negotiations between Bosnian Muslims and Serbs to lift the siege of Sarajevo, an agreement was reached and signed to remove guns "above 100 mm." The bone-weary American envoy, Richard Holbrooke, was pleased at what he considered a historic breakthrough—until an American general pointed out to him that what was required was the removal of "100 mm. and above."

What was the difference? Only some 250 of the 700 heavy weapons in the hills surrounding the city. Holbrooke went back to the Serbs and explained that what was meant was not "above" before the size but "and above" after it. Agreement to the change was elicited from Gen. Ratko Mladic, in a hospital suffering from kidney stones (which included the type of pain many of his victims wished on him). When he allowed the switch of the two words, the agreement went into effect. Words, even little ones, count.

And Also as Well, Too

"What is your opinion of Tom Brokaw's use of *as well* in lieu of *also*?" asks T. H. Scarbrough of Water Valley, Miss. (That's how you abbreviate *Mississippi*, and not MS, a coinage of Gloria Steinem.) "He always says, 'The Nasdaq was up *as well*.'"

Gee; that never bothered me, especially when it was going up. *Also* and *as well* are adverbs, and are synonymous—both meaning "in addition" and "too." But if you take a dive into syntax—that mysterious programming inside our heads that makes natives out of speakers—you will note a difference.

John Algeo, the neologism expert for American Speech, notes that the difference is "one of restricted privilege of occurrence." *Also* can go just about anywhere in a sentence; *as well* cannot. "*Also* looks in both directions," says Professor Algeo, "whereas *as well* is only retrospective or regressive."

Let's try it: "Jack Kemp also supports the flat tax." "Also, Jack Kemp supports the flat tax." "Jack Kemp supports the flat tax also." The placement affects the meaning, but the *also* fits naturally everywhere. Now go try that with *as well*: it fits everywhere except in front; nobody, not even Steve Forbes, would say, "*As well*, Jack Kemp supports my flat tax." Nor would you say, "Jack Kemp is *as well* supporting the flat tax." It must follow the focused-on word or phrase, not precede it: "Jack Kemp *as well* supports the flat tax" if you're emphasizing the supporter, and "Jack Kemp supports the flat tax *as well*" if you're emphasizing the range of positions the supporter supports.

That's not my rule; that's not the dead hand of some grammarian telling you what's correct; that's your internal voice of syntax, sometimes stronger than your conscience, telling you, "*As well* always comes behind the word it focuses on." Even poor little kids who much prefer a progressive tax code know that.

A related subject: now that we know that *also* goes anywhere, should you start a sentence with it? Good grammar is not always good style; I would use *also* as a sentence adverb only if I wanted to give the impression of an afterthought. "Jack's a great guy. Also, he supports the flat tax." Also, Prof. Dennis

Baron at the University of Illinois in Urbana says, "I hate it when people start sentences with *too,* though it is a common and accepted practice."

If you want to add an afterthought but not make it seem like an also-ran, use *besides.* Front or back.

There is more subtlety to "as well" than your comment on this adverb. The following anecdote about Lord Birkenhead (F. E. Smith; 1874–1930), Lord Chancellor in the 1920s, may show another dimension to the term:

Birkenhead discovered the Athenaeum Club and got in the habit, whenever he was in the Pall Mall, of going there to use the facilities [i.e., toilet]. Eventually a member challenged him, saying, "Are you aware, Lord Birkenhead, that this is a private club?" "Oh," answered Birkenhead, "is it a club as well?"

Of course Birkenhead knew perfectly well that the Athenaeum was a club (even Lord Chancellors are not that stupid), so the "as well," which must always end a sentence, appears to carry an implication of paradox, perhaps irony as well.

The story seems to date from the 1920s, since Smith was ennobled in 1919.

Paul J. Korshin
Philadelphia, Pennsylvania

When we were last in Ireland, in 1993, I noticed that people would begin sentences "as well. . . ." I recall a cooking program on television where the chef told us that an herb was especially good for flavoring, then added, "As well, it is good for the digestion."

Paul A. Lacey
Richmond, Indiana

Arklatex Nugget

The Whitewater case is producing locutions as well as prosecutions. Joe Pinder of Washington sends along an article from the *Washington Times,* filed from Little Rock, Ark., by Hugh Aynesworth. In it, the assistant independent counsel, Jackie M. Bennett, asked an investment partner of Jim Guy Tucker, then Governor of Arkansas, "Would it be fair to say that Governor Tucker kind of *rolled your pant leg up* on that one, didn't he?" The witness, R. D. Randolph, glumly replied, "I came out on the short end of the stick."

The *short end of the stick,* which first appeared in print in the mid-1800s, refers to the old custom of fighting with sticks or staffs; whoever holds the *short end* is at a disadvantage. Less familiar is *rolled up your pant leg,* which, according to Aynesworth, means "saw what you had, looked at your hand—it's Arklatexan, colloquial for this area, meaning 'took advantage of.'"

He referred me to Guy Bailey, a native of Oklahoma, now dean of liberal arts at the University of Nevada at Las Vegas, familiar with idioms of Oklahoma and the Arklatex region (southwestern Arkansas, northwestern Louisiana and northeastern Texas). Dean Bailey directed me to the song "Deep Elm Blues" (the *elm* is pronounced (ELL-um), recorded by the Shelton Brothers, from northern Louisiana, in the early 1930s.

"When Dallas was becoming the first urban community of the Southwest in the late '20s," says Dean Bailey, "folks were drawn there to have a good time. The song alerted them to the evils of the big city and advised them to protect themselves while there. It warned them of what could happen to careless country people."

The telltale lyric: "Now when you go down in Deep Elm, put your money in your socks/Or the women in Deep Elm, well, they'll put you on the rocks."

And how do you get the money out of the poor innocent's socks? First you roll up his pant leg.

Delicious dialectical discovery. Who says Whitewater is a waste of taxpayers' money?

You opined that the phrase "the short end of the stick" derived from the old custom of fighting with sticks or staffs, so that whoever held the shorter of the sticks was at a disadvantage. Another, and in my opinion, more likely, source for this phrase, since it seems to have originated in the United States, is the explanation given in connection with a display of mid-nineteenth century artifacts in the old courthouse museum in Vicksburg, Mississippi. There are displayed various devices for removing felled timber from the forests which populate the area. One such device consists of two stout poles carried by two men each, with a felled log resting on each of the poles so that the men carry the log much as stretcher bearers carry a stretcher. If the log were not centered from side to side and one man thereby bore a disproportionate amount of the weight, he was said to be getting "the short end of the stick." This derivation sounds far more plausible to a southerner like me since 19th century Americans were more given to fighting with fists, pistols and knives than with sticks or staffs.

Donald F. Wiseman
Memphis, Tennessee

I've got to question the "short end of the stick" derivation, which you proposed without citing authority. If it's a fight, wouldn't it be "short stick"? The "end" portion doesn't make a great deal of sense. Then again, as you are wont to say, Idioms is idioms.

Other alternative: consider baseball, where two players on opposing teams grab it and go hand over hand to decide some issue (such as who is first at bats—at least that's what I did as a kid). Or, "drawing straws." But with neither of these does the "end" make much sense, nor does it justify the means.

Gary Muldoon
Rochester, New York

As We Know It

"Ending the IRS *as we know it*" was a centerpiece of Bob Dole's economic plan, later driven home in his acceptance address with "You will have a President who will end the IRS *as we know it.*"

This was, of course, a play on Bill Clinton's pledge, made in his 1992 acceptance speech and carried out as his re-election campaign began in 1996, to "end welfare *as we know it,*" and repeated mockingly by Republicans in Congress as he vetoed their first two efforts to pass welfare-reform legislation.

"Many people heard only the first two words: end welfare," wrote Jason DeParle in the *New York Times Magazine* about that '92 promise, "but Mr. Clinton was mindful of the *as-we-know-it* qualifier. He was talking about new training programs, expanded child care, universal health care."

The earliest use I can find applying the qualifier *as we know it (AWKI)* specifically to welfare was by David Stockman, before his term as the frequently woodshedded Reagan budget chief, in 1978: "Welfare *as we know it* should be abolished," he asserted in an article for an economics journal, "for all but the nonworking—the aged, blind and disabled—whose eligibility can be ascertained by reference to physical characteristics."

We have come to know *as we know it* all too well. In *Independence Day* (the movie blowing up the White House, not the Pulitzer Prize-winning novel about a real-estate salesman's rites of passage), a computer expert persuaded a fictional U.S. President not to employ nuclear missiles against the Martian spaceships hovering over Earth, warning that it would mean "the end of life *as we now know it.*" The rock group R.E.M. (the initials stand for "rapid eye movements" that take place in sleep) recorded a song in 1987 titled "It's the End of the World *As We Know It* (And I Feel Fine)."

AWKI originally meant "as it is understood today," then was used as an intensifier, then (in Mr. Clinton's case) as a qualifier and often—as it gained cliché status—as a self-mocking dramatizer.

What was it before we knew it? In tracking back the source, before *welfare, life* and *the world* came *civilization.* Elizabeth Knowles of Oxford University Press cites Orson Welles, in his 1941 *Citizen Kane,* proclaiming: "I've talked with the responsible leaders of the Great Powers. . . . They're too intelligent to embark on a project which would mean the end of *civilization as we now know it."*

The screenwriter Herman J. Mankiewicz popularized, if he did not coin, that use of the phrase. More than half a century later, it is used with a tongue-in-cheek connotation: reviewing a $24-dreadful thriller, *Triangle of Death,* by Michael Levine and Laura Kavanau, in a recent *New York Times Book Review,* Colin Harrison refers to a fictional genetically engineered drug that simulates a 20-minute orgasm and wryly notes, "Such a drug would no doubt imperil morally upright *civilization as we know it."*

The hawkshaws of the Phrasedick Brigade led me to an early etymological source.

When I queried the American Dialect Society's bulletin board on the Internet (send queries to ads-1@uga.cc.uga.edu, and subscription inquiries to list-serv@uga.cc.uga.edu), a writer on gardening, Duane Campbell, dug up and sent back a citation from Oscar Wilde's essay "The Decay of Lying," in his 1891 book, *Intentions,* in which a character says, "The 19th century, *as we know it,* is largely an invention of Balzac." (You didn't think this laid-back language maven was hip enough to use this resource? You thought I was computer-illiterate? Better not nuke them Martians, Mr. President.)

Pretty soon the cliché will wear out, phrase makers will turn to fresher material and that happy day will spell the end of *as we know it* as we know it.

Been There. Done That.

The headline over an Op-Ed column by Maureen Dowd in the *New York Times* about the reappearance and disappearance of the campaign aide Mary Matalin from Republican politics read, *"Been There, Done That."*

A few days later, Playboy's founder, Hugh Hefner, was quoted in *U.S. News & World Report* about giving up his freewheeling life style at 70: "Once you can say, *'been there, done that,'* it becomes kind of pointless doing it over and over again."

In a now-classic monologue at the Radio-TV Correspondents' dinner in Washington, the radio "shock jock" Don Imus made sport of President Clinton's half-brother Roger with "If we were to have speculated on which member of the First Family would be the first . . . to receive a subpoena, everybody in this room would have picked Roger. I mean, *been there, done that.*"

To Charles L. Knapp, a professor of contract law at New York University, the phrase that has become a rage raises a handful of basic journalism questions: "*Who* was there first? *Where* were they? *What* did they do there? *When,* and *why?*"

The data banks are of no use in tracking the origin of this ubiquitous phrase because its words are too common to be "searchable." Yet in the vocabulary of world-weariness, the phrase has surpassed *same-o, same-o,* so I ran the traps of etymon-hunters in the Phrasedick Brigade.

"Somewhere in the dim, dark recesses of my tiny memory," reports David K. Barnhart of Lexik House Publishers in Cold Spring, N.Y., "I recall the expression *'been there, done that, have the T-shirt, won the trophy.'*" He attaches a page from *The MacQuarie Dictionary of New Words,* from Australia, defining the four words as "a phrase indicating familiarity with some activity to the point of boredom." MacQuarie cites from what seems to be a movie review in the Oct. 21, 1983, *Union Recorder,* from the University of Sydney: "We've *been there done that.*"

In the Winter 1995 issue of *American Speech,* the great language quarterly, John and Adele Algeo define the term as "an expression of prior experience, sometimes with an implication of boredom or reluctance to repeat it." They include this 1994 explanation by Linda Shrieves in the *Orlando Sentinel:* "The term may have originated in California five years ago, but it has only recently begun to become part of the East Coast lingo—thanks, in part, to a television commercial for Diet Mountain Dew."

Been there, done that, with its prior use from Down Under, was indeed popularized by the soft drink sold by the Pepsi-Cola company. William Bruce, senior creative director of BBDO (formerly BBD&O, even more formerly Batten, Barton, Durstine & Osborn), the ad agency responsible for the 1993 Diet Mountain Dew campaign, recalls: "We started with an ad picturing a guy making a base jump with a parachute off the rim of the Grand Canyon, followed by four grunge-type guys saying: 'Did it. Done it. Been there. Tried that.' The idea was 'So what?' A later ad showed a James Bond type saying, 'Child's play,' the same idea of boredom with other things."

To recap where we have been and what we have done: we have the first printed use (so far), and the way it was widely disseminated in the United States. Now to origins. What was the predecessor phrase?

Tom Dalzell, a slang expert in Berkeley, Calif., pored over his extensive language library and found *been and gone and done it,* a popular catch phrase in Britain in the late-19th and early-20th centuries. In Eric Partridge's *Dictionary of Catch Phrases,* P. G. Wodehouse was cited using that older form in a 1903 pre-Jeeves novel: "Captain Kettle had, in the expressive language of the man in the street, *been and gone and done it."* Partridge compared this with Caesar's *Veni, vidi, vici,* "I came, I saw, I conquered," but that triumphant laconic cry is far from the blasé sense of *been there, done that* today. In the mid-1800's, *seen the elephant* was used to express supreme indifference, a clip of "I've been around the world and seen something as exotic as an elephant; therefore, what you say does not impress me."

The immediate predecessor of *been there, done that,* which combines past participles with an adverb and a pronoun, lingers as a kind of competitor in the bible of the blasé: *same old, same old.* In John Guare's 1992 play, *Four Baboons Adoring the Sun,* a character's dissatisfaction with middle-class life is expressed with "We're tired of being the *same old same old* people." In a *New York Times* article by Robert Suro that appeared about the same time, a Texas voter said, "Somebody has got to decide where this country is going, instead of giving us the *same old same old."* An earlier citation, provided by Frederick Mish of Merriam-Webster, is from a 1988 *Rolling Stone* article about a 1967 Buffalo Springfield song by Stephen Stills, "For What It's Worth" (with its familiar refrain "Stop! Hey, what's that sound?"): "And what of the song's applicability to events of the present day? *'Same old, same old,'* Stills says, chuckling."

Thanks to Jesse Sheidlower, formerly of Random House (the troops really turned out on this), we have a use in W. D. Lasly's 1956 Korean War novel, *Turn Tigers Loose,* in which a character says, *"Same-oh, same-oh."* And in the 1970 play *Jello* by the poet Imamu Amiri Baraka, formerly known as LeRoi Jones, a more Westernized clip occurs: *"Same ol same ol."*

The repetition makes the phrase sing; searching for origins in an unrepeated state, one thinks of the Army expression *S.O.S.,* which referred not only to the initialized derogation of creamed chipped beef on toast, but also to *same old stuff* (a bowdlerized form).

One thing about today's on-line ennui: its staccato vocabulary is not bor-ing (hyphenated to make it more boring).

The xerographic copy enclosed shows a printing of the relevant phrase "Go there, do that," which antedates the 1983 October 21 reference in yesterday's column. It is a copy of a flight bag from a tour to Australia and Papua New Guinea which departed on 1983 May 21.

As appropriate for an agency in the tour business it is in the imperative rather than the past tense, but obviously the phrase was current then and I'm sure that an earlier example will turn up from down under. (I have seen sentences end with more prepositions, but they were trying.)

Edward P. Wallner
Wayland, Massachusetts

When I was in Korea in 1953, "same-O, same-O" had great currency as a response to "How's it going?", or some such greeting, and meant "the same old shit." It was derived, though, from the pidgin-English preferred by G.I.s in discourse with indigenous folk anywhere in the Orient. G.I.s repeated words and added a vowel to the ends of words or phrases to simulate the sing-song sound attributed to any Asian tongue, thus supposedly making English easier for them. A barracksmate of mine once told our Korean houseboy, "you washy-washy clothes, bring back here," and happily explained to me he was "teaching the kid English." I said, "Why don't you just tell him to 'do the laundry'?" He looked at me and, perfectly straight, said, "He wouldn't understand that."

Samuel W. Gelfman
Los Angeles, California

When I was growing up in London in the late '30s, early '40s, *"been and gone and done it,"* had nothing whatsoever to do with Caesar's *"Veni, vidi, vici."* It meant *"Now, look what you've done!"* yelled, shouted, or screamed, in impeccable Cockney English, to or by us, as the result of some kind of disaster or injury, to or by us. *"Nah, yer've bin 'n gon 'n dun it!"* to which was added: *"Nah yer ginna ge'(t)."*

It's been a long time—I can hear it in my head, but I'm not sure how to write it!

Eileen C. Prinsen
Dearborn, Michigan

Behind the Title

The quondam Clinton adviser Dick Morris (he doesn't use "Richard"; I don't use "former") has titled the memoir of his rise and fall *Behind the Oval Office*.

What bothers me about this book, written and published in jig time, is not that it is unabashedly self-serving and manipulative—there's a certain honesty about that—but it is the title itself.

Does it mean "Behind the closed door of the Oval Office"? A popular song and a television show during and soon after the Nixon Administration was "Behind Closed Doors," and that word-picture of activity hidden from public view is grammatically sound.

Does *Behind the Oval Office* mean "the true story of what goes on inside the Oval Office"? If so, a more apt title would be *Inside the Oval Office*, but perhaps the ghost of John Gunther has dibs on that.

Does it mean "the untold story of winning the right to occupy the Oval Office after a stunning setback in 1994"? If so, the title could be *Winning Back the Presidency, New Lease on 1600 Pennsylvania Avenue* or the like.

But *Behind the Oval Office* just doesn't work for language lovers, even if it intends to be an ellipsis of "The Man Behind the Man in the Oval Office." Surely the Random House book titlers, abetted by Mr. Morris himself, tested the title on focus groups, but there comes a time when such in-depth marketing studies go too deep.

The only book that would fit that title is by a landscape architect. *Behind the Oval Office* is a real place: it's called the South Lawn. Adjoining it is the Rose Garden, which songsters of the '70s could remind President Clinton and Mr. Morris they were never promised.

Between She and Her

In the Associated Press account of the speech Newt Gingrich gave to the House after being re-elected Speaker, he was quoted praising Robin Carle as clerk: "in the interchanges between she and Chairman Fazio." But when published in the *Congressional Record*, it came out "interchanges between *her* and Chairman Fazio."

The fix was correct: as the object of the preposition *between*, the objective pronoun *her* is called for, not the subjective pronoun *she*.

But between you and *me* (objective, not subjective), who fixed it? Didn't Republicans in the House decide last year to print proceedings verbatim, instead of allowing members to alter and sometimes radically rewrite remarks made on the floor?

Yes, but. The new rule permits "technical, grammatical and typographical corrections"; in this case, the editors of the *Record*—without even telling the Speaker—stepped up and did their duty to the English language. That's as it should be; it's the damnable media that report what was said, grammatical warts and all.

Black Is Back

Headline writers, who search for short words (nobody else uses *decry*), were having fits. In the '80s, *African-American* (15 characters plus a hyphen) had replaced *black* (five characters) as the self-description of preference among leaders of the race that was once called *Negro*, from the Spanish word rooted in the Latin *niger*, meaning "black."

Having established the preferred usage in news media generally unresistant to the change, most African-Americans found the handle to be a mouthful in a linguistic era that tends to shorten long terms. When the Department of Labor surveyed 60,000 households about the names of race and ethnic categories to use in job statistics, *black* was the choice of 44 percent of blacks. Those who preferred *African-American*, added to choosers of the earlier *Afro-American*, totaled 40 percent, an impressive showing for a relatively new designation. (Only 3 percent picked *Negro*, and 9 percent had no preference.)

The Government figures substantiate what language mavens have been hearing and seeing in the '90s: even when the longer term is used on first reference, *black* is the noun of second reference and is almost always used in headlines. It's safe to say that, even among those most sensitive to group preferences about nomenclature, *black* is back.

Meanwhile, in the *Hispanic* community (58 percent in the Labor survey; the term *Spanish-speaking* is politically charged, and was chosen by 12 percent), the newcomer, *Latino*, has been making a move (to 11 percent from a standing start). But the growing usage may hit a glass ceiling: "The difficulty is," writes John T. Rourke, professor of political science at the University of Connecticut, "that two female graduate students tell me that they are not *Latinos*, but *Latinas*. These Latinas contend forcefully that the use of the male *o* to designate all members, male and female, of that group is egregiously sexist."

Here's a thought: former *Cubanos* and *Mexicanos* who live in the United States use the sex-neutral terms "Cuban" and "Mexican" before the hyphen; why not refer to a *Latino* as a "Latin"?

Your column quotes Professor John T. Rourke of the University of Connecticut to the effect that two female Hispanic students find it "egregiously sexist" to refer to them as "Latinos" rather than "Latinas." It is true that each of the students is a Latina, not a Latino. However, the use of the plural *Latinos* to refer to all Latin Americans collectively, regardless of sex, is very much in keeping with Spanish grammar. For example, *hijo* and *hija* are the respective words for "son" and "daughter," but the correct term for a batch of offspring of both sexes is *hijos*. Similarly, *hermano* and *hermana* are the words for "brother" and "sister," but siblings are referred to as *hermanos* even if they are of both sexes. Most astounding of all, *padre* and *madre* mean "father" and "mother" respectively, but the plural *padres* is the word for "parents."

Louis Jay Herman*
New York, New York

*Louis Jay Herman died on May 13, 1996.

"She's a Latin from Manhattan," written in 1935 by Al Dubin and Harry Warren, antecedes your inspired use of the term, evading thereby the "egregiously sexist" and "politically charged" terms decried by some in the Hispanic community.

Notwithstanding the different motivations—yours of thoughtful social significance, theirs, a lighthearted rhyme—it proves there's nothing new under the sun.

Oh yes, to give the term added currency, the great Al Jolson sang it in a snappy tempo in a movie called *Go Into Your Dance.*

Teddy Diamond
New York, New York

Bloopie

Here's the copy in a television commercial from Bayer Aspirin: "Only Genuine Bayer can help save your life when taken regularly."

The problem here is the misplaced modifier. I would have no problem with "Only Genuine Bayer, when taken regularly, can help save your life" (though cheapskates like me think a generic can also do the trick). However, following "life" with "when taken regularly" suggests the copy was prepared by the Kevorkian Advertising Agency. Fix it, please; it's causing grammatical heads to pound.

The Bloopie Awards

Now is the moment for the dread Bloopie Awards, formerly the coveted Bloopie Awards. (And why do we drop the *-ed* from *dreaded?* Because the shorter and simpler *dread* shifted to adjective use in the 14th century.)

First, a note about a disturbing trend: What's the matter with advertising copywriters. What have they got against question marks.

"Who says you can't afford dental insurance," half-asks Crest, which needs to see its interrogator twice a year. Luv's diapers tries the same trick: "Isn't it great to be in Luv's," it says, but does not ask. What's with these guys. Pontiac, on a well-balanced kick of noun-to-verb functional shift, states, "Why just sedan, when you can Grand Am." Mistic advertises its bottled-drink product with "Tastes good, doesn't it." And Snackwell's fat-free cookies assert, "So good, can we ever make enough." Is there a new charge by magazines for the use of question marks. Shouldn't something be done about this before the trend gets out of hand.

And now—push the envelope, please.

The snake-eyes award for state-sponsored grammatical corruption while undermining the morals of minors with a promise of something for nothing goes to New York State's Lotto croupiers for "Tomorrow night, someone could win 6 million of dollars." What illiterate card shark on the public payroll infixed the unnecessary *of?* (Nice to use a question mark again; I was getting a sinking inflection.)

For the financial institution whose name was most likely to go out of date, the Bloopie goes to Twentieth Century Mutual Funds for confusion between number and amount: "When today's 30 year-olds retire, there will be less than two workers per beneficiary." *Fewer* workers, of course, and are the funds dealing with the 30-somethings or with 30 squalling year-olds? Better put a hyphen after the *30;* that hyphen will be needed even in the Twenty-First Century. (And while I'm on this outfit's case, "If you're approaching age 50, and want to enjoy your retirement . . ." won't do. The contraction *you're* cannot also be the subject of *want;* the funds should drop the contraction and use *you are.* Example: "If you are approaching the millennium and want a new name. . . .")

In a related gaffe, a runner-up Blooperette is awarded to the quasi-governmental entity known familiarly as Sallie Mae, which underwrites loans to college students, for its overreaching "Over the past 20 years . . . by helping over 20 million students." The first *over* is O.K., because it is a permissible substitute for "during," but the second *over* flunks: with numbers, like "20 million," the correct form is *more than.*

Funniest stretch of a noun: to Kraft salad dressing, which hyped its creaming ranch with cheese and announced, "Your salads are even *funner." Fun* is acceptable as an adjective, because it seems like an attributive noun in "Writing ad copy is a fun job," but raising the stakes to *funner* should be resisted because it invites confusion with *funnier.* (Handing out the annual Bloopies is, of course, the funnest of all.)

Subjunctive junk bond of the year shared in this triple dead heat: (1) Whirlpool's "Ever wish there was a team of you . . . ?" The subjunctive mood is used to express a condition contrary to fact. Since there is only one of you, no matter what you may wish, it should be "Ever wish there *were* . . . ?" But give the writer credit for a question mark. (2) Ford's "But it wouldn't be the Best-Selling Truck 16 years running if it wasn't built Ford Tough" suggests to subjunctive fans that Fords are not built Ford tough; should be "if it *weren't."* Those truck windows are befogged by (3) Windex, which offers, "How to make a room smell like the windows are always open." When a whole clause—subject and verb—follows a conjunction, *like* is incorrect; it should be *as* or *as if.*

In this case, it should be *as if:* "How to make a room smell as if the windows [hold it—you are now in the subjunctive, because the windows are not really always open] *were* always open."

The fiercely glaring eyes over the bulbous nose of J. Pierpont himself deploring the practices of variant spellers Bloopie to the banking house of J. P. Morgan for "You've just come into a sizeable sum of money." In American English, the preferred spelling is *sizable,* no extra *e.* Because you may get a defense of the variant in some dictionaries, the Bloopie is shared by the United States Postal Service for its stamp of the "Keystone Cops." For visual as well as aural alliteration, these slapstick comedians who cut to wild chases in films from 1912 to 1920 styled themselves the *Keystone Kops,* with two capital *k*'s. (Lucky thing the snail-mailers spelled *Nixon* right.)

The compounded abuse of sentence fragments Bloopie to Kotex Security Tampons for "Smooth and simple outside. Conforms to your body inside." Remember the fumblerule: No sentence fragments. But if you are impelled to leave your sentences in shards, at least observe the rule for parallel construction. "Smooth and simple outside" doesn't have a verb, while "Conforms to your body inside" does. If you began the first one with the verb *Stays,* the two fragments would be parallel.

It's been a banner year for the Comma Bloopie. Donna Karan: "Introducing simply the fastest easiest most gentle and effective cleanser on the face of the earth. Period." Even if you are hooked on fragmentation, as so many ad copywriters are, a list of superlative adjectives must have its entries separated by commas: "fastest, easiest, most gentle and effective." (Most of us capitalize *Earth* when referring to the planet, but maybe the writer had in mind the material for a mudpack.)

Contrariwise, Morton Salt used a comma when none was called for: "Removing ketchup from plush, nylon carpeting." Here, *nylon* is an attributive noun bound to *carpeting;* you would not say *nylon, plush carpeting.* Drop the comma.

The Uofallpeople Bloopie bestowed by dozens of Gotcha! gangsters to an errant language maven for an o-solecism mio: "Recently I was reading, and disagreeing, with a *New York Times editorial* about standards for teaching history."

Shows how important a comma can be. No, you don't need a comma after the sentence adverb *recently;* that comma is considered optional. The first comma is fine, beginning the separation of a verb and its object by a parenthetical phrase. The trouble with the second comma is its placement. *With* belongs in the parenthetical phrase with *disagreeing;* as it now reads, removing that phrase would leave "I was reading with a *New York Times* editorial."

Change that to "Recently I was reading, and disagreeing with, . . ." Copywriters can feel free to read, and disagree with, the strictures herein, but the complainers don't get to put a Bloopie on their mantel.

Whirlpool's "Ever wish there was a team of you . . . ?" demands the subjunctive mode, but *not* because it is a condition contrary to fact. Rather it demands the subjunctive mode because it is an *unfulfilled wish,* as in "I wish I were in Paris," or even "I wish I were an Oscar Meyer wiener."

Thomas C. Hoster
Palo Alto, California

I think you too merit the Uofallpeople Bloopie award for questionable (or worse) use of *Since* to begin a sentence in the paragraph on Subjunctive junk bonds. It seems to me that *As* would have been more appropriate, since it is . . .

T. V. Madhavan
Edison, New Jersey

Nowhere is this banner Comma Bloopie year more apparent than in your column and in the pages of the *NY Times.*

To cite just one of many examples, you write that "you are now in the subjunctive, because the windows are not really open. . . ." That comma after "subjunctive" is dead wrong. The "because" adverbial clause is restrictive in the end-of-the-sentence position. It gets a comma only if the writer disturbs syntax and moves it to the beginning or to the middle of the sentence.

You jump on some poor wretch for a pronoun problem in the sentence "If you're approaching age 50, and want to enjoy your retirement. . . ." However, you do not recognize that the comma after the number "50" is wrong because it separates a compound verb, not a compound sentence. You often fall into this kind of error yourself, Mr. Safire. Such superfluous commas puzzle me because I thought newspapers bent the punctuation rules to save space and would omit this incorrect comma for space economy just as they do not spell out "50" as people writing standard English would do.

If you're wondering whence comes my interest in the comma, I am an English teacher who has labored twenty-five years in the valley of the comma splice. We English teachers take commas seriously and protest their abuse.

Lee Drury De Cesare
Madeira Beach, Florida

You write, "What illiterate card shark on the public payroll infixed the unnecessary of?" It is my understanding it is card sharP (but pool sharK).

John Kendall
Port Angeles, Washington

In the process of rebuking yourself for a bloopie, you committed another one: The verb *bestow* always takes the preposition *on* or *upon*, not *to*.

Louis Jay Herman
New York, New York

Exclamatives

I'm a pop grammarian and word maven who makes no pretense of living in syntax.

Every now and then one of my innocent pitches gets slammed out of the park by a heavy hitter in the field of linguistics. In this year's Bloopie Awards, I noted the trend among advertising copywriters against using question marks at the end of interrogative sentences. One was "Isn't It Great to Be in Luvs," which seemed to me to call for a little squiggle with a dot under it at the end.

Wrong, I'm told. "That slogan is clearly an exclamative sentence and not an interrogative," writes Prof. James D. McCawley* of the University of Chicago's linguistics department, author of the seminal *Syntactic Phenomena of English*.

"While two of the major exclamative patterns in English evolved through the adaptation of interrogative structures to exclamative uses," Jim notes, losing me before he even gets to his sentence's subject, "they now diverge from interrogatives both phonologically (the word with the primary stress, here, *great*, is pronounced with a fall in pitch, not the rise that an interrogative would normally have) and syntactically (the inverted exclamative, as in the Luvs example, allows a use of *ever* that doesn't mean what *ever* in an interrogative means: *Was I ever hungry!* vs. *Have you ever been arrested?*). . . . If the Luvs copywriter had used the question mark that you demand, he/she would have thereby pinned an unwarranted and misleading badge of interrogativity on the sentence."

I disagree; the Luvs ad asked for a response, if only "Yes!" But criticism from geniuses who could give short festschrift to Noam Chomsky doesn't faze me; I am a synstrategist, not a syntactician.

McCawley's insights are also accessible to the layman, however; after an observation about metaphoric inflation in a piece I wrote about "$40 words," he conjectures, "The obsolescence of the expression 'Dollars to doughnuts' is partly due to the narrowing of the gap between $1 and the current price of a doughnut: it no longer is a bet with long odds."

---

*Professor James McCawley died on April 10, 1999.

Bloopie Preview

Ralph Lauren, the designer, is alive and well and not planning to retire.

I hasten to assure his customers of this because of the mail coming in about a recent advertisement: "Introducing Ralph Lauren Purple Label. . . . The penultimate collection from this master of distinctive style."

Penultimate comes from the Latin *paene,* "almost," and *ultimus,* "last"; its meaning is "next to last." That is its only meaning. *Penultimate* does not mean "best," "top-flight," "most wow-ee," "highly fashionable," "drop dead" or even "quintessential."

If the Purple Label collection were indeed Mr. Lauren's *penultimate,* that would mean only one more collection to go. I checked when Adam O. Emmerich of New York sent me the ad with a request to forward it to the obituary page, and I determined that there is no cause for alarm. (This is the *penultimate* paragraph of this item.)

What do you call the paragraph that is two from the last? The *antepenulti-mate.* If Mr. Lauren's copywriters saved all their second-from-last graphs, they could claim to have "the *antepenultimate* collection."

Blue Dog Demo

"The blue dogs are poised to bite Newt Gingrich," Jackie Calmes wrote in the *Wall Street Journal.* The Republican House speaker has had the votes of these self-described 'Blue Dog Conservative Democrats.' "

Twenty-three Democrats in the House of Representatives who were eager to reduce the Federal deficit sported lapel pins depicting a blue hound. Lest observers miss the point, the symbol was surrounded by the words "Blue Dog Conservative Democrat."

Early in the Eisenhower Administration, members of a group of similarly unopposing members of the political opposition led by Howard Smith of Virginia called themselves the Boll Weevils after the beetle with a long snout that bored from within the seedpods of the cotton plant grown in the South. In the early 1980s, Representative Charles Stenholm of Texas reapplied the term to Democrats, specifically those supporting Ronald Reagan's tax-cutting conservatism.

In the mid-'80s, another term to describe maverick Democrats began to surface in Louisiana. According to W. J. (Billy) Tauzin, a Louisiana Congressman, a local artist of expanding reputation named George Rodrigue began doing paintings of a blue dog with yellow eyes; a large signboard advertising his home and studio became familiar along Interstate 10 near Lafayette. On that sign was a picture of his favorite subject: the blue dog. (Reached at home, the artist tells me: "The dog I paint was my dog for 10 years. He died, and I started to paint him as a ghost dog, on his journey to try and find me. I've been painting him now for about seven years. His name was Tiffany.")

A Louisiana constituent recently supplied local politicos with a representation of the Rodrigue dog on the aforementioned lapel pin, identifying the wearer as a "Blue Dog Conservative Democrat."

The term is boosted from *yellow dog Democrat*, which is not a derogation, though *yellow dog* has a long history in American slang of denoting a cur. (A *yellow dog contract* is a labor organizer's derisive term for an agreement by employees not to join a union.)

That political phrase was coined in the 1928 Presidential campaign of the New York Democrat Al Smith, a Catholic and a "wet" whose nomination angered many regular Southern Democrats. When Senator Tom Heflin of Alabama (uncle of Howell Heflin) bolted the party rather than support the nominee, other Alabamians who remained grimly loyal to the party popularized the line "I'd vote for a yellow dog if he ran on the Democratic ticket."

According to Representative Tauzin, a clear distinction exists between the yellow and blue dogs: "A blue dog Democrat is a little more discriminatin', more open-minded." Representative Stenholm, the former boll weevil and blue dog, says the blue dog Democrat "has a little better sense of smell than a yellow dog, and sometimes will bite you, which a yellow dog Democrat won't do." The name of the group, reverberating with American political history, was far better than the other title the 23 mavericks went by, the Coalition, making up part of the Mainstream Forum, moniker for a loose amalgam of centrists.

A related phrase is *brass collar Democrat*, perhaps derived from the usage noted by the slang lexicographers Barrère and Leland in 1895, "Big Dog With the Brass Collar," meaning "Democratic leader"; it has come to mean "proud party loyalist," though not so determinedly regular as *yellow dog Democrat*.

If a *blue dog* is in play, what about a *red dog*?

That is reserved for football: it is a pass rush by linebackers, synonymous with *blitz*, although that defensive play often has one or more defensive backs rushing the quarterback. According to Tim Considine's *Language of Sport*, the phrase originated during the 1949 season when the New York Giants guard Red Ettinger, filling in at linebacker, bolted from his position to rush the quarterback; asked about the play, he replied he was "just doggin' the quarterback a little," giving rise to "Red's doggin'," which became the verb and noun *red dog*.

A skilled dialectologist would make political sense out of the following sentence, if the party loyalists decide to put political heat on the mavericks: "The yellow dogs decided to red-dog the blue dogs."

With respect to the coining of the term "yellow dog," it had to have been before the 1928 presidential election and the reference to Al Smith that you cite. Moisei Ostrogorski, a Russian analyst of American and British political parties, traveled in the United States in the 1880s and 1890s. In 1902 he published in England a two-volume work on *Democracy and the Organization of Political Parties,* volume one being on Britain and volume two on the United States. Although Ostrogorski praised American parties for their role of sustaining democracy, he was critical of what he perceived was the great strength of the doctrine of "party regularity" and voting the "straight party ticket." This doctrine, Ostrogorski complained, was held in the United States with the intensity of "religious dogma." He went on to complain that even voters "of the better element all end by voting for the 'yellow dog' run by the Machine," meaning for him in this context, the completely unqualified candidate. (Anchor Book edition, Volume II, p. 225.)

Demetrios Caraley
Editor, *Political Science Quarterly*
New York, New York

In the British General Election of 1970, a son of the landed gentry called Andrew Fountain stood for the west Norfolk seat representing the National Front, a small and nasty Party with nothing to offer the voters but thinly disguised racism. His mother, the redoubtable Lady Fountain, responded to her son's political foray by festooning the hedgerows of the family estate with bunting and blue placards extolling the virtues of the Conservative Party candidate for the constituency. Asked by a youngish television reporter why anyone should vote for him when even his mother had indicated that she would not, Mr. Fountain replied: "My mother would vote for a baboon if it had a blue backside," blue being the Party colour of the Conservatives.

I can testify to the above because I was the television reporter. Your piece "Blue Dog Demo" brought the incident to mind. During 20 years with the BBC reporting from 105 countries I found that I often preferred American usages of English and sometimes American pronunciations, for instance of the word "adult." I enjoy the story of Mrs. Dorothy Parker who, having had her pronunciation of "schedule" corrected by a bold British reporter, replied: "Oh skit!"

Michael Cole, Director of Public Affairs
Harrods Knightsbridge
London, England

It happens that I learned about both kinds of red dog at the same time in my life. After attending a prep school in a rather isolated spot in California (Carpinteria) I wound up at the University of Pennsylvania in the early fifties, when Penn was playing football against Notre Dame, Penn State, Duke, Navy, Army and other strong non–Ivy League teams. There was a lot of red dogging of our poor quarterbacks, and Penn didn't win a single game in 1954 and 1955!

At the same time, at the poker table in the fraternity house, I was introduced to the game of red dog. It is brutal because the pot keeps growing, you bet against the pot depending on how much confidence you have that you can beat the next card in its own suit, and failing having four aces (the only perfect hand) you can always go down in flames unexpectedly.

I also note that the *Random House Unabridged* treats the card game as the first meaning. I don't know how other reputable dictionaries rank the meanings.

Paul A. Rubinstein
New York, New York

"Blue Dog Demo" has fun with both blue and yellow dogs, but only as democrats, and doesn't mention the railroad built into W. C. Handy's "Yellow Dog Blues," Copyright 1914. "Where the Southern cross' the Dog" is a famous line in the jazz world.

James B. Weaver
Sarasota, Florida

You have brought up the term "yellow dog Democrat" and left its origin and meaning hanging on a note of speculation, thus leaving me twice surprised, as my great-grandfather, an old Missouri Confederate veteran and survivor of Shiloh, Vicksburg and a pestilent Union prison camp in Indiana was said to have used the expression more than a few times. His exact words were, so I have been told, "I'd vote for a Democrat if he was a yaller dog."

Missouri furnished 50,000 troops to the Confederacy, and the men who returned after the surrender had not much choice when they voted. Either they voted for a Republican (not likely) or they voted for a candidate in the "Copper head" category who had avoided the conflict—a "yaller dog" Democrat.

A possible source for the "yellow dog" element might be found in the term "yellow dog money," the tie-in here being that both money and party were of questionable legitimacy— politically or numismatically speaking at least.

Carey Allan Bunker
Tucson, Arizona

Another color of "dog": "black dog" is how Winston Churchill referred to his periodic bouts of depression.

Daniel Sachs
Bethesda, Maryland

The Boontling Jargon

If you're feeling featherleggy, pike down to the Horn of Zeese and harp Boontling.

Translation: If you're feeling feisty, walk down to a cafe called the Cup of Coffee and speak Boontling, a unique American jargon preserved in Boonville, a town in Anderson Valley in Mendocino County, Calif.

The argot, created in the late 19th century to make outsiders unwelcome, was studied by Charles C. Adams, English professor emeritus at California State University in Chico. English words are clipped front or back (tobacco is "tobe"), or phonemically reshaped (a quarter is "toobs," from "two bits"; a dollar is a "hig" from "higler," from "hog dollar"), or eponymized ("flories" are light-bread biscuits, named for Flora, a local woman who made them). Adams considers it a lingo, not a language, "a deliberately contrived jargon."

In *The Spring,* a riveting mystery novel by Clifford Irving, a form of Boontling, called Springling, is spoken by characters hiding a town secret. "The Colorado variant, if you have a keen ear," writes Irving in an author's note, "can still be heard southwest of Aspen near Springhill and the ghost town of Crystal City." Helpfully, he includes a glossary of Springling words used in the text at the end of his book, including *barney* (kiss), *cain* (to kill), *mollies* (breasts) and *socker moldunes* (especially impressive mollies).

Cliff is my boyhood chum who perpetrated the "autobiography" of the billionaire Howard Hughes years ago, figuring the nutty old recluse would never come out of hiding to blow the hoax. But he did, and Irving was *high-heeled* (arrested) and learned about the criminal mind from the inside of jail. Now, on the "also by" page, he lists 10 novels, 5 works of nonfiction and, proudly, 1 "other"—*The Autobiography of Howard Hughes.*

The Boontling expert, Adams, was unaware of the Colorado variant: "I wonder if it is possible that the two versions have a common ancestor. I have long suspected that the lingo was spoken in some form by immigrants to Anderson Valley before they settled there. They have roots in the renegade movement of the Reconstruction South. Some settled in the Wyoming–North Arizona area."

Thus do novelists spark searches for missing linguistic links. Adams's dictionary *Boontling: An American Lingo,* is in paperback (Mountain House Press, in Philo, Calif.), and Irving's novel is published by Simon & Schuster.

Bridge to Past Tense

Nowhere was the drug issue of greater concern in the Presidential campaign than among grammarians. When President Clinton was asked in the second joint TV appearance why he had delayed for three years a bill requiring certain warning labeling on cigarettes, he replied: "We took comments, as we always do, and there were tens of thousands of comments about how we ought to do it. That's what *drug* it out."

One school of thought holds that *drug* is a regional dialectical variant of the past tense, as well as being the past participle, of the verb *drag.* Thus: I *drag,* I *dragged* (or I *drug*), I have *drug.*

E. Bagby Atwood, in his acclaimed 1953 "Survey of Verb Forms in the Eastern United States," argued that *drug* was "popular regional," which meant "extensive in the noncultured types but relatively uncommon among the cultured."

However, another scholarly group points to a nonelitist history of the verb set forth in the *Oxford English Dictionary.* The first use of *drag* in the sense of "to lag in the rear" was in 1494: "that none should *dragge* or tary after his hoost." But the first recorded use of *drug* in this sense occurred more than two centuries earlier, in the 1240 *Lofsong*, or love song, and I won't trouble the reader with the Middle English. That suggested to the *OED*'s Sir James A. H. Murray in 1897 that the Scottish dialect use, though apparently the past tense of *drag*, "may have some different origin."

Therefore, in using "That's what *drug* it out," Mr. Clinton may have been drawing on a deep-structured linguistic impulse that causes many grammarians to pause.

Relatedly, the past tense of *bring* was injected into the campaign when Barbara Walters of ABC asked the President about the time after the elections of 1994 when he was said to have felt he had lost his way. He replied, "I needed to make a clear assessment of what had happened and why, and understand what people felt, and I decided I needed to dance with what *brung* me, as we say at home."

Though the past tense of *bring* is *brought* in Standard English, in regional speech in Britain and in the United States the verb has been conjugated like the Standard *sing/sang/sung* for centuries. In a 1927 edition of the quarterly *American Speech*, the Ozarks conjugation was listed: "[Present] Bring [preterite] brang, brung [past participle] brung." We still occasionally hear *brang*, as in Neil Diamond's 1972 hit song "Play Me" ("Song she sang to me,/Song she *brang* to me"). Less common, but like *brung* still prevalent today in the Eastern states, are *broughten* and *bringed*.

Mr. Clinton made clear he knew he was using non-Standard English with "as we say at home," contrary to his unflagged *drug* use. (Better fix that last phrase: "contrary to his non-Standard use of what most think is the past tense of *drag*.") But the *Dictionary of American Regional English*, with its third volume available, finds most usages of *brung* to be Eastern; how come the usage is "at home" in Arkansas?

A dialectical clue was found in a discussion the PBS interviewer Charlie Rose had with the *Wall Street Journal* columnist Al Hunt this summer. When "dance with the girl you *brung*" came up, Hunt said it was a favorite saying of the University of Texas football coach Darrell Royal.

That led me to Austin and a chat with Coach Royal, who recalled popularizing the phrase before the New Year's Day game in 1970: "Running was what got us to the Cotton Bowl, so I was determined to stick to a running game against Notre Dame. There was a press conference, and they asked me whether or not I would change my strategy. The most to-the-point answer I could come up with—which the media would naturally want, something vivid and quick—was 'We're gonna dance with who *brung* us.' Poor grammar, but it worked."

A fan sent Coach Royal the origin of the phrase, which he then vouchsafed to me. The front page of the 1927 sheet music reads, "The Gum Chewer's Song: I'm Gonna Dance Wit De Guy Wot *Brung* Me. A Knock-Out Novelty

Song With Ukulele Accompaniment, Lyric by Walter O'Keefe, Music by Harry Archer. You Can't Go Wrong With Any Feist Song." Pictured is a flapper with rolled-down stockings who is pulling a long string of chewing gum out of her mouth, to the horror of her dancing companion. (*Ukulele* is Hawaiian for "jumping flea," from the 1879 nickname of Edward Purvis, a popular performer in the court of King Kalakaua.)

Prof. Michael Biel of Morehead State University in eastern Kentucky, an authority on popular recordings of that era, has a copy of the Billy Murray–Aileen Stanley recording. "On the recording," he reports, "Murray—an Irish Bostonian—puts on a certain Brooklynese, while Stanley chews and pops her gum."

Where does this etymological detective work take us? First, we know that irregular English verbs confuse those learning the language, who often form past tenses and participles by analogy to similar verbs. Since *bring* rhymes with *ring* and *sing,* the past participle (which is then misused for the past tense) would seem to be *brung,* like *rung* and *sung.* The language may not be logical, but its learners often are.

Next, we now know that the phrase "dance with de guy wot *brung* me" was the work of an Irish-American lyricist from Hartford, who was writing for a singer putting on a Brooklyn accent. How did it get attributed to Brooklynese, the lingo of the locale of so many German and Eastern European immigrants?

The Teutonic language is the root of much German-Yiddish usage, and it profoundly affected the Saxons. "Old English had also a rare strong past participle *brungen,*" notes the *Oxford English Dictionary,* "to which later dialects have added a strong past tense, so as to conjugate *bring, brang, brung.*"

No wonder Dizzy Dean, the great pitcher and a master of malaprops, announcing a baseball game, made linguistic history by saying, "He *slud* home!"

Is it simply a coincidence that, six pages later in the magazine, Michiko Kakutani's article "The United States of Andy" is subheaded "Warhol as Patron Saint of Middle America—Who'd Have Thunk It?"

Jack E. Garrett
Jamesburg, New Jersey

Bumf

The Economist magazine considered the impending issuance of a lengthy report by the Intergovernmental Panel on Climate Change and warmly welcomed it as "two thousand pages of *bumf.*"

"Is the *Economist* playing a little joke?" asks Marjorie Pastel Martin of Westport, Conn. "The pronunciation is very awkward."

My first thought was that *bumf* was a recent derivation from *bomfog,* an Americanism meaning "bombast, bloviation, empty talk," rooted in an acronym used by reporters covering Gov. Nelson Rockefeller, who liked to use the expression "brotherhood of Man, fatherhood of God."

In an 1889 dictionary of slang by Barrère and Leland, however, the word is described as schoolboys' slang and defined as "paper. . . . A *bumf-hunt* is a paper-chase." The *Oxford English Dictionary* supplement provides an up-to-date definition and a grittier etymology. *Bumf,* also spelled *bumph,* is "toilet-paper" (which Americans have euphemized to *toilet tissue,* and further to *facial tissue; down the toilet* has gone *down the drain*).

In 1912, the novelist Virginia Woolf wrote to Lytton Strachey: "Is this letter written upon *Bumf?* It looks like it." The etymology is *bumfodder,* with *bum* meaning the buttocks, and *fodder,* originally "leaves and stalks," now "stuffing."

In current British usage, *bumf* is a contemptuous reference to a stack of documents, and is a useful contribution to the political lexicon.

Cataloguese

I spend an inordinate amount of time reading Victoria's Secret catalogues, looking for errors. (To avoid disapproving stares from colleagues, I slip the catalogue inside my copy of *Hustler.*)

"Weekend Prequisite" is the caption beginning copy under a picture of a model in a "heather grey" hooded sweatshirt, "prewashed for extra softness."

There is no such thing as a *prequisite.* You can sit around in your "poly fleece" (*ester* was long ago clipped) and claim its extra softness as your *prerequisite:* that means "a necessary condition" or "a requirement beforehand." A *prerequisite* implies, however, that some action is expected when the condition is met.

Maybe Victoria's secret meaning is *prequisite.* That term, familiar to politicians, means "prerogative attached to office or status," like a parking space at

National Airport or the inlaid wood floor in the office of the budget director. Because it has an elitist cast, *perquisites*—clipped by insurgents to *perks*—has become a politically dirty word.

Is wearing this hooded sweatshirt a *prerequisite* to having a warm and comfy weekend? Or is it a *perquisite* possessed by a woman powerful enough to sit around in a sweatshirt with a drawstring hood and leather skirt? ("Poly wants a perk!") We may never know, any more than we will know what the company means when it describes the accompanying leather skirt as "one of fall's *absolutes.*" I suspect this is intended to mean "you *absolutely* must have this"—taking the hyperbolic "an *absolute* must" and clipping the *must.*

Now to *heather grey.* I have no cause to cavil at the British spelling of *gray*—Victoria was a British monarch—but the color of a heather flower is purplish pink, and the sweatshirt in the catalogue looks plain gray to me. The rule in cataloguese is never to leave a color alone; always make it part of a noun phrase. Hence "Heather Grey" (good name for a model). J. Crew now offers a shirt in "oatmeal heather," "berry heather," "indigo heather," "spruce heather" and "black heather"—they've gone *heather* happy.

Finally, *prewashed.* That means "we wash it before we sell it." This is in the category of *prerecorded* tape, which has been recorded on before sale. Why not say, simply, *washed* or *recorded?* Because, I think, we did not protest when *preshrunk* made its debut two generations ago. Too late now: the Columbia University Press catalogue says "*prepayment* must accompany all orders"; PC Mall announces you are "*preapproved* for $1,000 of credit," and Home Depot's catalogue claims "everything is *predrilled,*" leaving us in the post-drilling era. *Pre-* is a very big prefix in cataloguese.

Turn now to the Neiman Marcus catalogue. (I use the *-ue* ending, because it helps with *cataloguese,* but most cataloguers prefer *catalog,* making them *cataloggers.*)

"Jacket has yolk detail."

Do not be alarmed; the designer has not slopped an egg over the jacket. Rather, the copywriter has made a homophonic error, substituting *yolk* for *yoke.* To *yoke,* as every user of ox power knows, is "to join"; in fashion, the noun *yoke* means, according to Merriam-Webster's 10th Collegiate, "a fitted or shaped piece at the top of a skirt or at the shoulder of various garments." (It was one of fall's albumens.) Wearers of jeans know the *yoke* to be the piece of material that joins the legs to the waistband, and it contains no cholesterol.

Lapses in grammar are not confined to the elite catalogues. Here's Shoppers Food Warehouse: "You will be amazed with the huge selection." You can be amazed *at* or amazed *by;* you are not amazed *with,* unless the person pushing the cart ahead of you is equally amazed. And while we're on idiomatic prepositions, here's a chocolate kiss to Hershey's gift catalogue, which "guarantees delivery between Dec. 6 to Dec. 22." The preposition *between* takes two objects, connected by an *and;* by inserting a *to,* the chocolatier throws off the sense. And any mechanic should take umbrage at this Sears claim: "Our 120-pc. mechanic's tool set has more of what you want!" Ever met a 120-piece mechanic? Make that "Our mechanic's 120-pc tool set" or, if you have room for just a few letters more, "our mechanic's tool set of 120 pieces."

The PBS Home Video catalogue, which presumes to teach students to "conquer the new S.A.T.," claims that its tape "could add as much as 100 points to your college-bound youngster's score!" Flunks the Safire Aptitude Test: *much* works with quantity, and *many* with a countable number. One hundred points would be "twice as many as 50," not "twice as much"; watch for this on your next exam, college-bound youngsters. And watch those word skippers at Blackstone Audio Books: "Our rental prices are lower than our primary competitors." Unless the folks at Blackstone Audio (can you hear this?) are suggesting that their primary competitors are a bunch of lowlifes, they might try "lower than those of our primary competitors."

Cata-writers have a lot of trouble with *either.* From Fingerhut Corporation, this pledge: "You either like what you order from us, or we make things right." The *either* should come before the *you,* to give the *or* a chance to link the two complete clauses; if the writer likes the colloquiality of starting with *you,* he has the option of using "You either like what you order from us or get a refund." From Alan Marcus: "Any fine watch you desire is either stocked in our vast inventory or is readily available." Again, what follows *either* must be parallel to what follows *or:* make that "either is stocked . . . or is readily available."

"Famous for innovation and quality, you'll find products that make life easier," says Hammacher Schlemmer. Unless *you,* the reader, are famous for innovation and quality, which most of us are not, that opening modifier is misplaced. Make it "famous for whatever, Hammacher Schlemmer offers products" etc.

I have nothing against the direct-mail advertising industry other than that it is undermining literacy and wrinkling the language. I set aside Victoria's Secret long enough to riffle through my L. L. Bean catalogue, thinking about getting a waffle-stitch knit shirt, which I see comes in oatmeal, elderberry and eucalyptus. I presume these names are intended to describe colors, unless my choice is "lumpy, winey and fragrant." And there was the flat statement from the catalogue pioneer: "All waffle knits are not alike."

Would old Louis Bean, in his original clodhoppers, have insisted that no waffle knits are alike? Hardly. With the lining of his shoes wicking away moisture, he would have advertised, correctly, "Not all waffle knits are alike." He knew how to tie a *not.*

There was the item in which you would replace *much* with *many*—

"could add as much as 100 points to your college-bound youngster's score!"

My quibble is that I would classify *100 points* more as a point in a continuum than as a countable number. Some examples that are perhaps less arguable are

"could add as much as 100 dollars to your bank account!"
"could add as much as 100 gallons to your swimming pool!"

Don't you prefer *much* over *many* in these two particular cases? They have the form of countable numbers, of course, but they feel like continuous quantities. Like most other arguments over grammar, this seems like a conflict between old-time rules and a gut feeling of what sounds right and sensible.

Walter Steuber
Springfield, Pennsylvania

Your point that "washed" is right and "prewashed" is wrong is well taken. It reminds me of Dizzy Dean's frequent comment when he was announcing baseball games, that "he is taking his preliminary warm-up pitches."

Arthur R. Carmody, Jr.
Shreveport, Louisiana

True or false: All waffle knits are alike? A: False. Therefore, it is true that all waffle knits are not alike. There is no tertium quid between "are" and "are not," and there is no difference in meaning between "All waffle knits are not alike" and "Not all waffle knits are alike." Nevertheless, your proposed correction is acceptable, even desirable, because everyone does not think logically (I mean, not everyone thinks logically).

Donald S. Dowden
New York, New York

The Certainty of "I'm Not Sure"

From the hushed halls of the Central Intelligence Agency to the corridors of power in the House of Representatives, a form of reverse English is taking hold. It is the language of uncertain certainty.

"*I'm not sure* that I am totally comfortable," said former Speaker Newt Gingrich to Tim Russert of NBC, "with people who think that God has told them what to do."

The meaning of *I'm not sure,* in this context, is the opposite of what the phrase usually means: the Speaker, in this case, *is* quite sure that he is *not* totally comfortable. But Mr. Gingrich, in this construction, pulls his punch ever so slightly. He does not come out and say, "I'm uncomfortable with . . ."; he is only "not sure that I am totally comfortable with." It is a formulation that seeks to give slightly less offense.

Master of the technique, which swept Washington vogue-talk, was John Deutch, Director of Central Intelligence. Aware that he was described in the *New York Times* as "loud, brash and confrontational," Director Deutch—in a Q. and A. before the National Press Club—was determined to be unloud, not brash and nonconfrontational. For help in this deceptive endeavor (such deviousness is considered a good quality in a CIA man), Deutch turned to the uncertain certainty.

Asked about the idea of merging the CIA with the Defense Department, he replied, "You have to have an agency responsible for strict management controls over human intelligence and spying, and *I'm not sure* the Defense Department is the place to do that."

That's not to be taken literally, of course. Deutch used to be Deputy Secretary of Defense in his previous, brash incarnation, and is as sure as hell that the Defense Department is the last place in the world to exert management controls over anything, especially spying. But he didn't want to upset old colleagues in his new, nonconfrontational stage, so he used the unsure surety.

When asked if he thought the CIA budget—then $28 billion a year, but a secret—ought to be made public, he drove home his mastery of the device: "*I'm not sure* that it's a good idea to go down the step of beginning to reveal that intelligence budget." That is a warm, winning way to dissociate oneself from the notion, far less brash than "That's a lousy idea" or "I believe we should not."

Keep an ear cocked for this oxymoronic rhetorical trick in your own cocktail-party circuit or academic seminar. It's the nice way to heave a pail of cold water on a suggestion.

In "The Certainty of 'I'm Not Sure,'" you refer to "this oxymoronic trick." Wouldn't it be better to describe it as "litotic"?

Gary Muldoon
Rochester, New York

"The Certainty of 'I'm Not Sure'" reminded me of a technique used by French government officials back when I worked for Reuters and the International *Herald Tribune*—then, in the late 1940s and in the 1950s, the European Edition of the *Herald Tribune*, although widely known as the *Paris Herald*.

The expression was, *"En principe, oui."* Favored especially by striped pants spokesmen at the Quai d'Orsay (there weren't any spokespersons back then, and probably aren't now), it meant, with few exceptions, *"Non!"* The demands of Parisian *politesse* were met, and reporters could, with considerable confidence, inform their readers that the French had no intention of joining the European Defense Community or of accepting whatever else was being proposed, especially if it came from *les amerlochs, les ricains,* or whatever other impolite phrases were used to describe Americans when they weren't present.

Robert H. Yoakum
Lakeville, Connecticut

Doubt Is Out

Alarm shown here about the vogue use of *I'm not sure that* to mean "I'm fairly certain that's a lot of hooey" has failed to dampen the delight in this locution shown by practitioners of sly derogation.

"I'm just not sure whether Sky is a mass-market service," a media-securities analyst was quoted regarding Rupert Murdoch's planned satellite service that might draw viewers from the cable industry. Note it was not the forthright *I doubt that* or the even more resolutely opinionated "Sky won't fly"; just that certain uncertainty.

The verb *doubt* is obviously out. Not since *when all is said and done* was shoved aside by the Britishism *at the end of the day* has the tried-and-true been so thoroughly ousted by the trendy.

My philosophy: If you can't stop 'em, correct 'em. Should it be *I'm not sure that,* or *whether,* or *if?* The answer rests on whether you want to express uncertainty or disbelief. (I just used *whether* because I am in genuine doubt about which you want to express.) If you're sincere about not being sure about the future of Rupert's Sky venture, use *whether* or *if.* (I like *whether* better because it's less ambiguous than *if.*) But if you're not really uncertain in your own mind, and your purpose is to cast doubt on or spread disbelief about Mr. Murdoch's enterprise, use *that.*

Am I splitting hairs? Sure; that's what mavens do. But on this, I'm backed up by Randolph Quirk, the usagist who sits in the British House of Lords as an independent spokesman on education: "When *I'm not sure* is followed by *that,* the meaning of *I'm not sure* is 'I doubt,' a polite denial. But when *I'm not sure* is followed by *whether* or *if,* the meaning is either 'I wonder' or 'I don't know.' There's a subtle difference."

Chinky Chose

Years ago, Joan Stricker of Great Neck, Long Island, asked about an expression in use among children in the Bronx: "*Chinky chose* always shows." She recalled, "It was used as a kind of comeuppance, in an in-your-face manner, in the playground," and wondered if it was rooted in an ethnic slur.

A query to the *Dictionary of American Regional English (DARE)* at the University of Wisconsin drew much head-scratching until Donald Rubin of Oakland, N.J., who grew up in the Bronx in the 1930s, told his daughter Ann, my editorial assistant, that " '*Chinky chose,* odds or evens' was the expression. You'd select odds or evens and, simultaneously with your friend, shoot out one or two fingers. If the choice was the same, it was even; if he stuck out two and you one, it was odd. Two out of three won. It was used to choose up sides, to determine who would bat first, like that." Thus, *Chinky chose* was used to choose.

"Your explanation from your dad was just what we needed!" wrote Joan Houston Hall, the editor assisting chief editor Fred Cassidy, America's folk laureat. "It may be that *Chinky chose* has nothing to do with racial slurs, but comes instead from *chinquapin*. See *DARE,* Volume II, at *hull-gull* to see how *chinquapins* were used in guessing games."

A *chinquapin* is an edible nut from the shrubby chestnut tree, varieties of which are found in the Southeast and California. In the game known as *hull-gull* in the Ozarks and Appalachians, smooth stones or hazelnuts or *chinquapins* or even store-bought marbles were held in a closed fist, and the holder would challenge his opponent to guess the number; if the guess was accurate, the winner won the handful.

But kids in the Bronx (of which I was one) never saw a *chinquapin,* so I held the dossier on this expression for more research. Then in came this query from Helen L. Gritz of Yonkers: "I have exhausted every reference work in the library to find the derivation of '*Chinky chose* always shows'; you are my last resort. In New York City during the '30s, when a play was disputed (for example, when I hit the ball and thought it was fair, but the other team called it foul), you'd agree to a 'do-over.' Then if I got a hit, my team would shout, '*Chinky chose always shows!*' But if I struck out, the other team would give voice to that chant."

In both the Stricker and the Gritz examples, the phrase seemed to mean "the truth will out, you see?" An editor at *DARE,* Leonard Zwilling, who grew up in the Bronx, was consulted by Professor Cassidy and reported, "I recall when there was a 'do-over' that was unsuccessful, that team would be taunted with '*Chinkee chose, Chinkee chose,*' as if that failure demonstrated—showed—the nonlegality of the disputed play."

Cassidy made a cautious guess about the etymology: *"Chinky* is probably a variant of *chintzy* and/or *chinchy* (and probably related to *chino* and *chintz*, the fabric), which all have Chinese or Oriental connections." An ethnic stereotype about Chinese immigrants dating back to the gold rush was that they were clever and penny-pinching. "So in the Bronx game," says the great dialexicographer, *"Chinky* may very well mean *Chinaman* who 'always shows' or contests an adverse decision in a game, trying to get all he can."

O.K., the ethnic slur is the *Chinky,* but what about the *chose?* The French word for "thing"? Cassidy explains: *"Chose* is most unlikely to be French. Mostly it seems to be a rhyme—the word to go with the key element of the whole phrase, *shows."*

In the dimly remembered chants of children are clues to a civilization's past prejudices and superstitions. We have to nail down the meanings while we can.

Thanks for granting me a "cautious" guess. It was no more. Not a "wild surmise." I have never heard the expression; it was reported from the Bronx, and that's where Zwilling knew it.

My experience with *chink* and *chinky* is from Jamaica, West Indies, where a *chink* is a bedbug, and *chinky* means bug-infested, therefore nasty-smelling, stinking. In Jamaica a Chinese, in the folk speech, is a *Chinee (man)*, a shopkeeper, and the word is quite distinct from *chink.* I have never heard this little verse. As I understand it (from Zwilling and others, Bronx use), it's a derisive snarl against the loser of a test. The A team or player challenges a play by the B team. They try the play over and the challenger (A team) loses. The B team snarls "Chinky chose always shows!" meaning "You were wrong! You challenged falsely; you knew we were right." Any further guesses would be incautious.

Frederic G. Cassidy, Chief Editor, *DARE*
University of Wisconsin
Madison, Wisconsin

Somewhere in the middle years of my sandlot baseball career in a nearly rural suburb of Hartford, in the mid-1930's, a bunch of kids started yelling something under circumstances similar to those which evoked chants of "Chinky chose" in the examples you cited in your recent column. I hadn't heard it before; when I asked one of the kids near me what they were saying, he said, "Cheatin' proves." Whether that's what they were really saying, or whether he had never heard it before either and had to keep up a front by making up the most sensible answer he could is at this point unknown and unknowable. If he was right, "Cheatin' proves" or "Cheatin' shows" are other potential sense-making etymologies for "Chinky chose."

John Strother
Princeton, New Jersey

Two youngsters would be choosing, using the "odds-or-evens" method, involving the simultaneous exposure of one or two fingers. The issue might be who goes first at a game, who gets the one mitt, or whatever. A dispute might arise if the loser of the choose insisted he wasn't really ready, or expected it to require two wins out of three, or claimed that his opponent exposed his fingers too slowly, giving him an unfair advantage, etc. At this point one of the disputants would say "Pinky chose," and the two would hook their right hand pinkies together. With his left hand one of them would swipe down on the linked pinkies, separating them and saying "Pinky chose always goes." This meant that the next "odds-or-evens" choose was absolutely decisive. If the loser of this last choose complained in any way, the winner could say: "Look, you agreed that 'Pinky chose always goes.'" The linking of the pinkies was taken as tacit agreement that the next result was final and determinative.

You can see how this expression could evolve alliteratively into "Chinky chose always shows," as it spread from block to block or from generation to generation of children, with the original pinky ceremony lost in history, but with the idea of decisiveness extended to any competitive encounter.

Hugh Horowitz
Mountainside, New Jersey

In my early teens, more than seventy years ago, all of us kids knew the phrase and were well aware of its real meaning. My personally authenticated source was my mother. But it was common knowledge that if any of us little ones did something unfair that went wrong, the appropriate catcall was "Chinky chose," meaning, of course, "cheating shows."

Arnold Forster
New York, New York

You refer to a letter from a woman from Yonkers who recalls that, in New York City during the '30s, when a play was disputed and a replay was agreed to, it was called a "do-over." Well, I grew up in Queens in the late '50s and early '60s, and I recall that before a play could be done over, a "do-over" had to be requested. The way to request a "do-over" was to shout "Hindu" during or right after the play. It seems all but certain that the term "Hindu" in this context refers to Hinduism, what with a central tenet of that religion being reincarnation—a replay or "do-over" on a cosmic scale.

John J. Di Clemente
Tinley Park, Illinois

I am not surprised that those raised in the Bronx haven't the foggiest idea of what they are saying. Those of us raised in Brooklyn, where articulation and comprehension of course were the best of the five boroughs, know perfectly well what "chinky chose" means—but we pronounced it properly. The easy language of children in the street turns "cheating shows" into the apparent ethnic slur "chinky chose." Indeed, when we had a "do over" and the villain was shown to be a villain, we would triumphantly say CHEATING SHOWS, or have it thrown back in our red faces, as the case might have been. In any case, the term has no relation to Asian cuisine or to French things. I have so informed my colleagues at *DARE*, whose own red faces cannot, I am glad to say, be attributed to cheating. Yes, we need to nail down the meanings of children's chants while we can, but clearly the argument on authority cannot come from where the wicked Yankees bombed in the Bronx.

Howard D. Weinbrot
Vilas and Quintana Research Professor
University of Wisconsin
Madison, Wisconsin

The problem with all the explanations you received was that they did not recognize that this was the second line of the verse and simply a humorous version of the first line: *"Pinky square is always fair."*

When there was a disagreement as to whether someone was safe or out and the parties agreed to a replay, or when there was a disagreement about a fact and the parties agreed to a third party deciding, they would pledge their compact by forming a square with their right pinkies. And they would agree: *"Pinky square is always fair, chinky chose always shows."*

In the schoolyard at P.S. 95, you never violated *"Pinky square."*

Howard C. Kaplan
Stamford, Connecticut

When I was growing up in the Bronx in the late '20s and early '30s, we played odds-evens by counting in Italian, though we were all Jewish. The counting went: *uno, due, tre* (pronounced uno, dua, tray) for the first display of finger(s); followed by: *quattro, cinque, sei* (pronounced katro, chinka, say). The rhythm of the count was: get ready, get set, GO! It was imperative that the displaying took place simultaneously so as not to change one's choice after seeing the opponent's. It seems to me that the *cirque, sei* became changed to chinky chose. I don't remember whether we displayed twice or three times. My belief is that it was twice and the contest began over in a tie.

I never heard "chinky chose always shows," nor even "chinky chose." We used "chinka say" for the name of the game.

Arthur Centor
Minneapolis, Minnesota

In Brooklyn, whether a "do-over" resulted in a "three-sewer" home run or a weak dribble to the pitcher, the winner of the "do-over" had good reason to impugn the honesty of the opposing team by shouting "cheating shows" ("see, there is justice").

Barry H. Mandel
New York, New York

As I read your piece, it dawned on me that my childhood friends and I had used a similar expression for the same purpose: as a chant of derision following a do-over in a game. The team with the favorable outcome would taunt the other team by shouting *"Cheating always shows!"*, with the first word usually pronounced CHEET-un.

I haven't a clue as to the origin of the expression I used as a child, but that won't stop me from giving you my two cents worth. I grew up in the '50s and '60s in Southampton on Eastern Long Island, some ninety miles from Manhattan and the Bronx. Like those who came before and after us, my friends and I had occasion to play games with kids from the City whose parents had summer homes in the area. Those contacts offered the opportunity for the exchange and mixing of colloquialisms. While "Chinky chose" would surely have sounded alien to our ears, "Cheating" would have been tauntingly familiar. It certainly makes a nice substitute in the churlish child's "Chinky chose" chant, changing the alliteration by half but the intent not at all.

Stephen L. Ham III
Southampton, New York

There is no possible doubt that the origin of *chinky chose* was "cheating shows." The ch-words are an echoic alliterative popularization of the simple original taunt. On *my* block (West 83 between Central Park West and Columbus Avenue), I heard, "Chinky shows, everyone knows." My authority rests on my having been born in Manhattan in 1924.

Deborah Karp
Bronx, New York

In the 1940s, the expression went as follows: "Chinky chose up your belly and down your nose." This, of course, was shouted by the successful team after a "do-over."

Alfred D. Fierro
Old Tappan, New Jersey

New York childhoods could probably provide endless grist for your mill. In my part of Brooklyn in the fifties we played a variation of handball in alleys, in which the ball—a "Spauldeen," of course—had to bounce once before hitting the wall, and be returned after no more than one bounce. We called the game "Kings and Queens" since each person had a position that moved up or down as he hit or miss.

When the ball hit a crack or was otherwise unnaturally obstructed, you could yell "Hindu" pronounced Hindoo, which allowed for the point to be played again. I have no idea why. But "Hindu" was a common expression indicating outside interference beyond one's control that merited a replay. If only we could get a "Hindu" as we grow older.

Needless to say, when we were done we would play a round of "caw caw [call call] ringo-lee-veo," a version of hide and seek in which if you got to home base and yelled "Olley olley home free all free all" you could release all the prisoners captured to that point.

Robert M. Herzog
New York, New York

I remember the phrase as "Chinky toes always shows." It was a derogatory word for Chinese people and I still hear fools use that term related to a local hand laundry or Chinese restaurant. Chinese people wore sandals which exposed their toes. The expression was used to tell someone who tried to fool someone or trick someone that the truth will out and if he's wrong, he will be exposed.

Al Winter
Bayside, New York

In the beautiful Borough of Queens we said it another way.

On the sand lot behind Jamaica High School, hard by the then new and quite grand Grand Central Parkway, a disputed call, strike or ball, foul or fair, was settled thus:

A. The challenge—"odds or evens?"
B. The action—on the count of three, flip out one finger or two.
C. The triumphant call, by the winner, of course—"Chinky shows! Always knows!"

We knew not of derivations, nor of ethnicity, except that the Chinese had a reputation for wisdom, hence all the "Confucius says . . ." jokes. Chinky shows, not chose, was the one accepted way to settle a dispute, short of the ultimate challenge: "Ya wanna good bust inna mout?"

Martin Schrader*
Croton-on-Hudson, New York

* Martin Schrader died on May 28, 1998.

If the youngster who demanded that a choose take place lost the choose, his companion would say "Cheat and chose always shows" meaning that the first youngster was cheating by demanding that a choose take place and was "shown up" by having lost the choose.

Gerald B. Lechter
Fort Lee, New Jersey

We never heard "Chinky chose always shows." Perhaps it was used by the classier kids in the West Bronx, but not by us in the East—Van Nest and Boston Rd. areas.

The expression we always used was, "Chinky choose always lose."

M. Altschuler
Flushing, New York

I grew up in the Greenpoint section of Brooklyn in the 1930s. On disputed plays, you would do it over. When the result would be against the party of the first part, the party of the second part would shout, *"Chinky chose,"* which was a variant of *"Cheating shows"* or *"Cheatin' shows."*

George Olewnick
Poughkeepsie, New York

Sometimes, when a call was disputed, an agreement to do the play over would not be reached. Protesting, by storming off the court, would result in giving the court over to the next player waiting to challenge the winner. Therefore, one player would accede, under duress, to the other. (Hoping to ultimately win the game and retain the court.) If the victor won the next play the court was silent but, if he lost the next play the mumbled words *"chinky shows—never goes"* provided much satisfaction in the face of an angry glare.

In terms of ethnicity, one of the commonly disputed calls was a foul killshot called a Chinese. This arose because of a game called "Chinese Handball" in which it is required that the struck ball bounce on the ground once before hitting the wall.

Arthur Illiano, Jr.
Effort, Pennsylvania

Clone Clone
Clone Clone

Headline writers, faced with the epochal news story of the first cloning of a mammal (everybody did it with frogs, but how many more frogs do we need?), sheepishly fell back on a pun on *clown:* "A Thousand *Clones,*" "Send in the *Clones*" and other such *cloning* around.

But if we are heading into what *Business Week* calls "the Biotech Century," wordniks need a serious fix on *clone.*

The noun means "replica, duplicate"; in biology, "an organism produced asexually from a single ancestor"—which, up to now, most often meant "grafting," a nonpolitical term used by botanists. A duplicated cell can be good or bad: when the body produces cells to fight infection, they are *clones;* but so, on the other hand, are cancer cells. The essence of the word is "same genetic makeup"—more "replication" than "reproduction," and not involving sex.

The noun produced a verb, *to clone,* meaning "to propagate so as to form a genetic duplicate," which first appeared in the magazine *Nature* in 1959. The adjective *clonal* was coined in 1968 and slammed into the public consciousness in 1971, when the Nobel laureate James D. Watson titled a seminal article in the *Atlantic Monthly* "Moving Toward *Clonal* Man—Is This What We Want?" (The word *seminal,* meaning "original and influential," comes from *semen,* Latin for "seed," the fluid containing sperm cells, and my labored wordplay on asexuality is slipped in here to assert its correct pronunciation, SEE-men-ul, contrary to what you hear from bowdlerizing academics on the air.)

Confusion surrounds the coinage of *clone. The Century Dictionary,* first published in 1889, cited a scientist named John Ashburner, "Constitutions differ according to degrees of tone and *clone."* This referred to "the condition of *clonus,"* or spasmodic contraction and relaxation of muscles, rooted in the Greek *klonos,* "violent confused motion, turmoil." That *clonus* can be found in the most recent Merriam-Webster.

In 1893, first-edition *Oxford English Dictionary* lexicographers took a look at the *Century's clone* and decided one citation was not enough to rate an entry. They preferred an adjective found in an 1849 citation, *clonic* spasm. But in the 1972 *OED* Supplement, the word *clone* appeared with a different meaning and a different Greek root (for "twig"), coined in 1903 by the botanist H. J. Webber. The wide meaning: "Any group of cells or organisms produced asexually from a single sexually produced ancestor."

Clone already has grafted its way onto political metaphor. "Britain's Tony Blair is a Bill Clinton *clone"* is not a genetic analysis but a semantic stretch: in such use, the meaning of *clone* is *imitator,* or in its slang form, *wannabe.* Another sense is "robot, automaton, android" (and I'll be beamed up by Mr. Data's fans for that). In cyberlingo, a *clone* is "a computer designed to run the same software as a competitor's computer."

The propagation of this word is global: the Germans write their noun *Klon,* and the French *clone* (but they pronounce it their special way). The Russians lengthen it to *klonirovanie.* Japanese use a phonetic approximation—*kuron,* though some prefer *bunshi-kei,* which means "branching system," akin to the Greek for "twig." That linguistic creativity is also apparent in Chinese: *fu zhi* is represented by the characters for "copy" and "produce."

As its frequency of use rises, however, the intercourse-free meaning accents the sexual activity associated with the verb *reproduce.*

You quote Bloom and Watson, two obviously reliable sources. However, you omit the father of all cloning sources, Aldous Huxley—if you want to do some serious reading and thinking about cloning, pick up his *Brave New World* and read the first two stunning chapters! Food for thought, and not "fat free" food either.

Patricia Boyle
Windsor Locks, Connecticut

A Closing Note

"All three TV stations out here," writes Pat Quinlan Frye of Santa Fe, N.M. (Miss Rheingold of 1948), "are using *closure* for *school closings*. We desperately need your help."

In New York, Duncan Steck, formerly of Merriam-Webster, writes about *closure* from another angle: "Have you ever done anything on that word as it pertains to relatives coming to *closure* after the cruel deaths of loved ones?"

The time has come to open up on a word that arguably has become as voguish as *arguably*. Even nontraditionalist U.S. senators, straining to keep up with the most modern lingo, are invoking *closure*. What they mean is *cloture*, a French word that has come to mean, in English, "a motion to end debate." Some grammarians objected to the use of a French word when an English one exists, but *cloture*, pronounced CLO-cha in Washington, is a word that has gained a specific legislative meaning, getting a big play whenever a filibuster is undertaken, and seems to have a nice, clotting quality; let's keep *cloture*.

Closure is an act that brings about an ending. It offers a sense of completeness, a conclusion. The reason the word is heard so often, in the wake of disasters like the Oklahoma City bombing and the death sentence given to the perpetrator, is that the term is a favorite of psychologists and pseudoalienists. Frank Rich, another powerful *Times* columnist, titled a column "Rush to *Closure*" and awarded the term "national buzzword of the week."

In psychology, it is "the tendency to create satisfying wholes." In 1924, R. M. Ogden, translating from the German *The Growth of the Mind*, by Kurt Koffka, a founder of Gestalt theory, was first to use the term. He wrote of "laws of relationship which have to do with *closure* and *nonclosure*." Arthur Koestler wrote in 1964 that "according to Gestalt theory, we solve abstract problems by applying 'the *closure* principle'; the solution closes the gap." Our love of psychobabble has allowed *closure* to spread over *closing* and the specific *cloture* like the kudzu that is gobbling up my ivy.

Here we go: when you shut the doors, you have a *closing*. When you cut off debate, you achieve *cloture*. When you wrap up and tie a ribbon around an emotion, you have *closure*. Nowhere is it written that you are forbidden to use *completion* or *finish*. (And why have movies stopped using "The End" at the end?)

Nothing punctures the voguish balloon like a good cartoon. In *The New Yorker* of June 2, 1997, Lee Lorenz drew a cartoon of a lady opening the door to the Grim Reaper, draped in black with scythe on shoulder. The lady says to her husband, "It's the *closure* fairy."

That's a wrap.

Coffee Nerves

"Controversial Coffees May Stain Gore" was the headline in *Legal Times*.

Had the Vice President soiled his shirt while in his cups? Was he getting into a controversy about the importation of beans from Colombia?

No; the use of *coffee* is part of the lexicon of funny fund raising.

"Are you by any chance examining the Starbuckian rise of the word *coffee* in political journalism?" asked Pat Ryan of *The New York Times* News Service. She cited this front-page headline over a *Times* article by Stephen Labaton, the journalistic Javert on the trail of the fund-raising campaign trail: "No Background Checks Done on Guests at Clinton *Coffee*." And Leslie Eaton led a feature piece with "O.K., so you have had *coffee* at the Clinton White House, your photo on the cover of Fortune." This calls to mind Bunny Berigan's version of the 1936 Gershwin song "I Can't Get Started": "I've been consulted by Franklin D./Greta Garbo has had me to tea."

The noun *tea*, which meant a beverage, was given a new sense of "a meal or social entertainment at which tea is served" by Jonathan Swift in *Polite Conversations* (1738): "Whether they meet at . . . Meals, *Tea*, or Visits." In the same way, in our time and as a result of the Clinton-Gore fund-raising efforts, the noun *coffee* is undergoing the same sense-stretching treatment.

Compounds have long been formed based on this beverage, from *coffee break* to *coffee-cake* to *coffee-table* book. The White House gatherings are based on the German *Kaffeeklatsch*, or "*coffee* party." (*Klatsch* is German for "the noise of gossip," the sound of conversation that mingles with the clattering of cups and the measuring-out of life in *coffee* spoons, Prufrock-style.)

Coffee, not preceded by the article *a* or *the*, is the drink; *a coffee* or *the coffee*, meaning "the meeting at which *coffee* was served," is now the event. The new journalistic declension from first reference to third was illustrated by this passage from a *Times* article by Raymond Bonner in Jakarta and the relentless Labaton in Washington:

"Investigators have been struck by the timing of Mrs. Kanchanalak's contributions last summer," noted the reporters, "around the time that she had arranged the *Kaffeeklatsch* [first reference] that included President Clinton. . . . Around the same time as the *coffee meeting* [second reference] on June 18, Mrs. Kanchanalak gave the Democratic National Committee $135,000 . . . The main discussion at *the coffee* [third reference] was over United States policy toward China, one participant said."

The root word is the Arabic *qahwah,* originally meaning "wine," which was applied to a hot, thick beverage that the Turks called *kahveh* and came into European, especially Scandinavian, languages around 1600. The root word of *fund-raising unit* is the Latin *fundus,* "bottom."

You say, "*Coffee,* not preceded by the article *a* or *the,* is the drink; *a coffee* or *the coffee,* meaning "the meeting at which *coffee* was served," is now the event.

However, from 1958 on, I recall hearing my late husband, Irv Schram, asking me for "a coffee." He would say, "I'll have a coffee." Since I grew up in Connecticut, this was an unfamiliar way of requesting a cup of coffee. In fact, I used to tease him about this "New Yorkese." Then I would also hear "a coffee" from his parents who had come from the Ukraine.

When we made a visit to Israel in 1961, I recall his asking for "a beer." I commented on this too. Of course, it turned out that the Israeli beer was labeled "Abir" (not sure of this spelling).

Peninnah Schram
New York, New York

The term "coffee clutch" has been turning up in my local paper from time to time over the past six months. Your column suggested to me that the term is no malapropism, but a timely replacement for "Kaffeeklatsch," at least in political circles.

John Morressy
East Sullivan, New Hampshire

Clearly you haven't been to Ethiopia, or you would not have placed the origins of "coffee" so firmly with the Arabs, the Turks and the Scandinavians.

Actually "coffee" derives from Kaffa—a former kingdom turned province in Southwestern Ethiopia, where it still grows wild in the forests.

Margaret Snyder
New York, New York

Coinage Corner

"Where does the common man get a 'citation in the literature' of a play on words?" Robert Brothers of Philadelphia asks. "I'm submitting to your file cabinet, with the earliest postmark, the word *Whitewaterloo*. As far as I know, the only citation is in my kitchen in a conversation with my wife."

Will the Independent Counsel cause Bill Clinton to meet his Whitewaterloo? If so, brother Brothers is the acknowledged coiner.

The Coinage Game: Neologic Nellies

"Those hardhearted Hannahs are going to cut Medicare," say the liberals.

"We're not cutting a thing," say the conservatives. "We're reducing the rate of increase." This is followed by a labored explanation of how the net amount being spent is more, but less than it would have been if the current rate of increase were allowed to run amok.

"Might there not be a word in Greek or Latin," asks Otto A. Silha in Minneapolis, "that would mean 'reduced increase' for use instead of 'cuts' in future fiscal debates?"

I made a quick run of the traps. Frank Abate of Dictionary and Reference Specialists in Old Saybrook, Conn., responded: "I know of no such word. Do you like *deincrementalization?*"

No. Tried Hugh Rawson, director of Penguin Reference Books: "A new word for budget balancers to use when increasing expenditures in real terms, but not by enough to account for inflation or to cover projected costs of serving larger numbers of people?"

That's an artful restatement of the problem, but what's the word? "I offer *necrement*, from Latin *nec*, 'not,' plus *crescere*, 'to grow' (and also the root of *increment*). The budget balancer could explain that 'the *necremental* increase is such-and-such.'"

Good try, but *necrement* sounds too much like a euphemism for a scatological epithet. Maybe the Neologic Nellies can solve the problem. These are the people who go about coining words and waiting for them to become part of the language; when they don't, the Neologic Nellies send them to me and wonder what's wrong with the rest of the world.

Wordrobe, for example, coined by June Gundersen of Brooklyn in 1984, meaning "the vocabulary with which we cloak our emotions." Or *okayance,* a coinage of Darcy McGrath of Chicago that same year, meaning "the bureaucratic process of getting approval." Or *greedlock,* by David Ebbitt of Newport, R.I., to denote the state of overcrowding caused by avaricious builders.

These are good words that never made it. But be careful about claiming to be the coiner of your favorite neologism: I thought I had a beaut a few weeks ago—*digivision,* a shortening of "digital television." Used it twice in a column, admiring how it saved space and came easily to the tongue.

Then in comes a letter from Sherman E. DeForest of San Diego, president of DigiVision: "We own rights to the word in the United States, and limited rights worldwide. In Great Britain, another DigiVision produces computer monitors, and ITT has limited rights to the marque in Germany." He says to cease using DigiVision's trademark as a generic.

Maybe that tricky capital V in the middle weakens his case, but I won't challenge it; somebody else was present at the creation. Neologic Nellies soon find that is all too often the case.

You discuss "reducing the rate of increase" and you wonder how else to describe that. In first-year calculus we describe that as "first derivative positive, second derivative negative," or in symbols, $dy/dx > 0$, $d^2y/dx^2 < 0$.

The general public will not understand the calculus, but it is clear to whoever remembers that from calculus.

Jerome E. Tuttle
South Orange, New Jersey

The Concealment of Sex

Would you call Madonna a *sex god*? Of course not. Search through all the competing data bases—Dialog, Nexis, Datatimes, Dow Jones News/Retrieval—and you will find the enticing entertainer described thousands of times as a *sex goddess,* never a *sex god.* Hold that thought about the *-ess* suffix as you read this letter from Andrew Hughes of New York:

"When I was young, we had movies that had *actors* and *actresses.* Now we seem to have nothing but *actors.* Even the women are called *actors.* The word *actresses* seems to have fallen into disrepute.

"Also, there are stories from time to time about the Catholic Church ordaining women. However, they all talk of ordaining these women as *priests*. If they did ordain a woman, why would she not be a *priestess?* Is there some reason for this, or is it just a change in fashion?"

I came across that letter in my "sex concealment" file as I was inserting the latest entry: in the novel being ghostwritten for Newt Gingrich (part of his Contract With a Publisher, presumably to be delivered right after the school prayer amendment vote), a German female spy tries to seduce the White House chief of staff: "Suddenly the pouting sex kitten gave way to Diana the *Huntress.*" (Italics mine. The prose—who knows?) Note the suffix because *Diana the Huntress* is a unified mythical name with the old-style occupation locked in; however, if today Princess Diana were seen with a rifle in hand stalking a royal gossipmonger, she would be described as *Diana the Hunter.*

Why? Especially in the arts, the *-ess* suffix has come to be thought of as an insult, or at least a thoughtless put-down. In literature, there is no *poetess* laureate; *authoress* has atrophied because *writer* shrouds the sexual identity. But call a woman sculptor a *sculptress,* and you'll get a two-ton chunk of marble dropped on your head. In the same way, a woman who murders her husband insists on being called a *murderer;* call her a *murderess,* and you're next.

Again, why? The reason is that we have foolishly abandoned the idea that, in language, the male embraces the female. Sitting on the moon today is a sign I helped write in 1969: "We came in peace for all mankind." If we ever get up the money to go back, some astronaut is going to change my plaque copy to *humankind,* ruining the iambic meter. As a result of our laudable determination to end the imperialism of the masculine in everyday life, we have been contorting our tongues into laborious constructions like *him/her* and *"He or she* should say to *himself or herself,"* or—worse—into the concealment of sex.

What does the changing of *chairman* to *chairperson* or *chair* do for us? It says that the one who runs the meeting is not necessarily a man; good point, which needed to be made. It also makes the point that the job itself is not destined for a man: before women were allowed on stage, all *actors* were *actors,* with the male *-or* ending. Same with *doctor,* and it would be silly to suggest "woman doctor" be called *doctress.* (Yes, *woman doctor*—a *women's doctor* is a gynecologist. Contrary to *New York Times* style that prefers *female* as the modifier, I see no reason that *woman* should not be used as an attributive noun. The fight has certainly changed from a generation ago, when H. W. Fowler was defending *woman doctor* in place of *lady doctor.*)

In the same equal-opportunity way, it makes sense to substitute *worker* for *workingman* (whatsamatter with you laggards at Workmen's Comp?), *firefighter* for *fireman* and *police officer* for *policeman.* Plenty of women are in those occupations, and it misleads the listener or reader to retain the old form. *Female fireman* and *woman policeman* are awkward, even contradictory, and we are better off, in occupational titling, with the sex-concealing form.

But do we need *woman actor* for *actress,* or *female tempter* for *temptress?* And what's demeaning about *waitress* that we should have to substitute *woman waiter* or the artificial, asexual *waitron?* We dropped *stewardess* largely because the occupation was being maligned—a popular book title suggesting promiscuity was *Coffee, Tea or Me?*—a loss that also took the male *steward* out the emergency exit, and now we have the long and unnecessarily concealing *flight attendant.* We were better off with *steward* and *stewardess.*

The abolition of the *-ess* suffix tells the reader or listener, "I intend to conceal from you the sex of the person in that job." Thus, when you learn that the *chairperson* or *chair* is going to be Pat Jones or Leslie Smith, or anyone not with a sexually recognizable first name like Jane or Tarzan, you will be denied the information about whether that person is a man or a woman.

Ah, that's the point, say the language police, sex-eraser squad: it should not matter. But information does matter—and does it really hurt to know? What's wrong with *chairwoman* or *Congresswoman?* Let's go further: now that the anti-sexist point has been made in this generation, wouldn't it be better for the next generation to have more information rather than less?

I think it is more of a hypersensitive put-down to say *female master* than *mistress,* or—faced with confusion with *mister*—to cook up a bisexual *mastress.* English doesn't need it; every dog should have its *master* and *mistress.* Same with *hostess;* it's good to know whether a "guest host" will be a man or a woman. (In Irving Berlin's song about Perle Mesta, "The Hostess With the Mostes'," the actress and songstress Ethel Merman belted out the contrary "not the priestess with the leastes'.")

Contrariwise, I would use *woman priest* in discussing the ordination of women, because it focuses on today's issue centering on sex. After women become priests in many religions, and the issue dissolves, then *priestess* would be the natural and informative word.

Does this mean the suffix is in? Not yet; we are still caught up in the correctness copywriters' purging of *-ess.* My position is best described as reactionary, but I thought I'd trot it out while reaction is in vogue.

I was an actor for many years—and would have hated to play a love scene with another "actor"! I shall stick stubbornly to actress, sculptress, priestess—and even huntress or goddess—no matter what "they" say. Furthermore, when I play a comedy scene with a woman, she'll be a *comedienne!*

The other day The L.A. *Times* stated that Barbara Walters is a "hero"—and Charlene Hunter-Gault referred, on *McNeil-Lehrer,* to early Black Lib supporters as "Heroes and Sheroes." Oh, boy!

It's even happening in the gardening world. I planted a clematis vine with the "variety name" of 'Madame Baron Veillard.' It appears that "Baroness" is down the tubes, too.

Philip Truex
Carlsbad, California

Congenital, Liar, Punch

When the ghost of the vituperative columnist Westbrook Pegler seized control of an ordinarily temperate *New York Times* columnist readers were exposed to an opinion with the bark off. Pointing to examples of mendacity through 15 years of commodities trading, Travelgate and Whitewater, he concluded that the First Lady, Hillary Rodham Clinton, was a *congenital liar.*

The reaction that is of interest to language students centered on the meaning of *congenital.* An op-ed colleague called to ask: "Did you mean *inherited?* Shouldn't you have used *habitual?*" A White House spokesman also picked up this literal interpretation of the adjective, and Mrs. Clinton later chose to escalate the charge in a National Public Radio interview: "My mother took some offense, because being called a *congenital liar* seems to reflect badly on her and my late father."

From this neutral corner of scholarly tranquillity in the arena of hot controversy, we ask ourselves today: what does *congenital* mean?

First, the word's history: a doctor formed it in 1796 from the Latin *congenitus,* "born with," and the term was defined in the 1893 *Oxford English Dictionary* as "existing or dating from one's birth." In 1848, Charles Kingsley, in "Saint's Tragedy," extended the term into general use: "The mind of God, revealed in laws, *congenital* with every kind and character of man." Charles Darwin picked it up in his 1862 study of orchids: "The so-called *congenital* attachment of the pollinia by their caudicles." The critic Matthew Arnold used the adjective in an 1879 essay: "The French people, with its *congenital* sense for the power of social intercourse and manners."

As the above shows, the meaning has developed from the medical "existing at birth" to a more general "innate, inherent, natural-born." *Merriam-Webster's 10th Collegiate* uses two examples to show the expansion: first, "existing at or dating from birth (*congenital* deafness)," then "being such by nature (*congenital* liar)."

What was the political vituperator's semantic intent? Although he did not return repeated calls, it can be surmised that he rejected *habitual, inveterate* and *chronic* as too mild, *baldfaced* as too trite and *pathological* as too severe;

congenital, with its sense of "innate" and connotation of "continual," must have seemed just right. We know that he asked his copy editor beforehand to read him the definition in *Webster's New World Dictionary,* and she reported that it came down on *innate* as the synonym.

The Economist, which characterized the columnist's usage as "vicious and meant to shock," went on to use the adverbial form in its current sense in praising the extemporaneous grammar in an address by the First Lady: "It was the speech of an exceptionally clear mind—one, surely, *congenitally* incapable of mysterious lapses of memory."

Though *congenital* and *congenial* (as in "Miss Congeniality") were sometimes confused in the past, the former is akin to "genesis" and the latter to "genius."

I must take singular exception to your characterizing our First Lady, Hillary Rodham Clinton, as a "congenital liar." To do so, disparages the efforts and reputations of hardworking Genetics Counselors, everywhere. Furthermore, it partially absolves Hillary of responsibility for her actions (The fault, dear Brutus, lies in our genes, not in ourselves—or even in our stars) and also impairs the future and impugns the reputation of poor Chelsea, as potential recipient of some of those genes.

Had I been consulted, I might have suggested consummate liar, contumacious liar, convenient liar, compulsive liar, consistent liar, constructive liar, capable liar, capricious liar, contradictory liar, Chaucerian liar, or even "Cowardly Liar" of *Wizard of Oz* fame, but no, not never, "congenital liar."

Seth L. Haber
Palo Alto, California

Liar

"Congenital, conshmenital," said a caller more interested in nouns than adjectives, "did you have to use *liar?*"

Agreeing to take a call on this purely on background, with no direct quotation (he is evidently intent on keeping a firewall between linguistic and political worlds), the invectivist noted that his first, timorous inclination was to use *prevaricator,* from the Latin for "to walk crookedly," but the current sense in *Webster's New World* is "to tell an untruth; lie," a definition that straddles two meanings.

To *tell an untruth* is not necessarily to *lie.* Mrs. Clinton, in an exceptionally clear-minded riposte to the *congenital liar* blast by the columnist, said: "I don't take what Mr. Safire says very seriously. . . . I was working for the committee that impeached President Nixon, for whom Mr. Safire worked and, best I can tell, is still working."

That "committee that impeached President Nixon" is an indisputable *untruth*; Mr. Nixon was never impeached. However, her statement was not a *lie*, because she obviously meant "the committee that recommended impeachment to the House." An *untruth*, which can be an honest mistake, can be labeled a *lie* or a *falsehood* only where there is an intent to deceive.

The second euphemism for *liar* to come to mind was *dissembler*, from the Latin *simulare*, "to feign"; the current sense of *dissembler* is "one who disguises or conceals." However, the trouble with this bookish word is that many people confuse it with *disassembler*, "one who takes things apart."

At that point, claims my source, the columnist recalled the advice of Winston Churchill, who once satirically called a colleague to account for "terminological inexactitude," but who ultimately decided, "Short words are best, and the old words when short are best of all."

Liar, its two syllables often eliding into one, dates back to Old English. It is unequivocal and unambiguous. In 1988 the columnist denounced Nancy Reagan for accepting expensive designer gowns as gifts and then falsely denying it: "Nancy Reagan knew it, hid it for years, lied when caught." However, some who had accepted that as fair comment rejected its application to this First Lady as "clearly over the line," a tennis metaphor.

You referred to the phrase "clearly over the line" as a tennis metaphor. I'm not so sure. (My credentials are years of playing, serving as a ballboy at professional tournaments in Florida throughout my childhood and having a mother who has umpired at all the Grand Slam tournaments.)

"Over the line" certainly doesn't refer to a ball that has landed outside one of the lines of play—that's referred to as being "in" or "out." As you probably know, even if the ball lands on only the tiniest fraction of the baseline (or whatever line is in question), it is still considered good.

Perhaps it derived from the foot fault. In that instance, when either foot of the server touches any part of the baseline (or the court inside the baseline) before they have struck the service ball, they have committed a foot fault. Still, I've never heard this phrase used in connection with tennis and neither has my mother. Since most infractions are very minimal (at most, the server's foot usually just grazes the baseline) I doubt the phrase "clearly over the line" would have its origins here. Since so many sports use lined boundaries to regulate play, I'd want a very clear source before attributing the phrase to tennis—especially since it's not in use by players or umpires.

Michael Giltz
New York, New York

Punch

The President's press secretary, Michael D. McCurry, told reporters after reading the "Blizzard of Lies" column that "the President, if he were not the President, would have delivered a more forceful response to that—on the bridge of Mr. Safire's nose." President Clinton later confirmed this pugilistic wish, but as the First Lady later took pains to point out, "smilingly."

The usage issue here is prepositional. The *Washington Times* used "punch him *in* the nose," while *The Economist* wrote, "Were it not for the constraints of the Presidency, [the President] would be minded to defend the family honor by punching Mr. Safire *on* the nose."

Which is it—a punch *in* or *on* the nose?

"The set phrase is 'punch somebody *in* the nose,'" reports William Kretzschmar, working on the *Linguistic Atlas* Project at the University of Georgia. "'Punch *on* the nose' is simply a variant, not a regional difference.

"In this expression, however," says Professor Kretzschmar, "the use of *in* is more prevalent than the variant *on*."

Yes, but. These verbal fisticuffs also point up the difference in British usage (*on* is preferred) and the change in preposition when a spot is specified: McCurry spoke of "the bridge" of the nose—right between the eyes—and *on* lent exactness.

Conspiracy Theory

"I'm a screenwriter working at Warner Bros.," writes Brian Helgeland of Malibu, Calif. (and I'm leaving the "Bros." unchanged to "Brothers," contrary to *Times* style, as a favor to Ed Bleier of that firm, who should now stop nagging me about it), "on an original idea of my own [*sic*] entitled *Conspiracy Theory*. . . . I'm wondering if you've heard a particular Conspiracy Theory that has stuck with you over the years. I'm looking for the odd, the outrageous and the humorous."

He came to the right place. "Humpty Dumpty Was Pushed!" was a bumper sticker on my car in the '80s, and I am thinking of putting in a special fax line to receive Vincent Foster material from the narrowed-eyes crowd that knows it has a softie in me. (They never did find the bullet, you know, no matter how Mike Wallace pooh-poohs it all on "60 Minutes.")

The first use so far of the phrase—perhaps the bright coinage—lies amouldering in the invaluable files of Merriam-Webster. In the Oct. 22, 1945, edition of *The New Republic*, Henry Morgenthau Jr., the treasury secretary, was quoted predicting "the end of heavy industry in Germany will permit transfer of factories to the very places where they would have been located in the first place, if access to raw materials, markets, labor and power had been really decisive factors in European development." Heinz Eulau, assistant editor of *The New Republic*, waved this idea off: "Mr. Morgenthau's *conspiracy theory* simply does not hold."

According to the first *Barnhart Dictionary Companion*, published in 1982, *conspiracy theory* "has been widely used since 1973, perhaps sparked by the many theories about the worldwide energy crisis, which began that year." In 1979, *The New Republic* again used the term, this time in attacking President Jimmy Carter's handling of the energy crisis: "He has encouraged *conspiracy theories* about oil companies, by blaming them every time his energy proposals have run into opposition."

Gaddis Smith, in a *Times* book review in 1981, pooh-poohed a notion being hypothesized about Franklin Roosevelt's encouraging the Pearl Harbor attack. "A counterwave of historians," Smith wrote, "attacked the *conspiracy theory* as nonsense."

That's what you do when you call any expressed suspicion, especially a complicated one, a *conspiracy theory:* you dismiss it as nonsense, the product of an unduly suspicious or even paranoid mind.

Conspire is rooted in "to breathe together," and is older than Shakespeare, who had Brutus say in "Julius Caesar": "Conspiracy,/ Sham'st thou to show thy dang'rous brow by night,/ When evils are most free?" In criminal law, *conspiracy* is a catchall charge used by prosecutors whose case is too weak to prove the commission of what was conspired about.

Sustained suspicion about the official conclusions regarding the death of John F. Kennedy led establishmentarians to characterize the disbelievers as *conspiracy theorists* or *conspiratorians*. Judge Alex Kozinski, perhaps fed up with the notions of the likes of the fictional documentary moviemaker Oliver Stone, wrote in wonderment two years ago of "2,000 books (yes, two thousand) and countless articles and pamphlets that make up the J.F.K. *conspiramania.*"

Note that *pooh-pooh* is frequently associated with the phrase, as the verb describing the action taken by people who use it. This is a reduplication of the single *pooh*, an exclamation of contempt that came into the language around 1595.

What does somebody besmeared as a *conspiracy theorist*, which denotes a person who attributes an unexplained or unaccountable event to a sinister plot, call those who readily accept coincidence as an explanation? *Dupes*, from the French *duper*, "to deceive or trick."

You refer to a 1945 *New Republic* article as "the first use so far . . . perhaps the bright coinage" of the term *conspiracy theory*. However, a search on the Lexis legal database reveals uses of *conspiracy theory* as far back as 1924. In that year, a federal district court case, *Pennsylvania R.R. System v. Pennsylvania R. Co.*, contained the passage, "in the instant case other questions are raised than those raised by the conspiracy theory to which the Brotherhood Case was in effect confined." Lexis also yields the fact that in 1937 Howard J. Graham published an article in the *Yale Law Journal* entitled "The 'Conspiracy Theory' of the Fourteenth Amendment."

Fred R. Shapiro
Associate Librarian for Public
Services and Lecturer in Legal Research
Editor, *Oxford Dictionary of American
Legal Quotations*
Yale Law School
New Haven, Connecticut

Dear Allan Siegal:

In case you missed Bill Safire's reference to Warner *"Bros.,"* you ("Times style"), and me in his recent column (attached), I trust computer abilities will now enable you to change the style from a uniform "Brothers," even when it is properly "Bros."—for Lehman, Lever, Warner, et al.

Many years ago, you explained to Bill, Abe Rosenthal and me that, as a daily paper hurriedly checking facts on deadline, it was trivial and disconcerting to also require checking of the correct spelling of such mutual second names.

With Bill trying to end my nagging of him—can the *Times'* computers now make it even more accurate?*

Ed Bleier
President
Pay-TV, Cable & Network Features,
Warner Bros.
New York, New York

*In the new *New York Times Manual of Style and Usage,* "Brothers" is still spelled out unless the company name appears in a headline, table, or chart.

Construing the News

"News of my imminent departure or resignation," said former Secretary of State Warren Christopher, "are neither new nor accurate."

Maybe the ordinarily careful lawyer meant *reports,* a plural subject; maybe he mentally substituted an *and* for the *or* and incorrectly made that the subject of his sentence; maybe he was so deeply "into denial," as the psychobabblers say, that he engendered subject-verb disagreement.

The only other possibility is that the secretary construed *news* as plural, taking the plural verb *are.* (*Media,* for example, is construed as plural; one should never say, "The media *is.*")

Mr. Christopher would not be the first American public figure to treat *news* as plural. Legend has it that Horace Greeley, editor of *The New York Tribune* during the Civil War, sent this telegraph message to one of his correspondents near a battlefield: "Are there any news?" To which the reporter supposedly cabled back: "Not a new."

Covering Charlie

In the scandal some have given the dysphemistic headline "The Asian Connection" (based on the 1971 movie "The French Connection"), which other journalists slug "Lippogate" or "Indogate" (based on the Lippo Banking group in Indonesia), and which the most euphemistic call "the campaign fund-raising mess," one unfamiliar character keeps popping up: an entrepreneur in Little Rock whose Chinese restaurant was frequented by Gov. Bill Clinton.

His name is variously reported as Charlie Trie, Charles Yah Lin Trie and plain Yah Lin Trie. Reporters are uncomfortable with the nickname *Charlie,* as it seems to be an ethnic half-slur based on the title character in the Charlie Chan movie series of 1926 to 1944. Hence, the discordant *Charles* is fixed at the beginning of a Chinese name, which can't be right.

We may be reading a lot about Mr. Trie in coming months, because he was a big fund-raiser who took an arms dealer from Beijing into the White House to see Mr. Clinton at a "coffee" that some have suggested might have been related to campaign fund-raising. How to refer to Mr. Trie in first reference?

To solve this linguistic puzzle, I obtained a photocopy of a letter he wrote in Chinese to a prospective client or donor. The signature is in Chinese, and underneath its characters is the translation, presumably written by the man himself: "Yah Lin 'Charlie' Trie." He treats his English appellation as a nickname, not to be escalated to be a formal part of his name, and—on the theory that a person is the best judge of his own name—that's how to refer to him. Drop the *Charles*; infix *Charlie*.

Crumpled or Wrinkled?

For synonymists, the high point of the Simpson Murder Marathon occurred when Deputy District Attorney Hank Goldberg pointed to a plastic bag with an envelope inside and put this question to a Los Angeles Police Department criminalist, Dennis Fung:

"Now, sir, I want to ask you about the condition of that item when you first opened it up on the witness stand and saw it. And distinguishing between the word *crumpled*, as in 'an item that's folded in on itself and kind of bunched together,' and *wrinkled*, meaning 'an item that may be folded but has creases that are apparent in it,' was this——.' "

According to the *New York Times* account, Judge Lance Ito "winced" at this, but when the defense objected, the judge overruled the objection and allowed the question, to the relief of lexicographers.

"When you brought it out for the first time on the witness stand," the prosecutor continued, "was it *crumpled?*"

"No," said the witness.

"Was it *wrinkled*, as I've just . . . defined it?"

"There were wrinkles in it," Mr. Fung replied.

Apparently that was not the answer the prosecutor had hoped for. "O.K., but was it folded?"

"Yes."

I don't know if this will break the case in the minds of the jurors, but it has caused at least one language maven to break his head over the difference between *wrinkle* and *crumple*.

Wrinkle, the noun and verb, comes from the Old English *gewrinclian*, "to wind round, to twist," probably related to *wrench*. A wrinkle is a crease, a line that has been raised or indented on a surface by contraction or puckering. On skin, it is usually unwelcome, though Shakespeare wrote, "With mirth and laughter let old wrinkles come"; most references are pejorative, as in Nathaniel Hawthorne's "So yellow as she was, so wrinkled, so sad of mien!"

At the Blue Ridge Factory Outlets in Martinsburg, W.Va., I picked up a pair of pants from J. Crew labeled "wrinkle resistant"; at the Ralph Lauren outlet the same day, I bought a jacket (after checking it to make sure it was not made in Singapore) with the label proclaiming the garment was "guaranteed to wrinkle"; the fashion world is evidently torn over this word.

Crumple, from the Middle English *crump* and related to *crimp* and *cramp,* means "to bend, to press into small folds," sometimes with a sense of destruction: in Ben Jonson's 1606 play, *Volpone,* a character warns, "He will crump you like a hog-louse." In more recent slang, *to crump* means "to fold, to give up."

To crumple is "to fold haphazardly," while *to wrinkle* is "to make a crease in," often by crumpling. The difference is illustrated in this 1711 line from *Addison's Spectator* No. 130 about fortune-tellers: "My friend Sir Roger alighted from his horse, and exposing his palm to two or three that stood by him, they *crumpled* it into all shapes, and diligently scanned every *wrinkle* that could be made in it."

Crumpling (folding) causes wrinkling (creasing), not the other way around. And a "new wrinkle"—in the sense of "a fresh idea"—comes from the old Anglo-Saxon *wrenc,* "a trick," probably influenced by the original sense of *wrinkle,* "twist." Hairsplitters could spend months on this; no wonder Judge Ito was left shaking his head.

Cut and Paste

"To drop her now would almost certainly be criticized by Republicans as a self-protective maneuver by the President," wrote David Johnston and Todd S. Purdum in the *Times* about Attorney General Janet Reno. "Any replacement in those circumstances would be attacked as a political *pasty.*"

That was an inspired updating of the word-figure about cover-up too often expressed as the clichéd "fig leaf," I thought, but the word was misspelled. In 1954, erotic dancers or strippers started calling the small disks covering their nipples *pasties,* and the word is always used in the plural, as a single *pastie* would be in the category of one hand clapping. (The spelling ends -*ie* to differentiate the noun from the adjective *pasty,* "unhealthily pallid.")

When I offered this praise and correction to Johnston, he sheepishly replied: "The word I meant was *patsy.* It was a typo. Never would use a metaphor like *pasties* in the same sentence with the Attorney General."

From the frying pan into the fire. Whenever I use *patsy* to describe a pushover, as in "the patsy prosecutor," I get letters from Irish-Americans protesting that the word is rooted in *Patrick* and, like *paddy wagon*, is an ethnic slur. Informed of this dilemma, my colleague turned *pasty-faced*.

There's also *pasty* (pronounced PAST-EE), the plural of which is *pasties*.
This is a turnover-type little meat pie that is very popular in Michigan and perhaps other midwestern states.

Helen Galen
Washington, D.C.

Day 1

One is where it's at.

"The House has been up to the usual kind of political fighting," said Bob Franken, reporting on CNN, "even on *Day 1.*" This usage was given prominence by Newt Gingrich's promise to hit the ground running on his Contract With America; asked about welfare changes that could take two years, the Speaker said, "I'm closer to *Day 1.*"

The locution gained a purchase on the American vocabulary in the 1970s. "The game shows," *Forbes* magazine wrote in April 1975, ". . . make money from *Day 1* for everyone." That year, *The Economist* in London discussed wage and price controls, using the phrase in "values at *day one* of the freeze." *Business Week* at the same time wrote of assets that "belong to your child from *day one,*" suggesting that the phrase had its roots in the business world.

Those were the earliest Nexis citations, but a 1973 use was found in the Westlaw data base, searched by Fred R. Shapiro, editor of the *Oxford Dictionary of American Legal Quotations;* he found a judge's opinion about "experience . . . from *day one* until the end of time." A *Miami Herald* sportswriter, Scott Fowler, wrote on Dec. 31, 1993, "From *day one,* we knew there would be a market of people out there that would want to sit in the first couple of rows." (Everybody styles the phrase differently; *The New York Times* prefers *Day 1.*)

The phrase was popularized by the ABC television program *"Day 1,"* which began in 1993. But the Gingrich use seemed to trigger a proliferation of usages. "This Week With David Brinkley" on ABC titled a program "The 104th Congress—*Week One,*" and a *New York Times* editorial was headed "Governor Whitman at *Year One.*" (Here we are on the verge of Millennium Three, and nobody has yet referred to *Millennium One.*)

Has any phrasedick noted the use of *jump street* as a synonym for *day one*? I have heard this from police: "We identified him as a suspect from *jump street,*" meaning from the outset. This is not to be confused with identifying a suspect from U Street, and I wonder if any DCPD rookie, overhearing that a suspect has been identified from *jump street,* has gone off to apprehend the perp there, perhaps thinking it to be the chimerical roadway between I Street and K Street.

Allan A. Ryan, Jr.
Cambridge, Massachusetts

I would suggest that the earliest reference to "Day One" is found in the earliest reference to the first day—Genesis 1:5,

> "God called the light 'day,' and the darkness He called 'night.' There was evening and there was morning—Day One."

The phrase has been variously translated as "one day" or "first day."

The original Hebrew says "Day One," using the cardinal form of the number. On occasion, Semitic languages use the ordinal form of the number "one" in place of the cardinal form, but those details are unnecessary for this discussion. The meaning of this phrase is generally understood as the "first" day, but grammatically the term is "Day One"—*yom echad*—where *"yom"* means "day" and *"echad"* means "one." (Hebrew, like so many other languages, places adjectives after the nouns they modify.)

The expected ordinal form would be *"yom rishon"*; *"rishon"* means "first" (and, as a point of information for a fellow philologist [if I may be so bold as to catalog myself with you], *"rishon"* derives from the Hebrew word *"rosh"*—"head"—which in turn is familiar to so many people in the phrase "Rosh Hashana"—Head of the Year). In modern Hebrew, the days of the week are still referred to numerically. Sunday is "First day" (not day one).

The other days in the Book of Genesis use the expected ordinal form of the number, so that the second day is referred to as "[a] second day."

So, I propose to you that the earliest use of the phrase "Day One" dates back to the Book of Genesis.

Paul J. Fisher
Birmingham, Michigan

I believe that I can cite you the oldest such reference—by far.

Indeed, the reference is to (as the biblical expression might go) the Day One of Day Ones. I refer you to Genesis 1:4, and the phrase usually mistranslated as "and there was evening and there was morning, the first day" (e.g., in the NRSV). I say mistranslated because the relevant time reference in the original Hebrew is *yom 'ehad* and the literal rendering of the phrase would therefore be "and there was evening and there was morning, Day One." If the intent had been to express "the first day," a different Hebrew form would have been used, namely *yom ri'shon*, or the like as, for example, in Exodus 12:15, "on the first day . . ." *(bayyom har-i'shon)*. When the other days of creation are mentioned subsequently, the text goes back to the conventional form for enumerating, e.g., *yom sheni* ("second day"; Gen 1:8) *yom shlishi* ("third day" 1:13) and so on until resting time on "the seventh day" *(bayyom ha-shbi'i 2:1)*.

Biblical grammarians have long pondered how best to understand why a special phrase was used for the first Day One. Still the day is, after all, unprecedented at the time; indeed, one can wonder whether it makes sense to talk of a first day when there has yet to be anything beyond it. Most biblical grammarians will tell you that we should probably read the phrase "and there was evening and there was morning, one day," i.e., there was one day's worth of time. Only after you start adding other days to it does it make sense to form a queue involving precedence. Whatever the case, I would not be surprised to discover that the literal rendering of *yom 'ehad* may have found its way into western languages as being the ultimate in primary designations of time zero at ground zero.

Bruce Zuckerman
Rolling Hills Estates, California

Default, Dear Brutus

When Republican budget-balancers balked at automatically raising the Federal debt ceiling, many commentators warned direly that this inaction "raised the possibility of *default.*"

The cartoonist Tom Toles of the *Buffalo News* showed Speaker Newt Gingrich examining a paper labeled "debt ceiling" while President Clinton, in a Roman toga, orated: *"Default,* dear Newtus, lies not in our underlings, but in ourselves, that we are stars." This was an especially apt parody of Shakespeare's lines in "Julius Caesar," as Cassius says to Brutus, "The fault, dear Brutus, is not in our stars, but in ourselves, that we are underlings." The conspiratorial Cassius's point was that only their present political status as mere servants and subjects of Caesar, and not any vast destiny written in the stars, was the cause of their problem.

The erudite cartoonist, in addition to punning *default/the fault* and *Newt/Brut*, turned the meaning upside down, having the President say that the problem was rooted not in staff aides' mistakes but in the principal adversaries' lust for stardom. Brilliant cartoon. (Some Shakespearean directors tell their actors to accentuate the word *underlings*, shifting the emphasis to mean "the fault is our acceptance of subservience." O.K., Herman Utix, back to the budget.)

A *default* is a failure—to fulfill a duty, to meet an obligation, to appear in court, to pay what is owed. A newer meaning, familiar to users of computers, is "an action that a program has been set to take unless otherwise specified by the operator," from *default* as an absence of instructions. ("Can't I get this outdated hunk of machinery to *default* to a screen with narrower margins?")

The earliest English use, as *defaute* in a 1250 document, meant "offense, crime, sin," borrowed from the Old French *defaillir*, perhaps rooted in the Latin *fallere*, "to be wanting." The *l*, though recorded in 1393, was not pronounced for a few centuries; in Shakespeare's *Henry VI, Part 1*, it rhymes with "about": "Alanson, Reignier, compass him about,/And Talbot perisheth by your *default*."

The *default* in the news has been the "threat" that the United States Government, in a constitutional crisis, might fail to pay interest on its debt, like some kind of nationwide Orange County. That's not going to happen, and many feel that even discussing the theoretical possibility erodes confidence in the financial system unnecessarily.

But the recent focus on the word, in its sense of "failure to meet financial obligations," has led to usage in a more general sense. In an independent-minded *Washington Post* editorial that stunned the commentating class, the headline read "The Real *Default*." The point was that the way to reduce the deficit was to cut growth of middle-class entitlements, including Medicare. Not "to lull the public"; in an extension of the vogue word to its original meaning of general failure, the *Post* editorialist held, "If that's what happens, it will be the real *default*."

The word is pronounced with the emphasis on the last syllable. However, with its increased current usage, stress on the first syllable is sometimes heard. This is probably the influence of football fans yelling, "DEE-fense!"

Dee-cline
Dee-fense

"O my offense is rank," the king says in "Hamlet"; that *rank*, from the Old English *ranc*, meaning "strong," meant that his crime stank to heaven, and had nothing to do with the Middle French word *renc*, meaning "row, order," from which we get military *rank*. The word *offense* in that sentence is usually pronounced of-FENCE, as in "Don't take of-FENCE," but the noun is often pronounced OFF-ence, especially when used in contrast to its opposite, "OFF-ense is the best DEE-fense" (first promulgated in this century as "offensive is the best defensive" by Ernst August Lehman in his 1927 book, *Zeppelins*).

For most of this century, that was the only time *defense* was pronounced with the accent on the first syllable. In all other cases, *defense* was invariably accented on the *fense*. Try it: the Pentagon houses the de-FENSE department; in the O. J. Simpson trial, it's Robert Shapiro for the de-FENSE.

During the Super Bowl, however, we all know what team will decide the winner: it's the DEE-fense. This gridironmongery is taken from the pronunciation of the exhortation from the fans in the stands: the old college *hold that line* has been replaced by the chant led by professional cheerleaders, "DEE-fense, DEE-fense!"

When a noun formed from a verb beginning in *d* gains such a specialized sense, the accent shifts to the first syllable. But wait—how can anyone issue such a sweeping grammatical diktat? Where is the supporting evidence?

In "On the Other Hand," surely the wittiest series of essays bottomed on "the dismal science," the seeded-wry economist Herbert Stein titles his first chapter "My Life as a Dee-cline."*

"When I lived in Maryland," Professor Stein writes, "I was a Dee-cline. In Maryland one could register as Democrat, Republican or Dee-cline. If you were a Dee-cline, you could not vote in the primaries." (Similarly, in the armed services, if you had no middle initial, you were issued three on your identification card: N.M.I., for "no middle initial.")

"A *Dee-cline* seems to me to carry a different emotional connotation," Pro-

---

*Herbert Stein died on September 8, 1999.

fessor Stein informs me, "than *Independent* or *Mugwump*. I think it suggests more disdain for the political process." (The comedian Steve Allen defined *turnout* with the story of the feisty old woman who told a pollster, "I never vote—it only encourages them.") Stein concludes, "I suppose that now that we are confronted with a Democratic Party headed by Clinton, a Republican Party headed by Gingrich and a third party headed by Perot, there will be more 'Dee-clines' than ever." Sure enough, the first observer of this Maryland species pronounces it DEE-cline.

Where Credit Is Due

In the item above, the reader will note the history of "Offense is the best defense." I threw it in casually, as if I had it on the tip of my tongue.

Confession time. I had not the foggiest notion of where that American axiom comes from, and it isn't in Bartlett's or any of the familiar quotation books. Like all amateur etymologists, I get red-faced with frustration and hell to live with when unable to find the source of a famous saying. So I called my secret weapon, Jeanne Smith of the Library of Congress, a longtime member of On Language's Phrasedick Brigade.

She dug it up in *Modern Proverbs and Proverbial Sayings*, a 1989 compendium by Bartlett Jere Whiting from the Harvard University Press. Ms. Smith has the researcher's knack, also possessed by crossword-puzzle aficionados, of coming at a subject from all angles: not only under *offense* or *defense*, but also under *attack*. There, she found a clue to even earlier usage: in 1931, J. H. R. Yardley, in *Before the Mayflower*, wrote about "the old-age military axiom that attack is the best defence." (The Brits spell *defense* "defence," another good reason to break up NATO.)

Assuming I wanted more on the first use under *offense*, she called up on her library computer the book cited in Harvard's proverbial compendium; it turns out that the Lehman book on zeppelins was published in 1927, not 1928 as the proverb dictionary has it, and so the year appears correctly in my seemingly offhand parenthetical etymon. Also, her digging led to Professor Whiting's earlier book, *Early American Proverbs and Proverbial Phrases* (1977), which traces the saying to the 1700's.

What separates genuine phrasedicks from ordinary researchers? The ability not only to find the right book, but also to figure out what categories or entries to try. That's where Jeanne is Queen. For example, a fax came in to me from Jeremy Curtin, a United States diplomat in Helsinki, Finland: "Have you ever come across a saying something like 'There is no limit to what a man can do or where he can go if he doesn't mind who gets the credit'? My deep memory tells me the source is a former C.E.O. of G.M. or G.E., but I can't find confirmation, and my deep memory is often wrong."

That saying struck a chord. In 1966, when David J. Mahoney* was C.E.O. of the Canada Dry Corporation, he sent out a small bronze desk plaque with those words inscribed as a New Year's gift to key customers and suppliers. Mr. Mahoney, now chairman of the Dana Foundation supporting brain science research, saw that memento pictured on the desk of Ronald Reagan in the Oval Office, but was never able to trace the saying's source.

Back to Jeanne Smith at the L. of C. (I recently misattributed "National Information Infrastructure" to the library, but that title is a Clinton Administration infobahn pomposity. Peter Braestrup,† the great foreign correspondent now serving as a Library of Congress senior editor, reports that its program to reproduce some books as on-line digital bits is called the "National Digital Library.") Ms. Smith checked the standard quote books, as I did; no soap. Then to the specialized business quote books, on the assumption that a business leader was the source. But nothing in this sense of *credit;* most credit quotes had to do with collateral. She then tried accomplishment and bingo! In the *Handbook of Business Quotations,* compiled by Charles Robert Lightfoot (Gulf Publishing, 1991), is this quotation from Benjamin Jowett, 19th-century educator, master of Balliol College, Oxford, and the great translator of Plato: "The way to get things done is not to mind who gets the credit of doing them."

The modern, revised version—"There is no limit to what a man can do or where he can go if he doesn't mind who gets the credit"—is much punchier and more memorable because it has the *credit* at the end. Who edited the Jowett remark to a form suitable for tycoon mailings and chief executive desks? We may never know, because whoever did the editing never gave a hoot about who got the accolades, but I give the credit for this research and much other to Jeanne Smith, knight commander of the Phrasedick Brigade.

In today's excellent piece, you describe Ms. Smith as a "knight commander" of the Phrasedick Brigade. Since these United States have, generally, no knights and no knight commanders (not knights commander), one looks to Great Britain for the definition thereof, as used, for example, by such as the Order of the Bath, and the Order of the British Empire. Applying such an analogy, Ms. Smith is a "*Dame* Commander" of the Phrasedick Brigade.

William E. Walker, M.D.
Houston, Texas

---

*David J. Mahoney died on May 1, 2000.
†Peter Braestrup died on August 10, 1997.

Your reference to Lord Jowett's famous translation of Plato reminded me that he was considered, while Master of Balliol College at Oxford, the greatest of classical scholars, noted for the near-universality of his knowledge of Greek and Latin literature and philosophy.

To honor his achievement, the Oxford undergraduates composed the following verse:

> "Here I stand, my name is Jowett,
> What there is to know, I know it.
> I am the Master of this College,
> What I don't know isn't knowledge."

Leslie Klein
Lexington, Massachusetts

I admire the quotation—it described Phil Hart perfectly.

A few years ago, when I tried to track down its origin, I was told—I believe by a researcher in the Library of Congress—that it was contained on a plaque on the desk of Colonel C. J. George, an aide to General George C. Marshall in the 1950's. I assumed that General Marshall was the "Great Disseminator."

I checked with the Marshall Foundation in Lexington, Virginia, this week. Tom Camden, the Director, didn't know whether General Marshall himself had used the quotation, but said that visitors to General Marshall's office would have seen it on Colonel George's desk in the anteroom.

Edward M. Kennedy
United States Senate
Washington, D.C.

The Demon Made Me Do It

Prioritize had a nice run for a while, as bureaucrats tried to put first things first. Then *trivialize* had its moment in the vogue-verb sun until the usage of this older verb shrunk to the very occasional. Now we have the *-ize* of demons upon us, and *demonize* is where the hot word is at.

"Even by the standards of the people who most want to *demonize* me," said Speaker Newt Gingrich about his multimillion-dollar book deal, "it does seem at some point they are going to run out of this story."

Earlier, President Bill Clinton, who has also been singed by personal denunciation, told a gathering of centrist Democrats that they should engage Republicans in "a contest of ideas. But stop all this *demonization.*"

The word has historical resonance. "I hope to atone to them for my *demonizations,*" William Taylor, a British literary critic, wrote in 1799. Thomas Carlyle, in his 1837 history of the French Revolution, described "black *demonized* squadrons," and a British newspaper in 1888 wrote gloomily of a world "where men are brutalized, women are *demonized,* and children are brought into the world only to be inoculated with corruption."

For a century, the verbed noun meant "to render demoniacal," to make appear like a demon—an evil spirit of lower rank than a devil. Recently, a new sense has emerged: "to criticize excessively; to caricature unfairly." In this meaning, the verb is an attack on the attacker, and the villain is the one who engages in the exaggeration of faults.

This is another example of the Basher Reversal. To sully the motive or tactics of a critic of Japanese tariffs, for example, call him a Japan-*basher.* A critic can be fair, but a *basher*—rhymes with *slasher* and *masher*—is a certified meanie. In the same way, any disparager or critic of a modern politician is now subject to the countercharge of *demonization.*

Thus has the word been trivialized. Time for reprioritization: when out to savage the savagers, try *Satanize.*

I first heard the term "demonization" used in its present form by Dick Wirthlin in 1980. He was talking about coming up with tactics to prevent the Democratic strategy of "demonizing" the Gipper. I think it was shortly thereafter that they started including the "peace through strength" line in all the speeches. I guess it worked. Certainly the Carter people were not smart enough to think of a way to "Satanize" the old man.

> Howell Raines
> New York, New York

Dissing Dysfunction

Hardly anybody says "I can't stand him" anymore. Nor do we hear "She makes my skin crawl" or "I despise him with every fiber of my being." Instead, the same feeling is expressed in the coolly clinical "We have a *dysfunctional* relationship."

When the pseudonymous Mom Kallikak goes off on a toot and Pop tries to get his clutches on the cleaning lady, and as Junior blames parental neglect and sibling ribaldry for his drug-cultural descent, molested Sis sells the story to a publisher as "the saga of a *dysfunctional* family."

The prefix *dys-* is always bad news. From Greek, Gothic, Old English, Indo-European, Sanskrit, any root you like—a *dys-* is "bad, difficult, impaired," the opposite of the prefix *eu-*, which always provides a nice day. Doctors picked up *dys-* in 1916 and married it to *function,* and then sociologists and psychologists glommed onto it in a big way.

The *dysfunctional family* was a coinage of the psychiatric social worker Virginia M. Satir in her book *Conjoint Family Therapy* (1964). It became such a cliché that when Wendy Kaminer wanted to parody Thomas A. Harris's book *I'm O.K., You're O.K.* (1967), she titled her book "I'm *Dysfunctional,* You're *Dysfunctional*" (1992).

Politics was next. The *Times* reporter John Broder, investigating the archaic modernization at the Internal Revenue Service, used the vogue word to describe many of the agency's computers.

And on NBC's "Meet the Press," the District of Columbia's Mayor, Marion Barry, wedded the economist's 1932 *structural unemployment* to the *dysfunctional family* to come up with the reason D.C. government does not work: it is *"structurally dysfunctional."*

As Bert Lance might now say, "If it ain't *dysfunctional,* don't fix it."

Dominoes' Return

Robert Rubin, past Treasury Secretary, believed strongly that a collapse of investor confidence in Mexico would lead to similar dismay in other economies that need foreign investment.

"Not all of Mr. Rubin's friends on Wall Street," David E. Sanger wrote in *The New York Times,* "fully subscribe to what he calls this 'theory of *interconnectedness*'—'if that's a word,' he adds."

My job in this space is to reassure Cabinet members, insecure in their diction, that the words they use are indeed part of the 650,000-word English vocabulary. It's hard to put together a word that hasn't been used, and duly recorded, before.

The noun *interconnectedness* first saw the light of print in the English theologian A. G. Hogg's 1922 tract, "Redemption From This World," in which he averred, "We labor hardest to perceive the *interconnectedness* of events," a sentiment echoed seven decades later by Mr. Rubin. In the meantime, the poet Stephen Spender referred in 1952 to "the *interconnectedness* of Western and Eastern influences." A current catalogue of scholarly books describes one title as an exploration of "the *interconnectedness* of painting, prints and film as modes of art."

I predict that the Rubin theory, as presently stated, will not make it, because no noun of 18 letters can fit into a headline.

Why not the shorter noun, *interconnection?* That isn't exactly a grabber of a name for a theory, either, but it has the advantages of relative brevity and greater familiarity.

Why not, while we're compressing, drop the *inter-* and go directly to a theory of *connection?* Because it would be wrong. A clear distinction can be drawn between *connection* (from the Latin *nectere,* "to bind," and *con-,* "with"), which suggests a single link, perhaps initiated by one of the joined elements, and *interconnection;* by adding the prefix *inter-,* meaning "between," the longer word means "a mutual joining" or "a linking of internal parts at several places." (Watch the difference between *connection,* which can refer to the act of connecting, and *connectedness,* which is simply the state of being connected.)

Besides, *connection* has a sinister connotation: "The French Connection" was a movie about a drug dealer's method of doing business, its operative word based on the American underworld meaning of *connection* as "an inside source" for nefarious or corrupt dealings.

An even shorter word leaps to the political mind: *linkage.* But a word associated so closely with Henry Kissinger's diplomacy may not be desired in the Clinton Administration.

Another solution for former Secretary Rubin can be found in a figure of speech favored by the columnist Joseph Alsop and popularized by President Eisenhower in 1954: "You have a row of dominoes set up. You knock over the first one, and what will happen to the last one is that it will go over very quickly.

"So you have the beginning of a disintegration," Eisenhower said, explaining his decision to offer economic aid to South Vietnam, "that would have the most profound influences."

From the *domino theory* to *linkage* to *interconnectedness;* we've come a long way, Lone Ranger.

Wouldn't you have been justified in addressing, or referring to, Robert Rubin as "Loan Arranger"?

Mervin Block
New York, New York

Fire!

"I see 'shouting fire in a crowded theater' quoted in your paper—and every-where else—all the time," writes David Dreyer, who left the White House to join Robert Rubin at Treasury. (An interminable word was coined in 1922 by A. G. Hogg to describe the relationship of this to the foregoing item.)

"Have you ever done a column on the misuse of the phrase 'shouting fire *falsely* in a crowded theater'? Everyone drops the word 'falsely,' but never explains why it would be improper to warn patrons that their movie house is about to be consumed by flames."

Let us fully cite the great stricture written by Justice Oliver Wendell Holmes Jr. Note in his wording that *crowded* is not used to describe the *theater;* also, the word *falsely* appears before *shouting fire,* perhaps the reason that adverb is often dropped. In the 1919 case of *Schenck v. United States,* Justice Holmes wrote:

"The most stringent protection of free speech would not protect a man in falsely shouting fire in a theater and causing a panic. . . . The question in every case is whether the words used are used in such circumstances and are of such a nature as to create a clear and present danger that they will bring about the substantive evils that Congress has a right to prevent."

Downsized

"You shall mark many a duteous and knee-crooking knave," says Iago in *Oth-ello,* "that . . . wears out his time, much like his master's ass, for nought but provender, and when he's old, cashiered." Such is "the curse of service."

If the Bard were writing today, the conniving Iago would be saying, "and when he's old, *downsized.*"

Despite economic growth and low unemployment, the word that strikes fear into middle managers and white-collar worrywarts is *downsizing.* Though the word's connotation is positive when President Clinton speaks of "*downsizing* the Government," it has gained a pejorative aura when applied to layoffs of workers.

The word was born in a happy spirit. The United Auto Workers leader Leonard Woodcock was an early user, reported the quarterly *American Speech,* speaking of "the *down-sizing,* as G.M. calls it" on "Meet the Press" on Sept. 5, 1976. A month later, an ad for Ford LTD's in *Southern Living* asked, "Will '*down-sized'* cars have '*down-sized'* prices?" The raising of oil prices by the Shah of

Iran in 1974 sped the need to reduce gas consumption, and *Newsweek* in 1978 reported "the rush to *down-size* cars to meet tougher fuel-efficiency standards."

In the '80s, when the verb about making cars smaller extended its sense to making work forces smaller, it was greeted with enthusiasm by stock analysts and met with narrowed eyes by unions and by easily replaced managers. Britain's *Longman Register of New Words* dates the current sense to 1987, defining *downsize* as "to reduce (a work force) in size by redundancy." (That can result from *outsourcing*, based on a similar formulation of direction-and-verb, *outsource*, meaning "to manufacture elsewhere," and causing workers to be *outplaced*.)

The obvious reverberant coinage was *upsize*, which made an appearance in an ad in the March 1983 *Car and Driver*. Its meanings, however, were "to enlarge, amalgamate, conglomerate, grow," as in the 1996 *Variety* headline about the ballooning of showbiz: "The *Upsizing* of Hollywood." However, these related meanings are not the opposite of "to fire" in the current, personal sense of *downsize*. A newly hired person does not say cheerily, "I've been *upsized*," unless he has been putting on weight as well.

In *The Dilbert Principle*, the cartoonist Scott Adams writes of his years of employment at Pacific Bell: "Companies realized they had to make *downsizing* sound like more of a positive development in order to keep morale high. This was accomplished through a creative process of inventing happier-sounding phrases that all meant essentially the same thing. 'You're fired' (1980); 'You're laid off' (1985); 'You're *downsized*' (1990); 'You're rightsized' (1995). You'll see the following phrases used during the next five years: 'You're happysized!'; 'You're splendidsized!'"

The lexicon of layoff has a wide range. *Cashier,* the verb Shakespeare chose in the sense of "discharge," is from the French *casser,* "to annul," not from *cassier,* "to put in a money box" (which is why we don't *cashier* cashiers). The verb *cashier* is "to dismiss from a position of high rank, usually with dishonor." To *dismiss* is to let go without taint; to *discharge* lies between, to dismiss for cause but without tearing off epaulets and putting a reprimand in the 201 file. *Sack, bounce, give the heave-ho* and *can* are all informal synonyms for these verbs of peremptory riddance. The government bureaucracy's *rif* stands for "reduction in force" and imputes obedience to budget cuts rather than firing for cause. *Walking papers* is passé. *Ax* is still in use, a favorite of sports headline writers, and suggests that the owner doing the firing of the manager gets a sadistic kick out of the act.

All these are more vivid than *downsize,* which in turn has more blood in its veins than the recent *restructure* and *re-engineer,* leading to the even more vapid noun phrase *work-force imbalance correction.*

A counter-euphemism is called for to denote an opposite of dismissal. The language is struggling to come up with a verb expressing irate voluntary departure better than the currently muttered *I'm outta here.* Lexicographers can almost hear it now: "You can't *downsize* me—I [future euphemism]!"

Doyenne

Martha Stewart was described in the *New York Times* recently as "the *doyenne* of decorating and the kitchen." *Doyenne* is the feminine of *doyen,* and both are French for *dean,* which is derived from the Greek *dekanos* and the Latin in *decanus,* "leader of 10 monks in a monastery." (*Ten* is *deka* in Greek and *decem* in Latin.)

Setting aside its academic and church senses, *dean* and the infrequently used *doyen* mean "senior member of a group." Both words used to describe the "senior and most eminent member," but in current usage, *dean* refers mainly to the oldest of the bunch, showing respect but not necessarily conferring pre-eminence.

Doyenne, for "female dean," made its appearance in English in 1905, as Arnold Bennett wrote in *Sacred and Profane Love* of his character Mrs. Sardis, "that stately dowager, that impeccable *doyenne* of serious English fiction." For nearly a century, the distinction combined leadership with age.

Since the '60s, however, *doyenne*'s stress has been on seniority, even as the overtly feminine word drew criticism as sexist (from those who reject *murderess* and insist on *murderer*). The anti-sexist usagists suggested *dean* to cover both sexes, finessing the age-versus-eminence problem. "*Doyenne* seems to be fading out," writes Kenneth G. Wilson in the 1993 *Columbia Guide to Standard American English,* "because it is exclusive language."

Doesn't seem that way to me. It is finding a niche among writers studying society who use it to characterize "senior female" of a certain age whose years at or near the top require social deference or professional respect but do not assure group leadership.

Therefore, despite the nice alliteration of "*doyenne* of decorating," I would not apply that word to Martha Stewart. Give her another *decade.*

Draco vs. Stentor

Draconian, an adjective based on the somewhat severe disciplinary practices of the seventh-century B.C. Athenian lawgiver Draco, is coming on strong. For a long time, it cooked along in data bases at a rate of about 60 a year, then jumped to double that in 1994 in reporting about the caning practices of the Government of Singapore. One of my editors at the *Times Magazine,* Michael Molyneux, reports that the high frequency of *Draconian* sightings continues into this year.

Draco had the good idea that punishment should be meted out only by the state and not by the vendetta of private groups. To put the law across, he simplified it: all crimes were punishable only by the state, and that punishment would be death. No shades of gray; one size fits all. From this harsh discipline we get the adjective *Draconian.* (A legislator named Solon later eased up on the sentences, which is why we call our compassionate Congresspersons *solons.*)

Which brings up the question: Why, if the frequency of this heavy-hitting adjective is increasing and nobody remembers who Draco was in the first place, do we still capitalize the word?

We don't capitalize *solons* when we are writing about our legislators. Nor do we capitalize *stentorian,* "extremely loud, booming," to describe the voice that fills a room without benefit of electronic amplification, an adjective whose eponym is Stentor, a Greek herald in the Trojan War who the poet Homer claimed in the *Iliad* had the voice of 50 men.

So let's drop the *d* on *draconian.* And now to use it in a sentence: In an article about the decision of Parris Glendening, Governor of Maryland, to hang the oil portrait of one of his predecessors, Spiro T. Agnew,* in the state's historic hall, I erred in calling Governor Glendening a Republican. The following message was left for me by a *Times* clerk: "Chuck Porcairi, Governor Glendening's deputy press secretary, called to let you know that the Governor is a Democrat, and that there will be a hanging ceremony to which you will be invited."

How's that for *draconian?*

---

*Spiro T. Agnew died on September 17, 1996.

Duh

"*Duh* . . . NFL Players Really Aren't So Dumb," read a recent headline in *The Wall Street Journal* over an article about the measurement of cognitive ability given to football draft prospects.

Is *duh* considered paralanguage, like the uncertain *uh* or the interrogatory *hunh?* No. Is it what the sociologist Erving Goffman calls "a response cry," like *ouch* or *yecch?* Sometimes.

Most often, *duh* is an interjection, an exclamatory sound ejaculated for a lexical purpose—that is, to convey a specific message. For that meaning, let us turn to Frank Nuessel, professor of classical and modern languages at the University of Louisville and the leading, and perhaps only, authority on *duh*.

"The interjection *duh* appears to have a general meaning of 'Boy, am I stupid!'" notes Professor Nuessel. "It may also appear as a 'tag form' at the end of a sentence, meaning 'Don't you think I'm behaving in a stupid (ignorant) fashion?' This usage implies another person in a conversational dyad." (Duh? *Dyad* means "pair.")

In one use, *duh* is a response to which the person does not know the answer. Person 1: "Do you know the square root of 1188?" Person 2: "*Duh.*" (Meaning: "I don't know.") In the tag form, a person would say self-mockingly: "I'm really good at this. *Duh!*" (Meaning: "I really haven't the foggiest notion how to do this!") Here the interjection equals "Not!"

"The choice of this interjection is a calculated usage," Nuessel points out. "It represents a linguistic convention designed to symbolize ignorance. It differs from the paralinguistic form *um* because *um* is an automatic response while the use of *duh* is deliberate."

To avoid the need to assert ignorance, all I do is hit my Num Lock key and transform a portion of my keyboard into a calculator, thereby getting the square root of 1188. Done. So where's the square root key? *Duh!*

Fifty-five years ago, one of the more popular prime-time network radio programs began its weekly performance thusly:

Telephone (rr-i-ngggg!)

"Hello, Duffy's tavern, where the elite meet to eat. Archie the manager speaking, Duffy ain't here, Oh! Hello, Duffy."

Archie, of course, was Ed Gardner, the originator and writer of the program. He would shortly thereafter be joined by "Miss Duffy" (Shirley Booth), whose job it was to oversee the cash register and to make sure that Archie wasn't too liberal with the poured drinks.

They would soon be joined by a droopy, moronic-voiced character named Finegan, played by a radio character actor named Charlie Cantor, who was a "vocal Lon Channey."

Finegan's greeting as he entered the establishment was invariably: "Duh—Hello, Arch."
And that's how it all began.

Melvin Rosenberg
Roslyn, New York

Here in Texas, when some smarty pants tries to take you down a peg or two by stating the obvious, or makes a patently evident statement as if it were handed down from on high, the best retort is "Duh"—as in, "yes, you idiot, how stupid do you think I really am?" or "Any fool would know that!"

Mrs. Shan Shipp
Dallas, Texas

E Pluribus Pluribus

OLBOM—On Language's Board of Octogenarian Mentors—strikes again.

Ever on guard against voguist pomposity, Alistair Cooke has just landed on *multiple*. "Madeleine Albright used it the other day," he writes. "'We have made *multiple* protests.' And a cop reported 'he called the station house *multiple* times.' What's next—'In my father's house are *multiple* mansions'? The word *many* is vanishing from American."

For years, the snooty aversion to the plain English *many* (which appeared in 725 in *Beowulf* as *monig*) resulted in the rise of the august *numerous*.

Here's a corrective: when in need of a noun to denote the price-earnings ratio of a stock, feel free to use *multiple*. But when reaching for an adjective to mean "a large number of," eschew *multiple* and choose *many*. Tired of *many* and want an informal synonym to relate to a younger generation? Try *lotsa*.

Early Rap Artist

Hold on to your cigar—we may have discovered an unexpectedly early rap artist.

This is the sort of find that sends a frisson of delight through the entire

Phrasedick Brigade and causes lexicographers the world over to rejigger their computer files.

It concerns the slang verb *to rap,* which has led to *rap session* and *rap artist.* Though the noun *rap* dates back to Middle English, with meanings ranging from "a sharp blow" to "a rebuke" to the undeserved reputation of "a bum *rap,*" a criminal charge that is sometimes beaten, the slang or colloquial verb is a product of recent black English, especially in the music world. In the *Oxford English Dictionary Supplement,* the modern noun *rap* is defined as "a special style of verbal display, repartee. . . . More generally, impromptu dialogue, talk or discussion." The earliest citation in this sense of shooting pyrotechnic breeze is in a 1967 article in the magazine *Trans Action.*

This sense is rooted, I think, in a more general usage of *rap,* to mean "to talk freely and frankly." To back up this definition from *Merriam-Webster's 10th Collegiate,* here is a 1929 citation from Damon Runyon: "I wish Moosh a hello, and he never *raps* to me but only bows, and takes my hat."

Alistair Cooke, an active member of OLBOM—On Language's Board of Octogenarian Mentors—was reading "one of my bed books," presumably one he keeps handy for reading in bed. It was *Churchill at Large,* a collection of essays, newspaper articles and other writings by Winston Churchill.

In a piece dated Aug. 5, 1933, Churchill wrote about a Washington dinner party in 1931, at which "after the dinner was over, the whole company formed a half-circle round me . . . and for two hours we wrestled strenuously, unsparingly, but in the best of tempers with each other." In that admixture of controversy and camaraderie, he concluded, "The priceless gift of a common language, and the pervading atmosphere of good sense and fellow [*sic*] feeling enabled us to *rap* all the most delicate topics without the slightest offense given or received."

That's it: *rap* meaning "discuss" in the writing of a master of English letters. "Astonishing in Churchill," notes Cooke. "I never heard it used at all until about 15 years ago, and then from a jazz drummer."

Ah, those elegant Washington dinner parties, where the latest slang was tossed about in the rapt half-circles around an articulate source. Those days went out with Joe Alsop.

As founder (and sole member) of SCOLBOM—Septuagenarians Correcting "On Language Board of Octogenarian Mentors"—I have an interpretation of Winston Churchill's use of the term "rap" that is quite different from the one in your column.

When Churchill said that the good atmosphere enabled the group "to rap all the most delicate topics" without offense, his meaning is clear to anyone still in his 70's. Churchill would normally have said "to *touch on* all the most delicate topics." But since he meant that rather than just discussing or alluding to these topics, the opponents were *hitting* them pretty hard, he used the term "rap" in the sense of "hit."

If Mr. Cooke's interpretation were correct, Mr. Churchill would have to have said "rap about" the topics, rather than "rap the topics."

J. R. McCrory
Stone Mountain, Georgia

Elite Establishment Egghead Eupatrids

As is well known (as Communists used to say), the world is run by a snobbish arrogant clique of rich and powerful aristocrats—a network of the well born and overeducated—who maintain a stranglehold on the all-powerful media and sneer at downtrodden commoners condemned to a lifetime in entry-level jobs flipping Bilderburgers.

Welcome to the international language of populist resentment.

"Netanyahu as Victim of the Media Elite," headlined *U.S. News & World Report,* using the word *elite* as T. S. Eliot did in 1948 with the phrase "an *elite*-governed society." The conservative Israeli Prime Minister was reported to have used a Hebrew slang term, *branja,* to derogate what the newsmagazine called "the liberal, secular, moneyed *elite* centered in North Tel Aviv."

As the most popular synonym for *the Establishment*—a term attributed in 1945 to the '20s novelist Ford Madox Ford but popularized by the British political commentator Henry Fairlie in 1955—*elite* has a paradoxical etymology. It comes from the Latin *eligere,* "to elect," and became a noun meaning "elect, choice" but now means the opposite of "elected"—indeed, *unelected* is a common complaint of outsiders about insiders.

Although *elite* as a noun can be used proudly—radio's "Duffy's Tavern" advertised itself as "where th' *elite* meet ta eat"—*elitist,* the noun and adjective, and *elitism,* the nominative, are pejorative: the sociologist David Riesman wrote in 1950 that Sigmund Freud "shared with Nietzsche and Carlyle elements of an *elitist* position." In the 1992 Presidential campaign, Dan Quayle updated and broadened the idea in the phrase "cultural *elite,*" which radio's rambunctious Rush Limbaugh now calls "the dominant media culture."

The Japanese have adopted the French-English word, pronouncing *eriito* air-EE-ee-toe. "A young murderer had gone to the best high schools, medical school, and had secured a position in a first-rate hospital at an early age," reports Daniel Long, a language professor in Osaka, "and he was repeatedly referred to by the media as an *eriito.*" In classless Communist China, the ruling class is called *tongzhi jieji.*

Russia has been rich in characterizations of the inside wielders of power. From the *intelligentsia* of a century ago (used by revolutionaries to mean "the educated nonaristocrats") to the *nomenklatura* of the Soviet era to the *praviashchiy klas* more recently, the leadership class has long been recognized and resented. Today's term is the anglicized *isteblishment,* according to Natasha Simes of Johns Hopkins University, and *elitnaia midiia,* a term every American radio talk-show host will readily recognize. *Mafiozny,* in addition to its sense of "criminal," also means "powerful; united in a cause."

In the '70s, our homegrown *elitnaia midiia* were lumped with the *elitist* academic "effete corps of impudent snobs" by Spiro Agnew in a phrase created by Pat Buchanan. (*Effete,* meaning "pampered, decadent," was taken as homophobic, confused with *effeminate,* criticism rejected by the Vice President with "Check your dictionary.")

Insider was used in an 1848 book about Wall Street stock trading, playing off Jane Austen's 1800 term *outsider.* Though some media *elitists* pride themselves on being *insiders,* the word carries a sinister connotation to the *auslanders:* although the Spanish word *camarilla* is the equivalent of the British *old boy network,* the Mexican columnist Jorge Castañeda prefers the English term *insider.*

In France, the influentials and lords of creation traipsing through the corridors of power are called *les gros bonnets,* equivalent to the American *top brass,* from *brass hats,* for "fancy military helmets," or *bigwigs.*

In the past, populist resentment focused on a social aristocracy that became a political class: the *Bourbons* (from a town in France, Bourbon l'Archambault, which spawned a family that long held the throne) were segregationists who gained control of the Democratic Party in the South after Reconstruction. *Brahmins* (from the Hindu caste furthest from "untouchables") became an attack word of Irish politicians in Boston in the late 19th century against wealthy and socially prominent blue bloods.

But wealth and high birth—as exemplified by the *eupatrids,* or hereditary aristocracy of ancient Athens—are no longer the hallmarks of the inner circlers. Now what turns us off is brandished brains.

Like *old boy network* and *the Establishment,* the newer *chattering classes* is from the Thatcher era, popularized by Alan Watkins of *The Observer,* and has traveled the Atlantic to be adopted here. Nicholas Comfort, in his *Brewer's Politics* (1993), defines it as "the intermeshing community of left-of-center and middle-class intellectuals, especially writers, dramatists and political pundits, who believe their views should carry enormous weight and have considerable access to the BBC and much of the media."

Though intellectuals rarely gain power and liberal governments are becoming a rarity, liberal intellectuals are resolutely seen as part of the *power structure.* (*White power structure* was a '60s civil rights term, influenced by C. Wright Mills's 1956 title, *The Power Elite.*)

Hirsute anti-intellectuals have concentrated on the lack of hair on the foreheads of their targets of resentment: *high-brow* was used in 1908 in reaction to the disdainful *low-brow*, coined two years before to describe the uneducated. *Egghead* was defined in a circa-1918 letter from the poet Carl Sandburg as "slang here for editorial writers"; it was popularized in 1952 by the columnist Stewart Alsop, quoting his nonjournalist brother John saying, "All the *eggheads* love [Adlai] Stevenson. But how many *eggheads* do you think there are?"

President Clinton deplores "a world in which Big Bird is an *elitist* and rightwing media magnates are populists." He knows who takes the lead in blasting the powers that be. Catch us on the media; we breakers of the *Brahmin branja* are established as the *anti-Establishment elite.*

Exit Strategy

Bob Dole contended that President Clinton's timetable predicting that United States troops would be out of Bosnia in about a year was "not an *exit strategy.*"

That was not his first use of the phrase. In 1988, when the Dole campaign for the Republican nomination was running out of steam, Peter Goldman of *Newsweek* wrote, "While Dole went through the motions of carrying on, his mind was on what he had begun to call the *'exit strategy'*—a way to get out with as much leverage and as many options as he could preserve."

The phrase can be applied to personal decisions as well as to political or military strategy. "In the week before retired Gen. Colin Powell took himself out of the Presidential race," wrote Michael Kranish in *The Boston Globe*, "he began to ask associates about an *exit strategy.*"

The meaning of *exit strategy* is "plan for withdrawal." The predecessor phrase is *escape hatch*, a nautical term now little used by the politerati. The modern policy wonk who likes to keep an eye on the egress cannot merely announce *I'm outta here* or the more recent *I'm history*, nor is an old-fashioned *farewell* sufficient. (In Britain, the sign at an exit reads *Way Out*, but Americans cannot have a *"way-out strategy"* because of the slang meaning of *way-out*, "wild, weird, far-out.")

Enter *exit strategy*. When? The earliest use I can find is from a March 1979 *Harvard Business Review* article by Profs. Robert Hayes and Steven Wheelwright: "The company must now make two kinds of decisions. The first relates to both the entrance and the *exit strategies* for a specific market."

Reached in Cambridge, Mass., and notified that his is the earliest citation in the data bank, Professor Hayes says: "We did not coin the term *exit strategy* for that article. I'm sure I had heard the term elsewhere. We were writing for people out in the manufacturing field, and we used terms that would have already been familiar to them."

Honest Bob's firm disclaimer of what is surely a major coinage leaves us with an etymological mystery.

Experiment

A stealthy euphemism stalks politics: it's the verb *experiment with*. When chosen to be the GOP convention keynoter, Representative Susan Molinari—an eminently respected working mother—was asked about past indiscretions. The upfront New Yorker said in a written statement, "Yes, close to 20 years ago, I did *experiment with* marijuana, less than a handful of times." It was, she asserted, "the wrong thing to do," but a White House official, perhaps worried about Republican charges that incoming Clinton staffers used harder drugs, promptly labeled her *experiment* "drug use," which leaves the length of time open-ended.

Why is it, wonders *New York Times* reporter Neil Lewis, that the universal verb of choice in admitting to past drug use is *experiment?*

No politicians who recall actions involving drugs in the 1960s claim to have *used* illegal substances; that would make them *users*, which connotes addiction or at least regular use. Nor do they say they *tested* drugs, which suggests measurement for effectiveness. *Dabbled in* connotes a ho-hum carelessness and *fooled around with* is dismissive.

The most neutral term, *tried*, is rarely used. Nor does the careful public figure admit to *smoking pot* or *snorting cocaine* or, heaven forfend, *mainlining heroin;* those verbs are too vivid. Hence the innocent, antiseptic *experimented with*, implying a scientific examination, undertaken not for pleasure but out of curiosity or scholarly interest, and finessing questions of frequency or length of use.

It's a great euphemism, gone largely unremarked; listen for it during the next political confession. Perhaps mindful of the derision that followed Bill Clinton's 1992 "When I was in England, I *experimented with* marijuana a time or two and I didn't like it and didn't inhale," the White House press secretary fearlessly eschewed the euphemism at a briefing: "I was a kid in the 1970s. Did I smoke a joint from time to time? Of course I did."

But White House euphemists forced Mike McCurry to backtrack, and a week later he penitently apologized for having "communicated a cavalier attitude." Spokesmen everywhere took note: stick to the safe verb *experiment*. (I *smoked pot* when I was 19, doing an article about teen-age drug use, but that was before *experiment with* was cool.)

Eye of Newt Revisited

"Allow me to join the herd of herpetologists," writes C. Leon Harris, professor of biological sciences at SUNY-Plattsburgh, "who are no doubt giving you a forked-tongue lashing for your definition of *newt*."

The faithful reader will recall a piece on *eye of newt*, an ingredient tossed into the witches' brew in "Macbeth." The creature whose eye was used, I explained, was "a small lizard related to the salamander and sometimes confused with a spotted eft."

Belay that. "A *newt*, like the salamander, frog and toad, is a member of a class of animals called *amphibians*," writes John Tucker of New York in collaboration with David Grow, a herpetologist with the Oklahoma City Zoological Park. "A *lizard*, on the other hand, is a member of an entirely different class of animals called *reptiles*."

Leo Kretzner, biochemistry prof at the University of South Dakota in Vermillion, explains further that "Amphibians and reptiles, while both in the vertebrate class, are members of separate orders. Their common body form is an example of convergent evolution." He notes, "The metaphorical appeal of a politician named after a reptile is obvious," but it would be wrong. However, the satirical possibilities are there: "After all, as a bona fide amphibian, the newt is slippery skinned and abandons its young."

W. T. Edmondson, a zoology professor at the University of Washington in Seattle, agrees: "A lizard is a reptile with a dry, scaly skin, while newts and salamanders are amphibians, frequently described as being slimy."

Other herpetologists—it is fair to characterize my many correspondents on this as a herd—dispute the sliminess factor. But even worse: "The Shakespearean witches' brew was a toxic mixture," writes Myrna E. Watanabe of Yonkers. "Newts secrete the neurotoxin tetrodotoxin," the writer continues, adding slyly, "structurally the same as the toxin found in the puffer fish."

Now let's clear up the confusion that has long been bothering me between the *newt* and the *eft*. Back to herpetologist Harris in Plattsburgh: "An *eft* is the adult terrestrial stage in the life cycle of an otherwise aquatic *newt*"; apparently when a newt grows tired of life in the water and climbs up on land, it becomes an eft.

Professor Harris adds etymological illumination: "Considering an *eft* to be a *newt* is not the result of confusion. The word *newt* resulted from a misdivision of *an ewt*, which in Middle English meant *an eft*."

Facially Valid

Sometimes a lawyer gets hung up on a term of art and shoots it through his entire brief. "As long as the forms were *facially valid*," wrote Howard M. Shapiro, FBI general counsel, reporting on the bureau's curious handling of White House requests for its confidential files, "the FBI was legally entitled to assume that their author was acting within the scope of his or her authority." He added, "We have been institutionally inclined to process *facially valid* White House requests without reflection."

Three more times does his favorite compound modifier appear in Shapiro's short report, including his attempt to exculpate the bureau's anything-you-want file-givers: "It would be unconscionable to now fault these employees for not having somehow discerned that the *facially-valid* requests from the White House were made without justification."

The first question that leaps to mind in examining the report is: Why doesn't the FBI have a policy on the hyphenation of *facially valid?*

It takes no hyphen. That flat assertion (composed on the analogy of the title of the First Lady's personally written book) is made without equivocation because *facially* is an adverb, not an adjective like *valid.* "Do not use the hyphen to connect an adverb ending in *ly* with a participle in such phrases as *newly married couple, elegantly furnished house*," says *The New York Times Manual of Style and Usage.* "But adjectives ending in *ly* are another matter: *a gravelly-voiced, grizzly-maned statesman of the old school.*"

Not every usagist agrees; the loosey-goosey Associated Press manual holds that no hyphen is needed for all words ending in *ly*, but that fuzzes up a delicious distinction. In the preceding paragraph, *personally written* is not hyphenated because *personally* is an adverb; had I written *surly-toned*, I would have hyphenated because *surly* is an adjective and I am a nitpickingly certain, maddeningly mean maven of the old school. At any rate, if the G-men's grammarian disagrees (as if to say, "Drop the hyphen, Louie"), let him be consistent. Can't have *facially valid* two ways without being two-faced. (The University of London professor Randolph Quirk—Mr. Grammar himself—agrees with me on this.)

With the bureau's helter-skelter hyphenation now resolved, we can turn to the phrase's meaning. Asked for his definition, Mr. Shapiro replied by fax that *facially valid* is "a common legal locution meaning 'valid on its face' or, more specifically, in this context, those requests which, on the request form itself, are filled out in accordance with then-applicable regulations and bear no obvious indicia of being invalid."

In plain words, it didn't look illegal. The *face* in *on its face* is the surface, the front, the side with writing on it that can be looked at, or faced, by the viewer. The legal expression means "in the plain sense of," and *facially overbroad* means the same as "overbroad on its face."

But there can be a subtext to that meaning, with the focus on the surface including a connotation of "apparent" or even "supposed" or all the way to the suspicious "ostensible." What is on the surface may not reflect what is underneath—a value beyond "face value." The Latin phrase *prima facie* means "at first sight," suggesting a presumption that can be rebutted, or evidence sufficient to prove a claim if not contradicted.

Now that *facially valid* is in general play, the popular meaning will probably accentuate the negative: looks innocuous, but watch it.

Famously

"Most *famously*," the *New York Times* wrote about Senator Sam Nunn, "he opposed the war against Iraq, in part because he knew that Gen. Colin Powell and other military leaders were among those urging that sanctions be exhausted first."

In the same week in the same newspaper, a culture reporter noted "the *famously* low-budget film 'El Mariachi,'" a poet quoted something "Samuel Johnson *famously* said of a new translation of Aeschylus" and a foreign affairs writer asked, "Isn't this the Mexico that is *famously* proud of its 1910 Revolution?"

"What's with *famously?*" writes Joanna Williams, who teaches art history at the University of California at Berkeley. She notes that the *Oxford English Dictionary* cites the first two meanings as obsolete: one is "in a famous or celebrated manner, renownedly," and the second, also listed by Sir James Murray in the 19th century as out of it, "commonly, openly. Also, in a bad sense, notoriously."

Only the third definition of *famously*, listed as colloquial, covers the sense most widely known in our time: "excellently, splendidly, capitally," with the citation, "We get on *famously.*" That sense was used by Shakespeare in a play about Coriolanus, the Colin Powell of his ancient time: "I say unto you, what he hath done *Famouslie. . . .*"

What's with *famously*, Ms. Williams, is this: The old, obsolete meanings have come back with a rush and shoved aside the "modern" meaning. "To get on *famously*" still means to embrace heartily and sail along in a splendid relationship, but that usage seems stilted and bookish. The newest meaning is the oldest: "renownedly, celebratedly." Obviously, neither of those adverbs comes trippingly to the tongue, so *famously* is the modifier of choice.

Thus, in *The Times*'s sentence adverb, "Most *famously*," the meaning is "in what everyone knows him for." In the same way, what Samuel Johnson "*famously* said" means what everyone knows he said about the translation of Aeschylus: "We must try its effect as an English poem." (Is that familiar to you? Not to me; make that "not-so-*famously* said.") To the harmless drudges who write dictionaries, he more famously said, "I am not yet so lost in lexicography as to forget that words are the daughters of earth, and that things are the sons of heaven."

Fast and Louche

The vanishing art of virulent vituperation got a lift the other day when *The Sunday Times* of London took after Sarah Ferguson, the divorced Duchess of York. The newspaper became incensed when a book purported to reveal the dalliance of "Fergie" with a Texas millionaire while she was pregnant with her daughter Eugenie; this episode, coupled with the Duchess's continuing Concorde-jet lifestyle while more than $7 million in debt, moved the editorialist to decry her "puerile nature and incontinent ways" and to denounce her behavior as "louche and loose."

I have popped a few public figures in my day, and reached for unfamiliar adjectives to make phrases memorable (*nattering* and *congenital* come to mind), but frankly, *louche* was a new one to me.

The unfamiliar adjective, originally French for "cross-eyed," is rooted in the Latin *luscus*, "blind in one eye." In English, early in the 19th century, *louche*, pronounced "loosh," came to mean "oblique, not straightforward," and in a shameful linguistic abuse of a physical disability, has since pejorated to "disreputable, indecent."

(I have long needed a verb for "to worsen in meaning," and have just back-formed *pejorate* from *pejorative*, based on the Latin *pejorare*, "to make worse." Now I can pejorate all I want; is this a great language, or what?)

So there is our last Duchess hanging on *The Times*'s wall, not only *louche* but also *puerile*, "childish" in the sense of "silly" (not "childlike," which is cute), a 17th-century adjective from the Latin *puer*, "boy." The other adjective chosen to castigate her is *incontinent*. In olden times, this meant "failing to restrain sexual appetite," as in the 1380 usage "an incontinent monk," but in 1828 Noah Webster noted the word had also gained the meaning of "unable to retain natural evacuations." Because that meaning, especially regarding damaged bladders, is now dominant, I would no longer use it in the more general sense of "showing unrestrained behavior."

Your discussion of the word "louche" illustrates the danger of relying too literally on dictionary definitions and not usage. It also illustrates the declining standards of cultural literacy in British journalism. "Louche" in the original *sense* was a French import quite common in British upper-class parlance and by British upper-class writers like Harold Nicolson, Nancy Mitford, and Evelyn Waugh. Basically it connotes someone who is shady, socially suspect, and more or less conscious of the fact by an unstraightforward personal manner. Now this is about the last thing that anyone can say about Fergie. She is frank, straightforward, and blatant in her willingness to shock public mores and "*épater*" the Establishment and the Royal Family. English friends absolutely agree with me.

Charles Maechling, Jr.
Washington, D.C.

Fig Leaves

Somebody at the Republican National Committee has a tin ear. In a press release beating up on President Clinton for concealing specific budget numbers and hiding behind a declaration of vague principles, the GOP "talking points" writer snorted, "That's a fig leaf so small even Gypsy Rose Lee would be embarrassed to try to hide behind it!"

First, Gypsy Rose Lee is a name remembered with fondness by the advanced geezer generation, and remembered secondhand by those middle-aged musicalgoers who saw *Gypsy* in 1959, but it rings no bells with the majority of Americans. (Some aging flack at the Democratic National Committee may be preparing a riposte based on Sally Rand and her fan dance.)

More to the metaphoric point, a fig leaf was a device used by sculptors in an age of prurient innocence to hide the male genitalia. The covering used by women who disrobed for a living was the *G-string*.

Miss Lee (no anachronistic *Ms* allowed), who died a quarter-century ago, brought good taste to the art of striptease; her unbimbo air and literary interest (she wrote *The G-String Murders*) led the language authority H. L. Mencken to coin a word to describe her line of work in show business. *Ecdysiast,* meaning "serious-minded striptease artist," is rooted in the Greek word for "shedding an outer coating."

But in an era of full-frontal nudity and lascivious lap dancing, what political vituperator can get any rhetorical traction out of recalling the days of wine and Gypsy Roses?

Herewith my application for joining the I Gotcha Gang:

I, too, remember Gypsy Rose Lee with fondness, having been suitably impressed by her even though I was only about age thirteen when introduced to her at an annual meeting of the Mystery Writers of America, but H. L. Mencken coined *ecdysiast* for another stripteaser, Georgia Sothern.

Hugh Rawson
Roxbury, Connecticut

Gypsy Rose Lee had two mystery novels published—neither of which she wrote. The first, *The G-String Murders,* was actually penned by the successful mystery novelist Craig Rice. Indeed, Miss Lee had the good grace and humor to dedicate the book to her, stating: "To Craig Rice, without whom this could not have been written." Her second book, *Mother Finds a Body,* although also written by Miss Rice, had little success and spawned no further sequels.

Otto Penzler
New York, New York

You seem to have forgotten about the most famous fig leaves of all.

I refer you to the Book of Genesis, Chapter III, Verse 7, which is concerned with the results of man's first disobedience. After Adam and Eve had eaten of the forbidden fruit "the eyes of both of them were opened, and they knew that they were naked; and they sewed fig-leaves together, and made themselves girdles."

Matthew Aronson
Brooklyn Heights, New York

Fizzy Water Everywhere

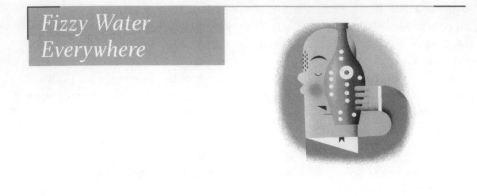

Soda water symbolizes sobriety. "Let us have wine and women, mirth and laughter," sang Byron's Don Juan, "Sermons and *soda water* the day after." These must be sober times. Never have we had such a variety of words to denote water with bubbles in it. In ordering your drink, of course, the word you choose signals your origins and sometimes your class.

Remember *seltzer?* It was the sole ingredient of a *two cents plain,* which is what residents of the Bronx called a glass of *soda water* that sold for 5 cents in the '40s, when I last ordered one at the High School of Science. The German word comes from mineral water from Nieder Selters, Prussia, called *Selterser Wasser.* It lives on in American English today in the last word of *Alka-Seltzer,* a tablet plunked into a glass of water that becomes an effervescent alkaline medication. (To the purist, *seltzer* differs from other bubbly beverages because it has no salt.)

But seated in an elegant restaurant at a power lunch, how does one order a calorie-free, fat-free, alcohol-free, custom-slavish drink? I tried "two dollars plain" but drew a blank stare from the person who wanted to be called a *waitron.* *Seltzer* is déclassé because it reminds late-night television viewers of wild attacks by the Three Stooges, who often brandished *seltzer* bottles; the word applies to the water given its bubbles by the process of carbonation invented by Joseph Priestley in 1767, and not from the natural bubbliness of underground springs. Only the outré stoop to mentioning a brand name, like Perrier, San Pellegrino, Quibell or Saratoga, because the cognoscenti at the Four Seasons or "21" eschew all designer labels.

You could say *soda,* or to add emphasis, *plain soda* (which also differentiates it from *bicarbonate of soda*), but somehow *plain soda* sounds plebeian or apologetic or cheap, recalling *soda pop.* The *pop* was the sound of the bubbles as they released their gas at the surface. The regional dialectician Jack Rosenthal wrote in this space in 1983 that *soda* was "a generic word for *soft drinks,* like *pop* to the Middle Westerner or *tonic* to the Bostonian, or *dope* to people from the South-Central states." In Wisconsin, according to Leonard Zwilling of the *Dictionary of American Regional English (DARE)*, the name for plain *soda,* as well as for the lemon-lime flavored 7-Up and Sprite, is *white soda,* to differentiate it from dark colas.

How about the Byronic *soda water?* That's a little more upscale, for almost three centuries meaning "water charged under pressure with carbonic acid gas." Also socially neutral is *club soda,* leading to the question: How is this beverage related to the weapon carried by Neanderthals? Answer: Cantrell and Cochranes Super Carbonated Club Soda was the trademark in 1877 of an Irish company, probably referring to the social clubs in which the gaseous new water was featured.

Much more impressive to flight attendants pushing fat carts down narrow aisles is *sparkling water.* Sometimes the carbonation is natural, but "the Food and Drug Administration allows bottlers of *sparkling water* to re-add carbonation to the water," says Jennifer Levine of the International Bottled Water Association, "so that the amount of carbonation equals the amount it has when it emerges from the spring's source."

The most recent term encompassing all unflavored effervescent beverages, *sparkling* or *club, mineral-enriched* or *seltzer,* is *fizzy water.* "Is the Age of *Fizzy Water* Ending?" was a recent headline in *The New York Times.*

Fizzle is of echoic origin, meaning it is a word coined to approximate a sound, and dates from a 1532 scatological use. *Fizz* came a century and a half later, followed by the adjective *fizzy,* which Rudyard Kipling used to describe Champagne: "The Captain stood a limberful of *fizzy*—Somethin' Brutt."

But what if all that *fizzing* causes you to belch? Or gives you that bloated feeling? How do you order plain water, which in bottles sells 10 times the amount of *sparkling water?*

If you're a swain out to impress a Southern belle, try *branch water;* a *branch* means a "small stream" in the Carolinas and Virginia, and *bourbon and branch water* is as familiar there as *Scotch and soda* is up North.

Few say *tap water* anymore; though *beer on tap* is fresh and desirable, water from the tap is rarely spoken of, though frequently given. When ordering water, if the waiter asks *"sparkling?"* it is more soigné to reply *still* rather than *tap* or *flat.* In France, *l'eau minerale* is *still,* usually Evian, and with *gazeuse* added it becomes *sparkling,* but an order of *mineral water* in the U.S. is an invitation to further interrogation of *"sparkling* or *still?"*

If you prefer the bubbles, the with-it term is *fizzy water,* an adaptation of British slang for Champagne. With or without minerals, unbruised by ice, its age is not yet done. (Urp.)

I am impelled to say, on the issue of defining mineral water, "You're all wet!" *Eau minérale* does not universally signify still water. Specifying the water remains an important part of the ritual of ordering, be it in the most modest bistro or in the most *huppé* and pricey restaurant. If you don't immediately designate your choice by brand or with a question as to which brands are available, the waiter will ask you to name your preference, using one of a number of for-mulae: "plate ou gazeuse, Madame," or "plate ou pétillante," or even, "avec ou sans bulles?" In Italy, you need to specify *aqua gassata* or *con gas or senza,* and in Madrid, I quickly learned to ask for *agua con gas.*

Mona T. Houston
Bloomington, Indiana

If you want the straight poop on *pop,* ask an old bottle collector, or even a young collector of old bottles. These antique glass aficionados will tell you that *pop* derives from the *pop* bottle, a uniquely designed glass vessel patented in the 1870's, and manufactured as a container for carbonated beverages. Instead of a cork stopper it had a solid, marble-sized glass ball impris-oned in the neck area which, when freshly filled, would be forced upward by gas pressure, firmly sealing it against an internal rubber ring at the bottle mouth to prevent leakage.

When one wished to have a drink from the bottle, he or she would press a finger down on top of the partially protruding glass ball which, with an exciting pop (like that of a pop gun, first heard of in 1662), would sink into a slot molded into the bottle neck allowing the soda to be poured. But that's not all this "smart bottle" could do. If one wished to drink only half and save the rest of the beverage, turning the bottle downward and to one side allowed the glass ball to reseat against the seal, ready to pop again later, so long as the gas pressure held it tight.

Needless to say, these fancy bottles were expensive to make and the beverage distributors depended on a healthy deposit to bring them back for reuse. This plan was thwarted unex-pectedly by a certain group: kids! Youngsters broke the bottles in vast numbers in order to use the glass balls to play marbles. Within a few years the whole enterprise went bust. Cheaper bottles with today's metal caps (patented in 1891 and called crown cork closures) soon took over, and kids had to get their marbles elsewhere. All that was left was the memory of that delightful sound and a new term for carbonated drinks.

Robert Gerard
Palisades, New York

Flea Circus

"Remember what Mark Twain said about dogs," said President Clinton not long after his re-election, perhaps thinking about press coverage. "Mark Twain said every dog should have a few fleas—keeps them from worrying so much about being a dog."

The report of Mark Twain's attribution is exaggerated. A. James Crawford of

Fairfield, Conn., writes that in *David Harum,* an 1898 book by Edward Noyes Westcott, the title character is advising a timorous friend to get up and lead the church choir, despite its challenges: "They say a reasonable amount of fleas is good fer a dog—keeps him from broodin' over *bein'* a dog, mebbe."

Twain on dogs: "If you pick up a starving dog and make him prosperous, he will not bite you," he wrote in *Pudd'nhead Wilson* in 1894. "This is the principal difference between a dog and a man."

Give Clinton a half-salute for a good quotation, wrong attribution. In another locution, however, he needs total correction.

Asked at a news conference about negotiations with Congressional leaders concerning a lowering of the capital gains tax, the President said, "I had no right to say that was a show stopper in a deal."

From the context, it appears that Clinton thinks that a *show stopper* stops a show, which is self-evident, but does so in a way that breaks up a deal.

As Barbra Streisand could tell him, a *show stopper* (first used by *Variety* on Aug. 19, 1926, in hailing the "itch dance" of the Dixie Four followed by Dave Apollon in a vaudeville show) means "a performance that receives such applause as to temporarily prevent the show from continuing."

A *show stopper* is cause for rejoicing and is definitely not a *deal breaker.* The earliest citation I can find of that term—referring to the admittance of an impediment that has blocked the marriage of many true corporate minds—is by Gary M. Hector in *The American Banker* of Nov. 18, 1980: "The Canadians collected money that encouraged the Europeans and Americans to label their dispute with the Canadians a *'deal breaker.'* "

I've run the usual traps of lexicographers, merger-and-acquisition bankers and labor mediators and can't come up with an earlier *deal breaker.*

Both *show stopper* and *deal breaker* are now often hyphenated, but within a few years should be treated as single words.

Come to think of it, I've heard "show-stopper" used in the software industry as follows: When you're testing the product before shipping it, a "show-stopper" is a bug that's so serious you *can't* ship the product with it, but have to "stop the show"—hold up the shipment, slip the schedule—till it's fixed.

Dr. Mark Mandel
Framingham, Massachusetts

"We chose to put our family first," said Dan Quayle, announcing his noncandidacy for President in 1996, "and to *forgo* the disruption to our lives."

The *Washington Post* picked up his verb in its headline: "Quayle *Forgoes* Presidential Race."

"Gotcha!" I cried at the breakfast table. *Forgoes* looked funny to me; what happened to the other *e?* I turned to my *New York Times,* and there it was: "and to *forego* the disruption to our lives."

I was mistaken; so was my colleague at the *Times.* The prefix *for-* means "away" or "wrongly" and refers to omission or prohibition, as in *forbid, forbear* and *forswear.* The verb *forgo,* without the *e,* comes from the Old English *forgan,* meaning "to pass by," or as we would say now, "to pass up"; it means "to do without, to give up."

What threw me off? There is an archaic verb *forego,* meaning "to go before," but it survives in the language as *foregone,* and that it will be a source of confusion is a foregone conclusion.

The prefix *fore-,* with an *e,* with its "to go ahead of" meaning, pops up in *forecast, foremost* and—as Simpson-potatoes can tell you—"the *foreperson* of the jury."

Pronounce *forgo* with the stress on the second syllable: for-GO. Brit Hume of ABC News mispronounced that verb right before the latest State of the Union address. He said President Clinton "will call on Congress voluntarily to FOR-go gifts from lobbyists now."

Many dictionaries list both spellings—*forgo* and *forego*—and helplessly suggest we pick 'em. Merriam-Webster, for example, has *forgo* as its main entry and a separate entry of *forego* as "a variant of *forgo.*"

None of that permissive stuff in the foregoing paragraph for me: what the noncandidate did was to *forgo* a run.

A nice choice of a word for a man who was publicly pilloried for adding an *e* to *potato.* Dan Quayle chose the apt verb, spelled it right and caught a few of us off base.

I suggest that you forgo the expression "publicly pilloried." It's no fun to pillory people privately. That's why it's not done.

Richard L. Jacobs
New Haven, Connecticut

$40 Word

Our search for the origin of *$40 word* is progressing.

The construction is in active use. Oliver Conant, an English teacher in New York, chastising me for using *argumentation* when *argument* or *reasoning* would suffice, notes that he looks to this column as "a solecism and obfuscation free zone" and not "as a place where I'm likely to stumble across verbal imprecision or the use of $50 words."

The price, of course, keeps inflating. Eric Widing of North Salem, N.Y., found the phrase selling for half price in William Strunk Jr. and E. B. White's 1959 *Elements of Style.* "Avoid the elaborate, the pretentious, the coy and the cute. Do not be tempted by a *twenty dollar word* when there is a ten-center handy, ready and able."

But here's a clue to the etymon, from Robert Goldman of New Rochelle, N.Y.: "Your reference to a '$40 word' evoked a fuzzy recollection of a radio program called 'Paul Wing's Spelling Bee,' where dollar values (none of which approached $40) were assigned to words."

The scent has been picked up; the hunt continues.

Four-Letter Words

"Work is a four-letter word" was a bumper sticker of the defiantly lazy in the '60s, based on a remark attributed to the Yippie Abbie Hoffman.

That illustrates the meaning of the phrase *four-letter word* as "vulgar, obscene," not for use in what used to be called *mixed company.* Of course, *work*—along with *hope, love* and thousands of other words of four letters—is not a *four-letter word.* That phrase (first used, Merriam-Webster says, in an 1897 book on flags) defines several sexually explicit or scatological terms, sometimes referred to as *barnyard epithets* or by using the first letter of the shocking term followed by the word *-word.*

These words are indisputably part of our language. "The obscene 'four-letter words' of the English language," *American Speech* wrote in 1934, "are not cant or slang or dialect, but belong to the oldest and best established element in the English vocabulary."

They are not included in most dictionaries, because publishers want to sell those books, and many parent-buyers are presumed not to want their children to pore through a book at home to look up the "dirty words." (Like all my prurient friends, I looked up *rape* in a dictionary when I was 8 years old, and was thrilled to learn it meant "carnal knowledge of a woman without her consent"; not until many years later did I learn what *carnal knowledge* was. That familiar experience caused the phrase to be used as a movie title in 1971.) The absence of these terms shames lexicographers but is considered our "sop to Cerberus"—an acknowledgment that some compromise is necessary between scholarship and commerce.

In the 70th anniversary issue of *The New Yorker,* the editor, Tina Brown, saw fit to print a couple of those four-letter words in a roundup of correspondence by the magazine's founding editor, Harold Ross. In this 1940 Ross letter to the humorist Frank Sullivan, I will bracket my omission of those terms for reasons to be given later: "Frank: Let me know about the ending—whether it was [past tense of a four-letter verb followed by 'up'] or not, and while I'm at it, I wish you and [John] O'Hara and a few other hardy boys would stop writing [two of the most familiar four-letter words] in letters to this office, because they have to be handled by pure young girls and I don't want to embarrass them, whatever the new attitude is toward such things. I'm a simple old double-standard boy. . . . As ever, R."

Seven years before, Ross had discussed the publication of such words in a letter to Frank Crowninshield, the editor of *Vanity Fair,* who also despaired that an editorial barrier to them was considered old-fashioned: "The use of daring words is one of our most serious problems, or at any rate, one of my most serious concerns. I, too, suspect frequently that I am a generation behind. Much of my activity the last couple of years has been fighting the use of words which I think are shocking in print."

In discussing a magazine's circulation "in mixed company," the careful editor (who evidently permitted the use of *which* to introduce restrictive clauses) wrote 60 years ago: "The hell of it is that in these days of frankness and disillusionment, when fathers insist that they want their daughters to have 'experience before marriage' and when Vassar graduates turn up with a vocabulary which you haven't heard since the old days in Fanny Brown's hook shop in California, I don't know how to gauge the standards of mixed company. I frankly suspect, however, that the present vocabulary is superficial socially, temporary and fadistic, and that the conservatives are in the majority."

They still are, but the increase in the published and telecast use of obscenities proves that it is not "temporary and fadistic." While the public use of racial slurs (described as "the true obscenities") has gained a greater taboo, the use of blunt sexual and excretory terms has been losing its taboo. The perfect example is the Ross discussion of four-letter words in *The New Yorker*, which he would never have included during his editorship.

So why don't I do the same? Am I a fuddy-duddy, a bluenose, an advocate of censorship? Why do I belabor you with arch, bracketed avoidances when you surely know the words and are no longer shocked by them?

Some would say the reason is that I like this job and want to keep it. Others would offer that I know that such fearlessness would be meaningless, as the forbidden words would be headed off at the editing pass. Those are cop-out excuses. Nor can I plead personal squeamishness, because I sometimes use these terms in private conversation and in writing fiction. I stand with the lexies: though there are dirty speakers and dirty writers, there are no dirty words.

But here is one reason to refrain from using four-letter words in the company of all ages, sexes and sensibilities (that's the new "mixed company"): it is a meretricious way of putting force in prose. (A *meretrix* was a Roman prostitute.) If a writer cannot shock with an original figure of speech, that writer pretends to be gutsy with the use of gutterspeak, relying on obscenity and profanity to reflect reality in dialogue. Screenwriters pepper their dialogue with street talk and project it into the theater and living room, debasing livingroom talk when it is treated as acceptable by the young. As a comedian said, he was raised to think *mother* was half a word.

Long ago, in the days of James Joyce and D. H. Lawrence, the four-letter word was avant-garde, true to life, artistically courageous; today, with its use by the phony-tough and the voguish, the former shockers are hackneyed, played out, artistically or reportorially demeaning.

Now we come to the practical reason for reinstating the taboo on four-letter words: we are robbing these great, short Anglo-Saxon terms of their power. Just as the key to sex appeal is artful concealment, not full frontal nudity, the key to shocking with language is the husbanding of taboos. Remember the classic Western movie *Shane*? Alan Ladd as the gunslinger did not pull the trigger until the end—and then the noise knocked you out of your seat. We were not inured to the shock by a hundred previous pops of the gun.

We need our disparaging epithets, our vivid vulgarisms and soul-satisfying expletives. If you stub your toe in the dark, lurch forward and knock over a table of glassware, what will you shout when a noun-verb obscenity—bandied about by children, grunted endlessly on cable television and rating 11½ pages in the *Random House Historical Dictionary of American Slang*—retains all the puissance of "Heavens to Betsy"?

Bring back muscular discourse. Save our abused and worn-out four-letter words. Declare them taboo again. They'll thank you by enlivening your language when you really need them.

Shane did not fire his gun for the first time at the end, but in the middle of the film when showing off to the boy, Joey.

The reason the shots in that scene were so loud was that director George Stevens told the sound man to record the shots as they were fired inside a metal garbage can, increasing the reverberation.

David B. Pittoway
New York, New York

Fuhgeddaboutit

"Will copywriters ever capture the vernacular of New York City?" asked a "reefer" (a boxed promotion referring the reader to an article on an inside page) in the *New York Times*. The answer: *"Fuhgeddaboutit."*

Undaunted, a copywriter for Cathay Pacific airlines gave it a shot: "Changing planes to Hong Kong? *Forgetaboutit."*

No way, José; if you are going to run the three words together in an attempt to capture the New Yorkese flavor, you have to change the spelling to conform to the local pronunciation. In New York, the *r* in *forget* is as lost as that letter in *York*. As every Noo Yawker on Madison Avenue knows, the mnemonic to copywriters trying to go local is *Nevuh fuhget!*

To spell the elided words correctly is to miss the point of this elision field. In the earliest use of this rampant run-together that I can find, the mistake of overcorrectness is made: Paul Attanasio, in a 1985 piece in *The Washington Post* about the director Martin Scorsese, reported the movie maker's "nailing home paragraphs with those shibboleths of resignation from the old neighborhood: 'Whaddaya gonna do?' 'Forgetaboutit.' "

The reporter transcribed *whaddaya* properly. This elision of "what are you," first noted as *whaddye* in the *New York Evening Journal* in 1913, could be presented as *what're yuh,* but that rye bread would not have the necessary seeds: the sound of *t* is changed to *d* in this dialect and the internal *r* is banished—thus, *"Whaddaya gonna do, Mardy?"* represents the sounds of "What are you going to do, Marty?"

But trying to express the fierce derision and unalterable dismissal of *fuhgeddaboutit* in the somewhat prissy *forgetaboutit* is the linguistic equivalent of accepting the assimilation of the bagel: that formerly hard-crusted ethnic treat with the distinct hole has, as it has overtaken the doughnut in popularity across America, been transformed into a doughbagel—a large, soft, sometimes sweet, nearly holeless pastry eaten by copywriters who pronounce their *t*'s and use *r*'s.

If I sound uncharacteristically prescriptive about this, it is because *fuhgeddaboutit* shows early signs of becoming one of those global Americanisms, like the last century's *O.K.* or this century's *no problem*, and it's important to get it right. Indeed, one of the senses of the phrase is, like one sense of *no problem*, "it's no trouble, glad to do it, don't mention it, piece of cake," expressed in French as *de rien* and in Spanish as *de nada*.

However, the main sense is a strong denial of possibility, with an admonitory overtone. With the first syllable separated, and the second syllable taking the stress, *fuh-GEDDaboutit* has eclipsed the infixed "abso-bloody-lutely nuh-uh," has driven out the crisply military "negative" and bids fair to replace "no way," with or without the rhyming emphatic of *José*.

It's a helluva coinage. *Helluva* is the elided form of *hell of a*, a phrase that suggested evil when it was coined in 1778, but its lumped-together form—first used by the humorist George S. Chappell in his 1926 book *The Younger Married Set* and noted by H. L. Mencken in 1947—has gained a connotation of admiration.

The practice of squeezing together words to form a name is in vogue at financial institutions (Citibank, Nationsbank) and among suspects in drug cases. "Sheriff's deputies and Franklin police searched the home of Efremzimbalist A. Randle, 27," *The Daily Iberian* in Louisiana recently reported. At the time of Efremzimbalist Randle's birth, the actor Efrem (not Ephraim, the usual spelling) Zimbalist Jr. was starring in "The FBI," a popular television series. Whaddaya know; helluva note. Gonna fuhgeddaboutit.

I don't know the origin of the phrase "a tin ear," but I think you have one. It is very annoying to be instructed by an expert who gets it wrong.

You make two mistakes. In your sub. head you say "talking like a New Yorker is not the same as talking like a Noo Yawker." No one who says *Noo Yawk* would ever say *Noo Yawker*. The correct spelling (and pronunciation) should have been *New Yawkuh* (or *Yawka*). The "r" would never be pronounced.

Similarly, in paragraph 5, where you write "Whaddaya gonna do, *Mardy*?" The name should have been written as *Mahdy*, with no audible "r."

Vivian Rothenberg
Brooklyn, New York

I have to ask why you promulgated a fine and absolutely correct rule for speaking Noo Yawk: "the internal r is banished" (a better guide, even, than the "t" to "d" usage) but flouted it in the next illustrative sentence: "Whaddya wanna do, Mardy?" "Mardy," by your precept and rightly, is "Mahdy" Every Martin I've ever known was and is "Mahtin" and that includes, from Boy Scout days, those invaluable assets in a birdwatching life list, the Pine and Purple Mahtins, and of course, the Stone Mahten, beloved by those un-P.C. retro folk who love to snuggle into their fuhs on a chilly Noo Yawk day in the gahment district.

Samuel W. Gelfman
Los Angeles, California

I wonder what Mr. Safire's reason was for mistakenly referring to the word "Nationsbank" as an example ". . . of squeezing together words to form a name . . ." I am sure most people know the word he meant to name is "NationsBank."

John J. O'Neill
Pinehurst, North Carolina

I'm shocked to find myself challenging you on your piece on "FuhGEDDaboutit."
You're dead right, as always, on the origins of the phrase and its evolution into a single word of admonitory denial. It is, though, all but impossible to pronounce it with the last syllable beginning with a "t." Trust me on this, Bill; absent an effort of will and a trained tongue, the whole phrase, especially compressed into one word, leaves the tongue lax below the teeth, to make sounds like "fuh", "duh", "ba", and "dit," not lifted as in a sharp terminal "t."

Charlton Heston
Beverly Hills, California

You seem to have "fuhgoddenabout" your own tenet regarding seeded rye (paragraph five—"t" becomes "d"). Only a New Yawker who spent too much time in Fargo would actually pronounce the "tit" at the end of the word. May I suggest that "fuhgeddaboudit" (note "dit") is the most accurate transcription of this word?

Richard J. Hyman
East Northport, New York

Full Bore, Small Bore

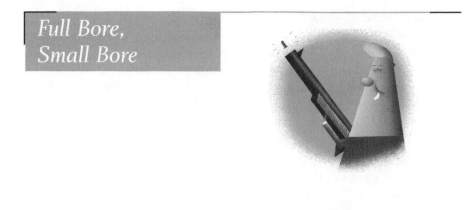

"Mr. Clinton proposes only *small-bore* reforms," opined the *New York Times* in an editorial about Medicare. A couple of weeks earlier, a cheerful harangue in the same space about tax cuts included a prepositional phrase: "But the economy is now operating *at full bore.*"

A dissymmetry is apparent. Shouldn't the opposite of *small bore* be *big bore*? Or shouldn't the opposite of *full bore* be *empty bore*? When a reader, Joseph D. Becker of New York, asked the editorial-page editor, Howell Raines, for the etymology, he bucked it on to me.

Full-bore, hyphenated when used to modify a noun, is a Britishism that Americans are adopting (like *not to worry* and *sendup*). Curiously, it is defined in an American dictionary, the Random House unabridged, but not yet in the *Oxford English Dictionary.* "Moving or operating at the greatest speed or with maximum power" is the Random House definition of the adjective. That "fullest extent" sense is expressed in the *Times*'s "the economy is now operating at *full bore.*"

Where is it from? "We are working on an entry on *full bore,*" says John Simpson of the *OED,* playing catch-up (an Americanism), "and our evidence shows that it derives from the *bore* meaning 'cylinder.' *Full bore* is the widest capacity of a cylinder." Some lexicographers think the *bore* first measured an engine cylinder (and have a 1927 citation), while others think that the origin is from the measurement of the inside of the barrel of a gun. "A .45-caliber gun can take a .44-caliber load," John Snyder of the gun lobby tells me, "so *full bore* would be the maximum-size load. In another sense, it means 'maximum capable powder load.'"

Whether from gun or engine, *bore* has an extended use attributed to the Royal Air Force in World War II: "I went after him *full bore,*" recounted the ace C. H. Ward-Jackson in 1943. There was a need for a new *full,* since *full sail, full blast* and *full steam* were obsolete.

Now what about those *small-bore* reforms? "Though *full-bore* and *small-bore* connect with each other technically as firearms terms," says Fred Mish at Merriam-Webster, "they are not opposites on the extended level. One means 'all-out,' the other 'trifling.'"

Winston S. Churchill wrote in 1898 of "a hundred men wounded by the *small-bore* bullets of a civilised force." The OED has a citation only two years later from the *Congressional Record* for the extended metaphor: "No *small-bore*, two-by-four, radical politicians can hurt that great court."

Unlike its big brother, *small-bore* is used only as a compound adjective and is almost always hyphenated. A nice usage was by Dick Morris, the triangulating political strategist: "The issues Washington speaks about every day are in many cases the true *small-bore* issues, or at least the boring issues."

Your column headed "Full bore vs. small bore: Is this wonky?" overlooks what is to many who know the Somerset and Gloucestershire area the most likely derivation of *full bore*. Anyone who has seen the Severn bore at *full bore* has no doubt at all that this is a tidal-wave moving "flat out" or at its greatest power. The OED should look earlier than to the Industrial Revolution and even to before the days of guns, to its own attribution of *bore* to the Old Norse *bara*, and to a more common usage of a similar expression *full flood* which surely would raise no question that a tide is incoming at its maximum power.

Barry G. Browning
Victoria, British Columbia, Canada

A choke is a device attachable to the end of the barrel of a shotgun to control the dispersion of the pellets fired therefrom. Full bore, or wide open, is the opposite of fully choked. Small bore is the opposite of large bore and refers to the diameter of the barrell.

Anthony J. Hope
Washington, D.C.

I just thought you might want to know that to a doctor, the opposite of small-bore is large-bore (*not* full-bore) as in a "large-bore needle" (or "hose," when we are being flippant).

Ben Z. Katz, M.D.
Chicago, Illinois

Funkmanship

"What a *funk* here is!" is the citation in a slang dictionary of 1698. "What a thick Smoak of Tobacco is here!" A century later, Francis Grose, in his *Classical Dictionary of the Vulgar Tongue*, defined *to funk*, from an old Flemish and

French dialect verb, as "to smoke, figuratively to smoke or stink through fear."

"The Funkie Butt Boogie" was performed by the jazz great Louis Armstrong, recalling the smell of a cigar butt in a place where blues was played. Thus, *funky* has a long-established meaning of "smelly," with special reference to the smell of tobacco smoke, and is associated with the good and bad times evoked by that smell. But it has another meaning, too, which floated out recently in the smoke-free atmosphere of Air Force One.

"I'm also trying to get people to get out of their *funk*," President Clinton told reporters on the Presidential plane. Alertly, one reporter asked, "Get out of their *funk*?" To explain what he was getting at, Mr. Clinton tried another metaphor: "What makes people insecure is when they feel like they're lost in the fun house. They're in a room where something can hit them from any direction any time." When this did not seem to sink in, he tried yet another word picture: "They always feel living life is like walking across a running river on slippery rocks and you can lose your footing at any time."

That last simile was especially vivid in evoking a feeling of insecurity, but the journalists were not inclined to admire the Presidential metaphors. Almost immediately, the Clinton use of *funk* was compared to Jimmy Carter's 1979 adoption of a memo by his pollster Pat Caddell in which the President's low popularity was blamed on a national *malaise*, or feeling of uneasiness. One pundit observed that the President could not very well use the other synonym, *depression*, a word long taboo at the White House. (One economic aide was told to substitute the word "banana" for that dreaded term.)

Give the Clinton White House credit: linguistic damage control went into action. Within hours after some of us headlined the word, Mr. Clinton got off the funkmanship kick entirely. "*Funk* was a poor choice of words," he announced.

"I feel very optimistic about the country," Clinton added, allying himself with a more Reagan-esque than Carter-esque outlook.

"That seemed to put an end to the Funk Monster," the columnist David S. Broder wrote in the *Washington Post*, covering a Presidential meeting with reporters at a breakfast for the columnist Godfrey Sperling Jr. "But Clinton was taking no chances. As he circled the room, schmoozing with various groups of reporters, he wanted to be sure they got the message. '*Malaise* is a state of mind,' he said. 'A *funk* is something you can bounce right out of.'"

In his effort to extricate himself, however, Mr. Clinton is getting into my lexicographic dodge. Not even the leader of the free world has the power of Humpty Dumpty, making a word mean "just what I choose it to mean."

A *funk*, noun, has a couple of other senses not connected to the smell of tobacco. One is "fear, panic": Grose noted in 1785, "I was in a cursed *funk*." In his 1856 novel, *Tom Brown's School Days*, Thomas Hughes gave the word its color: "If I was going to be flogged next minute, I should be in a blue *funk.*" Another, related meaning is "black mood, depression." I think this is what President Clinton originally had in mind, no matter what he said later to lighten it up. Other meanings abound—the *Historical Dictionary of American Slang* notes "to flinch," "to back down" and "to fizzle"—but "to be in a *funk*" usually means to be very gloomy, kicking the cat and muttering oaths. Sometimes, but not oftentimes, a red, white and blue *funk* seems to be the state of the Union.

The President—any President—should be encouraged to use such terms because they enliven our discourse. Mr. Clinton has a feel for metaphor; in the same chat with reporters on Air Force One, he referred to the complexity of managing change as "trying to hold 400 Ping-Pong balls in your arms." Many people see the President in power as an 800-pound gorilla, and the mental picture of an 800-pound gorilla juggling 400 Ping-Pong balls is one that deserves to be hung in the windows of our minds.

And that's not all: on that same funky flight, Mr. Clinton revivified a term I have never dealt with in this space. To reporters exhausted by early-morning jogging, he admonished, "Don't fall asleep—not fall asleep, but just don't get *blah.*"

This is not the *blah* of *blah-blah-blah,* the dialect form of the Latin *et cetera* or more precisely *ad infinitum,* "and on and on and on," leading to the definition of "drivel." This is rather the *blah* of the *blahs,* a state of boredom combined with minor heartburn first used by the manufacturers of Alka-Seltzer in 1967. (Will the copywriter from the Jack Tinker Agency step forward to take credit for a major coinage?) In 1975, *Forbes* magazine reported "a case of the economic *blahs,*" and in *Newsweek,* Maureen Orth wrote of a musician who "decided to escape the *blahs* of small-town stardom." In 1995, *Fortune* covered the AT&T breakup with "Wall Street has the long-distance *blahs.*" The *blahs* are surely with us, from "the August *blahs*" (Mel Elfin, *Newsweek*) to "the winter *blahs*" (Ellen Goodman, the *Boston Globe*).

The singular *blah* was popularized by *Variety* in the early '20s: "Pre-Holiday *Blah* Feeling Gets Into Amusement Stocks." In a verb phrase, as used by Clinton on what may have been his greatest metaphorical day, *to go* (or *get*) *blah* is "to lose all energy or zest for life, to crumple." It's what White House pool reporters do at 5 in the morning.

Several weeks before his Oct. 22 Funkmanship, Ms. Shelley Sutherland, a tall, beautiful, New York fashion designer in her mid-twenties, known for her frank observations, used a form of the word funk in an exclamation aimed at me. "Oh, Mister O'Neil," she piped up, not having seen my face since spring, "what a funky goat!" She was referring to my goatee, which I had grown over the summer to cover up a significant scar on my chin—the result of some July surgery.

Ms. Sutherland did not mean that my "goat" gave off a strong, unwashed, musty odor—I wash daily. She did not mean that it reeked of vile tobacco smoke—I gave up the weed more than 20 years ago. Nor did she mean that it filled her with fear. She simply meant that my newly grown chin whiskers were, well, "cool" (to borrow a word Maynard G. Krebbs might have hoped people would say of his 1950's TV beatnik chin wisp). She meant that my goatee was "fashionable, trendy" to quote a definition from the New Shorter Oxford English Dictionary.

J. Michael O'Neil
Vernon, Connecticut

I have something of an interest in the word "Funk" as it's our family name.

You listed "smoke" as among the various meanings. As the saying goes, "where there's smoke there's fire." Where there's a fire it's probably started by a "spark."

The OED, our mother-load of etymological information gives the earliest use of *funk* in 1330. It's meaning is "spark." As you and I as lexicographers know, words tend to wander from their original meanings. A strong smell or stink including tobacco smoke appeared in 1623. Cowering fear or panic appeared in 1743 as Oxford Slang: origin unknown. And the meanings proliferated over the years.

Peter Funk
Princeton, New Jersey

I think we can help on *funky butt*. While the odor of cigars doubtless permeated jazz establishments, so did other odors (see *DARE funky* adj. 1b). And Louis Armstrong's "The Funkie Butt Boogie" doubtless referred to body odors and their associated activities. After some backing and forthing, we finally decided not to include *funky butt* in DARE.

At any rate, here are a few quotations that we would have used had we put *funky butt* in as a separate entry (using quote 1970 that's now at *funky* 1b):

1939 (1959) Ramsey-Smith *Jazzmen* 13 New Orleans, There were several original tunes by Bolden . . . inspired by some "low-life" women . . . The words of the song, which later became his "theme" song, went: *I thought I heard Buddy Bolden say,/ "Funky'butt, bunky-butt, take it away."*

1959 Armstrong *Satchmo* 22 New Orleans (as of c. 1910), At the corner of the street where I lived was the famous Funky Butt Hall, where I first heard Buddy Bolden play.

Joan Hall, Chief Editor
Dictionary of American Regional English
University of Madison
Madison, Wisconsin

Like some other music terms, like jazz itself, funk also refers to sex—funky refers to the smell of sex. This usage became common in the sixties in the counterculture meeting of whites and blacks. Funk is a seventies black dance music. I am sure that Armstrong's tune is no reference to tobacco. Perhaps a researcher might find that the end of the smoked weed came to be called a butt from a similarity of function to our own buttocks.

Jazz musicians, African-Americans especially, have gotten great pleasure out of sneaking some of their funky—here in the sense of earthy and direct—terms into proper folks' social usage. I remember when Louis Armstrong made an appearance on (live) television in the squeaky clean fifties, he pushed the censorship envelope and gratified my watching family by telling someone, Jack Teagarden perhaps, that they were going to play the next tune "not too slow, not too fast, just half-fast."

Joel Latner
Princeton, New Jersey

You omitted what is perhaps the most common use of the noun, at least among African-Americans and rock fans: a specific genre of music that emerged in the early '70s, more rhythmically complex than '60s soul and less slick than disco.

Your Louis Armstrong reference hinted at this connection, but there's much more to it. First, at least to my knowledge, "funky" as an adjective in early-20th-century African-American slang denoted not the scent of tobacco but the aroma left behind by hot and sweaty sex. Mezz Mezzrow's 1947 autobiography, *Really the Blues,* defines it as "smelly, obnoxious." Its musical meaning is somewhat elusive for those not steeped in the genre (as Armstrong reportedly once said when asked to define jazz, "Man, if I have to explain it, you'll never understand"), but some combination of rhythmic vitality and African-American cultural resonance is about as close as I can come without specific examples.

I don't know exactly when the word passed into musical use, but it may have been in the late-1950s jazz scene, to signify music that was cruder and bluesier than the cerebral "cool" sounds prevalent earlier in the decade. In any case, by 1967 there was a dance called the Funky Broadway and James Brown was exclaiming "Ain't it funky now" at peaks in his live show. The beat of Brown's 1969 single "Funky Drummer" has been borrowed by numerous rappers, most notably Public Enemy. By 1970, the word had crossed over to white rockers, with the James Gang's "Funk #49" and Pink Floyd's "Funky Dung."

Brown's influence led to the genre specifically called funk, whose big beats, snappy bass lines and choppy, percussive guitars packed many a dance floor in the '70s. The musicians involved were predominantly, though not exclusively, black—a group called Wild Cherry had a 1976 hit with "Play That Funky Music, White Boy." Singer George Clinton crossed funky beats with psychedelia in his band Funkadelic. Later, he'd become the artist most identified with funk as a genre, leading two overlapping bands, Parliament and Funkadelic (eventually combined into P-Funk). "Make my funk the P-Funk—I want my funk uncut," a chorus exhorted on Parliament's 1976 album *Mothership Connection*. Clinton toured with the Lollapalooza traveling rock festival in 1994 and is a major influence on current million-sellers the Red Hot Chili Peppers.

Two other uses of "funky" as an adjective are worth noting. The first, decrepit but still cool (like my drummer's graffiti-bedecked van) is presumably derived from the musical/sexual dirt connotations. The second, less common, is defective or questionable. "That might sound funky, but I don't mean to mislead," Curtis Mayfield said on his 1971 live album. Thus, if my recording engineer says "the bass sounds funky," it's not necessarily a compliment.

Steven Wishnia
New York, New York

Gangsta-Busta

A certain violence-prone form of rap music is called *gangsta* rap. The earliest use with this spelling in the Random House files comes from the 1988 song "Gangsta Gangsta," by N.W.A. "It is certainly possible," admits Jesse Sheidlower, formerly of Random House, "that the term is earlier, perhaps even significantly earlier, but virtually every current use is based on the popularity of the term in rap music contexts."

Note that the spelling of the attributive noun *gangsta*, modifying another noun, *rap*, differs from *gangster*. That *-ster* usage, creating a noun meaning "member of a gang," was first cited in the *Columbus Evening Dispatch* in 1896 in an optimistic piece about political corruption: "The *gangster* may play all sorts of pranks with the ballot box, but in its own good time the latter will get even by kicking the *gangster* into the gutter."

The phonetic spelling of the attributive noun causes a fulmination from Robert E. Rhodes of Corpus Christi, Tex.; he is a past president of the Associated Press Managing Editors Association. He notes that, as editor and as journalism professor, he has "tried to instill within my reporters and students the use of proper and legitimate English words," and he wants to know: "How does the ever-so-cautious *New York Times*, which normally agonizes for years over style changes, accept with alacrity and with neither explanation nor apology the ghetto expression *gangsta* rap—instead of what logically would be expected to be *gangster* rap?"

Not my table; I'm an independent operator here allowed some leeway in pushing grammatical envelopes. The editor who speaks for the *New York Times* in these matters is Allan M. Siegal. "I'm reminded of the legend," he says, "about our reference to Meat Loaf, the rock singer, as 'Mr. Loaf.' When I first heard it, my reaction was that it was too good to check. But I checked, and it turns out that we were only kidding around."

What about the *-ster/-sta* controversy? *"Gangsta* rap is a new phenomenon," he explains. "It has little to do with gangsters. The people who perform it and sell it call it *gangsta*. If we imposed the *gangster* spelling, we'd be making ourselves risible. Proper and legitimate English words are fine when applied to existing concepts. New concepts justify new words."

Gauntlet/Gantlet

Will Shortz, who has brought zesty humor and modern sparkle to the creation of *New York Times* crossword puzzles, has stepped into a hornet's nest (What's a four-letter word for hornet? I ask waspishly) with his definition for *gauntlet* as a "paddling site."

When a reader, George J. Friedman of New York, objected—arguing that *gauntlet* means "glove," and a corridor of punishment is *gantlet*—Mr. Shortz replied: *"Gauntlet* (for a 'paddling site') is sanctioned by every dictionary I've checked, and it's the preferred spelling in Random House, *Webster's Third New International* and *Merriam-Webster's 10th Collegiate. Gantlet* is only a variant."

But to rely on those dictionaries about this, in my view, is to fall into confusage. Their etymologists make a great case for mere spelling variance, but writers of distinction prefer the judgment in *Webster's New World Dictionary* and *American Heritage Dictionary* (which has a fine usage note explaining the confusion): *gauntlet,* from the French, means "a glove with a flaring cuff," which you throw down when you want to issue a challenge or when your hand gets all sweaty; *gantlet,* without the *u,* comes via folk etymology from the Swedish-based *gantlope,* meaning "a course of discipline that you run past guys with clubs whacking at you from both sides."

Relatedly, Michael P. Dowling writes from Denver: "Interviewees on National Public Radio have 'run' both the *gambit* and the *gantlet*—while apparently trying out a range of options. Is this the opening move in a linguistic ordeal? What ever happened to *gamut?*"

A *gambit* is, as Mr. Dowling notes, an opening move in chess that sacrifices a pawn for some position; that has been extended to mean "an opening maneuver or statement to establish an advantage." *Gamut* comes from the Greek letter *gamma,* used by Guido d'Arezzo, a medieval Italian musician, to name the lowest note on his musical scale. Now it means "the full scale, the entire range." You can "run" the *gamut,* but nobody bangs you over the head with a club, the way people do when you run the *gantlet.*

Concerning *gamut:* the word is derived from the combination of "gamma" and "ut." "Ut" was Guido's syllable for the first note in a hexachord (a six-note scale, ut-re-mi-fa-sol-la; "ut" was later changed to "do"). Guido conceived of pitch in terms of interlocking hexachords based on G, C, and F (i.e., G-A-B-C-D-E, C-D-E-F-G-A, and F-G-A-Bb-C-D) and had a complicated system of naming individual pitches according to their place in these hexachords: thus (a certain) A was "A la mi re" because it was "la" in the C hexachord, "mi" in the F hexachord, and "re" in the G hexachord. The lowest G belonged only to the G hexachord; hence it was simply G (or gamma) "ut."

Mark DeBellis
New York, New York

A gambit is any move in chess that offers material for another advantage (even if only psychological). It can occur in the middle of the game. A gambit does in some fashion ask your opponent to put up or shut up. The word *ploy* does not quite apply either. Perhaps the simple word *challenge* would be best.

Gerry Meisenhelder
York, Pennsylvania

Gazillion

At a White House correspondents' dinner, President Clinton turned toward Al Franken, author of *Rush Limbaugh Is a Big Fat Idiot*, and said admiringly, "He's made a *gazillion* dollars on that book."

The counting began with a mere *zillion*, coined in 1930, about the time a Mr. *Zilch* appeared in the satire magazine *Ballyhoo*. In *zilch*, as in a sense of *zip*, the Z referred to *zero*. Looking at the productive morpheme *illion*, Fred Cassidy of the *Dictionary of American Regional English* notes that "Z, as the last letter of the alphabet, suggests 'as far as you can go,' therefore *zillion*, the highest possible number or variety." (In the other direction lies *zilch*, lower than which you cannot go.)

The escalation of *zillion* to *gazillion* took place, in as early a citation as John Algeo of *American Speech* can find, in a Feb. 25, 1980, Tom Shales column in the *Washington Post* referring to "gazillionaire Ellis Ikehorn." Says Shales now: "Using a made-up word instead of 'rich man' established a mocking tone. I could have used *zillionaire*, but I thought that *ga-* in front sounded funny."

Gazillion is in the 1996 edition of the *Random House Webster's Dictionary*, where it is defined as "an extremely large, indeterminate number."

To search Shales's linguistic subconscious: whence the intensifier *ga-*? Sol Steinmetz formerly of Random House says, "The *ga-* derives from the Scottish prefix *ker-*, as in *kerplunk* and *kerflop.*" The *Oxford English Dictionary* noted that *ker-* was the first part of an onomatopoeic formation to imitate the sound of a heavy body falling, and gives the variant *ca-*. Sounds to me that *ga-* is the newest variant.

Archimedes estimated the number of sands necessary to fill the universe at 1 with 51 zeroes after it. Mathematicians today can estimate with an overtone of infinity: a *gazillion* grains.

Your explanations for the *ga* on the front of *gazillion* seem to have overlooked another candidate, the *ge* on the front of the past participle of weak verbs in German, and presumably in Yiddish—e.g., gefuhlte fish. A prefixed *ge* has been used by a lot of amateur and professional comics to simulate a German accent or to accentuate the importance of the attached verb (or noun, it seems vaguely) throughout my lifetime. I don't think Will Cuppy started it, although he ran it lucratively into the ground while he was around, in his "Tales Mein Grossfader Told" series of short pieces and short books. Radio comics and high-school kids used it in attempts to deride Hitler and Nazi Germany during WWII. Whether one of your printed explanations is more proximate or not, I speculate that my submission might be related in dim linguistic prehistory to one or both of them, and may indeed have been the Grossfader.

John Strother
Princeton, New Jersey

Getting Real

Brandishing a brace of dead ducks, President Clinton said of his hunting experience: "I really started feeling like a real person."

Time for a reality check (a term that comes from Freud's *reality testing,* "to separate the real from the imagined"): *really* is an adverb meaning "actually" (not "figuratively"), but is used mainly as an intensifier. In British usage, the stressing word preferred is *indeed;* Prime Minister John Major would have put it: "Indeed, I started feeling. . . ."

Real is an adjective meaning "true, genuine, not apparent or illusory." As an adjective, it correctly modifies a noun, as in the President's "*real* person." However, you should not use an adjective to modify a verb; that's what adverbs are for. Thus, "I'm real tired" is incorrect; you should be *really* tired. Ignore advice to the contrary by roundheeled usagists.

What, then, is *real time*? Can time, which is known for marching on, be bogus? The term was used first in 1953 in a mathematical publication: "the solution of problems in 'real time', i.e., in conjunction with instruments receiving and responding to stimuli." That meant "right then" or "now," but it soon began to stretch: In 1960, the *New York Times* was writing about weather bureau attempts "to make 'real time' forecasts of the weather—forecasts fresh enough to be useful."

That same stretching is going on today. To most computer users, *real time* means "on line, interactively, without delay." To save money on service charges, some will dump a bunch of messages into a file and get off line; no longer in expensive *real time,* they can read and later respond at their leisure. Another way to avoid *real time* is to post a message in a public forum and later pick up all the replies, which may include replies to replies, in what is called a *thread.*

But not everyone uses *real time* to mean "immediate, going on at the moment." In the Senate Whitewater hearings, it was observed that witnesses would have been better off telling the truth "in real time" rather than dribbling it out over the course of months. John Wallace of Dallas notes, "The term has crept into our language to signify—as it does in physics and in engineering—the greater usefulness or higher quality associated with immediacy rather than delay."

In real reality, then, we really have two senses to *real time:* "live, not recorded," and "the value of being contemporaneous."

At ABC television, consideration must be given by Diane Sawyer and Sam Donaldson to changing the name of their show from "Prime Time Live" to the more with-it *"Prime Time Real-Time."*

For the TV and film industry, the common meaning for *real time* is "actual running time" as opposed to slow motion or fast motion (time lapse or animation), scan, shuttle or jog.

A real time sequence is recorded at the normal frame rate (30 frames/second for video, 24 frames/second for film) and plays back at the same speed as it was recorded. The action on seen film or tape takes the same amount of time as it took to do it: real time.

A common usage would be, for instance after screening a shot in slo mo or after scanning high speed through some footage, "Let's see that shot in real time."

Skip Blumberg
New York, New York

Coming from an historical period of computer development, perhaps I can shed a slightly variant history of this locution, "real time."

The matter revolves around the speed of the computer. In the early days, the speed of computing was so slow that most computing was considered as "historical" computing; that is, the data were all in before the computer was started. Payroll was an example of historical computing. The last hour had been already worked before the payroll computation could start. And the time required to compute the payroll was only limited by the patience of the employees who were waiting for their paychecks.

But as computing speed increased, we finally overtook the rate at which events occurred. A combination of radar and computer tells us at a given moment that a missile has left Moscow; it is now over the North pole; and in 18 seconds the missile will be on New York. At this point, there are 18 seconds to do something about the missile. Not much time, you say, but then retaliatory actions have become faster, too. This is real-time computing. And at this point the word *computing* can be replaced with the word *control*. We are dealing with "live data" instead of "dead data" as in the case of the payroll. We are now in a position to influence the outcome of the phenomenon by virtue of our greater speed of computation.

When Eckert and Mauchly left the Moore School to form their own company in 1946—having just finished the successful ENIAC—the company they formed was called Electronic Control Company, not Electronic Computer Company in recognition of their goal of producing computers of sufficient speed that they would be controlling devices rather than just computing devices. If you can get the answer before the phenomenon gets there, you are now in control; you are operating in real time. Automatic pilots in the airplane are real-time computers.

In other words, the antonym for *real-time* is *historical*. And the word *historical* in this case means *beyond control* or *beyond influence*.

Joseph Chapline
Newbury, New Hampshire

Go Reconfigure

When a word disappears from the Presidential vocabulary, does it mean a policy change?

In a speech at the Air Force Academy, Bill Clinton spoke of using United States troops in helping United Nations troops in both a withdrawal and a *reconfiguration*. After critics in Congress and the press focused on the second word, the President dropped it from his radio address a few days later.

A reporter noted the absence of the word and asked the White House press secretary, Michael McCurry, what that meant: "Is there a backing away from the commitment to consider using ground forces in a *reconfiguration*?"

The answer was a masterpiece of obfuscation. "The result of deliberations with the Europeans in the days following the President's speech," Mr. McCurry said, "indicated that *reconfiguration*—the requirement for United States assistance in the event of *reconfiguration*—could be limited to cases of emergency extractions and, as a last resort, because there was expertise and resources available from the European powers that could help accomplish that in a more orderly fashion if that was the scenario we were looking at."

A withdrawal, or "emergency extraction," is one military maneuver, sometimes euphemized as a "retrograde movement"; a *reconfiguration* is entirely different. In the first case, troops leave; in the second, they stay. Further linguistic confusion arose when Defense Secretary William Perry defined *extraction* as being "to points of safety in Bosnia"—which is not *extraction* but *reconfiguration*.

The Latin *configurare* means "to form from," rooted further in *figura*, "a figure." The noun *configuration* means "shape; the arrangement of parts." The verb *configure*, *Merriam-Webster's 10th Collegiate* says, means "to set up for operation esp. in a particular way." (Lexies save a lot of space by dropping the *ecially* from *especially*.)

Before uploading my political column, I bawl at the art department, "What's my *configuration*?" The answer will be "short and squat" or "tall and skinny," depending on the page's makeup that day. A *reconfiguration* means "remodeling, restructuring," a kind of *perestroika;* when applied to columns of troops, it means "assembling in a more defensible position."

After the negative reaction to the President's first statement, the United States commitment was limited to helping defend a withdrawal, not a *reconfiguration*. But the only way to tell that the policy had changed was to note the disappearance of the word.

Go South, Young Man

In the TV series "Murder, She Wrote," the character played by Angela Lansbury was accosted by a police lieutenant about a suspect she was helping: "When I sent some guys over to your place to pick him up," the cop complained, "he'd *gone south.*"

In the opposite direction, Adam Sandler wrote in *Variety* that the recent video release of *Snow White and the Seven Dwarfs* had sold more than 17 million copies and "generated *north* of $300 million in retail sales."

Now both ways: when the *Washington Post*'s media shoofly, Howard Kurtz, hoped that ratings of the O. J. Simpson trial would *"go south,"* Dan Rather on "48 Hours" on CBS responded, "The ratings were *going north*, not *south."*

Rather knows how to handle a compass: North is up, South is down. (I capitalize the directions, though not *southern* or *southward*.) Obviously, up is good news, down is bad. But this metaphor, now omnidirectional on television, has deeper roots than it seems. According to Fred Cassidy, editor of the *Dictionary of American Regional English (DARE)*: "Evidently a part of American Indian (Sioux) belief included *go south* = to die. The sense of deterioration is not far off."

The inspiring Professor Cassidy directed me to Mitford M. Mathews's *Dictionary of Americanisms*. In that 1951 lexicon, a 1746 citation, from David Brainerd's journal, about an aged Delaware Indian's opinion that the soul departing the body "would go southward" was elucidated in a *Harper's Magazine* article in 1894: "The Dakota tribes believe that the soul, driven out of the body, journeys off to the south, and 'to go south' is, among the Sioux, the favorite euphemism for death."

A sexual sense was added by whites who followed the American aboriginals. In the 1955 Broadway musical *Silk Stockings*, based on the movie *Ninotchka*, Cole Porter wrote, "I'd love to make a tour of you"; stops on this lyrical tour included "The eyes, the arms, the mouth of you/The East, West, North and the South of you." On the surface, an innocent lyric, and never banned from the airwaves; still, when Don Ameche sang the word *South*, the sexual innuendo about the nether parts of the body was unmistakable.

Financial reporters took up the compass metaphor to enliven their language about the direction of the stock market. "The markets headed south today" is an all-too-frequent usage in finance. Lou Dobbs of the CNN program "Moneyline" tells me, "While I've heard many analysts and market gurus talk about stocks *going south*, I've never heard anyone say a market is *going north."*

At least the directional metaphor of North (up, good news) and South (down, bad news) is clear. For example, when there is good statistical news on the jobless or inflation fronts, and those figures drop, you do not hear "Unemployment figures and inflation rates are headed south." Thus, the metaphoric meaning of "headed South" is not so much "downward" as "bad news."

That clarity cannot be claimed by *uphill* and *downhill*. "Your column and the crossword puzzle get my week off to a civilized start," Patricia Patricelli of Boston writes. "Usually it's all downhill from there. (Or is it *uphill*? I've never really understood that expression. Going *downhill* is easier, but it sounds negative to me, i.e., sinking, down in the depths.)"

It's all downhill from here. Does that mean "From now on, it's easy—no more struggling uphill" or does it mean "This is as good as it gets, and now we're headed for the pits"?

"I always thought that if someone were going *downhill*, that signified deterioration," Steve Conn of New York writes, "whereas *uphill* meant getting better. Tell me: should we prefer to go *uphill* or *downhill?*"

Allan Metcalf of the American Dialect Society notes that "*Downhill* has been going figuratively downhill since the *OED*'s first record of its use, in 1591: 'Th' Icie down-Hils of this slippery Life.' Whether we weep or rejoice in any particular instance depends on whither the icy downhills lead—to a decline, or to an Olympic skiing record."

John Algeo, the neologist of *American Speech*, points to the two-way working of the metaphor: "If one thinks that the top of the hill is the place to be, then *going downhill* is declining. But if one thinks about effort, then an *uphill struggle* is bad, and *coasting downhill* is good. The difference is between metaphorical place ('up' good, 'down' bad) and metaphorical effort to move on an inclined plane ('uphill' hard, 'downhill' easy)."

Though the first use of downhill, about the slippery life, was pejorative, a more famous use—by Daniel Defoe in his 1719 *Robinson Crusoe*—was upbeat: "a very short cut, and all down-hill," which was quicker and easier for the castaway and his man Friday than the long way uphill. "Perhaps a human tendency to look on the dark side favors the pejorative sense," Professor Algeo says. "Metaphorically, both work."

But they work at semantic cross-purposes. The hills are alive with the sound of confusion. My advice: forget the hill metaphor and try something nautical: *smooth sailing* and *rough sailing*, or if you go for the icy slopes, *easy sledding* or *hard sledding*. Ban the hills; if you want bad news, *go South*.

In connection with going south = dying, I seem to recall hearing that WWII slang included going *west* to mean dying: "He went west." (= "He bought the farm," but that's another story.)

Amy B. Unfried
Bronxville, New York

Your witty piece on whether going *downhill* is negative or positive sent me to one of my favorite books: *Downhill All the Way*, Leonard Woolf's autobiography.

With him, it is not either/or. It is *both. Downhill* is a glide—but toward deterioration. Like his wife Virginia, Leonard relished ambiguity.

Nardi Reeder Campion
Hanover, New Hampshire

May I offer one gentle correction regarding *Silk Stockings*, a musical I attended during its Broadway run with Don Ameche and Hildegarde Neff? Indeed, the directional phrase sung by Don Ameche was banned from the airwaves. I vividly recall the substitution, "I'd like to make a tour of you/The sweet of you the pure of you." At the time, I expressed an opinion that the original wording was a lot more innocuous than another verse in the lyric which ran, "I'd like to handle the heart and soul of you," which seemed manipulative, to say the least.

I should add, however, that the sexual connotation given to the word "south" sailed right over my head. Who could imagine that straightforward Don Ameche with his toothpaste grin and squeaky clean portrayals of all those upstanding American inventors could be capable of a leer? In retrospect, of course, the innuendo is inescapable in light of the author/composer's identity.

Eleanor Williams Hall
Bellevue, Washington

Going Negative

For the next edition of my political dictionary, due out in 2004, in time for Colin Powell's bid for reelection, an entry will be a phrase that was coined in 1984 but that really blossomed in 1996: *going negative.* "Mr. Dole has spent the better part of the race," wrote the *New York Times* in late October, "waiting desperately for someone to *go negative* about Mr. Clinton's ethical lapses."

The coiner (or first recorder, since he put the phrase in quotes) of this attack on attacks was Hendrik Hertzberg, during the Democratic primaries of 1984 the Washington diarist of *The New Republic,* now executive editor of *The New Yorker.*

"With a week to go before the New York primary," went this former Carter speech writer's negation of negativism, "the campaign has taken a nasty and depressing turn. Everyone is *'going negative.'* Mondale started it. . . . His campaign . . . has had only one thought on its raging metal mind: destroy. Destroy Gary Hart. Destroy him and his accursed new ideas."

The linguistic turnaround is in the wings: "In his Inaugural address today, the President *went positive.*"

The Goldilocks Recovery

Economics was labeled "the dismal science" in 1850 by the historian Thomas Carlyle, and its metaphors are suitably fearsome and depressing. An arrangement in the 1970s for exchange rates to fluctuate within a band within another band was called *the snake in the tunnel,* and the total of the unemployment and inflation percentages was called *the misery index.* In the '80s an aborted economic recovery was called *a dead cat bounce.* Even its euphemisms for recession give the users a sensation of seasickness, as in *rolling readjustment.*

How pleasant it was, in this sad trope-a-dope, to hear an economist introduce a happy figure of speech to the droopy discourse. It happened at a White House briefing by Robert Reich, the previous Secretary of Labor, and Laura Tyson, former chair of the Council of Economic Advisers. (Ms. Tyson was the chairwoman of the group, and not a piece of furniture, but the official Clinton terminology labels her *chair.* Although the White House press office, in its releases, used an *o* to spell *advisors,* her council styled itself *advisers,* the spelling preferred by *Merriam-Webster's Collegiate,* 10th Edition, and by American Heritage. *Advisors*—perhaps influenced by *supervisor*—is listed first by *Webster's New World Dictionary,* Third Edition, giving cover to the White House press office and to Anthony Lake, who used the controversial *-or* ending in spelling his informal title of National Security Advisor. However, most newspaper stylebooks, including that of the *New York Times,* use *adviser,* but who listens to the elitist media and its culture of personal destruction anymore? Amid this babble, a voice of cool authority is needed. My advice: in this devolutionary political era, don't knuckle under to any White House spelling diktat; spell it *adviser.* Live free or die. End parenthesis.)

Standing next to Adviser Tyson, whose hair is auburn, Secretary Reich made his sunnily hirsute contribution to economic jargon, referring to "the *Goldilocks recovery*—not too hot, not too cold. . . ."

This catchy figure of speech is drawn, of course, from the story of "Goldilocks and the Three Bears," in which a hungry young blond woman breaks into the home of an absent family of carnivorous furry mammals. She samples their porridge, their chairs (the furniture, not their discussion leaders) and their beds. The comparisons invariably lead her to the bowl, chair and bed of the smallest bear, which in the case of the cereal was neither too hot nor too cold, and in the cases of the furniture neither too hard nor too soft, but—*just right.*

The satisfaction of the bedtime story to the children of statisticians is in the discovery by Goldilocks of the perfect mean. (Others find in this story an example of the rip-off of third-world resources by the industrialized nations, but that could not be the Secretary's intent.)

Even as the Secretary of Labor was purveying the just-right picture of a Goldilocks economy, an anonymous White House aide was telling Todd S. Purdum of the *New York Times* about growing out of childish things, and adopting a less certain view of the political scene after the takeover of Congress by Republicans: "A lot of this is still seeing through a glass darkly."

Some spinmeister in that White House reads the Bible. This expression comes from I Corinthians 13, in which the Apostle Paul writes: "When I was a child, I spake as a child . . . but when I became a man, I put away childish things. For now we see through a glass, darkly; but then [we shall see] face to face. . . ." The point is that wisdom will come when a person wrestles with his personal angel and comes face to face with God's grace: "now I know in part: but then shall I know even as also I am known."

The phrase *through a glass, darkly* is used today to confess to uncertainty. But not even the most spiritually evocative phrase is above parody: Mark Twain, in his laceration of James Fenimore Cooper's obfuscatory prose a century ago, wrote about his target: "He saw nearly all things as through a glass eye, darkly."

You dealt with the phrase *through a glass, darkly.* Its biblical origin, and the way you indicated it had been used, got me thinking. I expect that many who use it today are not aware that *glass* in the phrase actually refers to a looking glass or mirror. Mirrors in biblical times were not as clear as those we are familiar with today. Ancient mirrors were often simply a piece of highly polished brass or another metal, and offered a less than ideal reflection. This is the point of the phrase in I Corinthians. Today *through a glass, darkly* seems often to be used as if one had in mind darkly tinted glass. This is a bit different from the original metaphor, though the basic idea of distorted vision is still present.

For those who follow such details, the Greek in I Corinthians 13 is *di' esoptrou en ainigmati*, which is translated "through a glass, darkly" in the King James Version. The Greek word *esoptrou* (used in the genitive, with *-ou* ending, in the phrase) means "looking glass," as rendered also by Jerome in the Latin Vulgate translation, where he used *speculum* for the Greek word.

Frank Abate
Old Saybrook, Connecticut

"Misdivision" is also responsible for the incorrect *apron* and *orange* which should, of course, be called by their ancient and proper names: *napron* and *norange.* (See *napkin,* related to the former, and *naranja,* Spanish for the latter.)

Arthur J. Morgan
New York, New York

Bears are, of course, *omnivorous*, not merely carnivorous, as your Sunday column advised. Carnivorous bears would hardly be eating porridge in the first place. But since bears **are** members of the order Carnivora, you at least have not made a newt-level error of taxonomic misclassification.

David B. Pittaway
New York, New York

Your treatment of the adviser/advisor topic skirted around a possible litmus test in deciding between use of the "-er" or "-or" tail.

The collegiate baseball league of which I am Commissioner has what it has called throughout its 28 years of existence an Advisory Board. Its membership is reviewed each year by a Board of Directors, and the chosen parties become Advisors.

Whenever a matter comes up that has elements which may have arisen within the experience of members of that body of Advisors, I feel full freedom and, in some instances a duty, to consult with one or more of them before proceeding unadvised. On most such occasions I am also receiving a lot of advice, solicited and unsolicited, from qualified and unqualified advisers.

Given this line of distinction—the "-ors" are a preselected, screened, and at least presumptively trustworthy source of advice, whereas the "-ers" include anybody who cares to give advice. Once I come to a decision and act on it, there is considerably more coverage for my posterior if I can cite the advice of an Advisor in support of my decision than if I cite advisers Tom, Dick and Harry, each of whose credentials I would then have to detail and validate.

John Belson*
Park Ridge, New Jersey

*Mr. Belson died in February 1995.

Goo-Goo Eyes

"Democrats want an outside *goo-goo* to determine the standards of right and wrong," I wrote in a recent piece about the ethics of Newt Gingrich. "But internal *goo-goos* are elected to do that job, guided by the public's sense of right and wrong."

That struck some readers as an ethnic slur.

"When I was growing up in San Francisco 60 years ago," writes William G. Ackerman of San Rafael, Calif., "some of the guys referred to Filipinos as *goo-goos.*" And "Back when I was in high school," writes Francis G. Hutchinson of Redwood City, Calif., "I had a friend of Filipino ancestry, for which I was from some quarters scorned for chumming around 'with that *goo-goo.'* Move me forward in the lingo. Is it now a term for *guru?* Or *goofball?* Or an infantile person?"

The slur they have in mind is *gook,* of unknown origin, reported first by *American Speech* in 1935 to mean "anyone who speaks Spanish, particularly a Filipino," and was later used in South Korea and Vietnam to denigrate all non-whites. (The return slur by Asians, based on *slant-eyed,* leading to the noun *slants,* is *round-eye.*)

A *goo-goo* is decidedly not a *gook. Goo!* is the sound often made by a satisfied baby, and it became part of imitative baby talk. Reduplicated, it came to mean "loving, enticing," as used in the phrase *goo-goo eyes,* and was turned into a verb by Mark Twain in *Huckleberry Finn:* "The duke . . . just went a goo-gooing around, happy and satisfied."

The word may have been influenced by *goggle,* "to stare with eyes bugged out," which was then caricatured in a comic strip, "Barney Google," by Billy De Beck, in 1919, and was further popularized in 1923 by the impresario and songwriter Billy Rose in "Barney Google—with the goo-goo-googily eyes."

The political term *goo-goo* began in New York in the 1890s after the City Club began to form district-level Good Government Clubs to press for reform.

The *New York Sun* dubbed the Good Government types *Goo-Goos,* a term of derision that was picked up by Theodore Roosevelt: "The Republican machine men have been loudly demanding a straight ticket; and those prize idiots, the Goo-Goos, have just played into their hands by capering off and nominating an independent ticket of their own."

Influenced by an older term, *goody-goody, goo-goo* has lost its capitals as a shortening of *Good Government.* It is now used in affectionate derogation of reformers and ethicists.

In the light of your recent discussion as to whether "goo-goo" can mean a Filipino, John Steinbeck uses the term "Manila Goo-Goos" in Act Two of *Of Mice and Men.*

WHIT: We don't never go to Gladys's. Gladys gits three bucks, and two bits a shot and she don't crack no jokes. But Susy's place is clean and she got nice chairs. A guy can set in there like he lived there. Don't let no Manila Goo-Goos in, neither.

In the novella version of *Of Mice and Men,* the term is simply "Goo-Goos." The "Manila" was added in the play version presumably to make it clear to an East coast audience that Filipinos were meant.

Ralph H. Orth
Burlington, Vermont

Your references to "gook" as "anyone who speaks Spanish," as indicated by American Speech in 1935 interested me. The use in Korea, during the Korean War, and the carryover to the Vietnam War is clearly understandable, it seems to me. The Korean word for "people" is "guk" or "gook." They call themselves the Hanguk, or the Han people (River Han). Americans, however, are Meguk, pronounced "Me Gook." One can immediately imagine the willing application to people who say to an American serviceman "Me Gook." Spanish is inexplicable.

Richard C. Fox
Los Angeles, California

Your musings on the term "goo-goo" failed to mention the most famous goo-goo of them all, and a tasty one at that!

It's Nashville's (and the South's) fifty-year-old "candy cluster" that has been advertised every Saturday night for many years on the WSM "Grand Ole Opry." Goo Goos even made it in the '70s movie *Nashville*, and is regarded as a delicacy in some upscale Manhattan food emporiums.

Bill Knowlton
Syracuse, New York

One word probably coined from *goo* is *googol*, the number one followed by one hundred zeros. The coiner was American mathematician Edward Kasner, who supposedly obtained it from a young nephew when the boy was asked to make up a name for a very large number.

To get an idea of the magnitude of this number, just consider that it is roughly one quintillion (one followed by eighteen zeros) *times* the number of electrons in the entire universe!

David Bernklau
Brooklyn, New York

"Goo-Goo Eyes": "The slur they have in mind is *gook*, of unknown origin . . ." Not to me. According to old Far East hands (pre-WW II experience), the term for Caucasians is *me gook saram* (long-nosed people). Or the origin may be Tagalog.

Arnold J. Lapiner
Trumansburg, New York

In the 1920s our smalltown ice cream parlor served goo-goos, the ultimate sundae: your favorite-flavored ice cream topped with chocolate syrup, a fluff of whipped marshmallow, your choice of crushed nuts or almonds (I always chose almonds) with a shiney-red maraschino cherry, all this for 15¢ (yes!).

M. B. Helms
Omaha, Nebraska

In the art world in NYC, "Goo-Goo" is the affectionate nickname for the Guggenheim Museum (where eyes are important).

Martin Ries
Scarsdale, New York

You thought the term "gook" had no clear origin. I've felt the word is an American creation that derives in part from the name of the Korean language—hangul—where the 'l' is abrupt and the sound is like "hangoo." This sound is associated with derogatory and less than acceptable things in our language (goo, goof, goober, goop). It acts like the Yiddish "schm-" sound and its derivatives. Whatever comes after this sound makes a term that is often derogatory and less than acceptable in Yiddish. Couple the natural negative nature of the "goo-" sound with a feeling by some that orientals were worth less than westerners and "gook" appears. If this seems like a bunch of gobbedlygook then I'm a shmegegge.

Marc Marcussen
Mansfield, Massachusetts

Gotcha! Gang Strikes Again

"You, of all people," begin the letters from the Gotcha! Gang, a hardy tribe obsessed with accuracy and a lust for catching error in others.

As longtime readers know, I occasionally stud my language and political columns with "mistakes" to see if anybody is paying attention, or to draw mail. It's a trap, of course. Here are answers to some of those caught in it during 1995:

1) "These sources have proven reliable," I wrote, trumpeting past leakage triumphs. From Bill Elder, copy editor of *The Vindicator* in Youngstown, Ohio, comes this response: "Wrong! *Proven* is an adjective; you wanted *proved* instead. Not to feel alone, though; many have *proved* that they can make this

mistake. The only *proven* remedy, of course, is to change your copy, as I did."
He's right; as it proved to be the case in the Scottish legal verdict *not proven*,
keep *proven* an adjective.

2) "The best place to hide anything," I wrote, ". . . is to leave it in plain view."
Asks David Leff of Framingham, Mass.: "How can the verb *to leave* be a place?
Shouldn't your keyboard have preferred 'the best *way*'?"

Yeah. Or to save space, "The best place to hide anything is in plain view," as
I told Edgar Allan Poe, who needed a plot about a purloined letter.

3) While flaying L. L. Bean for some bloopie in its catalogue, I tut-tutted
that "old Louis Bean" would never have stood for such stuff. "Do you suppose
the 'old Louis Bean' you wrote about," demands Rex Pinson of Waterford,
Conn., "could be related to the late Leon Leonwood Bean, the inventor of the
Maine Hunting Shoe and founder of the institution (I do not use the word
lightly) that bears his name?" (O.K., Louis, drop the gun, as Bogie never said.)

4) Sears advertised, "Our 120-pc. mechanic's tool set has more of what you
want!" and I sneered: "Ever met a 120-piece mechanic? Make that 'Our
mechanic's 120-pc. tool set.'" That pedantry drew a blast from no less an
authority than James D. McCawley of the department of linguistics at the University of Chicago: "*Mechanic's tool set*, I presume, is a compound like *catcher's
mitt* or *brewer's yeast*, and *120-pc.* modifies the whole compound, the same way
that *genuine leather* modifies the compound in *a genuine leather catcher's mitt* (a
catcher's mitt made of genuine leather, not a mitt for a genuine leather
catcher).

"Your correction of Sears' ad is a change for the worse," continues Professor McCawley, choosing not to write the possessive as *Sears's*, "since the
ambiguity that you point out isn't pernicious (no reference to a 120-pc.
mechanic could be intended), while the ambiguity in your correction *is (our
mechanic's 120-pc. tool set* has a plausible but unintended interpretation as
'the 120-pc. tool set belonging to our mechanic')."

5) "In your cute construction *sanhedrin of skinflints*," corrects William J. Slat-
tery of Jamestown, R.I., "*Sanhedrin* should have been capped."

I disagree. Capped words, like capped teeth, stand out; when you want to
use an unfamiliar word, avoid capitalization, quotation marks or italics—let
the word shift for itself. *The* Sanhedrin was the highest court of the Jews
before the destruction of the Temple and, as a proper noun, deserves a capital letter. When it's used to mean any high council, though, I think it should
be *a sanhedrin*. You don't capitalize a similar word, *synod*, also originally an
ecclesiastical council, now come to mean any assembly, and the Bible loses its
cap when used as "the bible of the computer industry." (The word I originally
had in mind was *witenagemot*, "a council of nobles advising the king," but I
couldn't think of a word beginning with *w* meaning "conservatives." One of
these days I'll find a use for *a witenagemot of wiseguys*.)

6) "Under the agents' eager aegis, political reputations would be made and destroyed," I wrote in a spy novel zestfully panned by no less an authority than the Soviet spy Aldrich Ames. A more appreciative reader was Jacques Barzun, the great usage arbiter, who nevertheless noted, "Seeing as how *aegis* is a shield, its eagerness is a bit hard to visualize." True; from the Greek for "goatskin," *aegis* was the majestic shield worn by Zeus and the breastplate worn by Athena; a more fitting adjective would be "impenetrable."

I kind of liked the sound of *eager aegis*, though; been reading too much poetry.

7) When I wrote that President Clinton had been *chastised* by the voters in the 1994 Republican election sweep, Dick Thornburgh of Pennsylvania circled that word and noted, "Don't you mean *chastened?*" (I could never get a call back from him when he was Attorney General; now he corrects my mistakes.)

Both *chastise* and *chasten* are rooted in the Latin *castus*, "pure," as is *castigate*. In the parsing of punishment, *castigate* is to tongue-lash, *chastise* is to discipline by the infliction of pain and *chasten* is to correct in such a way as to purify and strengthen ("We gather together to ask the Lord's blessing./He *chastens* and hastens His will to make known"). I meant to say that Clinton was *chastened* by the 1994 results.

8) I have also, in the recent past, berated Mr. Clinton for a general softness and wetness characterized as "all carrot and no stick." (Todd S. Purdum used the same expression in a recent front-page *Times* article about the budget impasse: "President Clinton used both *carrot and stick* on Congressional Republicans today by vetoing two more spending bills.")

This was a play on the Texan "all hat and no cattle," but it drew many Uofall peoples from Gotcha! Gangsters around the world who believe that the figure of speech is *carrot on a stick*—dangled from a stick tied to a donkey's neck, purely incentive, not reward or punishment.

Mine really was a fake mistake. (Most of the preceding, as cynics undoubtedly suspected, were bona fide boo-boos.) I have long held to the on-a-stick theory, daring anyone to come up with an early citation showing an *or-a-stick* usage. My associate, Jeffrey McQuain, author of the new Dove vocabulary tape, "Word Workout," found a letter dated July 6, 1938, from Winston Churchill, demonstrating that the metaphor originated as a reward-punishment combination: "Thus, by every device from the *stick* to the *carrot*, the emaciated Austrian donkey is made to pull the Nazi barrow up an ever-steepening hill."

Argue with Sir Winston? Never. Never. Never. Never.

Gotcha, Hobbes

Bidding an embittered farewell to his senatorial and media inquisitors, Anthony Lake alternated alliteration with apt allusion as he withdrew from consideration as Director of Central Intelligence.

He denounced the confirmation process as "nasty and brutish without being short." This alluded to Thomas Hobbes's 1651 description of the life of man in a state of nature as "solitary, poor, nasty, brutish, and short." Most citations of this quotation from *Leviathan* about ungoverned, primitive humanity leave out the "solitary, poor," as did Lake's, but his play on the phrase's last word had impact.

He hoped citizens would demand that "Washington give priority to policy over partisanship, to governing over 'gotcha.'"

As Lexicographic Irregulars know, an affiliate of the Nit-pickers' League calls itself the Gotcha! Gang, whose members are dedicated to finding errors in this column and who—unaware of "mistakes" planted herein to elicit their "corrections"—delight in hurling whoops and imprecations from their citadels of pedantry.

Gotcha! is a pronunciational spelling similar to *wontcha* ("*Wontcha* come home, Bill Bailey?") and *onganna* ("*Ongonna* dunk my bagel inna cawfee"). According to Prof. William Kretzschmar, director of the *Linguistic Atlas* Project at the University of Georgia, the reduced form produces significant change: "The stressed vowel in the pronoun, the *yoo*, becomes a schwa"—pronounced UH. "The *t* plus the *ya* of *you*, run together, turns into a *tch*, an affricate."

We all know that when it comes to language change, a mere running together of words, or elision, ain't nuthin' compared with an affricate, in which an explosive consonant (like *p, b* and *t*) is followed by a fricative consonant (like *th* and *f*) to transform both into a whole new ball game. Fistfights break out in American Dialect Society meetings over whether affricates like *judge* and *church* should be considered one syllable or two, and whether word blends like *gotcha* and *let's* have become grammaticalized, or fused into a unit.

"*Gotcha* is not slang," insists Jesse Sheidlower, principal editor at Oxford's North American unit and a slang specialist. "The eye-dialect spelling suggests informality, but it's actually standard usage, and wouldn't be entered in any of the slang thesauri." (So how come, Jesse, you can find it in the *Random House Historical Dictionary of American Slang? Gotcha!*)

The term can express understanding ("*Gotcha*, boss") or maintain a conversation with more piquancy than the grunted *uh-huh* ("*Gotcha*, keep talkin'") or be an exclamation of petty triumph similar to *aha!*—as used above to embarrass a source guilty only of being helpful, or mock-menacingly, as in the chess player's affrication of "I've *got you* where I want you." A specialized sense having to do with the sort of distracting maneuver demonstrated by the actress Sharon Stone in the movie *Basic Instinct* has a string of citations in the *OED*'s second edition on CD-ROM but has run into the V-chip that some paternal editor has placed in my computer.

Coinage? The earliest use found so far was by the mystery writer R. H. Edgar Wallace, in his 1932 *When Gangs Came to London:* "The plane . . . went down and it fell with a crash. . . . '*Gotcher!*' It was Jiggs' triumphant voice." The spelling changed in 1966 in the "I understand" sense and soon followed in all other meanings of this extraordinarily useful addition to the language, including Anthony Lake's alliterative *gotcha government.*

The nomination sank when a key Democratic senator threw up his hands at lapses in management competence, but the part-time farmer Lake insisted, "Washington has gone *haywire.*"

This Americanism is based on a farming metaphor. Bales of hay were bound with wire: when cut, the wire would spring loose crazily, endangering the farmer; when left lying around, it would become entangled about the legs of horses and cattle, irritating or even maddening them. A 1905 Forestry Bureau Bulletin used the metaphor to derogate a logging operation with poor equipment as "a *hay wire* outfit"; a 1929 *New York Times* article described a defective recording system as having "gone *haywire,*" and John O'Hara, in his 1934 novel, *Appointment in Samarra,* extended the metaphor to a man "absolutely *haywire*" over a woman.

Gotham Forever

"Gotham City," as all Batman fans know, is New York—particularly New York below 14th Street, from SoHo to Greenwich Village, the Bowery, Little Italy, Chinatown and the sinister areas around the base of the Manhattan and Brooklyn Bridges.

"Originally I was going to call Gotham City 'Civic City,'" said Bill Finger, collaborator of Batman's creator, Bob Kane, in *History of the Comics,* by Jim Steranko. "Then I tried Capital City, then Coast City. Then I flipped through the phone book and spotted the name 'Gotham Jewelers' and said, 'That's it,' Gotham City. We didn't call it New York because we wanted anybody in any city to identify with it. Of course, Gotham is another name for New York."

Of course; the Peninsula Hotel, formerly the Gotham, is there on Fifth Avenue. Gotham is a village in Nottinghamshire; in 1806, a Lancaster, Pennsylvania, newspaper referred to "the Man of Gotham, who prints *Freeman's Journal*"; that alluded to a Philadelphia editor. But a year later, Washington Irving, America's first satirist, located Gotham in New York: "They all capered to the devoted city of Gotham," he wrote, and in a collection of humorous essays he called *Salmagundi,* noted that the residents of New York reminded him of the strange English town of Gotham (as in "The Gothamites . . . have waxed to be most flagrant, outrageous and abandoned dancers"). The residents of the town feigned madness to discourage King John from building a castle there. Their exploits were recounted in *The Merrie Tales of the Mad Men of Gotham,* and Irving fancied these cannily foolish people to be similar to New Yorkers.

Perhaps the proper noun *Gotham,* like the adjective *Gothic,* derives from the Goths, a Germanic tribe that took over much of Europe from the third to the fifth centuries.

Washington Irving, popularizer of *Gotham* as the pseudonym of New York, later wrote a five-volume biography of George Washington. The writer would surely have appreciated this riddle: "What is the question to which 'Washington Irving' is the answer?" The answer: "Who was the father of our country, Shirley?"

You speculate that the origin of the proper name *Gotham* is perhaps from *gothic.* The authorities I have seen say that the name of the English town means 'goat town' in Anglo Saxon, *Got* + *ham,* the common suffix *-ham* meaning town, a form appearing in many English placenames.

Irving Lewis Allen
Storrs, Connecticut

Grotesquerie in a Box

Newt Gingrich is all wrapped up in boxes. Metaphorically, every day is Boxing Day to Newt. (In Britain, the first weekday after Christmas is called Boxing Day, after the tradition of giving boxes of gifts to servants and public employees.)

"Medicare will be put in a separate box," he told a group of elders called the Seniors Coalition, a conservative part of what is derogated as the Geezer Lobby.

That's one sense of the Gingrich box: a device to separate and protect. Earlier this year, he was using the box in another sense, more creatively, as his central idea-packaging device:

"Speaker Newt Gingrich, fond as ever of futuristic management consultant-speak," wrote the *Washington Post* columnist E. J. Dionne Jr., "addressed the Ways and Means Committee last week on the importance of 'thinking outside the dots.' This maxim is also often rendered as 'thinking outside the box.' The idea is to encourage people to junk their preconceptions."

The *dots* and the *box* are related. A brain teaser used in 1984 by Development Dimensions International, management consultants, showed eight dots forming a square, or box, with a dot in the middle. "Without lifting your pencil from the paper," the teaser went, "join all the dots with only four straight lines." It looks like this:

$$\begin{matrix} \bullet & \bullet & \bullet \\ \bullet & \bullet & \bullet \\ \bullet & \bullet & \bullet \end{matrix}$$

(I have tried to solve this and conclude that you have to be a liberal.) "To connect the dots," wrote DDI's Nancy Hrynkiw to Anne Soukhanov, an inquiring lexicographer, "you must go outside the nine dots, but most people automatically think that they have to stay within the nine dots." (See page 388 for the way it's done by visionary public servants and executives destined for the top or soon to be fired.)

Thus, *thinking outside the dots* or *outside the box*, Ms. Hrynkiw explains, means "thinking about a problem without the constraints that 'how things are now' sometimes imposes." According to a list of current corporate catch phrases assembled in the Nov. 4, 1994, *Management* magazine, *thinking out of the box* can be defined as "creating new processes, not just refining old formulas." The magazine adds, "However, challenging your bosses' processes is risky." (I would write that as *bosses's processes*, insuring a rhyme.) (The other corporate catch phrase I liked was *delayering*, which means "firing middle management.")

This sort of iconoclastic creativity in solution-seeking, also called *what-if thinking*, is the second sense of the Gingrich box. A third means "disciplined": when the former Speaker temporarily departed from the 10 points in his Contract With America, raising the issue of school prayer early this year, he quickly realized it to be a mistake and chided himself for *going outside the box*.

In this sense, a box is a plan, sometimes described as a *core message;* to go *outside the box* is to slop over, to lose focus. There is a seeming contradiction here: to *think* outside the box is laudable, but to *go* outside the box invites censure, and could lead to wholesale delayering.

The box or nine dots exercise was originally printed in a book of similar puzzles, but first used commercially by Wilson Learning around 1970.

Page W. Glasgow
Troy, Michigan

As an adjunct professor of human resource management at Mercy College, I took the opportunity with my summer class of graduate students to assign research topics. One suggestion was to find the earliest occurrence of the Nine Dots exercise.

One of my graduate students, Judith Hanna, asked Richard Lowry, Professor of Psychology at Vassar College (where Judith is Assistant Registrar) for any leads. He reports that the earliest direct reference is in G. W. Hartman's "Gestalt Psychology: A Survey of Facts and Principles (1935)," where it is attributed to a psychologist named Scheerer.

Tom Pison
New York, New York

A *geezer* is a rich, mean, stingy, grouchy, old, bald guy, with hair growing out his ears and nose, wearing an out-at-the-elbows cardigan and baggy pants; a codger is all of the above, rendered genial and lovable by the fact that he has designated you his sole heir.

Robert Gordon
Emerald Isle, North Carolina

Growing the Grotesquerie

"They will do anything to stop us," an irate Newt Gingrich said to the Republican National Committee in January, referring to Democrats in the aftermath of Republican election victories. "They will use any tool. There is no *grotesquerie,* no distortion, no dishonesty too great."

Months later, when a reporter suggested a link between criticism of the

Government and the Oklahoma bombing, Mr. Gingrich stayed in the box: "I think that's *grotesque* and offensive."

Both the adjective *grotesque* and its noun (*grotesquerie*, the French form, preferred by Mr. Gingrich to *grotesqueness*) spring readily to the Speaker's lips, and its popularization is a fine contribution to the American political vocabulary.

It begins in a cave. From the Latin *crypta* for "crypt, cavern," we get to the Italian *grotto*; the drawings on the walls were *grotesco*, in French *grotesque*. Archeologists revealing the grotto work found the art wildly formed, whimsical and extravagant. *The Century Dictionary* added "absurdly bold; often used in a sense of condemnation or depreciation," and cited this line in John Milton's *Paradise Lost* in 1667: "A steep wilderness, whose hairy sides/With thicket overgrown, grotesque and wild,/Access denied."

(Funny that *access denied* comes from Milton; it's an infuriating phrase that appears at the top of my computer screen when I try to call up a file and forget my code name. You often get wonderful stuff like this in the *Century Dictionary*, a 10-volume set published in 1897; I picked it up for $60 from a used-and-rare-book seller glad to get it off his shelf. If you have room, and can find a set, grab it; you'll one-up all your CD-ROM friends.)

From a description of the wild and woolly paintings on the cave walls, it was a short jump to "fantastic, antic, comically distorted," and then to "ugly, deformed, misshapen, twisted" and altogether "bizarre." (Recently discovered cave paintings are extraordinarily graceful and what we now call "artistic"; they are grotesqueries that are not grotesque.)

Because the word begins with the sound of a growl, it should have a greater appeal to orators than *bizarre,* a popular synonym that has a connotation of nuttiness; the connotation of *grotesque* is "extremely distorted and ugly." In Britain, the slang term *grotty*—usually followed by the sound of "yecch!"—may be derived from *grotesque.*

I believe the usage of the term "grotesque" is not from the "wild and woolly" at all, as the caves were not known when the term began to be used as it is. Rather, when the golden palace of Nero, Domus Aureus, I think it was called, was discovered in Renaissance times in Rome, broken into, and traversed, seen as a series of vast cave rooms, which it still remains today for the tourist, what was painted on the walls, the fanciful chimerical paintings of flowers and beasts, satyrs and nymphs of the grottos of these now roofless buildings, are what were termed *grottesco*, i.e., after the style of the decoration on the walls. At least that is what the book says (ACI), the best guidebook on Rome, as you stroll through what was once Nero's home.

It is worth an hour the next time you are in Rome, I assure you, because you will then see how those forms were swiftly adopted everywhere in Italy for wall paintings in the various

Renaissance palazzi. *Grotesque,* those decorations certainly are not. But they are *of,* or *from,* that grotto; indeed, were they adapted for good wallpaper, you could live with most of them happily, as they are far from what you might think of as bizarrerie. Moreover, the "growl" you speak of is the *gro* in English, in the throat; in Italian it is a sound that begins with the *g* in the throat, but is connected immediately with the trilling *rrr* at the tip of the tongue, rather more musical and not Neanderthal, not really.

Jaschu Kessler
Santa Monica, California

Growth Stock

"Why is it that when a C.E.O. announces that his goal is to *grow the company,* the phrase sets my teeth on edge," asked Joe Fox,* a senior editor at Random House, "whereas if a politician announces that he aims *to shrink the deficit,* it seems acceptable to my ear?"

I was breaking my head over this when two thoughts occurred: first, the opening quotation in the above paragraph is too long. It should read, " 'Why is it,' asked Joe Fox," followed by the rest of his question. The reader wants to know quickly who's being quoted. Second, why am I breaking my head to figure out the answer when I have access to the world's greatest grammarians?

"Your correspondent had a good sense of language," responds Jacques Barzun, author of the classic *Simple and Direct.*

"*Grow* seems one of those verbs that are both intransitive ('Children grow fast') and transitive ('The farmer grows wheat'). But that is an illusion. If you think a moment about the second sentence, you see that it means only *plant,* and this in a very abstract sense. If someone is planting bulbs, you do not say, 'Look at her growing tulips,' or again, if a sapling is doing well, you do not say, 'I will grow it taller with fertilizer.'

"*Grow* in transitive use is an idiomatic form restricted to the meaning 'make a crop of'—'They grow turnips in Zanzibar.' And that is why the CEO cannot 'grow his company' any more than he can grow his children."

But what about *shrinking* the deficit? Is *shrink* also one of those verbs that only seem to go both ways, transitive and intransitive?

"*Shrink,* on the other hand," says Professor Barzun (See? Just the right length of quote), "is a true transitive-intransitive verb. You instinctively *shrink*

---

*Joe Fox died on November 29, 1995.

from pain as the laundry *shrinks* your cotton shirt. Both uses have the same 'extension,' whereas transitive *grow* has only a single, abstract use warranted solely by idiom."

Under *Growth Stock,* you quote Jacques Barzun: "*Grow* seems one of those verbs that are both intransitive . . . and transitive. . . ." Here, shouldn't the verb ("are," in this case) agree with "one" and be "is"? You then repeat this yourself when you write, "Is *shrink* also one of those verbs that only *seem* to go both ways, transitive and intransitive?" In this sentence, it appears that "seem" should also agree with "one," and be "seems." I realize I am doubting two experts in this area, but I remember learning case agreement somewhat differently, and we did both go to the same high school.

Jonathan S. Silber
Bethesda, Maryland

Half in Love with "Full Frontal"

The state of Maryland seems to be in the pornography business. Here it is on the Motor Vehicle Administration's instructions for renewal of my driver's license: "You must be 21 or older to get a *full frontal* photo license."

I suppose what they really mean is a mug shot—just the driver's face, taken from the front, not in profile or three-quarter view, and surely not head to toe in total undress.

Full frontal—the two words occasionally separated by a comma, more often hyphenated as a compound adjective and most often left just standing there naked of punctuation—began with *nudity.* I remember going to an off-Broadway play in 1969 titled *Oh, Calcutta!* expecting to see what is initialized as "T.&A.," referring to bosoms and behinds, but startled to see the cast of perfectly nice young people lined up, facing the audience, with nothing covering anything. This was described, with a gulp, as *"full frontal* nudity." The show ran on and off, and around the country, for 20 years. It was a kind of breakthrough to finality in stripping; there was nowhere else to go.

Images of the naked performers fade (though not with all of us), but the linguistic impact lives on. The earliest citation of the phrase—*"full frontal* nudity on the stage"—was in William John Burley's 1971 British novel, *Guilt Edged.* A. Alvarez picked it up in a 1972 *Saturday Review:* "In these days of *full frontal* intimacy he [V. S. Pritchett] sticks to the unfashionable virtue of reticence."

The Times of London in 1973 began to extend the meaning beyond nudity by quoting a worried executive's "We're all in for some *full-frontal* management," and *Business Week* three years later gave the phrase a twist, using *full* to modify the military phrase *frontal attack*.

The extended usage is growing in frequency, gaining ground on "all-out, unrestrained, full-fledged." In a *Los Angeles Times* review of a book by Henry Roth, Stefan Kanfer writes, "Those who cannot endure *full frontal* history argue that Roth's writer's block had one cause—the inability to confront this sexual transgression." Even further removed from sex is the columnist Paul A. Gigot's use in a recent *Wall Street Journal* column about Pat Buchanan's Presidential campaign: "His Medicare ad is a *full-frontal* pander to seniors."

Unlike many phrases that lose their sexual connotation as they move into general use ("different strokes for different folks," "use it or lose it," "let it all hang out"), *full frontal* retains echoes of its origin. Writers not only mean "unabashed" but often intend to convey the sense of "intended to shock." Old-fashioned, full-figured strict constructionists insist on the hyphen.

Your droll commentary about "full frontal" brings to mind Archie Bunker's nonpareil observation, made in connection with some kind of protest demonstration in which she had participated, that daughter Gloria was in a state of "full nudal frontity."

Dana S. Wickware
Clinton, Connecticut

"Full Frontal Nudity" was the title of a *Monty Python Show*, recorded November 25, 1969, and aired December 7, 1969.

Kim Brobeck
Vacaville, California

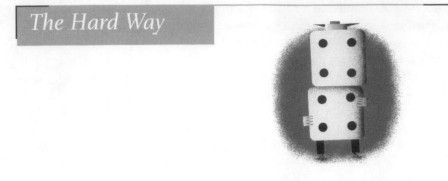

My informal job title in the Nixon Administration was Rejected Counsel. That's because, as a speech writer, I would occasionally put my head into the Oval Office to say: "Mr. President—Do the popular thing! Take the easy way!" Mr. Nixon would ritualistically throw me out of the office, allowing me to submit a speech draft that would truthfully report: "Some of my aides have suggested that I do the popular thing, that I should take the easy way. But I have rejected such counsel."

This happy memory came to mind as I listened to Bob Dole's eloquent announcement of his departure from the Senate to devote all his time to his Presidential campaign. In that talk, he referred briefly to his difficult travail as a wounded veteran in relearning to walk: "I trust in the hard way, for little has come to me except in the hard way, which is good because we have a hard task ahead of us." Later he recalled times of discouragement: "I have been there before, I have done it the hard way and I will do it the hard way once again." At the conclusion, he reprised the theme: "For the American people have always known, through our long and trying history, that God has blessed the hard way."

I reached Dole after the speech to ask who wrote it. He was at first reluctant to say because he didn't want the anonymous volunteer to get in trouble with his employer, but when I explained that it would only help the writer's career, and that people now understand that public figures get professional writing help, the Senator replied that drafts had come from Mark Helprin, a novelist who contributes op-ed pieces to the *Wall Street Journal*.

After I reported the source of this welcome change from the stilted style of most previous Dole speeches, the modest Mr. Helprin found himself inundated with media calls and requests for bylined articles. The *Wall Street Journal* proudly took a full-page ad in other papers reprinting its contributor's piece about Dole, demonstrating what little trouble his political involvement got him in. Only Richard Cohen of the *Washington Post*, one of the few pundits who have not had the exhilarating and instructive experience of having written for a politician, grumped that getting outside help made the Dole remarks less authentic.

Well, then—as a longtime derogator of "the easy way"—what can I contribute to the rhetorical origin of Mr. Dole's *the hard way*?

As *the New Deal* was rooted in card playing, *the hard way* is derived from rolling dice. In Damon Runyon's 1931 book, *Guys and Dolls*, a character familiar with the world of gambling is quoted: "'Charley,' he says, 'do you make it *the hard way?*'" In shooting craps, *the hard way* means "the most difficult way": narrowing the ability to make an even-numbered point by requiring the two dice to come up with a pair of equal numbers totaling the point. For example, if eight is the point to be made *the hard way*, the combination of neither six-and-two nor five-and-three will do; *the hard way* calls for two fours. What makes it "harder" is that the odds of achieving the point that limited way are higher. By extension, the phrase *to learn the hard way* means "through bitter experience," and *to come up the hard way* means "primarily by one's own efforts."

In an interview with *Newsweek*, Helprin recalled Dole's words when making the decision to leave the Senate: "If I'm going to run for President, I'm going to have to run for President."

This "if-then" construction has long been used in the expression of determination and grit. Said the 19th-century political economist William Graham Sumner, "If you ever live in a country run by a committee, be on the committee." Said Gov. Huey Long of Louisiana to a group of young politicians, "If you want some ham, you got to go to the smokehouse." Said Napoleon Bonaparte to a hesitant general, "If you're going to take Vienna, take Vienna."

You did say that two fours was the hard way to make an eight point, but you didn't say how much harder than the easy way. The answer is four times as hard. A six point is also four times as hard the hard way as the easy way. A four the hard way is twice as hard as the easy way.

Arthur J. Morgan*
New York, New York

*Arthur J. Morgan died on September 28, 1996.

From the bleak and poor village of Youyan, China, a *New York Times* correspondent, Patrick E. Tyler, wrote movingly that the school-age girls "who could be going to class from this village tend the water buffaloes that forage lazily on the *hardscrabble* mountainsides."

In a *Kirkus Service* book review of *Answers to Lucky* by Howard Owen, the reviewer used *hardscrabble* to intensify an adjective: "Tommy Sweatt grew up in the river-rat country, *hardscrabble* mean."

Writing about the pioneering country singer Patsy Cline, Dave Tianen of the *Milwaukee Journal Sentinel* observed that "some of Cline's mystique must rest on her tragic early death and *hard-scrabble* upbringing."

This Americanism's first citation was in the 1804 journals of Lewis and Clark: "Got on our way at *hard Scrable* Perarie." By 1812, it meant "effort made under stress," in a *Salem Gazette* headline: "Presidential *Hard Scrabble!*" Herman Melville, in *Moby Dick*, used the adjective form in the same sense: "While taking that *hard-scrabble* scramble upon the dead whale's back." Mitford M. Mathews, in his *Dictionary of Americanisms*, gave another sense an inspired definition: "a place thought of as the acme of barrenness where a livelihood may be obtained only with great difficulty."

Rooted in the Dutch *schrabbelen*, "to scratch," *scrabble* means "to struggle to survive by scratching or clawing"; the addition of *hard*, now no longer separated by a hyphen, intensifies the struggle.

Great word, but its power is being diminished by too frequent use. The vogue-word-sensitive Mary Ellen Greenfield* of Washington, when asked its meaning while striking it from some copy, replied, "A very difficult board game."

Harrumphisms

Clearly, something must be done; basically, the problem is this:

Clearly and *basically* have been reduced to throat-clearing, attention-demanding words. The new meaning of both is "I'm here. Shut up and listen."

A third harrumphism is *actually*. R. W. (Johnny) Apple, chief Washington correspondent of the *New York Times*, came barreling into my office to denounce the widely prevalent insinuation of *actually* into sentences where it adds no emphasis or intensification. "Kids use it all the time these days— '*Actually* I think I'll go out.' Or travel agents—'I can *actually* get you a flight tomorrow.'"

Is this not a variant of the British usage, pronounced *EK-chil-ee*? The Anglophile Apple thinks not: "The Brits use the word to cast doubt on what has gone before. 'Some say Gladstone was the greatest Prime Minister. *Actually*, he fell short.' But we just use it as filler."

---

*Meg Greenfield died on May 13, 1999.

Perhaps the rise of the need to assert actuality has been stimulated by the cyberese popularity of *virtual,* which is artificial actuality. But beware of harrumphisms and other words that do no hard communications work. As Alistair Cooke likes to say in making this point, "Long period of time no see."

Now that you have splendidly covered "clearly," "basically," and "actually," how about discussing the curse of "arguably"? The word is *everywhere,* and usually is incorrectly used (as a synonym for "without any question").

Florence W. Patrick
North Kinston, Rhode Island

With all due respect to Anglophile Apple, I don't believe he is correct. I distinctly recall an occasion in 1963, at tea in a Bermuda hotel, plodding desperately through a stilted attempt at conversation with a lofty young Englishwoman. Seizing on the banal as a last resort, I asked where she lived in England. Came the supercilious reply: "In Surrey, EK-chil-ee."

Pondering this apparent non sequitur, I eventually reached the tentative conclusion that the usage is a subconscious holdover from the Norman Conquest, stemming from the French *actuellement,* "at the moment," "currently," or "at present," but not used in this—or any—particular context.

Eleanor W. Hall
Bellevue, Washington

Heartland

"Terror in the *Heartland*" was the way both NBC and CBS titled their Oklahoma bombing coverage.

This word has a historical resonance. In 1904, the geographer Halford John Mackinder, in his *Democratic Ideals and Reality,* coined the word in propounding the notion that the Eurasian *heartland* was the pivotal area of history. This theory did not make a big impression in England and the United States, but was embraced by German geopolitician Karl Haushofer in the 1920s and was picked up by Hitler in *Mein Kampf,* closely associating the word with Nazi world dominance.

After World War II, George Orwell used the term, again in a geopolitical sense, in *1984*: "The territory which forms the *heartland* of each superstate always remains inviolate." In 1947, the New Zealand quarterly *Landfall* applied the term to the American Midwest: "We are in the frontier West, the *heartland* of the American myth." Dwight Eisenhower of Abilene, Kan., liked to say, "I come from the *heartland* of America."

Today, the word has two meanings: the first, "a central area with strategic advantages for defense," and the more recent, "the American Midwest, where traditional morality and 'mainstream' values ostensibly flourish."

The second meaning is now predominant, with a modification taking it away from the geographical to the demographic: the place, like suburbia anywhere, known for concern with, or lip service to, old-fashioned virtues. *Heart* not only means "center," but also has connotations of character and love; the *heartland* is the home of what the columnist Joseph Kraft called "Middle America."

Residents of "Bosnywash," the Boston–New York–Washington corridor, have not yet presumed to call their area the *brainland*.

You wrote that the word heartland "has a historical resonance." What resonated for me was the use of "a" before historical rather than "an," which to me seems preferable. In trying to figure out why this is, I concluded that to a professional narrator of books-on-tape and corporate and medical videos, flow is all. "An" softens the aspiration of the h and becomes less hiccuppy. And in the mouth of a radical "an"-user, the h might even become silent ("an istorical"), which is nicer still. But curiously, "an" works only before the adjective or adverb; "an history" is clearly wrong. In searching for the rule, I've concluded that "an" is preferable when the second syllable is stressed, "an hysterical passenger," "an holistic approach," "an hilarious joke," "an Hispanic candidate"; but "a hemophiliac," "a hypocritical reply," "a hologram," and "a humanistic attitude." "An hour" and "an honor" don't count because the "h" is silent to begin with.

By the way, you might have avoided this thoroughly inconsequential observation by eliminating the article altogether. Resonance resonates just fine all by itself.

Eric D. Conger
Weehawken, New Jersey

Heather Happy

Catalogue copywriters, wicking away the sweat on their brows, insist that every color be part of a noun phrase. In hooting at *heather gray* recently, I held that *heather* is a purplish pink flower—and the gray hooded sweatshirt using that noun phrase looked plain gray to me.

Not since *Newsweek* placed me high on a list of "the worst-dressed men in Washington" have I been so out of fashion.

"The adjective *heather*," writes Ken Gould of Fort Lee, N.J., "has always been used to describe a mottled appearance, or a two-tone color. *'Heather gray'* would indicate a cross-dye effect of both a lighter and a darker gray in the fabric as opposed to a charcoal or banker's gray."

Hope Einstein of Stamford, Conn., writes that heathered yarn "has a flecked or mottled look of uneven, blended color," and uses *heathered* to mean "speckled." Nancy Fryer Croft of New York agrees: "*Heathery* means 'flecked with various colors,' and 'heather gray' is a fitting description of the mixed-gray coloration of classic sweatshirts."

O.K.; *heather,* as an attributive noun modifying a color, does not mean "purplish pink," but means "flecked, speckled, mottled, varicolored, two-toned." However, Ms Croft then brings up a new fashion advertising controversy: "the misuse of the word *anorak* when *parka* is meant."

I always thought the two were interchangeable: *anorak* from the Inuit Eskimo for "a long pullover hooded jacket," and *parka* from the Samoyedic Russian for the same outerwear.

"Outfitters for outdoorsmen," argues Ms Croft, "have always used *anorak* to mean a parka in which the opening, usually closed by a zipper, extends only partway down the front of the jacket. You need to pull an *anorak* over your head to take it off. A garment that unzips to the bottom is called simply a *parka.*"

Dictionaries don't make these fine distinctions about outerwear; perhaps Esquimaux do. My question: who decides that an anorak is no anorak if it zips all the way down? Not the Eskimo, unfamiliar with zippers. Not the lexicographers. The fashion industry? The writers of ad copy? More about this if I find out.

Hello, Central

"If you want to get with it in terms of nomenclature," Richard Holbrooke, former Assistant Secretary of State, told me, "you're going to have to stop referring to the nations of Eastern Europe as being in *Eastern* Europe. They think of themselves as being *Central* Europeans."

Was I being subtly manipulated in some sort of bureaucratic power play? Rather than rushing out to the cutting edge of current diplomatic usage—possibly contributing unwittingly to the perpetration of a policy nuance—I waited for this major geo-semantic shift to work its way upward.

Sure enough, when the White House held a meeting to promote trade with what I used to call *countries behind the Iron Curtain,* or *captive nations* or *Warsaw Pact nations,* the designation chosen was not *Eastern Europe,* but a tentative, transitional, all-inclusive "White House Conference on Trade and Investment in *Central and Eastern Europe.*"

But in addressing that group in Cleveland, President Clinton threw out the *Eastern* and gutsily used the Holbrooke formulation: "Look at what is happening in Central Europe. . . . Just six years ago, the countries of Central Europe were still captive nations."

It's all very well for diplomats to issue diktats and for Presidents to get on usage ukases, but nothing changes until it changes in the *New York Times,* which does not treat geographic designations or names of countries lightly, especially when political implications impinge. (Took me years to get us to change the old spelling of *Rumania* to the *Romania* that Romanians prefer.)

"For my language column," I queried Allan M. Siegal, assistant managing editor and overall stylistic czar, "do we capitalize *Eastern* Europe and *Western* Europe?" That was an easy one, for openers; then the zinger, put offhandedly: "Where is *Central* Europe?"

Al Siegal solicited an opinion from Bernard Gwertzman, foreign editor, who replied, "Safire's question comes at a time when the foreign desk has been discussing using new terms for the geography of Europe."

In formulating his recommendation, Gwertzman queried Craig R. Whitney in Paris, the *Times'* European diplomatic correspondent: "Craig, the question is asked here, shouldn't we drop terms like 'countries of *Eastern* Europe' when we really mean, largely, countries of *Central* Europe? I know this is a semantic difference with all sorts of political implications, i.e., if Poland is part of Central Europe, shouldn't it be allowed in NATO sooner than if in Eastern Europe. What do you think?"

Whitney in Paris to Gwertzman in New York: "When you think that until 50 years ago, Kaliningrad and half of present-day Poland were actually part of Germany, then for Poland, Hungary, Czech Republic and Slovakia the situation is clear: they always were considered Central Europe and consider themselves that now. Romania and Bulgaria are another story. As for the Balkans: most people this side of the Atlantic refer to them as southeast Europe, or the Balkans. Historically, Eastern Europe is actually Ukraine, Belarus, and western Russia. The Baltics fit into this scenario as 'the Baltics,' since they are no more Eastern European than Sweden and Finland are. Cheers, Whitney."

Gwertzman to Siegal: "We will use common-sense geographic designations for parts of Europe. Clearly, there is a western Europe, a central Europe and an eastern Europe. The cold war had brought about a political division of Europe into East and West, with Berlin the implicit dividing line. The establishment of two alliances, NATO and the Warsaw Pact, allowed us to say 'Western Europe vs. Eastern Europe.' That meant that the classic center of Europe was more or less omitted."

With the cold war over, and with the countries of the old Warsaw Pact no longer tied to the Soviet "East," Gwertzman recommended: "The time has come to 'restore' the Czech Republic, Poland, Hungary, eastern Germany and Slovakia to *Central* Europe. I would say that European Russia, Ukraine, Belarus, Bulgaria, former Yugoslavia and Romania probably belong in eastern Europe but not as a political designation."

I have shared these ultrasecret internal *Times* documents with readers not only to show how this institution sweats the details of style and denotation, but also to give readers a chance to holler as diplomats and editors linguistically carve up the world.

At the State Department, nomenclature is an expression of foreign policy. "There must be an *Eastern Europe* somewhere," says a spokesman, Aric Schwan, "but where exactly that line falls became a matter of hot dispute." Does it take in the Baltic States—Latvia, Lithuania and Estonia—the forced annexation of which into the Soviet Union was never recognized by the U.S.? Because the Baltics want no part of being thought of as "Eastern," State's designation of them with that word has been dropped, and that area is now part of the "Nordic/Baltic desk."

But what of the area covering Ukraine, Belarus, Moldova and the other former Soviet republics? Wouldn't they like to be thought of as *Central* if it helps them get out of the Russian orbit? "As of now," admits the Foggy Bottom spokesman, "we have no real name for the other bureau. Jim Collins is the Ambassador at Large for what's being called *New Independent States*, but it's also referred to as the *East European, Caucasus and Eurasian* Bureau."

In *The Bloc That Failed*, Charles Gati saw the political meaning in Europe's loss of the word *central*: "Take 'Eastern Europe.' Before 1945 geographers had seldom identified such a region. . . . The map provides ample justification for questioning Eastern Europe as a geographic entity." Prague, capital of then-Czechoslovakia, part of the "East," is north*west* of Vienna, capital of Austria, considered part of the "West."

The use of *eastern*, Mr. Gati posited, was part of a Soviet pretense of political commonality with the six states of Central and Southeastern Europe. The word *central* once suggested they were greatly influenced by Germany; the word *eastern* asserted the domination of Russia.

When anybody asks for your position on the 1999 enlargement of NATO to include the nations of Eastern, or Central, Europe, play it semantically safe.

Here's my own mooring, updated and consistent: capitalize the noun, not the adjective. It's eastern Europe, central Europe and western Europe. (And whatever became of northern and southern Europe?)

Perhaps the time has come to resuscitate either the term Mitteleuropa or Middle Europe. These terms have a valid history, as is expressed in *Webster's New Geographical Dictionary*, and cover the geopolitical context you mention.

Thomas R. Claire
New York, New York

Hillary Speaks

I put it directly to the Dalai Lama, who was in Washington pressing for the protection of Tibetan culture: did Hillary Rodham Clinton's unexpectedly strong speech to the United Nations Fourth World Conference on Women, held in Beijing, help the cause of human rights in his country?

"Yes," the monk in red robes replied without hesitation. "The speech will have an enormous positive impact in the long run."

Having elicited and reported that ringing endorsement, I feel more comfortable dissecting the speech as a piece of oratory.

She made effective use of what speech writers call "the Kennedy let 'em." You will recall how J.F.K., in his *Ich bin ein Berliner* speech, thrice set up the straw men "some who" and demolished them with a "let them" construction: "There are some who say that Communism is the wave of the future. Let them come to Berlin."

In the same way, Mrs. Clinton found "some who question the reason for this conference" and pulverized them with "let them listen to the voices of women in their homes, neighborhoods and workplaces." And what to tell "some who wonder whether the lives of women and girls matter"? "Let them look at the women gathered here."

Another rhetorical device that worked was what the Greeks called *epanodos*, meaning "the road back," which is repetition in reverse. Shakespeare used *epanodos* in "Macbeth": "Fair is foul, and foul is fair." The First Lady used it in Beijing: "Human rights are women's rights. And women's rights are human rights."

Epistrophe is also a Hillary specialty. That's the ending of phrases with the same term. "If women are healthy and educated, their families will flourish. If women are free from violence, their families will flourish. If women have a chance to work . . . their families will flourish." Obviously, Mrs. Clinton and her speech writer, Lissa Muscatine, decided to push alliterative *epistrophe*.

With those positive elements noted, some constructive criticism:

"Women *comprise* more than half the world's population." The parts do not *comprise* the whole; the whole *comprises* the parts. (A book *comprises* its chapters, not the other way around.) *Comprise* is a synonym for *include,* and a smaller group can never "include" the larger group; instead, smaller groups "constitute" or "form" the larger one. Our nation *comprises* 50 states, but the 50 states constitute, not *comprise,* our nation. Because "population" is the whole of which "women" are a part, the correct verb is *compose* or *make up.*

Later, she got it: "Women and children *make up* a large majority"; they do not *comprise* it. (When Jimmy Carter estimated that "about 8 percent of our military forces are comprised of women," he was using an even more controversial construction: the passive "is comprised of." Even though "comprise" should not take "of," many dictionaries are now including "comprised of," sometimes labeled as a "loose usage." Substitute the synonym in that passive phrase, however, and "is included of" makes no sense; replace it with "is composed of.")

I will not cavil at her use, four times, of *raise* in connection with the upbringing of children. We in the rear guard of usage prefer *rearing* children and *raising* cattle, but this distinction is being worn down and may have been given a powerful clop on the head by the First Lady in this formal speech to a world body. However, her locution "fast-food chefs" is an oxymoronic euphemism; the 1951 modifier *fast-food,* like its predecessor *short-order,* applies to *cooks,* whether they work in "greasy spoons" or "fast-food joints"; *chefs* (from the French *chef de cuisine,* meaning "head of the kitchen") carries a clear connotation of gourmet cooking.

Mrs. Clinton urges women to "take greater control over their own destinies"; I would urge them to take control *of,* rather than *over,* or to exercise greater *power over.* This seems like a nitpick, but if you are going to empower an entire sex, you have to give it the proper linguistic tools. Same with her use of "caretakers for most of the world's children"; since you take care of someone, the better choice would be "caretakers of." The preposition *for* works better with "caregivers for," because you can give "care for."

She spoke of efforts to "bring new dignity" and "bring new strength" to women around the world. *Bring* should be used only for conveying something from somewhere else to the place of the verb's user. In this case, neither *bring* nor *take* fits; *give* or *add* would have been appropriate.

Her choice of "let us not forget" places her on the side of the prescriptive and eat-your-peas rhetorician; the verbal finger-wagging is surely not incorrect, but as the Reagan speech writer Peggy Noonan pointed out, "let us remember" is the warmer and more positive form.

Her use of *NGOs,* an abbreviation, before using the full phrase, "nongovernmental organizations," invited confusion in the minds of the worldwide audience; it's not a good idea to assume everyone knows what the local audience does. There are those for whom *NGO* stands for *Nongovernmental Observers, Naval Gunfire Officer* or *National Gas Outlet.*

Mrs. Clinton needs to address her *also* problem. "Women also are dying from diseases" suggests in the present progressive that women, as well as men, are dying. Her intended meaning, however, was that another problem facing women is disease; therefore, her word order should have been "women are also dying." Same with her use of "we also must recognize," which means "we, too, must recognize." She obviously meant "we must also recognize," which has the *also* modifying the *recognize* rather than the *we*.

"The voices of this conference," the First Lady told the delegates, ". . . must be heard loud and clear." Everybody knows what she meant because *loud and clear* is a fused phrase, but the problem is with the *heard.* A sound may be loud when it is made, but it is not "heard" loud; either the voices should be loud and clear without the *heard,* or the voices should "ring out" loud and clear.

Is any of this belated copy editing necessary? Wasn't it a good speech, well received by all except the repressive Chinese gerontocracy? The central message of Hillary Rodham Clinton's most important speech came across with courage and puissance (loud and clear, if clichés appeal), but when a representative of the United States steps on the world stage, he or she should pay attention to the details. "It is time for us to say here in Beijing, and the world to hear," she said, but could more clearly and forcefully have said, "and time for the world to hear." It's a little thing, good English usage in the service of oratory, but the little things add up.

Hissy Fits and Golden Oldies

"The people up there are having a *hissy fit* all over Washington," Pat Buchanan told "Face the Nation" on CBS. "They can't believe it—'The beast is coming.'"

This citation breathed new life into my *hissy fit* dossier. It was opened in July 1995, when Senator Orrin Hatch of Utah said, "If you file for cloture after five days of debate, that's no reason for anybody to get up here and pitch a *hissy fit.*"

Asked about this at the time, Senator Hatch said: "The term probably surfaced in the Appalachians, but it's been used in Utah for as long as I can remember. And if you really wanted to carry it out to the end, a *hissy fit* is an 'itty bitty fitty.'" Having ventured onto that thin ice, the Senator added, "I think I'll go back to plain and simple *temper tantrum.*"

I would not advise that; a *tantrum,* origin a mystery, means "a fit of temper," and a *temper tantrum* is both redundant and an example of fused words. Better choose to fly into either a temper or a tantrum, in describing a red-faced politician lying on the floor, banging his heels, waving his tiny fists and bawling at the unfairness of trade policy.

The Senator bottomed his opinion about the phrase's Appalachian origin on a citation in the *Dictionary of American Regional English*, which spotted it in a 1934 issue of *American Speech*: "*Hissy* is probably provincial slang. I have heard it for 8 or 10 years. *He threw a hissy* . . . means that the person in question was very disturbed and very angry." *DARE* speculated that it came from a hypocoristic, or pet-name, form of *hysterical*, or maybe from the echoic *hiss*. My guess is that the association with *fit* suggests hysteria.

The term is now in active use. An Internet posting (in the newsgroup *alt.showbiz.gossip*), under the heading "Madonna and Her Chihuahua," asks: "Does anyone have any details on Madonna's confrontation with airline officials about taking her Chihuahua on a flight? Supposedly she gave a *hissy fit*." Thus, the operative verb can be "to have, throw, give" such a fit, but the most vivid, in my view, is Senator Hatch's "to pitch" one.

Mr. Buchanan's follow-up line was to quote the Washington establishment as saying, in horror of his candidacy, "The beast is coming." That text cries out for deconstruction.

It has nothing to do with "Beauty and the Beast" or any rough beast slouching toward Bethlehem. Rather, it may be rooted in an 1815 skit, found in Louis Cohen's 1925 *Napoleonic Anecdotes*, purporting to show how Napoleon's return from Elba was progressively regarded in Paris; it can be found under "public opinion" in "Respectfully Quoted," the dictionary of quotations most frequently requested from the Congressional Research Service.

"What news? *Ma foi!*

"The tiger has broken out of his den" was the first report. Then: "The monster was days at sea. The wretch has landed at Fréjus." As Napoleon marched toward Paris, the newspapers treated him with renewed respect: "The General has entered Lyons." As he came nearer, the nervous press gave him back his name: "Napoleon slept last night at Fontainebleau." Next came the return of title: "The Emperor proceeds to the Tuileries today." And finally, "His Imperial Majesty will address his loyal subjects tomorrow."

This anecdote shows the vagaries of public opinion, especially as reflected in press coverage, and was expressed in shorthand by Buchanan's "The beast is coming," whether he knows it or not. (Deconstructionists don't worry about what authors intend; only the text counts.)

A rhetorical device that my former Nixon speech-writing colleague uses to deflect or derogate questions about the opinions he has expressed in print over the years is *golden oldies*. When Ron Brownstein of the *Los Angeles Times* began, "When you talk about immigration today . . ." Buchanan anticipated a quotation coming back to haunt him and interrupted with a smiling "The *golden oldies,"* giving the inflammatory opinion an aura of antiquity and thus irrelevance.

This is a show-business term for a song or movie of a previous era still regarded with fondness and surrounded with nostalgia. The first usage in the *Random House Historical Dictionary of American Slang* is from *Time* magazine of Dec. 2, 1966, describing the recording "Gallant Men," by Senator Everett Dirksen: "The platter . . . promises to become what the deejays call a *'Golden Oldy.'"*

Bob Shannon of WCBS-FM thinks the predecessor phrase was "oldies but goodies," at a time when the word *oldie* was pejorative. The music industry's new term was influenced later by the gold records symbolizing sellers of a million or more. My own speculation is that *golden,* a color associated with autumn's dying leaves, was reinforced by 50 years of marriage being called the "golden wedding anniversary" and led to old age being euphemized as "the golden years." In the phrase *golden oldie* (the singular is spelled with an *ie* or a *y*), the adjective gives a nostalgic glow to the noun, adding the value of gold to the age.

It shakes sere seers like me to hear songs from the 1980s, with which I am just beginning to get familiar, referred to with this phrase. Madonna's "Like a Virgin" is not even a brass oldie in my book; if it ain't "As Time Goes By," it's not vintage. (You must remember this. . . .)

Though Buchanan has avoided statements in recent years that could be construed as anti-Semitic (adding "Judeo-" to "Christian" in speaking of our heritage), one popped out when he was being heckled by unidentified youngsters at a rally in Lexington, Mass. He called their demonstration "a revolt of the overprivileged" and asked, "How did Brandeis's football team do this year, guys?" Brandeis is a university whose student body is 60 percent Jewish (the majority on financial aid) and has not had a football team since 1959; Buchanan's jab was taken as a derogation of his hecklers as rich Jewish sissies.

In South Carolina, the intellectual anti-intellectual attacked his opponents for the "vapidity and hollowness" of their campaigns. This criticism caused Cokie Roberts and Charles Gibson on "Good Morning America" to marvel at the use of an unfamiliar word on television in a political campaign.

Unfamiliar? *Vapid* is a word used more in writing than in speech, but its seeming closeness to *vacuum* and *vacuous* gives most listeners the idea that the meaning has something to do with emptiness. That's true, though the words are unrelated.

Vapid is rooted in the Latin *vapidus,* "tasteless" (in its original flavor-free sense), and may be related to *vapor,* which also has no zip. The synonym is *insipid,* also rooted in "lacking in taste or savor." The noun, on the analogy of *rapid-rapidity,* is *vapidity,* which—if spoken with scorn and backed up with a familiar synonym like *hollowness*—may be used on the campaign trail.

I grew up in the '40s in the Midwest (Southern Indiana). Redundant or not, "temper tantrums" was the common usage in our area; most often, they were thrown by children. On the other hand, we would have considered "hissy fits" redundant; when we had one, we "threw a hissy." In all my years in that region, I never once heard anyone say "hissy fit."

Jack E. Garrett
Jamesburg, New Jersey

"The beast is coming" does not refer to anything as obscure as Napoleon's return from Elba. More likely it refers to Revelations 11:7, "And when they shall have finished their testimony, the beast that ascendeth out of the bottomless pit shall make war against them, and shall overcome and kill them." Lock and load.

Byron D. Coney
Seattle, Washington

In Danish, and possibly in other Scandinavian languages as well, the word "hidsig" (pronounced as spelled in English) means hot-tempered. The origin is the German "hitzig." I wonder whether the English word came from Scandinavian or German settlers.

Gretel Jantzen
Gentolte, Denmark

About 1958, top forty rock 'n' roll radio was just starting and jive-talking, motor-mouthed d.j.s (as opposed to the stodgy, deep-voiced, slow-talking announcers of old) took over the airwaves.

Looking for a snappy way to mix an occasional older record into their tight playlist, but wanting to assure their quick-on-the-dial-changer listeners that they were about to hear a "gen-you-wine classic," radio jocks used a number of terms: golden gasser, golden goodie, golden great, goldie and golden oldie.

In both the radio and record industry, "golden oldie" won out, probably because of its strong alliterative effect. Besides, d.j.s could easily transpose "golden oldie" into "old gold" as in: "This is Jerry Jingo spinning some romantic old gold for all those submarine-race watchers out at Harvey's Lake tonight."

As far as "oldies but goodies" (immortalized by Little Caesar & the Romans in the classic "Those Oldies But Goodies Remind Me of You") the term is still very popular today and probably ranks second to "golden oldie" in describing a classic pop tune of years gone by.

Though radio friends have assured me it was used earlier, the oldest reference I've seen to "golden oldie" is in Goldmine's Rock 'n' Roll 45 RPM Record Price Guide by Neal Umphred where I found a listing for a record album simply called "Golden Oldies" released on Decca Records in 1960.

Richard Chisak
Kingston, Pennsylvania

In our use of its recent slang sense, we have come to the end of history.

History, the with-it user of vogue lingo will recall, was a cheery term for "goodbye," as in "I'm *history*"; another sense was "out of it; passé," as in "Nobody hums that tune anymore; it's *history*." A more extreme version of that sense was "finished, washed up, wrung out and cast aside," as in "Forget about her; she's *history*." The word's demise seemed to be further hastened by Francis Fukuyama's amusing musing about Clio in his provocative book titled *The End of History*.

But *history*, in its sense of "hopelessly old-fashioned; last year's craze" is back in the mists with *twenty-three skidoo*. In our breathless run-up to the millennium, the hot term for outcastedness—expressed in a combination of scorn and revulsion—is *toast*.

"Hey, dude. You're *toast*, man" was a passage in the *St. Petersburg Times* of Oct. 1, 1987, the earliest citation the *Oxford English Dictionary* research staff has of this usage. "Actually, the trendiest way of saying someone is finished is to say 'He's *toast*,'" wrote the columnist George Will the following year. "The women in Bush's entourage also are turn-you-to-*toast* toughies."

Nearly a decade later, Tom Friedman, foreign-affairs columnist for the *New York Times*, envisioned Secretary of State Madeleine Albright urging Jiang Zemin, the Chinese leader, toward the next stage of economic development because "if you can't deliver that next stage you're *toast*." The columnist concluded his imaginary dialogue by having Jiang ask, "What does it mean to be *toast*?"

It means "burned, scorched, wiped out, demolished" (without even the consolation of being remembered, as *history* offered). Makers of a movie about a volcano in California wrote the tag line "The Coast Is *Toast*." When Ted Turner, the magnate who enjoys sailing, almost fell overboard, he told an interviewer in 1992, "I thought I was *toast*—I would have died"; five years later, firing his own son after a merger, the tough-loving father said, "He's *toast*."

Thus has the simile *warm as toast* been thrust aside. The noun's standard meaning—"sliced bread singed by heat," from the Latin *torrere*, "to burn"—is being temporarily overrun by its slang meaning. A less torrid Caribbean sense was described by Roger Abrahams in the July 1962 *American Folklore* magazine as "the long narrative poem called the *toast*." However, the verb *to toast* continues to mean "to salute with a glass in hand and an encomium on the lips"; a similar sense of the verb can be discerned in the Caribbean meaning "to accompany reggae music by shouting."

If *toast* comes after the end of *history*, what will come after the final scraping of *toast?*

A far more horrific term: *roadkill.*

Representative Peter King, Republican of New York, used the term as he played Casca to Newt Gingrich's Caesar: "As *road kill* on the highway of American politics," he wrote in the *Weekly Standard*, "Newt cannot sell the Republican agenda." This followed the metaphor used by Mr. Friedman, whose *toast* usage is cited above, referring to nations that fail to get their international economics right as "*road kill* on the global highway." Frequent use of *roadkill* with *information superhighway* can be expected, especially in Internet prose.

The original meaning was "an animal killed by a motor vehicle and lying on a roadside." The first *OED* citation is from 1972, as Richard and Rochelle Wright wrote in the book *Cariboo Mileposts* about magpies: "They . . . usually feed on carrion or *road-kills.*"

Now the metaphoric sense means "no longer viable," with a second sense of "easy victim"; Charlie Nobles, a sportswriter for the *New York Times*, described the Miami Hurricanes college basketball team as "formerly viewed as Big East *road kill.*" Drop the hyphen; close up the space and write it as *roadkill.*

Will the vogue meanings of the nouns *toast* and *roadkill* follow the course of all-but-forgotten *history?* We'll know when all is said and done. (*At the end of the day* is *toast,* but *roadkill* will not soon be shunted aside by *pavement pizza.*)

Hole Card

Tom Brokaw of NBC called to ask me about Vice President Al Gore's charge that the Dole-Kemp suggestion to cut Federal income tax rates by 15 percent would "*blow a hole in* the deficit."

Because that charge was repeated by Clinton surrogates, it is safe to assume that Democrats carefully considered that phrase. But the figure of speech is off key: *to blow a hole in* means "to destroy" or at least "to diminish"; the image is that of a torpedo striking a ship below its Plimsoll line.

However, *to blow a hole in* the deficit is to reduce the deficit, a consummation devoutly to be wished by just about everyone in politics. The meaning Mr. Gore intended was that the Dole tax-cutting idea would increase, balloon or even skyrocket the deficit—thereby *to blow a hole in* hopes of balancing the budget.

Mr. Brokaw's observation was sound, and he was right to torpedo the overblown rhetoric. This did not stop the House majority leader, Dick Armey, from subsequently telling David Brinkley of ABC, perhaps tongue in cheek, that the Clinton agenda was "likely *to blow a big hole in* the deficit and result in the need for massive tax increases."

How "Shrunk" Snuck In

"*Trivialize* had its moment in the vogue-verb sun," I wrote, "until the usage of this older verb shrunk to the very occasional."

Louis Jay Herman, noted Gotcha! Gangster, objected: "Permit me to join the Uofallpeople Club, to upbraid you for *shrunk*. All usage manuals consider *shrank* the preferred or exclusive past tense of *shrink*, *shrunk* being the past participle." Kerry Wood of Palo Alto, Calif., adds, "I never thunk you'd have done such a thing."

For the irregular verbs *shrink* and *sink*, the simple past tense is "He *shrank* the material and *sank* the boat." The past participle is the form of the verb used in the present perfect tense, which shows action completed at the time of speaking: "He has *shrunk* and has *sunk*." Thus, the natural progression is *shrink-shrank-shrunk, sink-sank-sunk.*

At an embarrassing moment for the prosecution in the O. J. Simpson trial, Christopher Darden gulped, "The gloves appear to have *shrank* somewhat." Incorrect; the past participle is *shrunk* or *shrunken*.

Shrink-shrank-shrunk is orderly enough; why, then, did Iofallpeople sink into using *shrunk* as the past tense? Because Walt Disney got to me, I guess: the 1989 movie *Honey, I Shrunk the Kids* did to *shrank* what Winston cigarettes did to *as:* pushed usage in the direction of what people were casually saying rather than what they were carefully writing. Mr. Herman dutifully objected to one and all about that Disney title (adding a note of praise for the well-placed comma).

In the past-tense dodge, usage is all. The learner of English, having mastered *sink-sank-sunk* and *begin-began-begun* and *drink-drank-drunk*, would assume *fling-flang-flung* and *swing-swang-swung*. But there ain't no such animal as *swang* or *flang*, except in some far-out dialect; in those and other cases, the past tense hops over the expected word to the past participle.

"*Shrunk* is much less common as a past tense than *shrank*," notes Fred Mish of Merriam-Webster, "but *sunk* has somewhat greater frequency of occurrence in relation to *sank*. These occurrences can be unsettling at times. A local sportswriter here likes to say of high-school athletes that they 'shined in the contest' instead of 'shone.' "

In the face of the language's weakness of grammatical discipline, what's a poor usagist to do? Be a stiff. Make the new form work for its acceptance. Stick with *shrank* in the simple past, at least until the movie and its offspring— like the Heritage Foundation's "Honey, I Shrunk the Tax Base!"—fade from memory, even if it snuck up on us and makes us feel like something the cat dragged (not *drug*) in.

Snuck up? "How did *snuck* ever sneak in?" asks Doris Asmundsson, professor emerita of English at Queensborough Community College in New York. (So that's the feminine of *emeritus*.) "Words like *creak, critique, eke, freak, leak* and *tweak* do not, in the past tense, become *cruck, crituck, uck, fruck, luck* and *twuck*. Why then *snuck*? Eventually a *sneaker* might turn into a *snucker*."

Evidently Charles M. Schulz,* the cartoonist of "Peanuts," agrees; Rerun says to Charlie Brown, "If you *sneaked* up behind him, you could hit him with a stick." This is formal English.

On the ABC sitcom "Step by Step," however, a teen-ager tells her parents, "I know I shouldn't have *snuck* out."

Here's a perfect example of a usage that has crept (informally *creeped*) up on us. "He grubbed ten dollars from de bums and den *snuck* home" is the first print use cited in the CD-ROM *OED*, in an 1887 edition of the *New Orleans Lantern*. The novelist James T. Farrell used it as the past participle in the first part of his Studs Lonigan trilogy, the 1932 "Young Lonigan": "They had all *snuck* in and were having a good time, making trouble." Raymond Chandler, the great mystery writer, used it in the simple past tense in his 1940 *Farewell, My Lovely:* "I *snuck* in there and grabbed it."

The Random House Webster's notes this in accepting the term as a standard variant: "*Snuck* occurs frequently in fiction, in journalism and on radio and television, whereas *sneaked* is more likely in highly formal or belletristic writing."

John Algeo of *American Speech* goes further: "*Snuck* is now educated, standard use; *sneaked* is rare." He notes that *sneak* has mysterious origins; it first appears in Shakespeare's *Henry IV*, Part 1: "A poor unminded outlaw *sneaking* home." Professor Algeo notes that the Old English verb *snican* meant "to crawl," but that word would have become *snike*, not *sneak*, in Modern English; curiously, the past tense of *snican* would have become *snuck*.

Thus, we should hold off a few years before caving in to *shrunk* as a simple past tense; I'm sorry, it snuck up on me.

---

*Charles M. Schulz died on February 12, 2000.

You tried to sneak in "professor emerita" when dealing with a female professor.

Nay, nay, oh wise one! Emeritus qualifies professor, which is a male term and therefore always emeritus, whether applied to a man or a woman. If you want to be precious, you would have to use the word "professoress" (yuck!), who would then be indeed "emerita," if the term applies.

John T. Dentay
Willowdale, Ontario
Canada

Now that you have accepted "snuck" as proper American English usage, I look forward to similar recognition for "slud," as in "and he slud into first" (Jerome Hanna Dean, radio baseball commentator and retired N.L. pitcher).

Robert J. Wolfson
Professor Emeritus
Syracuse University
Syracuse, New York

I'm on your side about *shrunk-shrank* and I'm sorry you gave in to the minicarpers. There are several verbs that tolerate variation in the past tense vowel (e.g., *dove, dived; planked, plunked; drank, drunk,* and a few others). The fault—if any—is archaism and not ignorance. It is even possible to say "I have showed," just as it is possible to write *shew* and not *show.* You proved the desirability of free choice when you used *snuck* in place of *sneaked,* which in certain contexts would be ridiculous.

Jacques [Barzun]
San Antonio, Texas

You used *shrunk* as the preterit (simple past tense) of *shrink.* Collins permits it as an alternative to *shrank,* but I'm afraid I do not. The principal parts are *shrink, shrank, shrunk. Shrunken,* which Collins allows as an alternative past participle, I do not. *Shrunken* is a *passive* participle.

A "shrunken head" is one that someone shrank, or has shrunk. And you're welcome to it.

Arthur Morgan
New York, New York

Or What?

"Pork rinds and Perrier," muses a redneck in a TV commercial for 7-Eleven stores, "is this heaven *or what?*"

On the ABC sitcom "Family Matters," a teen-age girl tentatively challenges a boy: "Do you want to go to the dance with me *or what?*" Viewers recall a daughter on "The Cosby Show" a decade ago defying her parents with "Is this America *or what?*"

In a *New York Times Book Review* assessment of the 1991 novel *A Hollywood Life,* by David Freeman, Chris Chase writes: "They make love. She in the skirt. Every time. Is that dumb *or what?*"

"We have entered the world of *or what,*" notes George Feldman of New York. Adds Sheldon Rosen of Brooklyn: "This is a very overused and misused expression. I don't really believe I know the meaning."

Am I here to provide the meaning and the etymology or what?

The phrase is known to lexicographers as a *tag question,* like the *won't you?* after "sit down" or the *isn't it?* after "today's a scorcher." It is akin to the German *nicht wahr* after "Kissinger one-upped the world by escorting the Queen to Ascot," meaning "isn't that so?"

The function of a tag question is to follow a statement with a question eliciting confirmation, approval or assent. When the tag is part of a sentence that is itself a question—like *Is this fun or what?*—the tag is used to add emphasis. Readers who follow these columns with scholarly intensity will remember Prof. James McCawley's exposition of the *exclamative*—a question with more of the force of an exclamation than an interrogation.

"The *or* suggests an option," says Frank Nuessel, professor of modern languages and linguistics at the University of Louisville, "and the *what* functions as a type of pronoun, standing for a deleted clause—as in 'Is this fun or is something else fun?'—with an ironic tone implied.

"*Or what* looks for an obvious answer," says Nuessel, "suggesting a rhetorical question most of the time." Sometimes, however, it can request an answer: for example, told about a new book, a person might ask, "Is it a biography, *or what?*"

Prof. John Algeo (am I pulling out all the academic stops on this or what?) planted a query about the *or what?* epidemic in his column "Among the New Words" in the quarterly *American Speech,* where he defines it as "a tag emphasizing the preceding question or implying that its answer is obvious." In the second volume of Jonathan Lighter's marvelous *Historical Dictionary of American Slang,* the catch phrase's earliest citation is an inscription on a 1965 napalm canister in Vietnam: "Hot Foot. Do You Need This *or What?*"

When Algeo hit the button on his CD-ROM edition of the *Oxford English*

Dictionary, early etymology leaped out. As the last member of a series, the phrase implied an open choice among a series of options. In an entry in his 1766 diary, John Adams asked himself about the quality of a Massachusetts lawyer, Robert Auchmuty Jr.: "In what is this Man conspicuous? in Reasoning? in Imagination? in Painting? in the Pathetic? *or what?*"

In the same seriatim way, George Bernard Shaw, in a 1902 letter to a hypochondriac, wondered about the work of a Dr. Buzzi: "Is it starvation cure, or overfeeding cure, or water cure, or grape cure, or faith healing, *or what?*"

However, by 1922, James Joyce was using the phrase more as an emphasizer than as a pronoun for another option. The slang phrase *get the horn* meant "get horny, become sexually excited"; in "Ulysses," a character asks, "Got the horn *or what?*"

Algeo concludes: "It seems likely that the emphatic use of *or what?* to highlight a preceding rhetorical question grew out of the statement of an alternative when in fact no alternative was conceived by the speaker. So *Is that dumb or what?* begins with the sense 'Is that dumb or what else can explain it?' but as a rhetorical question, no real alternative explanation is imagined. Thus *or what?* becomes purely a signal of emphasis, a sort of lexical exclamation mark." An exclamative tag.

The final sentence of this item, ending in a reprise of the phrase under study, writes itself.

Did you hear that Sylvester Stallone is going to play Hamlet?
Really?
Yeah. "To be . . . or wha'!"
(Add Rocky shrug and final glottal stop.)

Michael Posnick
Manhattanville College
Purchase, New York

I think you were right in the question-mark or exclamation wrangle. Fowler is on your side and so am I. Against the three of us, who stands a chance?

Jacques [Barzun]
San Antonio, Texas

The Hunting of the Grouse

The season of elections in Russia, Israel, the United States and probably Britain brings with it the language of complaint. As the punster at the O'Meara Camping Equipment Company in Dublin wrote in an advertisement for a sale at this time of year, "Now Is the Winter of Our Discount Tent."

The vogue verb for complaining on both sides of the Atlantic is *to grouse*. Stephanie Strom of the *New York Times* wrote from London about a charge made by John Preston, deputy leader of the Labor Party, that a preview copy of a report critical of a Government cover-up was made available to the Conservative Party chairman: "'People will want to know whether Mr. [Brian] Mawhinney has been given prior access to the Scott report so he can run a political damage-limitation exercise from Tory central office,' Mr. Preston *groused*."

We are not speaking here of the noun denominating a game bird, like the sage hen, or of the Australian slang adjective for "excellent," as in the 1947 use of "a real *grouse* brush she was, with bonzer black eyes." The verb *to grouse*, often labeled "informal" in dictionaries, was first cited as British Army slang by Rudyard Kipling in his 1899 *From Sea to Sea* in a passage written 12 years earlier: "That's the only thing as 'ill make the Blue Lights stop *grousin'* and *stiffin'*." Kipling went on to define his character's terms: *"Grousin'* is sulking, and *stiffin'* is using unparliamentary language."

Grouse is akin to *grouch*, which is derived from *grudge*, rooted in the Old French *groucier*, "to envy, resent." Many words beginning with *gr* carry that growling connotation, including *groan, grunt, grimace, gruff* and *grumble*.

If you want to disparage the plaintiff mildly, try *grumble*; if you want to ridicule that person, try the plaintive *whine*. To subtly support the complaint, use the brave *protest*. For a characterization of the complaint as excessively minor, there's *nit-pick*; to add an element of noisiness, consider *bellyache* or *gripe*, and to derogate plainly, the slang verb *bitch*. In newspaper reporting, which strives for objectivity sometimes at the cost of color, a simple *complain* will suffice.

Disgruntled readers are free to *grouse*, a verb that has moved uncomplainingly from slang in Kipling's time to colloquial usage today; within a generation (grumble, mutter), it will be Standard English.

The other day I tried to slip "grutching" into a piece about negative ads, and the copy desk turned it into "grouching." But no use groaning about it. They assumed I don't spell good.

Walter Goodman
New York, New York

You nominate John Preston as deputy leader of the British Labour Party. No doubt he was happier than the present deputy leader John Prescott. As they say, though, what's a cott between friends.

Heidi Kingstone
London, England

Regarding the use of "grouse." Almost every English pub has low ceilings, especially those that are *very* old. Each pub also displays a sign that reads: "Duck or Grouse."

Joyce Z. Weil
Oxford, England

Hush Money

Thomas Jefferson was furious.

He had given some money over the years to a scurrilous Scottish journalist, James Thomson Callender, out of the goodness of his heart. Now Callender was hinting that Jefferson had passed him the funds to keep him quiet about his earlier support of Jefferson's anti-Federalist cause, which had encouraged the journalist to attack Alexander Hamilton and even to cast aspersions on President Washington.

"He [Callender] intimated that he received [the money] not as a charity," the newly elected President Jefferson wrote his friend and anti-Federalist colleague James Monroe on May 29, 1801, "but as due, in fact hush money." Not another nickel would be forthcoming, vowed Jefferson, who considered himself unfairly maligned by an ingrate: "Such a misconstruction of my charities put an end to them forever."

The author of the Declaration of Independence once observed: "I am a friend to neology. It is the only way to give a language copiousness and euphony." He was the coiner of such useful nouns as *doll-baby, Anglophobia* and *breadstuffs,* and the verbs *belittle, reticulate* and *neologize.* But in the case of *hush money,* Jefferson was calling up a figure of speech long familiar to everyone in the new American Government.

It was first recorded in 1709 in England. "I expect *Hush-Money* to be regularly sent," wrote Sir Richard Steele in the *Tatler,* "for every Folly or Vice any one commits in this whole Town." Jonathan Swift put it in a 1731 poem to John Gay: "A dext'rous Steward, when his Tricks are found, / *Hush-money* sends to all the Neighbours round."

Following the term's steady course through the language over three centuries, the *Oxford English Dictionary* defined it as "Money paid to prevent disclosure or exposure, or to *hush up* a crime." (A century before, Shakespeare used the echoic *hush* as an adjective in *Hamlet* to mean "silent"—"as *hush* as death"—and as a verb in *Twelfth Night*, "My dutie *hushes* me.")

The hardy phrase of accusation was central to coverage of the 1972 break-in at Democratic headquarters at the Watergate complex in Washington. After an interview with Charles Colson, who had been President Nixon's special counsel, a *New York Times* reporter, Christopher Lydon, wrote on June 9, 1973, "Payments by Nixon associates to the Watergate defendants could be construed as criminal '*hush money*,' he [Colson] remembers telling Haldeman." The subsequent euphemism for payments requested by the conspirator Howard Hunt to the jailed Watergate burglars to encourage their silence was "humanitarian relief."

Here we are a generation later and the phrase is once again in the headlines. The *Washington Times* put it in quotations: "Subpoenas focus Starr's probe on '*hush money*.'" The *Memphis Commercial Appeal* headlined a column by William Rusher "*Hush Money* for Hubbell?" In an article about fees in excess of $400,000 paid to the former Associate Attorney General Webster L. Hubbell after he was forced to leave the Justice Department, Jeff Gerth and Stephen Labaton of the *New York Times* delicately avoided the accusatory term as they wrote of money "intended to discourage him from helping investigators who were looking into the Clintons' finances."

The term is always strongly pejorative, which is why it is put in the form of a question or described as an allegation. Payments so described are always defended, as in Jefferson's letter, as charity, relief or other instances of simple generosity to one in need that are given a sinister motive by the uncharitable.

A related term, *hush puppies*, refers to small deep-fried balls of cornmeal dough. They gained the name when used to quiet yapping dogs hanging around the kitchens of Southern homes but are not recommended by modern veterinarians.

Hyphenated Heritage

We could tell that Republican candidate Pat Buchanan was reaching out to Jewish voters when he amended *Christian values* to *Judeo-Christian values*.

Comes now the Rev. Donald L. Roberts, president of Goodwill Industries–Manasota Inc., before the Senate Finance Committee: "I would be less than responsive to my high calling if I did not daily remind myself and others of the words of our Judeo-Christian-Islamic heritage that justice should roll down like waters."

Notes Daniel Patrick Moynihan, ranking Democrat on Finance: "It's now official. Ours is a *Judeo-Christian-Islamic heritage.*"

If anybody feels left out, we've got some more hyphens.

Odd that after discussing $40 words you talk about "hyphenated" heritage. Fowler says "hyphened" and that does the job, it seems to me. The American mania for adding syllables should be good for a column some day.

> Don Shannon
> Washington, D.C.

I Wrote It Myself

President Clinton has taken to running down his speech writers in public, boasting about rejecting prepared remarks and doing the writing himself; this is to show that what he says comes from the Real Him. I suspect that these lines are written by speech writers falling on their pens, mightier than their swords.

In Mr. Clinton's pre-Christmas "Middle Class Bill of Rights" speech (bottomed on Nixon's "Economic Bill of Rights" statement, which we stole from F.D.R.), I was pleased to hear his pickup of the "government that is leaner, not meaner" phrase; was ambivalent about his "raise their children" (purists differentiate between *raising* cattle and *rearing* children, and in formal speech that distinction should be made, but Mr. Clinton, even when wearing a dark suit in the Oval Office, prefers the folksy), but was stunned, stunned (one cut above "shocked, shocked") by "Some people do take advantage of the rest of us by . . . flaunting our immigration laws."

To *flaunt* means "to show off, to parade ostentatiously"; the verb the President meant was *flout*, "to disregard contemptuously, to mock or scoff at." Even kids raised with the laid-back *Merriam-Webster's Dictionary of English Usage* are told that mistaking *flout* for *flaunt* is "a genuine error" and, by confusing these verbs, "you do run the risk of giving some of your listeners the mistaken impression that they are smarter than you are."

If You've Got It, Flaunt It

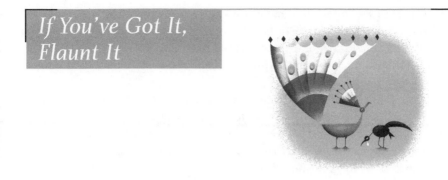

"Oscar Wilde was jailed, exiled and ruined," wrote John Lahr in *The New Yorker*, in a piece about Woody Allen, "for flaunting sexual convention offstage as brazenly as his epigrams undermined social convention on it."

That's a finely honed sentence, contrasting differing conventions by stressing the adjectives *social* and *sexual* and playing the syllable *off* against the concluding stressed word *on*. Even the de-emphasized last pronoun *it* was well chosen, because its alternative—*onstage*—would have made the sentence too determinedly balanced.

Only one problem: *flaunting* was a mistake.

To *flaunt* means "to display proudly, even ostentatiously," the way a peacock shows its feathers; indeed, an early use of the word in 1576 was set in the phrase "whose fethers *flaunt,* and flicker in the winde."

The word that fit the context of *The New Yorker*'s piece on Allen was *flout*, which means "to jeer, deride, scoff at, show contemptuous disregard for," first cited in a 1551 translation of Sir Thomas More's *Utopia:* "in moste spitefull maner mockynge . . . and *flowtinge* them."

The substitution of *flaunt* for *flout*, a mistake made frequently enough, irritated Ann Kirschner of Brooklyn. "*The New Yorker* used to be a bulwark of elegant, not to mention correct, usage," she wrote the magazine. "Then, little by little, cracks began to appear in that edifice. With the substitution of the word *flaunting* for *flouting* . . . the destruction is now complete."

That somewhat hyperbolic denunciation drew a cool reply from a copy editor (whose name is safe with me; ever since I blithely titled a piece "Let's Kill All the Copy Editors," I've been worried that some nut would take it seriously). "Our use of *flaunt* is correct," insisted *The New Yorker*. "According to Webster's Tenth New Collegiate Dictionary, *flaunt* may mean 'to treat contemptuously,' which is the meaning we had in mind. The accompanying usage note points out that, although this use of *flaunt* undoubtedly arose from confusion with *flout*, the contexts in which it appears cannot be called substandard."

Kirschner took that to be a throwing-down of a *gauntlet*. (Or, as they might now say at *The New Yorker,* of a *gantlet.*) What do readers do when good usage gives way to common usage—when error triumphs, dictionaries drop the standard, things fall apart and the center cannot hold? They come—in high dudgeon, puzzlement, sometimes whimpering in pain—slouching to language mavens for support or solace.

Ann, your little friends are wrong. They have been affected by the skepticism of a skeptical age. R. W. Burchfield in the latest *Fowler's Modern English Usage* says flatly that *"flaunt* is often wrongly used for *flout."* And in that very usage note cited to you by *The New Yorker,* Merriam-Webster goes on to say, "If you use it, however, you should be aware that many people will consider it a mistake."

That warning label is expounded fully by E. Ward Gilman in *Merriam-Webster's Dictionary of English Usage:* "This is one issue about which there is no dissent among usage commentators. All of them regard the use of *flaunt* to mean *flout* as nothing less than an ignorant mistake. . . . Even those commentators who are relatively liberal in other matters take a hard line when it comes to *flaunt* and *flout."*

The mistake is undoubtedly alive and well, made every day, but even Gilman—a superb historical usagist often derided in this space as Old Roundheels—opines that "we think you well advised to avoid it, at least when writing for publication."

What, then, is *The New Yorker*—in whose pages some of our best authors write for publication—to do? Brazen it through? Ignore the whole thing, secretly placing both *flout* and *flaunt* on the magazine's taboo list? Turn upon and savage its own copy-editing department, causing much internal anguish at a management that won't stand up to fuddy-duddy grammarians and semantic stiffs?

I empathize with the *New Yorker* editor in a case like this. I once referred to Oliver Cromwell as "the Pretender." As the swarming Gotcha! Gang promptly pointed out, Cromwell was "the Protector"; it was the son of James II, claiming the British throne against the house of Hanover, who was known as the Pretender (and his son—Bonnie Prince Charlie—was known as the Young Pretender). I have been waiting for a moment like this, dealing with another subject, to sneak in a correction that few will notice. It's hard to admit factual error, even harder to lay your head on the block—recalling the treatment of Charles I by supporters of the Protector—and confess to misjudgment of English usage. The justification of error is not limited to political figures.

When does the frequency of error reach critical mass and transform the mistake into a "new sense"?

Should we, for example, preserve the distinction between *gantlet,* "a punishment run," and *gauntlet,* "a heavy glove sometimes thrown down in challenge"? Do only pedants insist on *masterly* to mean "skillful" while *masterful* means "domineering"? Is it worth breaking our heads to remember *continuous* as "incessant, uninterrupted" while *continual* is "repeated with brief intermissions"? Where is it written that *refute*, "to disprove by argument," must never be used as a synonym for *deny* in its sense of "to declare untrue"?

Right here is where it's written, in the animadversive annals of the defenders of distinctions. We prescriptivists are aware that semantic shift is a signal called by the living language; we lie on Jespersen's couch of metanalysis as *a napron* becomes *an apron* through repeated error over the centuries. But we ask, Why should the slurring of sharp lines of definition take place on our watch? A *stalacite* won't become a *stalagmite* in our time, no matter how lost we get in the Luray Caverns.

Fearlessly do we *flaunt* our *gauntlets* before flinging them down in challenge to the louts of *flout*. They may be in *denial*, but we're in *refutation*.

Internettled

Every culture develops its own vocabulary. Computer users in 1980, looking for a word to describe the transfer of data from a large computer to a smaller one, came up with *download;* that's still what it means, though the large computer is now called a *host system*. A nice verb, and the transmission in the opposite direction is called, with admirable consistency, *upload*. (This is on the analogy of the judicial metaphor: to hand *up* an indictment—to the bench—and to hand *down* a verdict.)

A new vocabulary soon develops barnacles. Certain words from other cultures are adopted with such frequency that they become clichés.

"To think faster and work faster the physical link between you and the machine must be *seamless,*" a Microsoft ad read, racing past the comma that belongs after the second *faster*. (They may have spell checks and grammar checks, but not punctuation checks.)

An ad for "Johnny Mnemonic," a CD-ROM game based on the short story by William Gibson, promises "a multi-million dollar, *seamless,* non-stop movie that you play." (Drop the hyphens from both *non-stop* and *multi-million;* make it "multimillion-dollar.")

Seamlessness is next to godliness on the Internet. What does *seamless* mean?

Originally, it meant "without the stitches showing." The 15th-century word got a boost from the phrase *seamless stockings,* which filled a too-brief period between silk stockings—with seams that seemed always to need straightening—and panty hose. Its opposite, *seamy,* coined in 1604, meant "showing the rough side of the seam."

By metaphoric extension, the adjective *seamy* came to mean "squalid, sordid," as befits the underside of life, while *seamless* has come to mean "perfectly smooth, without awkward transitions," as every network became a *seamless web.*

In my book, *seamy* is still a lively adjective, but *seamless* could use a rest.

Let me not knock Internettese, however; in some cases, word choice is apt and careful. In addresses, the last part, called the *domain,* is separated from the middle part, called the *site,* by what most old-timers would call a *period.* But a period is a punctuation mark that ends a sentence; this mark does not perform that function. Internet users call it a *dot,* and rightly so (from the Old English *dott,* "head of a boil," influenced by the Old German *tutta,* "nipple"). It's not a *period;* it's a *dot,* saving two syllables in leaving a message on voice mail.

A vocabulary also develops conventions. Just as management consultants have incorporated *not to worry* in their lingo, Internet users—called *browsers, lurkers* and *cruisers,* and perhaps some of them will send in other suggestions for a name—like to say *Film at 11.*

To explain this term, I turn to the *Electronic Frontier Foundation's Guide to the Internet,* though I am loath to quote directly because what I have downloaded carries such stringent warnings about copyright. These guys are very stern about that. But let's take a chance: *"Film at 11.* One reaction to an overwrought argument: 'Imminent death of the Net predicted. Film at 11.'"

I like that. Many times we hear "overwrought arguments" by doom-saying friends, and it is useful to have a lighthearted put-down available. *Film at 11* is the close of a promo for a news show, hurriedly interjected by a television announcer between commercials. Its use as a signal by Netties tells a lot in a little phrase.

Now this: The on-line (soon to be *online*) vocabulary suffers from initialese. *R.T.M.*—"read the manual"—is unimaginative, even when infixed with an initial for an obscenity. Same with *F.A.Q.,* "frequently asked questions." *IMHO*—"in my humble opinion"—is at least an acronym (pronounceable as a word) but is smarmy.

We can close this item with a *smiley,* a happy neologism for "a way to express gladness on a keyboard." A colon, a hyphen and a right parenthesis, observed by tilting your head to the left, will cheer your day.   :-)

Invasion of the Cuddlies

"*Warm and fuzzy* math meets Cold Resistance" was the headline of a recent article in *Insight* magazine about traditionalist objections to the teaching of mathematics that skips over the basics of arithmetic.

In another context, the two words were joined again by Tom Hayden, the California politician, who spoke of "community-based economic development," admitting that the phrase sounded "a little *warm and fuzzy.*"

The first printed use found so far of the cuddling adjectives was in a 1979 Associated Press article about a competition among electrical engineers to make mechanical mice that "bore little resemblance to the *warm, fuzzy* creatures they're named for." Soon a children's book by Claude Steiner was titled *Warm Fuzzy Tales* and an acting company called itself the *Warm Fuzzies*, turning the second adjective into a noun.

The words are used together so often that the acting-company formulation has taken over: "Hard-bitten East Coast trade negotiators," wrote a *New York Times* book reviewer in 1988, "will want to dismiss some of their arguments as typical California '*warm fuzzies.*'" The *Times* likes the phrase: "Even 'gambling,' the term that once conjured up green visors, cigar smoke and gumball-size pinkie rings," wrote Gerri Hirshey in 1994, "has been buffed with *warm fuzzies*. We call it 'gaming' these days."

The *warm fuzzies* in business use are "compliments intended to reassure and motivate" and in more general use "lovable, squeezable, cuddly items or ideas." Originally a description of the feel of a child's soft and furry plaything, the phrase is now used in derision and has become a derogation of the treacly or overly empathetic.

The origin of *fuzzy* is sharp and clear: its Scottish dialectical kin, *fozy*, derives from the Dutch *voos*, "spongy, loose textured." *Fuzzy* thinking is imprecise. *Fuzzy* writing is an abomination. Nobody knows why the police are called the *fuzz*.

Closely associated with the rise of the *warm fuzzies* is *security blanket*. "Perhaps the best idea I ever had," the creator of "Peanuts," Charles M. Schulz, said in 1971, "was Linus and the *security blanket*. It suddenly made *security blankets* and thumb-sucking O.K. all around the world."

Asked if he recalled the moment of coinage, Schulz replied: "I think it was readers who called it that. Looking back now through our early reprint books, it seems that Linus had a blanket in 1955; therefore, I assume it was because our first little boy had a blanket. His older sister had a small pillow that she carried around. This is all I remember, and I hope it helps."

Clutching my own small leather pillow, a sentimental item I have lugged through life from my first office about that time, I now turn to another tactile expression that is used to castigate New Age executives: *touchy-feely.*

"*Touchy-Feely* Justice" is the cover-story headline in the May 5, 1997, *Forbes* magazine, as its editors blast "vague do-gooder laws."

What is this tactile textuality? The best early definition was by John Algeo in the summer 1991 issue of *American Speech:* "association between persons based upon emotional sympathy rather than intellectual relationships, and expressed by physical contacts such as hugging." His earliest citation is a *Los Angeles Times* article in April 1972 about sensitivity training: "Faculty critics deride it as '*touchy-feely*' education."

I presume it comes from the phrase, prevalent in the '60s, *to get in touch with your feelings.* Professor Algeo, reached in Wheaton, Ill., agreed: "It's all very Marin County. Something is *touchy-feely* if it values the physical and emotional above the logical and the intellectual. It also values 'interpersonal relations' (which seems to presume that there can be 'extrapersonal relations'). It values the *warm fuzzies.*"

James Crotty, a slanguist who goes by the sobriquet "the Mad Monk," reported that the '80s synonym was *woo-woo:* "The phrase *touchy-feely* was first used to describe therapy sessions at Esalen, a 'retreat center' in Big Sur, Calif. That's where *get in touch with your feelings* was born, with the *touch* referring to kinesthetic feeling and the *feel* to affective feeling. Now the transpersonal psychology, the hot-tub encounters and the New Age movement, all are scorned with the compound adjective *touchy-feely.*"

An early and frequent scorner was Meg Greenfield, a columnist for *Newsweek* and editor of the *Washington Post* editorial page. In 1977, she used the phrase to draw a word-picture of the actions of members of the U.S. Senate during the Carter Administration, "always engaged among themselves in a kind of forced, *touchy-feely* bonhomie—a back pat here, a handclasp there, a playful minishove, an earnest clutch of the other fellow's lapel."

It became a noun on television. In an episode of "Roseanne," the title character and her husband have had an argument. When their son-in-law soothingly says that neither one should be blamed, Roseanne's sister replies, "We don't need the *touchy-feely* right now."

You cite a 1979 Associated Press article as the first printed use of "warm fuzzy." We own a book that contains an earlier printed use: *T.A. for Tots: And Other Prinzes,* by Alvyn M. Freed, Ph.D. (copyright © 1973 by Alvyn M. Freed; Jalmar Press, revised edition, 1974).

Chapter 3 of *T.A. for Tots* is titled "Warm Fuzzies." "Good strokes give us warm feelings. Feelings of being OK, of being loved. We call those feelings warm fuzzies" (page 64 and 65). Bad strokes are cold pricklies, i.e., cold pricklies are the opposite of warm fuzzies (page 66 and 67).

Warm fuzzies and, to a lesser extent, cold pricklies are still a part of our family's vocabulary.

Greg Papanikolas
Tucson, Arizona

Ish Bin Ein Punster

"Labor is talking the *ish,*" said Benjamin Netanyahu in his campaign for Prime Minister in Israel, "and we're talking the issues."

That was a bilingual pun. *Ish* means "the man" in Hebrew; Netanyahu was saying that his opponents were turning away from the issues of the campaign to concentrate on him as an individual, as an *ish.*

A few years ago, after making a mistake that seemed to cast scorn on a former colleague, I admitted to a *Schadenfreudean slip.* That was a play on the German *Schadenfreude,* "guiltily taking pleasure in the suffering of friends," and *Freudian slip,* "a mistake revealing subconscious attitudes," based on teachings of Sigmund Freud, the one-man Prozac of his day.

Islamic English

Arabic is a language that has contributed many words to English, from *admiral* to *algebra, sofa* to *sugar.*

What about *fatwa?* Though not yet in most leading college-size dictionaries (Random House includes it), the word has been used frequently in connection with the call by the Ayatollah Khomeini of Iran in 1989 for the murder of the novelist Salman Rushdie. According to Judith Miller, author of *God Has Ninety-Nine Names: Reporting From a Militant Middle East, fatwa* means "an Islamic ruling," which can include, but is not limited to, "a death sentence."

The proper names of organizations much in the news are instructive. *Hamas* is an acronym for five Arabic words meaning "Islamic Resistance Movement" and is a play on the Arabic and Turkish words for "zeal." Transliterated from Arabic, the noun *hezb* refers to a political party, and *Allah* is God. Thus, *Hezbollah,* the name taken by the Iranian terror organization active in Lebanon, means "Party of God." (I would spell it *Hisballah,* but the U.S. press resists my fatwas.)

Ms Miller's on-the-scene reporting is studded with these fascinating linguistic asides. The Arabic word *taqiyya* means "religiously sanctioned dissimulation"—that is, "lying to protect one's faith or its adherents." *Haram* means "forbidden," covering strictures against alcohol, drugs, extramarital sex and dancing; its opposite is *halal,* the Islamic rough equivalent of the Hebrew "kosher."

How did Libya come to be known as *Splaj?* That acronym is used by Western journalists in the area as shorthand for Muammar Qaddafi's name for his country: the *Socialist People's Libyan Arab Jamahiriya,* the last word meaning "gathering of the masses." After a U.S. bombing attack in 1986 failed to kill Colonel Qaddafi, he added a "Great" to the nation's name, and some Westerners now refer to it as "the Great Splaj."

The Jade and the Jaded

"We will see a legion of men," wrote the *New York Times* columnist Maureen Dowd in high dudgeon, "prompted by the President's lawyer, come forth and accuse Ms [Paula] Jones of being a jade who wore short skirts and flirted. Imagine."

A *jade?* Many of us have given a gift of jade, which is a green gemstone. Its name comes from the Latin *ilia,* "side," based on the ancient notion that the wearing of the green cured a pain in the ribs. (That's a stitch.)

And all of us world-weary sophisticates know what it's like to feel *jaded*—senses dulled from too many self-indulgent experiences, satiated with sex, booze, lies and videotape.

But the noun *jade,* in reference to a woman? Sounded Elizabethan to me; sure enough, there it is in Shakespeare: "I know he'll prove a *jade,*" Petruchio is told in *The Taming of the Shrew,* in a line I expurgate to avoid double entendre. In *City Gallant* (1614), by John Cooke, a woman is derogated with "She's good for nothing, then, no more than a *jade.*"

Why this sense of worthlessness? The origin is the Icelandic *jalda* or Finnish *alda,* "a mare." Starting with Chaucer in 1386, it became a contemptible name for a horse, like those that later dragged themselves around Hackney (whence *hack,* as in *hack journalist*). Tired, overworked, whipped *jades* led to the current sense of *jaded,* but the noun derogation of mares also took off in another direction—to put down human females.

The *OED* gives a 1560 description of a wanton: "Such a *jade* she is, and so curst a quean, She would out-scold the devil's dame I ween." The diarist

Samuel Pepys in 1668 derided "a most homely *jade* as ever she saw." The slang word's meaning degenerated into "worn-out prostitute," though it sometimes means the less pejorative "hussy" or "minx."

In the synonymy of misogyny, *harlot* is a professional, now called a *sex worker;* a *strumpet,* a *bimbo* and a *slut* are "unchaste to the point of being debauched"; a *trollop* and a *slattern* are "sloppy but not necessarily immoral"; a *wench* is archaically "sexy without a judgment of promiscuity," and a *jade* is "plain worn out," whether from honest or oldest-professional labor.

After publication of Dowd's blast, the President's lawyer, Robert Bennett, backed away from his threat to Ms Jones to "put her reputation at issue," reducing it to questioning her veracity only. I went down the hall to salute my colleague for her puissance and—more to the point of this column—to ask if she had been reading a lot of Shakespeare lately. Prepared for my query—on a hair trigger, actually—she replied: "I got *jade* from Edith Wharton's 'The Gods Arrive.' She also used *coquette* as a verb, *coquetted.*" Having won her point in the sexual politics war, my colleague was no longer in high dudgeon. (O.K., hold off the postcards: that phrase maybe comes from the French *en digeon,* "with hand on the dagger's hilt." There is no "medium dudgeon," although, thanks to Damon Runyon, there is a "medium hello.")

You wrote that "jade" came from the Latin *ilia,* for "side," "based on the ancient notion that the wearing of the green (you left out "stone") cured a pain in the ribs." I learned this derivation a bit differently.

The "pain in the ribs" part was okay because jade was first called *piedra de ijada* ("stone of the loins") by the Spanish who first saw jade when about to pillage the Mayans. In 1863, the French chemist Damour first noted and published the chemical and gemological differences between the two varieties of jade (today called jadeite jade and nephrite jade).

Continuing the old belief that jade, if worn, would cure diseases of the kidneys, Damour named the more precious form of the stone as *pierre de l'ejade.* He was, after all, French! Then, by the principal in linguistics known as "back-formation," this became *pierre du jade* (itself a form of *de le jade*). Evidently the apostrophe in *l'ejade* moved to the right. And so, *le jade* came into English as "jade" (today, correctly called jadeite jade). The other form of jade was called *lapis nephritus,* Latin for something like "stone of the kidneys." That came into English as nephrite jade, and is simply called nephrite, today.

Don Krakowski
Denver, Colorado

Further to your discussion of jade, and its relationship to pain in the ribs.

Jade occurs in two crystalline forms, one being jadeite and the other being nephrite. You will note that nephrite relates to the kidney, as in nephritis; the basic unit of the kidney is the nephron.

As I dimly recall from previous readings, jade may have the appearance of a kidney stone passed in the urine. Kidney stones often cause pain below the ribs. Jade have been prized for warding off this disease entity.

I hope this contribution entitles me to membership in your crew of word nerds.

Stanley C. Fell, M.D.
Bronx, New York

Janus Lives

"I'm pondering the difference between *boned* and *boneless* chicken," writes Alan Levy, editor in chief of *The Prague Post*. He is even more troubled about words like *sanction*, which is a verb for "allow, authorize," and a noun for "punishment," almost the opposite. "Is there a lexicographical term for words that become antonyms of themselves through distortion, if not misuse?"

The word is *contranym* or *antilogy*, but the popular phrase for it is *Janus word*. Janus was the Roman god of beginnings; in Latin, *ianus* is "gateway," and *January*, the opening month of the year, is named after this bearded custodian of the universe. The face of Janus was on the gates of his temple in the Roman Forum; they were open in wartime and closed when Rome was at peace, requiring a head with two faces. One sense of *Janus-faced* is "deceitful, two-faced," and another is "sensitive to dualities and polarities."

In *Crazy English* (1989), Richard Lederer told of Queen Anne's supposed comment in 1710 on seeing the completion of Sir Christopher Wren's magnificent edifice, St. Paul's Cathedral: "awful, artificial and amusing." At the time, that was a royal compliment with *awful* meaning "awe-inspiring," *artificial* "artistic" and *amusing* "amazing."

Those are merely words that flipped their definitions to the opposite, but *Janus words* retain both the original and the changed senses. In his book *Power Language*, the best short course you can take in good writing and strong speaking, Jeffrey H. McQuain gathers up words that face in two directions. One is *oversight*: either "something overlooked" or the quite different "function of overseeing." Another is *arguably*, which McQuain urges should be replaced by *certainly*, if that's your drift, or *hardly*, if you intend the opposite. A third is the political verb *to table*, which in Britain denotes "to put on the table for active discussion" but in America means "to chuck it on the table to gather dust."

If words exist to communicate meaning, *Janus words* are not good words. They communicate confusion. We're stuck with the ones mentioned here so far, at least until one sense sinks and the other dominates, as "breathless in adoration" did with "yucky" in defining *awful*. But we don't have to encourage the coinage of new *Janus words*.

Consider *showstopper*, "spectacular performance that causes the audience to interrupt the show with applause," which President Clinton used to mean "deal breaker," and for which he was roundly abused in this space. But "as any computer nerd could tell you," wrote Vicki Meagher of Bedford, Me., "a *showstopper* (one word, no hyphen) is a bug so egregious that even avid users of a piece of software will find the product unusable. A *showstopper* stops the show, all right, and causes people to throw up their hands—but in disgust, not to applaud."

Can it be that this new word—barely seventy years old—has developed an opposing sense? Apparently so; when Prof. Richard Gambino of the State University of New York at Stony Brook was awarded the National Medal of Technology at the White House in 1995, and began to talk tech, President Clinton pointed to Vice President Gore and said, "Talk to Al about that; he's interested in all that information technology." Writes Gambino, no mere computer nerd: "I suggest President Clinton may have picked up this usage of *showstopper* from the technology wonks he works with—perhaps Al Gore, who did in fact ask some informed technical questions.

"*Showstopper* is often used in engineering parlance," Professor Gambino continues, "in the sense of 'something that presents an insurmountable obstacle.' For example, a boss might ask a young engineer in a project review, 'Is this problem a potential *showstopper*?' I heard this term at I.B.M. Research in technical discussions at least as early as 1975."

Clarity lovers, awake! Stop this *Janus word* before it splits the lexicographical screen. Ensconced in my Queen Anne chair, I say it's awful, artifical and arguably amusing.

Jersey's Vanishing "New"

"If there were five Steve Jobs [*sic*] or one Bill Gates in Harlem," observes Newt Gingrich in his capacity of Author, not Speaker, "the entire nature of the community would change." The columnist Richard Cohen commented sourly, "Yes, it would have moved to Jersey."

Catch the usage: *Jersey*, not *New Jersey*, the full name of the state. Robert Wallace of Albany alerted me a few weeks ago to the widespread clipping of the Garden State: "How come a guy in Brooklyn can say, 'Hey, Gino, what say we go over to Jersey today?' and it sounds all right? But if the same guy is in Hoboken and says, 'Hey, Gino, what say we go over to York today?' it sounds wrong. Why?"

First, some history: *Jersey* is the name of the largest of the English Channel Islands, taken from the Caesars. *Jers* is a corruption of *Caesarea;-ey* is a suffix meaning "island." (Jersey cows were long hailed for the high fat content of their milk, and a worsted material produced there took the island's name; a jersey is a close-fitting tunic or vest originally made of jersey cloth. "The Jersey Bounce"—without the *New*—was a song popularized by Benny Goodman in the 1940s.)

York, originally Eboracum, was the name of an outpost of the British province of the Roman Empire visited by the Emperor Hadrian in the year 120. It became a royal house, symbolized by a white rose, central to British history. When the Brits set out to take the area of North America known as New Netherland from the Dutch, a royal charter for the colony was granted by King Charles II to his brother, the Duke of York, and renamed New York. But while the expedition was still at sea, the Duke of York ceded a portion of his colony to Sir George Carteret and another noble, because Carteret— when Governor of the Channel Island of Jersey—had entertained Charles as a Prince in exile.

Carteret, the Jerseyan, already had a patent on a couple of islands off Virginia and had named them *Nova Caesarea*; the tract that split off from York's colony was named the same, and promptly adopted the English translation, New Jersey.

So Eboracum and Caesarea became New York and New Jersey. How come one is keeping the *New* and the other is not?

My theory to explain the selective dropping of the *New* is this: when the name following the *New* begins with a vowel (*a, e, i, o, u* and sometimes *y*), the *New* elides with the second word and is preserved within it: that's why residents of New Orleans say "Nawlins" and denizens of New York say "N'yawk." But when the second word begins with a consonant, the *New* remains distinct—*New Rochelle, New Zealand*—or gets clipped entirely, as in *Jersey*. (This lightly substantiated theory is worthy of scholarly refutation in *American Speech*, the linguistic quarterly.)

Another theory is advanced by a lexicographer who lives on the other side of the Hudson River. "New Jersey's dropping of the *New* goes back a long way," says Robert Chapman, who has revised *Roget's Thesaurus*. " 'To Jersey' is found in the U.S. as early as 1784 and had a longer time to be established. New York has also been used without the *New* in the past. The first use of 'to York' is from 1838, and 'York' was used in 1855 inside quotation marks in the life story of P. T. Barnum; in the early 1900s it had some underworld use by tramps and criminals, but it never really got established beyond the slangy stage."

Chapman suggests a distinction between the two names: Jersey, an island off England, is less known than the heavily traveled city of York. "Americans could say 'Jersey' and assume they'd be understood; to avoid ambiguity, though, 'York' needed to be 'New York.'"

How do Jerseyites feel about the clip? "I've lived here a long time," says Professor Chapman, "and found no resentment about the clipping to 'Jersey,' certainly not the reaction that San Francisco residents have to 'Frisco.'" The director of the state's Division of Travel and Tourism agrees: "Taking a poll of the lifelong residents of the state here in the office," reports Linda Mysliwy Conlin, "I find the consensus is that 'Jersey' is like the familiarity of an old friend or a family member; it's a positive term indicative of the friendly people you'll meet here."

Gov. Christine Todd Whitman (who prefers *Jerseyan* to *Jerseyite*) isn't having any of this shortnin' bread: "No one calls it Hampshire; no one calls it Mexico or York—so why call it Jersey?" I have tried to explain why herein, but conservatives traditionally resist change.

In suggesting that New York hasn't been shortened to York because the Y acts as a vowel, you are flying in the face of what I had thought was standard wisdom on how Y is used as a vowel and as a consonant.

I have long thought and taught that Y should be considered a vowel only when it makes a vowel sound, as in Egypt (short i), reply (long i), or worry (long e). When it makes the sound we hear in yellow or yes, it is not standing in for a vowel sound and so should be considered a consonant.

Does this ring true with you? If so, your theory on the dropping of "New" finds its exception in New York.

Mark Rigg
Pottstown, Pennsylvania

There is no "vanishing 'New.'" Rather, it has been used or not used, depending on the preference of the speaker and the formality of the occasion, for the last 320 years. The only element of a place name that I can think of to which a valid analogy might be drawn is the "Great" in Great Britain. Since it has probably been many centuries since anyone felt a need to distinguish the name of Great Britain from that of Little Britain (i.e., Brittany), the use or nonuse of "Great" seems to depend on how formal one wishes to be. (That the "Great" is almost always dropped may well reflect the fact that the full name of the country is the United Kingdom of Great Britain and Northern Ireland, which is probably called by its full name about as commonly as is the State of Rhode Island and Providence Plantations.)

Michael L. Ticktin
Roosevelt, New Jersey

The proprietary colony of New Jersey was separated into two colonies when Lord John Berkeley sold his half to Edward Byllynge in 1674. The new colonies were known as the Eastern Division of New Jersey and the Western Division of New Jersey. They shortly were being referred to as "the Jersies" and this continued even after Queen Anne reunited East and West into a single (now royal) colony in 1702. The Jerseys described the united colony and, after 1776, the state well into the nineteenth century. I believe this was the beginning of the practice of calling New Jersey simply Jersey. Over time the shortened name became applied to a variety of things which would properly call for the inclusion of "New." (Jersey Lightning, Jersey Devil, Jersey Blues, Jersey City, Jersey Justice, Jersey Bounce, Jersey Girl, etc.)

Dr. Claribel Young
Professor of History
Georgian Court College
Lakewood, New Jersey

Just a Moment

"Fasten your seat belts," the flight attendant announces. "We will be landing *momentarily*."

Sir John Kerr, the former British Ambassador to the United States, who left his post to be Britain's top diplomatic civil servant, departed—or deplaned— with one gripe about the American language: "It's the abuse of *momentarily*. When the stewardess says that, I think to myself: 'We'll be on the ground for only a moment before the plane rushes off again. I'd better hurry.' But she doesn't mean that at all."

She means *"in a moment."* Purists, most language mavens and British diplomats use *momentarily* to mean *"for a moment."*

I am prepared to bail out here. When a word's meaning is in such flux, you can't say which definition is correct. If you're deeply in the moment, and have to use that word, say "We'll be landing *in a moment,* if we don't crash"—or if "fleetingly" is your intent, forget the adverbial form and try "I'm only staying *for a moment*—don't get up."

Soon is such a beautiful word. Try it, briefly.

Just Driving By

It began with a slip of the tongue by President Clinton. At a campaign visit to a Rhode Island hospital, he joined the criticism of limiting maternity stays to 24 hours. But instead of reading his derogation of *drive-by deliveries,* a phrase first directed in print in 1995 at hurry-up hospitals by Carol M. Ostrom of the *Seattle Times,* Mr. Clinton mistakenly used the term *drive-by pregnancies,* a quite different, not unknown but hitherto unlabeled problem. A Dole-Kemp news release called attention to this minor gaffe under the headline "Much More Fun Than a Drive-In Movie."

This focused the attention of lexicographers on the adoption of a compound adjective by speakers who like to be on the cusp of English usage: *drive-by.*

"Two men were shot to death on Hollywood streets in separate *'drive-by'* incidents" was the lead of an Associated Press article from Los Angeles on Feb. 12, 1981, in the first citation I can find of the term; its use within quotation marks indicates it had been in spoken use earlier. From its first, literal meaning—"gunfire from a vehicle driving past the target"—*drive-by shooting* soon assumed the meaning of "random, senseless violence aimed not at a particular victim but at any individual nearby."

Drive-by delivery was preceded by *drive-through delivery,* first cited in June 1995 in the *Chicago Tribune,* and defined as a "shortened hospital stay for childbirth" by John and Adele Algeo in their *Among the New Words* feature in the Spring 1996 *American Speech* quarterly. *Drive-through* began with fast-food chains (based on *drive-in,* coined in 1933 by a New Jersey movie theater operator) and was picked up by banks (which also use *drive-up*), both serving customers who never had to leave their cars.

But it is *drive-by,* not *drive-through,* that is getting metaphorical extension in the language. In a January 1994 article on "squeegee men," *Newsweek* reported on a "new fad—*drive-by haranguings.*" A year later, Anne H. Soukhanov reported in the *Atlantic Monthly* Michael G. Gartner's use of *drive-by hatred,* which she defined as "seemingly motiveless acts of loathing typically directed at a victim not personally known to the perpetrator." Margaret Carlson of *Time* later that year wrote of "liberal baby-boomers, who thought *drive-by* sex and drugs were fine for them but want limits for their offspring."

As it is used more often, the compound adjective is losing its frightening quality and is accentuating its random or casual sense: "You can hear," wrote the *Washington Post* of Jack Kemp's debate performance, "an increasing volume of *drive-by* criticism like this on the Republican side."

Keeping Your Powder Dry

The return of the regular, monthly Presidential news conference is a fine thing, not the least because it gives us a chance to instruct the Chief Executive—and one another—on the use of famous phrases.

Pleased at the prospect of bipartisan cooperation, President Clinton said, "Now both sides are *keeping their powder dry* enough to create the possibility we can reach a balanced budget agreement." Later, he returned to the phrase: "I would ask our friends on the Republican side and the Democrats who care as passionately as I do, just *keep our powder dry.*"

His meaning in both contexts is clear: "remain calm, keep cool." But that is only half the meaning of the phrase and misses the most telling part.

Oliver Cromwell, at the Battle of Edgehill in 1642, is supposed to have told his Roundhead troops in that opening fight of the English civil war, "Put your trust in God, my boys, but mind to *keep your powder dry.*" (Nobody wrote it down at the time, and its first report came in 1834, but I say let's give it to him.)

The Pretender wasn't talking talcum; gunpowder was his subject, and when the powder is wet, the gun does not go off and the ammunition just sits there. The attraction of the phrase was its combination of what Bergen Evans called "piety and practicality." That combination was repeated in World War II in the saying and song, "Praise the Lord and pass the ammunition."

The purpose of keeping powder dry is to be able to blaze away at the proper time. Thus, the phrase *keep your powder dry* is not limited to "stay calm" but carries an implicit, most ominous threat: "and be prepared to blow the enemy's head off at the propitious moment."

That cannot be the message that Clinton, in his bipartisan mood, intended to convey. On the other hand, in this column I'm a lexicographer and usagist, not a mind reader.

I enjoyed learning the origin of "keep your powder dry." It called to mind another adage I've heard that makes the same point: "Trust Allah, but tie your camel."

Paul D. Hess
Natrona Heights, Pennsylvania

Kiduage

More popular is *POG*, which I have noted on many little T-shirts. Pronounced to rhyme with *dog*, this term is an acronym, formed in Hawaii, from the initials of a popular drink of Passion Orange Guava. *POG* refers to a kid's pastime of collecting bottle caps.

The *-out* formation is still with us. Oldsters who remember being *freaked out* can work out its current synonym, *weirded out*, but the *-out* is sometimes dropped in the latest kiduage. *To hang out*, familiar to those now concerned about reductions in the growth of Medicare, based on *to hang around* and associated with *to hang tough*, no longer has an auxiliary word: "We decided to hang at the mall" is the formulation heard by *mall doofs* (from *dufus*, "a loser").

If your kids are unable to differentiate among a *nerd* ("social outcast"), a *dork* ("clumsy oaf") and a *geek* ("a real slimeball"), you might want to establish your expertise by trying these more recent (and in the process of being replaced) examples of kiduage: *thicko* (nice play on *sicko*), *knob*, *spasmo* (playground life is cruel), *burgerbrain* and *dappo*.

Professor Marcel Danesi, who is author of *Cool: The Signs and Meanings of Adolescence*, treats kids' slang as a social dialect that he calls "pubilect." He reports that one 13-year-old informed him about "a particular kind of *geek* known specifically as a *leem* in her school who was to be viewed as particularly odious. He was someone 'who just wastes oxygen.'"

If you want to stay on the generational offensive, when your offspring uses the clichéd *gimme a break*, you can top that expression of sympathetic disbelief with *jump back* and the ever-popular riposte *whatever*.

I'm tempted to conclude with *I'm outta here* or *I'm history*, but Connie Eble in her *Slang and Sociability* shows how that usage is dated. She notes that *I'm history* is "a parting phrase modeled on an underworld expression referring to death," and it has inspired *I'm archives*.

Other farewells include alterations of foreign terms: *chow for now* (based on the Italian *ciao*), *hasta, pasta* (from the Spanish *hasta luego*), *osmosis, amoebas* (from *adios, amigos*) and *my feet are staying*, a loose translation of the German *auf Wiedersehen*.

James M. Edwards, a correspondent from Pittsburgh, was just wondering: is he just persnickety, or is the word *just* just being tossed into sentences unjustly, with just no thought to its proper function?

He points to an article quoting the chemical-company executive Ray Aiken, saying, "You *just* can't keep pumping out the old stuff." Mr. Edwards suggests that Aiken has placed his *just* too early in the sentence, and his meaning would be better expressed as "You can't *just* keep pumping out the old stuff." (Even better: "You can't keep pumping out *just* the old stuff.")

Just so. In that sentence fragment, *just* means "exactly, precisely." The adverb can also mean "merely," as in *"just* wondering," or in the title of the posthumous collection of more than 50 short stories by the novelist Shirley Jackson: *Just an Ordinary Day*. This ubiquitous modifier has another sense of "barely," as in *"just* a hair's breadth," and another of "nearly," as in *"just* about there," and "really," as in "I'm *just* fine—I only look sick," and more. (Forget about the adjective *just;* we're doing justice only to the adverb here.)

When used in the sense of "only," *just* is properly placed where the *only* should go. This presumes you pay attention to the position of your *onlys*. If you sing "I *Only* Have Eyes for You," you fall into romantic error; it should be "I have eyes *only* for you," or "I have eyes *just* for you." (Another possibility of placement—*"only* I have eyes for you"—can get your face slapped.)

For more help with *only* placement, try Patricia T. O'Conner's useful grammar guide, *Woe Is I*, which moves *only* around from *"Only* the butler says he saw the murder" (no one else says it) to "The butler says he saw *only* the murder" (he saw nothing else).

Mr. Edwards submits another citation, this from Howard Stern, the broadcaster: "Why don't you let me *just* work the equipment?" Since the shock jock presumably wants to speak on the radio and work the equipment simultaneously, shouldn't he pull the adverb up before the *let* and say, "Why don't you *just* let me work the equipment?"

Yes. When you use *just* in the sense of "merely," place it *only* before the part of the sentence you intend to modify.

I am being grumpily prescriptive here, firing off diktats perhaps without proper obeisance to sloppy usage that has reached the refuge of idiom. Ordinarily I would wait six months for a response from the University of Chicago linguist Professor James D. McCawley, who saves up his anti-prescriptive harangues at my pop-grammarian conclusions and then looses a MIRV'd barrage. In this case, I ran the placement of *just* past him beforehand, rather than have legions of readers exposed to *just* one side (not *"just* exposed to one side").

The linguistic giant begins setting me straight with *"Just* has other meanings besides the ones you list. A relevant one is that in 'You've *just* got to help us,' meaning 'damn well,'" which a charitable reader will take to have been Mr. Aiken's meaning.

Just right. "In the Howard Stern quote, *just* probably has its 'only' meaning, but since we don't know what Stern was contrasting *work the equipment* with, the fact that he clearly wanted to talk as well as work the equipment need not conflict with what he said."

Say wha'?

"For example," goes McCawley, who knows his students need f'rinstances to grasp the heavy stuff, "if Lyndon Johnson had said, 'I *only* drink bourbon,' you wouldn't have been entitled to infer that he didn't drink, say, coffee: the implicit set of alternatives that *bourbon* is contrasted with can plausibly be interpreted as 'liquors' or 'whiskies'—thus as not including coffee. Maybe Stern meant 'work the equipment and not listen to your kibbitzing.'"

Aha! Aren't you, heavy linguistic hitter, separating *only* from its focus, the way the lyricist Al Dubin mistakenly did with the Harry Warren melody in "I *Only* Have Eyes for You"? If you snatch *just,* when it means "only," away from its focus, aren't you creating ambiguity? (Let's see him *just*—meaning "damn well"—handle that.)

"Triple red herring. First, in spoken language, 'contrastive stress' marks the focus, irrespective of where *only* is placed. Second, even in written language there is most often *only* one plausible focus—what else could *eyes* be contrasting with? Third, keeping *only* adjacent to its focus sometimes creates ambiguity, as in 'Mary lets John drink *only* bourbon,' which could mean 'She doesn't let him drink anything else' or 'It's O.K. with her if he doesn't drink anything else.'"

McCawley then applies his crusher: "In its musical setting, the line 'I *only* have eyes for you' is unambiguous, since Harry Warren set the words *only* and *you* to rhythmically stronger beats than *have* and *eyes,* creating a musical counterpart to stresses on *only* and *you.*"

Just one minute, Jim. You got me on a poetic technicality on the song title. But why do I afford you this valuable space to accuse me of fostering ambiguity when I am trying to sharpen the focus? You members of the deep-structural workers' union may find that "contrastive stress" (nice phrase—thanks for that) marks the focus, but we prescriptivists say it's the placement of the *just* and the *only* where they belong in the sentence that clearly marks the focus.

McCawley argues that "focalizers" like *just* and *only* have not only a focus but also a scope, and that my hang-up about placement in this case is perverse. But the purpose of today's drill is to show, in microcosm, the debate that goes on between descriptive linguistic scientists and prescriptive language mavens about the way language is used and the way it might better be used. Could help build a bridge. *Just* maybe.

Professor McCawley has a supporter in H. W. Fowler. On page 405, writing about a letter to the editor complaining about the misplacement of *only*, Fowler comments, "There speaks one of those friends from whom the English language may well pray to be saved." I have never understood why those who say they revere Fowler never pay him any attention when he is commonsensical.

E. W. Gilman
Springfield, Massachusetts

Let a Simile Be Your Umbrella

Investigations always turn up interesting words and lively figures of speech.

At the Senate Whitewater hearings, the Democratic counsel, Richard Ben-Veniste, argued that Rose Law Firm payroll records found in the storage room of the White House residence supported Mrs. Clinton's contention that she had done little work for the corrupt Madison Guaranty savings and loan. "Yet there is a question mark about how these records came to be produced," he admitted, concluding, "What we have here, in my view, is an *anomaly.*"

Anomaly, rooted in the Greek for "uneven," was coined by Leonard and Thomas Digges in 1571 to describe the unevenness in a cannon's construction. Astronomers picked it up to cover what could not be explained in the motion of celestial bodies, and now it is a useful word for something beyond "irregularity": an *anomaly* is something "hard to explain, peculiar, difficult to classify." The Democratic lawyer's choice of words was "spot-on" (a Britishism), as was his subsequent use of a mysterious Californianism.

The Whitewater committee, Ben-Veniste acknowledged, had a right to determine "whether there were any *shenanigans*" in the handling of documents. (Next day, on CNN's "Capital Gang," the columnist Al Hunt asked, "Are there any *shenanigans* in his tax returns?" referring to the Republican candidate Steve Forbes.)

This word first surfaced in *Town Talk,* a San Francisco journal, in 1855: "Are you quite sure? No *shenanigan?*" A year later, in a Sacramento newspaper: "These facts indicate that there is some *shenanegan* going on." Mark Twain, who had worked in California, used it in an 1862 letter: "Consider them all . . . guilty (of 'shenanigan') until they are proved innocent." In the 1920s, the word meaning "skulduggery, deception, fast one" began to be used in the plural, in the merrier sense of "high jinks, tomfoolery, kidding around."

Origin? Some lexicographers think the Irish *sionnachuighim,* "I play tricks," may be the source; others speculate that it is from the slang German verb *schináglen,* "to work," or the Spanish *chanada,* "a trick or deceit." But nobody knows, and the frustrating "origin obscure" appears in most dictionaries. This department will happily entertain other speculation, because the word is in frequent use and fills the semantic space between dirty tricks and dirty doings.

Ben-Veniste correctly used this delicious Americanism. At the House hearings into Travelgate, however, a Virginia Republican was linguistically off-base in grumbling about the decision of a subpoenaed witness, David Watkins, to ban cameras and microphones. "Committee member Tom Davis called the rule that allows individual witnesses to shut down broadcast coverage *arcane,*" noted a press release from C-Span, "and we agree."

I do not. *Arcane,* from the Latin meaning "secret, hidden in a chest," means "mysterious, obscure, knowable only to insiders." The plural noun form used by inside-baseball players is *arcana.* Though he might argue that the origins of House rules are lost in the mists of time, the word the Congressman probably had in mind was *archaic,* from the Greek for "ancient," now meaning "antiquated, out of date."

At the Senate hearings, Carolyn Huber, a former Rose Law Firm office manager and now a White House aide, said of the subpoenaed records she had found, "I just picked them up and plunked them down in that box that was already there with the knickknacks in it."

Plunk, an imitative word, came into the language in 1805 to denote plucking a string or striking a hollow object to emit a short, metallic sound, and is now used about the pizzicato sound of a violin. Toward the end of the century, *plunk down* appeared, meaning "to drop abruptly" (plunk it down) or "to set down firmly" (plunk down a dollar bet) or "to settle into position" (she plunked herself down in the witness chair).

A *knickknack* is a 1618 reduplication of *knack,* a word first used by Chaucer. It originally meant "an underhanded trick, a device to deceive, a crafty artifice," later moderating to "a dexterous performance; something adroit, clever." The reduplication veered away from the fast-and-loose meaning to a new sense of "trinket," in British usage "gimcrack, kickshaw," in American usage "ornament," or as my mother used to call my cherished possessions, "dust collectors."

Rivaling Mrs. Huber as the most colorful speaker at the hearings is Lauch (pronounced lock—the name is Scottish) Faircloth, a Republican Senator from North Carolina. Francis X. Clines of the *Times* made a collection of his similes about getting information out of the White House: "like eating ice cream with a knitting needle," "like skinning a hippopotamus with a letter opener" and my favorite—"like teaching a kangaroo to do the limbo."

Lying Flat

"Lying prone on beds or cots" was the caption of a drawing in *Newsweek* showing a body lying toes upward, accompanying its coverage of suicides in the "Heaven's Gate" cult near San Diego.

"I sent a rather cranky complaint to *Newsweek*," reports Donald Crosby of Springfield, Va., "that it had incorrectly used the word *prone* to describe the terminal position of the suicide victims."

The magazine responded: "While your suggestion, *supine*, would also have been correct, our use of *prone* was based on the meaning 'lying flat or prostrate, in a horizontal position' given in *Webster's New World Dictionary*. . . . We stand by our usage, though we appreciate your concerns."

Mr. Crosby is not placated. "When my drill instructor screamed at me to assume the *prone* position when I was firing the M-1 rifle in 1945," he writes, "his physical well-being (and mine) would have been jeopardized had I arbitrarily chosen to fire my M-1 in the *supine* position on the assumption that *prone* and *supine* are synonymous."

They are not. *Newsweek* chose to cover its error by pointing to the *Webster's New World* second, or fuzzy, definition, ignoring its first: "lying or leaning face downward."

Moreover, in a note about synonymy, the dictionary reports that *"prone*, in strict use, implies a position in which the front part of the body lies upon or faces the ground; *supine* implies a position in which one lies on one's back." *WNW*, now published by the Macmillan division of Simon & Schuster and edited by Michael Agnes, goes on to illustrate the latter with "he snores when he sleeps in a *supine* position," an observation with which my wife grimly agrees. (A pillow acts as a kind of muffler when one snores in a *prone* position, but it makes it hard to breathe.)

Supine has another sense of "mentally or morally inactive; listless." That does not describe the irate Mr. Crosby, a retired university professor, who asks: "If *prone* and *supine* can be used interchangeably, what's next? *Infer* and *imply*? *Loan* (the noun) and *lend* (the verb)? Will *hot* and *cold* become synonyms, with their once-specific qualities regulated by the subjective caprice of the user?"

Nosirree, prof., not with MASS—Mothers Against Semantic Shift—manning the ramparts. Only recently, at a meeting of the Judson Welliver Society of Former White House Speechwriters, an editor of *The New Yorker* assured me that his publication will never again confuse *flaunt*, "to make an ostentatious display," with *flout*, "to show scorn." The good usage fight is always worth fighting.

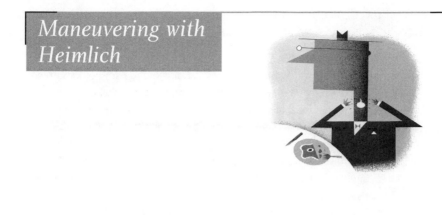

Maneuvering with Heimlich

You're sitting at a luncheon given by the Eleanor Naylor Dana Charitable Trust. You sneak a look at the place card of the guy next to you. It says, "Henry Heimlich, M.D." To make conversation, you pop the question he must be asked by everybody: "You any relation to the Heimlich of the *Heimlich maneuver*?" He replies, "I am he."

Here is the guy who developed the technique to save the life of someone who has a piece of food stuck in the windpipe. The rescuer gets behind the person who's turning purple, places a fist between the lower ribs and upper abdomen, exerts sudden pressure upward—and out pops the foreign object, enabling the swallower to breathe.

You choke down the urge to point out that "I'm him" is replacing the formally correct "I am he" and ask instead the question on the mind of every language maven: why is it called the Heimlich *maneuver*, and not the Heimlich *method* or *technique* or even *squeeze*?

"My original name for it was *subdiaphragmatic pressure*," the doctor replied. "In June 1974, three editors of the *Journal of the American Medical Association* called me to say that they wanted to name it after me, and did I want to call it a *method* or a *maneuver*? I asked what was the difference in meaning. They said that a *maneuver* was a procedure involving an expert movement, while a *method* involved a series of steps, as in a urinalysis, and I shouted, 'Call it a *maneuver*!' "

This thoracic surgeon's name is in almost all the dictionaries now, like the liveryman Thomas Hobson of *Hobson's choice* (no choice at all), the engineer Edward Murphy of *Murphy's law* (if anything can go wrong, it will) and the astronomer Edmund Halley of *Halley's comet*. (Lexicographers are still unsure about Werner Heisenberg of *Heisenberg's uncertainty principle*.)

In Hispanic countries, the sharp upward yank is called *Heimlich maniobra*, and in Germany, *Heimlich Handgriff*; since the doctor's name means "secret" in German, the phrase translates as "the secret handclasp."

"My name, a proper noun, has now become an adjective modifying *maneuver*," notes Dr. Heimlich, 75, who is now working on a treatment for AIDS using malarial fever. "It is also a noun, as in 'I gave him the Heimlich,' and a verb, 'I Heimliched him.' A great thrill, really."

Having one's name become part of the language is certainly not a common occurrence, but it does happen, as your examples show. What's interesting about the phenomenon is that there is a certain hierarchy involved. Lowest on the totem pole are people whose names have been somewhat modified as they enter the language. Consider Guillotin, Volta, and Macintosh who gave us guillotine, volt, and mackintosh.

Next are the people whose names became adjectives but remained capitalized. Heimlich and Hobson are certainly good examples. Note, though, that without the customary accompanying noun (maneuver, choice, etc.) the word has little, if any, meaning.

Higher yet are the people whose names became nouns and lost their capitalization. But even among this group there are two echelons. Lowest are those whose names have become units of measurement. Among many are watt, ampere, and joule.

Highest, and at the top of the totem pole, are the people whose names could come up in everyday conversation. My list of these people, which I am sure is far from complete, includes bloomer, shrapnel, martinet, boycott, zeppelin, diesel, vernier, hansom, brougham, sax, and silhouette. It also includes words that were originally part of people's titles. For example, the orrery was named after the Earl of Orrery. Other such patrician words are sandwich, derby, chesterfield, and cardigan.

As a separate category altogether, there are the words that have come from the names of fictitious characters. This list is short. To date it is comprised only of shylock, knickerbocker, and scrooge.

Finally, there may be a unique name-to-noun instance that is best illustrated by the sentence "William Safire is a Dr. Jekyll and Mr. Hyde."

Howard Waddell
Miami, Florida

Many Icons, Few Iconoclasts

"The iconography of her face," the film critic Gene Siskel wrote in *TV Guide* of Marilyn Monroe, "red lips, platinum hair, blue-shadowed eyes—resembles an American flag."

That, I suppose, is why we all felt so patriotic to be lusting after Ms Monroe; she resembled a new Old Glory. And just as movie reviewers are now called "film critics," an array of icons, or the study of the effect of icons, has come to be called *iconography*. We are all *iconographers* now.

Mary Tyler Moore was described in this magazine by Jonathan Van Meter as "an insecure, talented person trapped in the aura of an *icon*, struggling to find her way out." David Brinkley was said by Peter Jennings to be reducing his workload "after 15 years as the *icon* of Sunday-morning television." An *icon* need not be a person: Apple Computer's difficult moments early this year were profiled in *Business Week* under the title "The Fall of an American *Icon.*"

Carol Schoen of New York, who teaches an Elderhostel course called "*Icons* of the 20th Century," writes: "I am troubled by the vagueness of the term. Should it refer only to people, such as Albert Einstein or Marilyn Monroe? Do the people in the picture have to be readily identifiable or can they be as unknown as the girl weeping over the fallen student at Kent State? Or can it be used, even, for pictures of events without people, such as the mushroom cloud created by the first atom bomb?"

In 1989 in this space, under "I Like Icon," the origins of the vogue word were explored. Born in the Greek *eikon*, "to resemble," the word's earliest meaning was the material representation, or image, of a saint or angel in the Eastern Orthodox Church; that meaning evolved into "revered symbol," like a cross, crescent or star. I remember, at a summit conference in Moscow in 1972, sneaking into an antique shop on the Arbat and asking the dealer for the item in its original sense: "*Ikony yest?*"

The breaker of religious icons in the eighth century was called an *iconoclast*, a meaning applied to the religious rebels known as Protestants in the 16th and 17th centuries, and more recently to attackers of any venerable institutions like marriage or government.

Academics latched on to *icon* in 1954, when W. K. Wimsatt called his collection of essays in the New Criticism *The Verbal Icon: Studies in the Meaning of Poetry*. In semiotics, the study of signs, the form of a symbol suggests a meaning to the viewer. A poem is a "verbal icon" in the way it uses words to form figures of speech, and uses phrases to create images—all to suggest emotional meaning that words used in the prosaic way are powerless to convey.

But after two generations in the iconing tower, the word is getting worn out from overuse, and its meaning is growing fuzzy.

Icon today has at least three senses. One is simple enough: "a graphic representation of an idea," like the little dingus on the computer screen that shows a garbage pail; when you click on it, the material is deleted. (I never click on it, for fear that it really means the writer gets trashed.)

Another meaning, of greater concern to literary types, is "symbol," a sign that represents, or a token that stands for, something else. A symbol ("an eagle of liberty") accentuates a likeness, while a metaphor ("swimming in scandal") finds a similarity in quite different things. I like to get specific about symbols: an *avatar* is the embodiment in a person of some idea. An *archetype* is an original model, or prototype, of a quality, much as the picture of a screaming student stands for protest or the image of a mushroom cloud represents destruction in Ms Schoen's query.

"Over a thousand years after the introduction of the *icon* to the Slavs," writes the lexicographer Anne H. Soukhanov (whose Henry Holt book is *Word Watch*), "the word *icon* in its newest cultural sense reflects exactly the reverence that was accorded the saints at a time when 'visuals' were as important in communication as they are today in a world governed by electronically generated imagery."

A third sense of *icon*, which slops over on the second, is "idol." By this most of us mean "living idol, superstar," and its subset, "media celebrity, the famous famed for being famous." The sloppiness comes from applying icon status to a representative of a passing fancy or conferring it all too quickly on a possibly incipient icon: *Newsweek,* in an article on "The Carolyn Style," announced, "J.F.K. Jr.'s Bride Is Already a Fashion Icon for the 90's."*

Sorry; in my book, the newest Mrs. Kennedy will have to earn her iconhood. She's still only an idol. If we're not careful, we'll be swimming in a sea of icons (which is a metaphor).

> Shouldn't the study of icons, as well as the study of the effect of icons, be called iconology, while *iconography* is related to how the icon looks when written or printed?
>
> *Melvyn S. Goldenberg*
> Riverdale, New York

May Day! Might Day!

Exhuming a report from a law firm that cast a benign light on the Clintons' Whitewater actions, Mortimer Zuckerman, editor in chief of *U.S. News & World Report,* opined, "This report may well have been written in invisible ink for all the attention it has had."

Attention must be paid to his misuse of *may*. That auxiliary verb—same as other "helping verbs" like *can, be* and *do*—is designed to help fix the tense or mood of verbs that it accompanies. In *may's* case, the big function of that modal auxiliary is to describe the degree of likelihood.

---

*John F. Kennedy Jr. and his wife, Carolyn Bessette-Kennedy, were killed in a plane crash on July 16, 1999.

You *may well* find that you can use this information one day. In the preceding sentence, the *may*, especially emphasized by the *well*, indicates a fair likelihood. Some little doubt; no certainty, but the modal auxiliary *may* helps push the action verb *find* toward the subjunctive mood—the sub-subjunctive, as it were—with the meaning somewhere between "could" and "probably will."

While *may* leans toward probability, *might* leans toward unlikelihood. Mr. Zuckerman, with "*may* well have been written in invisible ink," was trying to express an imaginary condition, contrary to fact: we know the report was not literally written in invisible ink (or even lemon juice, which the budget-conscious CIA now uses). To help propel that act of writing into the figurative world, the construction needed is "it *might* have been written in invisible ink for all the attention it has had."

Try it this way: "Dole *may* pick a centrist as his running mate" allows for the active possibility of picking Colin Powell, but substitute *might* in that sentence and you turn the general into a very long shot.

A good reason for preserving the difference between *may* and *might* is to avoid confusion between the two meanings of *may*. Besides indicating doubt, the helping verb *may* has a sense of permission: "You *may* take one giant step." That could mean "I give you permission to take one giant step" or something quite different: "Who knows, you *may* take a giant step or you *may* not." (But you didn't say, "May I?")

Here's a recent ad for Intel, quoting a line in a 1949 *Popular Mechanics* magazine: "Computers in the future *may* weigh no more than 1.5 tons." The intention there was to express less doubt than *might*, but note how it sounds like the permissive *may*, as if computers were allowed to weigh no more than that. (As it happens, my old laptop seems to weigh 1.5 tons when carried with its bricklike adapter.)

What causes confusion is this: The past tense of *may* is *might*. "I *may* throw up" expresses the fearsome possibility of regurgitation; "I *might have* thrown up" discusses that bygone possibility in relaxed retrospect. (Don't misuse *may have* for *might have*; it would be like saying *do have* when you mean *did have*. Keep Whittier's use of the past in mind: "For of all sad words of tongue or pen/The saddest are these: 'It *might have* been!'")

The title of this piece includes "*May* Day!" referring to the international radio signal for help. That distress call has nothing to do with May, the fifth month on the Gregorian calendar, named after the Roman earth goddess Maia (not the Greek mother of Hermes by Zeus, the first expositor of "Might makes right"), and the month first signified as "merry" in 1598. The emergency "*May* Day" (or "Mayday") is based on the French *Venez m'aider*, "Come and help me," which I have been glad to do for Mr. Zuckerman.

I'm afraid I lose my temper with baseball announcers who say: "If he'd played closer to third, he may have caught the line drive."

Since he didn't play closer to third base, he could never have caught the drive, and so *may*, which leaves open the possibility of his catching the ball, is foreclosed, and *might* is right.

Art Morgan
New York, New York

Militia

The Latin noun *miles*, pronounced MEE-lays, means "soldier" and led to the terms *military* and *militia*.

Originally *militia* was used for any military force, but by the 1700s, the term started to separate itself from official armies. The novelist Horace Walpole wrote in a 1759 letter, "I am one of the few men in England who am neither in the army or *militia*." Gen. George Washington, in 1776, made clear his preference for "regular" soldiers in a letter to the president of Congress: "To place any dependence upon *militia*, is, assuredly, resting upon a broken staff."

However, the framers of the Second Amendment to the Constitution wrote in 1791, "A well-regulated *militia*, being necessary to the security of a free State, the right of the people to keep and bear arms, shall not be infringed."

(That famous sentence, today revered by some and resented by others, is poorly constructed; the commas throw us off. I would amend it to read "Because a well-regulated militia is necessary to the security of a free State, the right of the people to keep and bear arms shall not be abridged.")

The key modifier is *well-regulated*; evidently the Founding Fathers were mindful of General Washington's skepticism about militias.

Today's embattled militia members, muttering about the Government-media complex, might turn to the humorist Finley Peter Dunne, writing in 1902 as Mr. Dooley, cited in dictionaries for a dialect spelling of *militia*:

"The newspaper does ivrything f'r us. It runs th' polis foorce an' th' banks, commands th' *milishy*, controls th' ligislachure, baptizes th' young, marries th' foolish, comforts th' afflicted, afflicts th' comfortable, buries th' dead an' roasts thim aftherward."

Mistake Sandwich

"This stark refutation of the First Lady's response," wrote the Pegler-esque vituperator in a recent essay, "was corroborated by contemporaneous notes ... of Susan Thomases telling McLarty, 'Hillary wants those people fired.'"

"I recognize the violation of a rule," writes John LaRosa of New York. "Use the possessive of a noun or pronoun before a gerund. I learned this rule from you. You pluralized the name when it should have been possessivized."

Got me. The gerund in question is *telling*, which is a verb acting as a noun, as in "Telling could get you in trouble." When Mrs. Clinton's confidante Susan Thomases (not plural) does the telling, her name should be made possessive—that is, followed by an apostrophe and then an *s*. (The *Times* uses only the apostrophe with a double sibilant.) Though pronouncing it sounds as if you're falling asleep, the correct form is *Thomases's*.

I must have had politics on the brain. What do you expect from a student of poetic allusions who turns Robert Frost's "Mending Wall" into "Mending Fences"?

Modem, I'm Odem

We can learn from sitcoms.

In a new NBC series titled "Hope and Gloria," Hope asks Gloria's ex-husband, Louis, for advice on what men want. Louis says he can respond only for himself: "A big-screen TV, 800 pixels to the inch."

When Hope asks what *pixels* are, Louis explains, "That's what they call those little dots."

A *pixel* is a word created from "pictures," or "pix," and "elements." The phrase "picture element" was first used in 1927 in the magazine *Wireless World*, writing about "the mosaic of dots, or picture elements." By 1969, *Science* magazine was describing how it was possible to tape-record "the analog video signal from each *pixel*" in photos sent back from space by Mariner 6.

A *pixel* is the smallest part of the video screen than can be turned on or off or varied in intensity. It is what seems to be a single dot on your computer screen or TV set; if it's a color screen, it's really three dots together, or clusters of red, green and blue—the triad of colors that, when energized, add up to white or, when the set is turned off, show as black.

"The most common computer resolution," Bill Howard, executive editor of *PC Magazine*, tells me, "has 640 pixels across by 480; this is the Video Graphics Array, or VGA. Higher-resolution monitors may have 800 by 600 (SVGA, S for "super") or 1,024 by 768 (no abbreviation or acronym commonly agreed on yet for this)."

(I am writing this on a 1,024 by 768 computer screen, which I call HBVGA, for "Hoo-Boy Video Graphics Array," an appellation I happily commend to the computer world, which seems to be groping madly for a superlative above "super.")

We're talking here about resolution, or the sharpness of an image. It used to be expressed in the number of lines to the TV screen; a good picture for a regular broadcast had close to 500 lines. Nowadays people count pixels, and the more available the better, from Louis's 800 pixels to my own computer screen HBVGA standards.

If the noun is here, can the verb be far behind? In a review of Mick Jagger's performance in a Rolling Stones concert, Jon Pareles of the *New York Times* wrote, "*Pixilation* effects on the video screen also make him look more hyperactive than he actually is."

"Alert!" signals Judith Economos of Scarsdale, N.Y. "A wonderful word is about to be commandeered by a formation on *pixels*. Do something!"

No; *pixilation* has been kicking around the language for a half-century to describe a technique of cinematographers and stage managers to make human performers appear to move as if artificially animated. Using a stop-frame camera, the pixilator can distort and speed up the motion of actors, thereby making Mr. Jagger, perhaps growing lethargic with the years, look more frantically animated than ever.

Based on that noun, the modern verb *pixilate* invites confusion with an earlier *pixilated:* "bemused, fey, whimsical" or "slightly and happily drunk." This is formed from the noun *pixie*, a mischievous sprite or fairy, who is pictured with a pointed, conical hat; it is not known if the *pixie* got his name from the *pixie cap* or vice versa.

In coining the modern verb, did cinematographers intend the jerky movements of the subjects to reflect the older meaning connoting whimsy and tipsiness? This is like asking what came first, the pixie or the pixie cap.

The solution to the confusion is this: Spell *pixilated* from the sprite, meaning "intoxicated," with an *i* after the *x,* and spell *pixelate* derived from the photographic technique with an *e* after the *x.*

I'm inclined to put this useful distinction on line, introduced by Gary Muldoon's near palindrome, "Modem, I'm Odem," coined on the analogy of "Madam, I'm Adam." I cannot enforce this spelling split, but good sense sometimes prevails; put on a funny hat and give it a pixie-esque shot.

"Pixilated"—the one reference I recall for that is *Mr. Deeds Goes to Town,* with Gary Cooper, and maybe Jean Arthur? Cooper comes from a town where, as it turns out, everyone is a bit off—"pixilated," as one of the characters describes the townspeople.

Gary Muldoon
Rochester, New York

The Most Optimistic Man

"Pangloss for Veep" was the headline above George Will's column in *Newsweek,* commentating on Bob Dole's selection of the buoyant Jack Kemp as his running mate.

(Normal people *comment;* commentators, in their role as pundits, *commentate,* a new verb. If I say "Jack's an upbeat guy," I'm merely commenting; if, in my capacity as language maven, I excoriate the crowd at Cliché Corners by saying "How come nobody can find a synonym for *ebullient* in describing Kemp?" I am *commentating.*)

However, something happened to Dr. Pangloss on the way to the cover of *Newsweek.* The columnist, cultivating his garden of readers, had written: "Conservatism needs cheerfulness. So, Pangloss for Vice President."

Will's allusion was to Voltaire's philosophical novel *Candide,* satirizing in 1759 the optimism of the followers of the harmony-peddling philosopher Leibniz. In the novel, Dr. Pangloss (meaning "all tongue" in Greek) is the tutor of the innocent young hero Candide (from the Latin for "glowing with innocence"). Although every calamity befalls his student, including the enslavement of his sweetheart to wash towels in Turkey, the resolutely optimistic Pangloss maintains that "all is for the best in this, the best of all possible worlds."

So much for the savage satire by Voltaire in our national newsmagazines. When it came to putting the title of the column among other election reports across the top of the magazine cover, the editors made a striking editorial decision, changing the name to "Pollyanna for Veep."

It was as if one of the columnist-novelist Joe Klein's anonymous bosses said: "Who knows from Voltaire these days? How many of our readers are familiar with *Candide,* much less with the character of Pangloss, and who is Leibniz anyway? Who are we writing for, a pack of literary elitists? Give me a cockeyed optimist that everybody can relate to. Is there another one beginning with *P,* so nobody'll notice the change?"

Enter *Pollyanna.* She is the title character of the 1913 novel by Eleanor Hodgman Porter who exuberantly espouses "the glad game" and was portrayed on silent film by Mary Pickford in 1920 and in a 1960 talkie by Hayley Mills. The name also was helped into eponymhood by songwriters. First, Ira Gershwin, the lyricist of the sad song "But Not for Me" in the 1930 show *Girl Crazy* (reworked as *Crazy for You*), has the disillusioned lover sing: "I never want to hear from any cheerful Pollyannas/Who tell me fate supplies a mate, it's all bananas." And in 1958, Doris Day recorded a bouncy tune, "Everybody Loves a Lover," with lyrics by Richard Adler: "Ev'rybody loves me . . . I feel just like a Pollyanna."

With this powerful pressure from lyricists, *Pollyanna* came to be defined in *Webster's New World Dictionary*, Third College Edition, as "an excessively or persistently optimistic person" and, slightly less pejoratively, in *Merriam-Webster's Tenth Collegiate* as "a person characterized by irrepressible optimism and a tendency to find good in everything." In another word, *Panglossian*—an easier adjective to use than *Pollyannaish* but one that requires recognition of a hero unsung in popular song.

Eponymy—the coinage of a word after a person's name—is big in politics.

An example: *Maudlin,* as tear-jerking passages in speeches are often described by unmoved opposing partisans, comes from the Old French *Madeleine,* and in turn from the Greek *Magdalene,* referring to Mary of Magdala, portrayed in medieval paintings weeping by the sepulchre of Christ before His resurrection.

Another example: *Pander,* a verb that Democrats and Republicans hurl at one another about generous entitlements or tax cuts meaning "to gratify the voter's greed," comes from Pandarus, who helped the Trojans in their war against the Greeks and who was used by Boccaccio, Chaucer and later Shakespeare as the go-between arranging a love affair between Troilus and Cressida. Shakespeare's character, having appealed to baser passions, demands eponymy—"let all pitiful goers-between be call'd to the world's end after my name: call them all Pandars." What the Bard wants, the Bard gets, though the noun is now more often *panderer.*

The resolute sunniness of the Republican convention—Kempian *ebullience* comes from "bubbling, boiling over"—was exemplified by Susan Molinari, the New York Representative described in the *New York Times* as "a *template* of the kind of swing voter the party needs: a young, moderate, suburban working mother."

The reader will note the use of the word *example* in this piece, which, along with *illustration,* is considered bor-ing in modern prose. Livelier words include *avatar,* from the Sanskrit for "reincarnated," now meaning "the living embodiment of," which used to be right on the cusp but has been supplanted on the cutting edge of newspaperese by *template.* This word—originally *templet,* or "little temple"—for a while meant "pattern used to make accurate copies," but its primary sense is now "plastic crib sheet formed to fit over computer keys to help doddering journalists figure out how to interpret the fast-changing keyboards."

We who used to call ourselves writers and now defend our electronic rights as "content providers" shall prevail. Like Bob Dole (who proclaimed himself a plain speaker but who used chiasmus, the inversion of word order in parallel clauses popularized by John F. Kennedy, to good rhetorical effect), I am the most optimistic man in the world. My new byline, aimed at both populists and elitists: Pollyanna J. Pangloss.

Mulling Over "Mull"

Headline writers are language's Great Compressors. They look for verbs with great character and few characters. Convicts do not anticipate, they *face;* visionaries do not envision, they *see;* politicians do not promise, they *vow.* The shorter the sweeter.

Sometimes the Squeezer Squad falls into cliché. At the *New York Times,* the forces of freshness were pleased when the usage czar Allan M. Siegal issued a diktat against three of the weariest of overworked headline verbs. *Decry,* a verb used mainly in headlines and not in normal speech, is out; try *deplore* or, if there's room, *disapprove,* but avoid *whine,* which is pejorative. Another new taboo is *score;* instead, try *denounce, brand, attack* or *condemn.* Replacing that worrier's favorite, *beset,* are the verbs *trouble, plague, irk* and *vex;* though those last two are rarely used in spoken English, they have the advantage of brevity.

When the anti-cliché hit list was passed around copy desks ("U-Czar Bars Trite Heads"), some of the masters of the art were concerned that favorites among older verbs might be endangered. Not to worry: William McDonald, now deputy editor in Arts and Leisure but still the *Times's* legendary horseless headsman, assured his colleagues that *assail* and the past tense of *slay* were in good shape. ("*Balk, vow, ponder* flourish; *hit, rip, nab, craft, downsize* slain.")

The hottest verb in the headline world? That's easy: it's the short word for *think about, contemplate, cogitate* and *consider.* Though *ponder* is big—evidently pensiveness is coming on strong in the news—the word of the year is *mull.*

"*Mulling* the Death Penalty Option," headlines *Legal Times.* "Ford *mulls* recall due to ignition fires," writes *USA Today* (eschewing "owing to"). "Kentucky Legislators *Mull* Map," notes *Congressional Quarterly.*

"Recently I notice many headline writers have been doing a lot of *mulling,*" writes Ellis Butler of Oneida, Tenn. "'City Council *Mulls* Sewer Seepage.' I can live with that, but now they've started *mulling* people." He encloses a clipping from the *Knoxville News-Sentinel* about a movie for which "Arnold Schwarzenegger, Jean-Claude Van Damme and Sly Stallone are all being *mulled* for the title role."

Mr. Butler finds two senses of *mull* in his dictionary: "to heat, sweeten and flavor with spices," as in "*mulled* wine," and "to grind or mix thoroughly, pulverize," which he says "might be fitting for Mr. Van Damme or Mr. Stallone, judging from their recent action epics." He adds, "Let's *mull* it over."

The grinding of a mill was the origin of *mull*; the metaphor was extended in America in 1873 to mental grinding; the novelist Jack London used "*mull* it over" in that sense in a 1910 letter. But ponder that long form of the verb: "mull *over*." *In the sense of "consider with care, turn over in one's mind," mull over* used to be the usual usage, though the *over* was sometimes dropped. It struck me that modern usage is killing the *over*. I ran this notion past Dr. Frederick Mish at Merriam-Webster, and he said, "I would probably never use *mull* without *over*." But when he surveyed his data base of print media to find out how often *mull* has been used nakedly in the past 10 years, he came up with a near tie.

That means editors now generally accept *mull* without *over*. Not my style: when conveying a message of "thinking long and hard," pulling my chin, going "Hmmmmm," I would never use the clipped form; it goes counter to the meaning of "examining in detail," and the word picture loses the turning, stirring connotation.

But that's where the headline writers took over. They needed another word for *ponder*, which was working too hard. No room for *ruminate*. And I think that's why they adopted *mull* and moved *over*.

Neck That Down

Asked recently about dependents of Department of Defense civilians remaining in Kuwait, Gen. John M. (for Malchese) Shalikashvili, Chairman of the Joint Chiefs of Staff, told *Army Times:* "The vast majority, if not all, are on a long accompanied tour. We're going to *neck that down* to those that are absolutely necessary."

The ever-vigilant Joseph C. Goulden of Accuracy in Media sent in that clip and noted: "When I was a slip of a lad in rural East Texas, 'neck' was something you did with a nubile maiden at the Fox Drive-In Theater, or on a blanket in a pine copse at Scout Lake. Pray tell where the Hon. Shali found this term, and how it got into military speak."

Perhaps A.I.M. is reluctant to slam the top brass against the wall about their usage, but on such matters this former corporal has a tradition of fearlessness verging on the foolhardy. I put it to the general: What's with *neck down?*

"It is possible that I first heard the term *neck down* as an artillery officer," the man known as General Shali responded cheerfully, despite having been calumniated as "General Shilly-Shally" by this columnist writing in another space last year. "However, the phrase is actually used by both military and civilian shooters. *Necking down* is the practice of reducing the diameter of a cartridge case at its neck, allowing a smaller diameter bullet to be fired from it. This is frequently done to increase the velocity of the projectile."

The J.C.S. Chairman, an immigrant from Poland who "learned English from the silver screen under the expert tutelage of John Wayne," directs us to "ABC's of Reloading," by Dean A. Grennell, for pictures of cartridges going through a *necking down.*

Etymology unsupported by the Pentagon confirms the general's definition. Mitford M. Mathews, in his 1951 Dictionary of Americanisms, defines *neck* in an 1812 citation as "to cut the *neck* (i.e., the excrescence at the point where the lead was poured into the mold) off an old-fashioned round bullet for a muzzle-loading rifle." The *OED* has a 1938 use from a metallurgical text: "The contraction begins to concentrate at some one point on the bar, [and] the piece begins to *neck down.*"

"The phrase has also crept into the civilian lexicon," notes the general, zeroing in, as riflemen say, on the extended metaphor of interest to lexicographers, "meaning 'a reduction to increase efficiency.' Good examples might be *to neck down* a lengthy column—or in my case, this letter."

Because Shali had in his cross hairs the readers of a publication directed at members of the armed forces, he could be confident that his figure of speech would be understood. Corporate executives seeking a synonym for *downsizing* less euphemistic than "work-force imbalance correction" might strike a Patton-esque pose and say, "Sorry, old-timer, but this place needs a *necking down.*"

As for the media watchdog Mr. Goulden, happily entwined in his memory with a nubile maiden on a blanket in East Texas, the slang verb *to neck* as "to indulge in amorous caresses," which dates from 1910, is now obsolete, gone with *sparking, spooning, courting* and *petting.* (*Nubile*, from the Latin *nubere*, "to marry," once meant "marriageable" but now usually means "young and sexy.")

What do we now call a combination of kissing, stroking and fondling—with hands outside the clothes—punctuated with sighs and moans, all in the spirit of affectionate fun? In the '80s, the odious *sucking face* held sway, and that self-mockery is perpetuated with today's *swapping spit,* but a note of sportsmanship has been added with *boxing tonsils* and *tonsil hockey.*

Mugging (which dates back to 1821 in England), *mauling* (without a violent connotation) and *grubbing* are current, along with *going for sushi,* based on "tongue sushi," a mutual rolling-up of tongues, which seems anatomically difficult.

Recently the most popular national usage has been necking down to *hooking up,* which retains a kind of innocence, though this department will entertain competing regional entries for what used to be *light petting.* Just about everything else comes under *having sex.*

Ductile materials like steel, when subjected to more tension than they can bear, fail in a process which has always been called "necking down." *Resistance of Materials* by Fred B. Seely, published by John Wiley & Sons in 1925, shows an illustration entitled "Neck-down Section," so called because the failed section appears to have a head, shoulders and neck. I believe this phrase was in common engineering use long before modern high-powered cartridges, and I suspect that the phrase comes from a 19th century engineering origin.

Charles D. Snelling
Allentown, Pennsylvania

We all know how the word *peccadillo* is now often used: as a minimization, or dismissal as insignificant, of a brief, secret extramarital affair by a politician. In the synonymy of political sin, it is more than an *indiscretion* and much less than a *zipper problem*. And yet all our major dictionaries shy from this current meaning, preferring the more general "trivial offense," "trifling fault" or "minor sin."

Lo—there is the word in the third edition of *Fowler's Modern English Usage* revised by New Zealand's gift to the English language, Robert W. Burchfield, the man who edited the great four-volume supplement to the first edition of the *Oxford English Dictionary*.

But in this linguistic bible, Burchfield deals with usage, not meaning. Therefore, the entry on *peccadillo* concerns itself not with the gradations of playing around, but with a deeper question that all of us in the language dodge have been pondering: how do you spell the plural of *peccadillo*?

"At one time or another we are all in difficulties," writes Burchfield, "with the plural of words which in the singular end in -*o*." Short words like *no* and the verb *go* take the *e*, as *noes* and *goes*. "Polysyllabic words tend to have -*os*," the newest edition observes, adding *punchinellos* to the earlier editions' *archipelagos* (although *Webster's New World Dictionary* prefers *archipelagoes*), *armadillos*, *generalissimos*, and *manifestos*.

Thus, while many dictionaries fudge the plural of *peccadillo*, giving both ways, Fowler's usage bible takes a stand: its preferred spelling, confirmed by Burchfield, is *peccadillos*, not *peccadilloes*.

What about *potato*, which drew so much attention to Dan Quayle? "Completely naturalized English words," according to Fowler's, get the *e*: therefore, *potatoes, tomatoes, vetoes, heroes*. But "curtailed words," usually made by dropping the last syllable, get no *e* in the plural: *memos, photos, rhinos* and—better get this right—*typos*. Same with alien-looking words: *fandangos, mikados, placebos, weirdos*.

Now we are into the pleasures of Fowler (known as *A Dictionary of Modern English Usage*, by Henry W. Fowler, when first published in 1926, lightly edited by Sir Ernest Gowers in 1965, more thoroughly rewritten by Burchfield.) This has never been a handbook; it is a body-and-soul book, rambling through the byways of usage with a delight in the detailed discovery of difficulty, written with a style all its own: certain, authoritative, unafraid to make decisions. Burchfield is less prescriptive than his predecessor, more inclined as a lexicographer to rely on historical evidence and electronic evidence of usage. He asks, "Why has this schoolmasterly, quixotic, idiosyncratic and somewhat vulnerable book . . . retained its hold on the imagination of all but professional linguistic scholars for just on 70 years?"

My answer: In an age of semantic shift and grammatical drift, this has been a book that offers moorings. In changing it, the editor-rewriter invites the wrath of all who like their grammatical scripture pristine. But there is still steel in this volume's spine; the ebullient New Zealander's original entries offer conversation without tergiversation.

That brings us to "hard words" like *tergiversation* (from the Latin words for "turning back," now meaning "equivocation, weaseling," a useful political term). Burchfield, like Fowler, studs his work with short essays like the one on "hard words," taken from the title of the first English dictionary, by Robert Cawdrey, in 1604. (Think of that—for most of his writing life, Shakespeare had no dictionary to turn to.)

To someone who asked, "Why does Anita Brookner use hard words like *rebarbative* and *nugatory*?" Burchfield responds, "One possible answer is that the famous novelist does not regard them as 'hard.'" That's his style—he replaces Fowler's "long" with "polysyllabic"—but he chooses a position somewhat short of the writers who enjoy using hard words. (O.K.—*nugatory* means "trifling" or "inoperative," and *rebarbative* is "repellent, irritating," presumably coined by a woman whose lover had a scratchy beard.)

You stated that *tergiversation* came from Latin words for "turning back."

I think that that should have been "turning the back." The word comes from "*tergum,*" the back, and "*versare*" or "*vertere,*" to turn. *Tourner le dos* instead of *reculer.*

Frederich J. Ortner
Bronx, New York

The New Gulag

"I want *laogai* to become a word in every language," said Harry Wu, the Chinese dissident, to Gerald F. Seib of the *Wall Street Journal.*

After a stretch of 19 years in labor camps for being a troublemaker—that word is the title of his book—Mr. Wu found refuge in the United States. He returned four times to China to document conditions in the camps, where prisoners are "re-educated" doing menial work in fields and factories; on his last trip, he was arrested and became a cause célèbre for two months until his release.

Why does he want to publicize the Chinese word *laogai*, which rhymes with "now-guy"? (It means "reform through labor," a phrase that seems to suggest healthful exercise but is a euphemism for "humiliation by being forced into menial labor for no pay." According to Charles Laughlin, who teaches Chinese literature at Yale, "The word is particularly applied to intellectuals who are sent to labor camps located in isolated areas in the countryside.")

Perhaps because he understands the power of a word to define and then become a rallying point for an international protest.

When Alexander Solzhenitsyn wrote *The Gulag Archipelago* in 1973, his investigation of the network of Soviet prison camps made famous the acronym for *Glavnoe Upravlenie ispravitel'-no-trudovykh LAGerei*, meaning "chief administration of corrective labor camps." The word-picture of an archipelago—a sprinkling of islands in a large sea—combined with the acronym suddenly brought into geographic focus what had been an amorphous idea of prisons everywhere. After that, "the Gulag"—no *archipelago* needed—became the word-symbol of Communist oppression.

That is what Harry Wu is seeking with *laogai*. By making famous the unfamiliar word, he seeks to dramatize the discomforting fact of slave labor. Political scientists have no difficulty with that—many human rights activists urge him on—but linguists wonder if any Chinese word lends itself to adoption in the West. (One that has is *coolie*, the Anglicized spelling of *kuli*, found in both Chinese and Urdu, meaning "low-paid worker," used mainly in English now in the phrase "coolie wages." Another is *gung-ho*, originally taken by U.S. marines in 1942 to mean "work together" and now meaning "enthusiastic," which comes from *gonghe*, a clipped form of the Chinese words for "Chinese Industrial Cooperative Society.")

Another word appearing in articles about campaign finance scandals called "the Asian connection" (a play on the 1971 movie *The French Connection*) is *guanxi*, pronounced gwahn-shee. This means "the network of personal, familial and commercial relationships used by East Asian men to advance their interests," and is being applied by muckrakers to the network of political and business associations in Little Rock, Washington and Jakarta, Indonesia. Headline writers have called this "the Asian connection," and those who insist that all scandal bear the *-gate* suffix slug it "Indo-gate" or (after the Lippo Bank) "Lippogate."

Although the term *guanxi* as used by Asians has a benign connotation as the interplay of favors, jobs and status among the upwardly mobile, its use by Westerners carries the clear connotation of bribery, political fixing and general corruption.

We thought we'd mention a few additional words: "mango," from the Mandarin *"máng guǒ"*; "won ton" from *"hún tun"*; and, of course, "chow mein" from *"chǎo mi'an."* (Although, the Chinese version of "chow mein" is literally what its words suggest: fried noodles; the Americanized version, which contains the usual gloppy vegetables and corn starch, is not true to its linguistic roots.)

Robert Badner and Xie Dong
Bloomfield, Connecticut

The New Old Testament

What do you call the *Old Testament*? I noted that "the *Old Testament* Job was a Gentile" in a column and got a letter from Michael Berenbaum, who teaches theology at Georgetown.

"To Jews, there is no such thing as the *Old Testament*. Job is a book and a character in the *Hebrew Bible*," he observes, arguing that "*Old Testament* is a Christian term that presumes that the *Old* has been supplemented by the *New Testament*," a view that Judaism does not hold.

I ran that past Prof. David Marcus of the Jewish Theological Seminary in New York. "I use *Old Testament*," he said cheerily, "but many people have a problem with that because *old* assumes *new*. Strict Jewish people use *Hebrew Bible;* however, they do say *New Testament*."

Next source: the legendary Prof. Jacob Neusner of the University of Florida, author of a shelf of books, including *The Price of Excellence* (Continuum). "Nothing is incorrect about your correspondent's complaint, but the use of *Hebrew Bible* in the context of religious studies is not a whole lot better than saying *Old Testament*. Here's the reason: Parts of the Scriptures of Judaism are written in Aramaic, so if you say *Hebrew Bible*, you're leaving out that part."

Hmm. I'd be willing to write "the *Hebrew Bible*, plus parts of Daniel, Ezra, Jeremiah and the others that were written in Aramaic," but others might find that formulation taking a lot of space.

Prof. Michael O'Connor of the Union Theological Seminary in New York recognizes the "prejudicial" problem in the 14th-century term *Old Testament* and notes that Roman Catholicism accepts as canonical more *Old Testament* books than do the Jewish and Protestant faiths. "In the next generation," he predicts, "Christians will probably more often refer to the *First Testament,* a term coined in the early '80s by James Sanders at Claremont."

I checked with Professor Sanders at the Claremont School of Theology in Claremont, Calif. "I cannot use the term *Hebrew Bible*," he explains, "because the Jewish canon is arranged in an entirely different way from the *First Testament* Scriptures in Christian religions." The books of the prophets, which come in the middle of Judaism's Scripture, were placed at the end of what Christians call the *Old Testament* because they predict the coming of a messiah and make a natural transition to the *New*.

The Rev. Bernard Lee of Loyola University in New Orleans agrees: "For Catholics, the *Old Testament* contains additional books ordered differently than in the Jewish canon. I like to call the *Old Testament* and the *New Testament* the *Early Scriptures* and the *Late Scriptures* because that seems the least ideological approach."

"Face it," responds Prof. Mary Boys at the Union Theological Seminary, "'*First* and *Second* Testaments' is short on poetics. And when we offered a course at Boston University titled the *Hebrew Bible,* many students said they did not sign up for it because they did not know Hebrew. On the surface, it seems a simple question—What do you call the *Old Testament?*—but it's truly complex."

I will leave the religious complexities to the theologians and deal with the simple problem as a card-carrying prescriptive usagist. Evidently *Old Testament,* as a proper noun, is beginning to offend some Jews, and we see sensitive Christians becoming aware of it. In the *Dictionary of Global Culture,* edited by Kwame Anthony Appiah and Henry Louis Gates Jr., we read, "The Bible is divided into two parts, the *Hebrew Scriptures* and the *New Testament.*"

The terms *Hebrew Bible* and *Hebrew Scriptures* may be knocked as suggesting they do not include Aramaic books or may not be translated into English, but most people get the drift that they are "the Bible of the Hebrews." And nobody objects to *New Testament.*

Therefore, in my mental stylebook, I'll go along with others who use *Hebrew Bible;* however, because I am a traditionalist and do not find objections from co-religionists upsetting, my personal preference remains *Old Testament.* (Many strongly traditional Jews reject both *Bible* and *Testament* and choose *Tanakh,* an acronym for the three divisions of the sacred writings: Torah, the five books of Moses; Nebiim, the books of the prophets, and Ketubim, the other sacred writings.)

But the handwriting is on the wall (Daniel 5:25–28). I foresee, in this eagerly inoffensive age, a widening use of *Hebrew Bible* and *New Testament* as the description of Scripture in the future, with Christians continuing to use the *Bible* to cover the *Good Book* (or *Books,* as the case may be).

If *Hebrew Bible,* its usage now spreading among theologians and other academics of many faiths, does ultimately replace *Old Testament* for the proper noun, I hope the old Middle English phrase lingers on as an acceptable compound adjective, as in "the *Old Testament* Job" or "the *Old Testament* prophets," with the two words meaning "fearlessly uncompromising in matters of justice and morality."

You don't agree? Decide for yourself; this is the voice of the language maven, not the Voice from the whirlwind. Having thus solved the *Testament* problem to my own satisfaction, I now plan to turn to another linguistic controversy in religion: the use of *B.C.* after a date before the birth of Christ.

Should it be *B.C.* or *B.C.E.*? Does the latter stand for "Before the Christian Era" or "Before the Common Era" or "Commander of the British Empire" or what? Should *A.D.* be placed before or after the Year One, or does that abbreviation of the Latin *Anno Domini*—"in the year of our Lord"—step on Jewish, Muslim and other non-Christian toes?

Jehovah's Witnesses use *Hebrew-Aramaic Scriptures* rather than *Old Testament*, and *Christian-Greek Scriptures* rather than *New Testament*. Also, B.C.E. for *Before the Common Era*, and C.E. for *Common Era*, are used in dating, thus by-passing the issue of stepping on "Jewish, Muslim, and other non-Christian toes."

> *Maryam Mansour Stager*
> Scranton, Pennsylvania

The Jehovah Witnesses have the final word on your column. They designate the divisions of the Bible in terms of their original languages: the Hebrew-Aramaic Scriptures and the Christian Greek Scriptures.

While on the subject of religion, I have two corrections to make to your column. The *anno* in A.D. is not capitalized, i.e., *anno Domini*. And the B.C. and A.D. abbreviations are usually not printed as regular capitals, but as small capitals.

> *Will Greene*
> New York, New York

Your reference to bathroom signs reminds me of the ones in Riverside church, where quite a few years ago they were changed from *Ladies* and *Gentlemen* in ornate brass to *Men* and *Women* in plastic. At the same time, in a bow to multiculturalism, they put in Spanish ones: *Caballeros* and *Damas*. Clearly, *Hombres* and *Mujeres* was out.

> *John E. Ullmann*
> Professor Emeritus of Management
> Hofstra University
> Hempstead, New York

No Problem

The 1996 Presidential campaign has blessed us with its first addition to the English language.

Arlen Specter, the Pennsylvania Senator who announced his candidacy for the Republican nomination, was chairman of the Senate Intelligence Committee. In an interview, he noted that the long delay in filling the post of Director of Central Intelligence was "especially *problemsome*."

That word triggered the ire of Louis Jay Herman of New York, godfather of the Gotcha! Gang. "I find it bothersome and troublesome (and then some)," he writes, "that a Presidential hopeful should think that *problemsome* is an English word. Please zap him at once."

Not me. (Or "Not I," as nominative freaks would insist.) Here is the long-sought answer to the *problematic* problem.

The problem with *problematic*—a word much in vogue among academicians and foreign-policy wonks—is that it has two different meanings.

The first is "difficult; having the nature of a problem; hard to grasp or solve." Example: "Devising a strategy for capturing the Republican nomination when you are a former crime-busting prosecutor is easy, but when you are unequivocally pro-choice, it becomes *problematic*."

The second meaning is given in *Webster's New World* as "not settled; yet to be determined; uncertain." Example: "That Specter will be supported by Barry Goldwater in Arizona is likely, but an endorsement from Anita Hill is *problematic*."

Merriam-Webster's Tenth Collegiate covers those two senses and adds a third: "expressing or supporting a possibility," as in "The notion of an Eastern moderate capturing the nomination may now seem remote, but some observers say it's still *problematic*."

Presented with one word burdened with three meanings, the listener or reader must examine the context to figure out the correct sense every time; what kind of word is that?

It's a word to avoid. But now, thanks to Senator Specter, we have a new word whose meaning is unambiguous: *problemsome*, coined, as Mr. Herman suggests, on the analogy of *bothersome* and *troublesome*. It should be defined only as "presenting a problem; difficult." No other senses to intrude and confuse.

Down with *problematic*, which sounds like the brand name of a camera with a flash that never goes off. Here's a write-in vote for *problemsome*, the word that solves. (Pity it's not easier to pronounce.)

I find your ready acceptance of Arlen Specter's coining of *problemsome* fraught with problems. As you noted, it's practically unpronounceable; when I try to say it I sound like Demosthenes before he got the hang of the pebbles.

I resist using a non-word when a few simple alternatives do the work: don't *prioritize*; set priorities. Don't *calendarize*; schedule. No need to *incentivize* the employees; give them incentives, inspire them. And away with *potentialize*; reach your potential. You may have guessed from these examples that I spend far too much time hanging out in the business world. In fact I am a corporate trainer, teaching employees first to recognize jargon and then to dejargonize their writing. My job is full of problems.

Judith R. Birnberg
Sherman Oaks, California

No Way, V-J

"Our whole effort in this thing," an unidentified American official in Tokyo told *Washington Post* correspondent T. R. Reid, "is to commemorate an event, not to celebrate a victory. So we have assured Japan that nobody in the U.S. Government or military will use the term 'V-J Day' this year."

That struck me as prettification of history by government fiat, and especially insensitive to veterans' groups recently incensed by Enola Gay–bashing at the Smithsonian Institution.

I called Michael McCurry, the White House press secretary, who said: "The dropping of 'V-J' is a canard quacking through the cosmos. My suspicion is that it started with the embassy in Tokyo trying to be delicate and not using 'V-J' in official statements."

Presumably, a Japanese official had pointed out that "V-E Day" (May 8) denoted Victory in Europe, and did not directly tag the loss on Germany and Italy; on that analogy, the terminology for the defeat of Japan would be "V-P Day" (Aug. 15), for Victory in the Pacific (though Al Gore had nothing to do with this).

Mr. McCurry hastened to repair the damage: "It will still be V-J Commemoration Day, but the formal title will be something longer, like 'V-J Day, comma, Victory in the Pacific, comma, End of World War II Commemoration.'"

When other reporters braced him with this at his daily briefing, the press secretary was able to produce planning documents referring to "V-J Commemoration Day." A crisis of politically correct euphemism was averted.

The "canard quacking through the cosmos" figure of speech showed a nice sense of double meaning in the Clinton White House.

A *canard* is the French noun for "duck," originating in the verb *caner*, "to cackle or quack." In English, however, the noun *canard* means "lie."

This is said to have come from the French expression *vendre des canards à moitié*, "to sell half-ducks" or "to half-sell ducks"—meaning "to swindle, to deceive." English writers have cited the French phrase since the early 1600s when the half-seller of ducks was called a "guller" or "lyer." Thus, Mr.

WILLIAM SAFIRE 198

McCurry's "canard quacking through the cosmos" dealt subtly with the bifurcated etymology of the word, playing on a quacking duck and an untruth.

The temptation is to slyly continue here with the origin of *lame duck*, but this column is scrupulously nonpartisan.

Noah's Arcane

Daniel Schorr, dean of electronic pundits, designated the word *arcane* as the newest addition to the lexicon of scandal speak.

Data bases show a rush of uses of *arcane* within 50 words of the name *Gingrich*. That demonstrates how defenders of Newt Gingrich, in their campaign to keep him as Speaker of the House, universally embraced that adjective to apply to "a tax law too complicated to hope to master."

The mysteriously ubiquitous word is rooted in the Latin *arca*, "chest, box," which is also the root of *ark*, a boat Noah built to enclose, or hold in, two of every species. The synonym is "secret," but because that word is stamped on just about every document around Washington, the unopened box behind the unfamiliar *arcane* gives the word a connotation of deeper mystery understood only by the initiated. The noun form, commonly used only in the plural, is *arcana*.

Opponents of Newt used three related terms that need separation here: he was urged to *step down*, *step aside* and *stand down*.

Step down, dating back to 1400 in its primary meaning of "to go from a higher level to a lower," gained its extended meaning of "to withdraw or retire from office" in 1890: "Let . . . the lunkheads *step down* and resign."

Step aside, in 1530 meaning "to move out of the path," has an extended meaning, not yet in many dictionaries, of "withdraw temporarily" or "make room for a replacement." It is ambiguous in its conclusion, a step short of the decisive *stepping down*. If the 25th Amendment ever came into play, a disabled President would step *aside*, letting the Vice President assume his powers as Acting President, but would not step *down*.

Stand down began in 1681, telling a witness to "step down from the box after giving testimony." It was picked up by sports a century ago to mean "give up one's place on a team" and in World War I gained its present sense of "relax, come off duty after a state of alert," in contrast with *stand to*; after the Armistice, the opposing forces *stood down*.

Used in connection with a call for a politician to step down or aside, *stand down* is, in the adjectives carefully chosen by the House Ethics Committee, "inaccurate, incomplete and unreliable."

Non-Bloopie

This department has savaged advertising copywriters for the debasement of adjectives (*colossal* to mean "medium-sized"), but in good spirit, a salute to the makers of Le Sueur peas, who describe their product on the label of the can in no uncertain terms: "Very Young Small Early Peas." (Maybe they could toss in a couple of very teensy-weensy baby commas.)

> Comments on usage are made by
> fools like you and me,
> But only God can make a pea.
>
> Justin G. Huber
> Cedar Rapids, Iowa

Not So Special

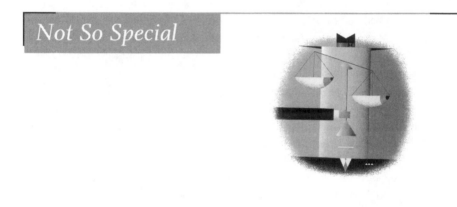

"You were wrong about Janet Reno's powers as Attorney General," whispered Daniel Schorr, senior correspondent of National Public Radio, seated next to me at a speech Henry Kissinger was giving to the Nixon Center for Peace and Freedom in Washington.

In the moment when Henry turned from a castigation of multilateralism to the necessity of the expansion of NATO, I whispered back I was rarely wrong, but sometimes mistaken.

Next day, Dan called with the citation of my error, which appeared in the lead of a harangue about the never-ending cover-up of long-forgotten blunders: "Janet Reno's wrongheaded refusal to appoint an Independent Counsel in the Iraqgate scandal. . . ."

The whole idea of an Independent Counsel is that he or she is *not* appointed by anyone in the executive branch, the veteran of Watergate coverage explained. The law directs the Attorney General, when confronted by credible evidence of wrongdoing by certain high officials, or when pushed hard by Congress, to ask a special panel of the Court of Appeals in Washington to name and empower an attorney of its choice to investigate. Thus, the formulation of my lead should have been "Janet Reno's wrong-headed refusal to *seek the appointment of* an Independent Counsel" etc.

Not content with Gotcha-gangsterhood, Mr. Schorr suggested: "But why not turn your error to constructive use in your language column? Confusion reigns on *Special Prosecutor, Special Counsel* and *Independent Counsel.* Straighten it out."

It goes back to Watergate, when Attorney General Elliot Richardson appointed Archibald Cox to be *Special Prosecutor,* a term long used in Justice Department regulations. After the Special Prosecutor Act of 1978 gave appointment power to the judicial branch, it occurred to legal minds that not all investigations led to prosecutions, and the title of the appointed attorney unfairly imputed guilt to those being investigated. The title was amended to *Independent Counsel,* a less menacing choice.

Meanwhile, at the Justice Department, it occurred to appearance-conscious officials that the word *special,* so long associated with the independence of special prosecutors, could be used to give the illusion of independence to appointees chosen (*handpicked* is the pejorative verb) by the Attorney General, and remaining under Justice Department control. Hence, *Special Counsel.* That was the title given to Frederick Lacey in 1992, when the Bush Administration resisted the extension of the Independent Counsel Act and wanted to give the appearance of having its Iraq actions reviewed by an outsider.

When I offered him the sobriquet Patsy Prosecutor, using *patsy* as an attributive noun (a noun that modifies another noun), some hypersensitive readers objected to *patsy* as being derived from *Patrick* and therefore a slur on the Irish, on the analogy of *paddy wagon,* and so should be used only by Irish pundits. The *Oxford English Dictionary* Supplement gives "origin unknown" for this slang word, but inaccurately defines it as "all right"; the great dictionary's citations prove that to be a sense in the past, but the predominant meaning of *patsy* is and always was, as Eric Partridge defines it, "dupe or 'fall guy,'" citing a 1925 play of that name by Barry Connors. But I digress.

In the Whitewater investigation (called "the Whitewater *matter*" by White House aides, "the Whitewater *scandal*" by partisan Republicans and "the Whitewater *affair*" by sly subliminators), *Special Counsel* Robert Fiske, who was appointed by Attorney General Reno, was replaced when the Independent Counsel Act was renewed by *Independent Counsel* Kenneth Starr, appointed—at Reno's request—by a judicial panel.

In terms of adjectives striking terror into the hearts of Presidential aides and Cabinet officers, *special* is soothing and *independent* is terrifying. But can Mr. Starr be properly called a *special prosecutor*?

Yes, though the phrase should not be capitalized as if it were a title. Once a court-appointed counsel has persuaded a grand jury to hand up an indictment on anyone, it strikes me as fair to call him a prosecutor—and not just a run-of-the-mill prosecutor, but one made special by virtue of his appointment in an extraordinary manner.

"Anchorpeople reach for *special prosecutor*," white-haired Dan Schorr says, "because it sounds more sexy."

Does the scourge of Watergaters, conscience of the networks and out-mavener of language mavens prefer *anchorpeople, anchorpersons* or *anchors*?

"Hate 'em all," he says, playing the curmudgeon.

Of "Of a"

"Ace! It's an epidemic!" He doesn't have to sign the cover note; the only person to call anybody in Washington "Ace" is Ben Bradlee, better known as "Sport" to journalists who can remember the generalized appellations of the 40's.

The clipping attached to the submission from the former editor of the *Washington Post* contained this quotation from Kate Spade, designer of handbags (formerly *pocketbooks,* and before that *purses*), about the impression given by Carolyn Bessette-Kennedy, who became an overnight icon when her name was joined in happy hyphenation with that of John F. Kennedy Jr.: "It's called the 'editor look.' It's much more popular of a look than it used to be."

That "editor's look"—defined by Ms Spade as "very simple hair, very simple shoes, nothing that says a lot, but it all says great things"—did not trouble Bradlee, a man with very gray hair, very complex shoes and a lot of snazzy outfits that say nothing. It was the infixed *of a*—"more popular of a look"—that got to him.

What kind of a speaker, or what sort of a writer, sticks an unnecessary *of* between adjective and subsequent noun? In that very question is the probable source of the new idiom: *kind of a* and *sort of a,* locutions active for centuries, popularized *of a.* Then came *considerable of a,* used in 1766 as "about 6 o'clock *considerable of a* shock was felt in Boston" and in 1875 by Mark Twain in "A brick came through the window with a splintering crash, and gave me a *considerable of a* jolt in the back."

About 20 years ago, only in America and almost exclusively in spoken English, did the (adjective) *(of a)* (noun) construction take hold. "It won't be that long *of a* speech," said the former Brooklyn Dodger shortstop Pee Wee Reese in 1984; "How big *of a* carrier task force?" asked the newscaster Jim Lehrer two years later. In neither of those examples does the *of* add anything to the sentence's meaning.

Is it correct? No; in Standard English it is not. Is it epidemic? No, Sport, but it is making the transition from the spoken language to the written, as idioms do. Is it that big *of a* deal—or, as we purists would insist, that big a deal?

Could be, if the latest type, deepest-structure syntactician can figure out why so many Americans feel the need to insert *of a* into their sentences before nouns.

Wait; why didn't I follow the "latest type" in the preceding sentence with the words *of a*? Let's try another locution like that: when I asked the Russian politician Gen. Aleksandr Lebed when he employed the rejected Yeltsin confidant Aleksandr V. Korzhakov as his adviser, he narrowed his eyes and countered with a growl that was interpreted as "What kind adviser?"

That dropping of the *of a* sounds like English as spoken by a non-native speaker, and is often imitated by those who pick up cadences from parents whose first language was learned in Central or Eastern Europe.

There's poetic justice in English: for every expected *of a* dropped after *type* or *kind*, another *of a* is being inserted unnecessarily before a noun. Strange. Gives the language an "editor's look."

Of Galoots and Flaps

"The grilling of a useful *Galoot*" is how *Newsweek* headlined a column about Craig Livingstone, the former bar bouncer in charge of personnel security at the Clinton White House and the man responsible for the flap-caper-affair-scandal (choose one) that permitted nearly a thousand confidential FBI files to be examined by White House political operatives. "It was a moment," wrote Joe Klein, breaking new ground with the old slang noun, "when *galootery* had leverage."

A *galoot* is always big. "We can't resist the urge," wrote the *Boston Herald* about a Georgia Tech basketball star, "to make the big *galoot* happy." In 1978, the *Washington Post* television critic Tom Shales wrote of the "exposure of the big *galoot's* hairy chest." Andrew Heller wrote in the *St. Petersburg Times* in 1992 of a large dog that was "a slobbering, oafish, utterly lovable *galoot*."

Although the *Random House Historical Dictionary of American Slang* defines the word as "a person, usually a man, who is clumsy, unpleasant, stupid or the like," the above citations show that the word can also connote "an amiable bumbler," which is the way the White House hopes its Mr. Livingstone will be seen.

The word is defined as "a soldier" in J. H. Vaux's 1812 *Flash Language*. Used by Artemus Ward and Mark Twain, *galoot* became associated with raw recruits in the Army and the Marines; the 1867 *Sailor's Word-Book* defines it as "an awkward soldier . . . a sobriquet for the young or 'green' marine." This is a stretch, but it may be rooted in Krio, the creole of Sierra Leone, which defines *galut* as "a hefty person."

Are the *galoots* who brought us Filegate, as lazy writers automatically slugged it, involved in a *flap*, a *caper* or a *scandal*?

A *flap* originated in World War I as British aviators' slang for "air raid"; perhaps influenced by the earlier *flapdoodle*, "nonsense," it came to mean "minor crisis," with an overtone of "much ado about nothing"; a 1925 dictionary defines *flap* as "the familiar Navy term for the sudden 'liveliness' on board ship on the arrival of an emergency order involving general activity at extreme high pressure." Just as the Nixon White House initially dismissed the Watergate burglary as a *caper*, with its connotation of "madcap misdemeanor," the Clinton White House and some in the media preferred to disparage the reaction to the handling of the files as a *flap*.

Now to the first really thorough synonymy of political ruckuses:

A *flap*, etymology above, is the least important and most transient.

A *caper* (from the Italian-based *capriole*, "a playful gambol") connotes mischief but not sustained wrongdoing.

A *brouhaha* (probably from the Hebrew *baruch habba*, "blessed be he who enters," prelude to a noisy entrance) now means "minor uproar."

A *sleaze attack* (from the derogation of shoddy material made in Silesia) is an atmosphere or series of actions in which ethical transgressions short of crimes are committed.

Matter and *affair* are neutral characterizations made while the nature of the suspicious actions are being investigated.

Finally, *scandal* (from the Greek *skandalon*, "a trap with a springing device") is a series of crimes committed by people in public office and, when followed by multiple prosecutions, is usually modified by the compound adjective *full-blown*.

Those of us who are ready to apply the term *scandal* to fishy dealings and inexplicable cover-ups can take a lesson from the etymology of the word. The Greek word was adopted by Latin as *scandalum*, "the cause of stumbling," which led to the Old French *escandle*, and ultimately to the French *scandale*. But a variant of the Old French *escandle* was *esclandre*, meaning "a scandalous saying or report." That was the root of *slander*, "malicious utterance intending to defame." The two words are still entwined; one man's *scandal* is another man's *slander*.

Of Hacks and TK

Reader-friendly novelists whose characters wander through arcane worlds are now adding a new element to their work: glossaries, defining words not in most readers' vocabularies or available in standard dictionaries.

"Hackspeak: A Glossary" is right up front in the novel *Hacks* by Christopher S. Wren, a member of the foreign staff of the *New York Times* who uses his middle initial to avoid confusion with the architect of St. Paul's Cathedral. He refers to the argot of the *hack*, the foreign correspondent, which is Mr. Wren's occupation when filing dispatches for the *New York Times* in the daytime. It is a refinement of *hack writer*, or "literary drudge," derived from *hackney horses*, the worn-out equines that drew carriages along the cobblestone streets of London.

The *hack* that led to "journeyman writer" and now to "itinerant journalist" is not the same as *hacker;* that modern word for "cyberobber" comes from the verb *to hack*, meaning "to chop or cut crudely," which led to the sense of "to do a successful job," as in "That fellow can really hack it." Computer *hackers* are good at what they do until they get caught, while foreign correspondent *hacks* are ejected from totalitarian states when they are doing a good job.

A *ceasefile*, according to Wren, is an "agreement among reporters on a story not to file competitively," similar to, though more nefarious than, a *lid*, a press secretary's assurance that no news will be forthcoming for a specified time.

Fuzz and wuzz is "urban police reporting," with *fuzz* from "police" and *wuzz*, a spelling variant of the past tense of the verb for a state of being, referring to corpses; this usage was popularized among reporters by Dan Rather of CBS.

Another rhyme is *run and gun*, which Wren defines as "news coverage of homicides, fires, car crashes and other daily mayhem," recalling the TV assignment editors' credo, "If it bleeds, it leads." *To run in* has had a meaning of "to arrest" since World War I, and *gun* as a verb has a meaning of "to shoot." The combination of *run-and-gun*, hyphenated, may have begun in basketball, where it means to play aggressively, to run at the basket and shoot.

Not in the glossary, but recognizable to members of the trade, is the novelistic hero's name, T. K. Farrow. The initials *TK*, as the copy editor of this column knows all too well, are used without periods for "to come," with the "come" laid down in a way—"kum"—to meet the approval of a spelling reformist who never puts the story in the lede. Whenever I have a hot hand—that is, writing with easy passion and at high speed—I hate to stop and look up a fact, preferring to put in *TK*, thereby promising the editor to supply the missing item later. (Sometimes I forget, and the researcher and copy editor don't catch it, and we all look like jerks.)

A *mushroom journalist* is defined as a "reporter assigned to hard, thankless stories." This delicately put definition is rooted in British stock-market lingo for a trader who appears spasmodically on the floor and is liable to make mistakes. Paul Beale, in his *Concise Dictionary of Slang*, published in 1989, noted the U.S. T-shirt usage in the 1970s: "I feel like a mushroom: everybody keeps me in the dark and is always feeding me [barnyard epithet]."

A *rocket* is the bane of a foreign correspondent's existence: "a message from editors alerting a reporter to a competitor's story." Whether this is caused by the other guy's enterprise or by his dirty betrayal of a *ceasefile*, the *rocket* from home necessitates what journalists call a *catchup* or *matcher* or *follow*, usually spelled "folo."

A *laptop* is denoted as a "portable computer." That's obvious enough, but I note it here to illustrate a difference between makers and users. Five years ago, a 12-pound computer was called a *laptop*, to differentiate it from a *desktop*. (Both are adjectives that have become nouns.) When the six-pounders were introduced to save a whole generation of humans from lopsidedness, the manufacturers called their product *notebook computers*, with their even smaller and lighter cousins, *subnotebooks*. But persnickety journalists tend to resist official nomenclature, and today's six-pounders are called *laptops* as in olden days, and the little ones are called *the little ones*.

Wren defines *suit* as a "senior news executive, especially one without field experience." I don't want to be a lexicographical bigfoot (that's a media biggie who treads on the toes of local correspondents), but the gentle definition leaves out some of the scorn felt by reporters for the consultants and top brass who think journalism not merely a noble calling but a business that should turn a profit.

This is a natural segue (a noun based on a verb in music for "to follow immediately," but in the news business, especially in radio, "to use a word or related theme as a smooth transition to another topic") to a novel by William Hood, a veteran operative for the C.I.A. and its predecessor, the Office of Strategic Services, titled *The Sunday Spy*. The author includes espionage argot that cries out for a glossary.

A *suit*, in spies' lingo, is a *P.C.*—not "politically correct," but a military intelligence officer in "Plain Clothes," not in uniform. I would speculate that the underworld use of *suits* to sneer at plainclothes detectives is the basis of the pejorative connotation of the term.

A *treff* is a "contact," its derivation unexplained in the text. A call to Mr. Hood, who is no longer under cover, reveals that the slang noun's origin is in the German verb *treffen*, "to meet."

A *wafflebottom* is defined in Hood's novel as O.S.S. slang for a communications engineer, and the term gradually broadened to any intelligence officer involved in technical work; the C.I.A. usage now includes "specially cleared personnel who deal with codes and ciphers." It is rooted in the imprinting of a chair on the seat of its occupant, and was first recorded in espionage use in TK.

Your column begins by noting that "Reader-friendly novelists whose characters wander through arcane worlds are now adding a new element to their work: glossaries. . . ."

Actually, the practice isn't new, especially in foreign editions. With the baseball playoffs in full throttle, it's especially timely to cite these two examples: *The Natural* by Bernard Malamud (London: Eyre & Spottiswoode, 1963) ("Some notes on the game of baseball," pp. 239–48); *The Universal Baseball Association Inc. J. Henry Waugh, Prop.* by Robert Coover (London: Rupert HartDavis Ltd., 1970) ("Glossary," pp. 247–62).

Each of these classics of baseball fiction by American novelists contains a glossary of baseball terms for English readers unfamiliar with baseball lingo.

The use of glossaries in these two critically acclaimed mainstream novels was, you might say, a defining moment in the practice.

Richard Dannay
New York, New York

You derive "hacker" from the "hack" use meaning "to do a successful job," and say that computer hackers "are good at what they do until they get caught." However, for years, in personal-computer circles, a hacker has been someone who likes computers so much that he keeps hacking (chopping away, continuing) for hours at a time. From that, it came to mean someone who is good with computers, probably because those are the people who keep on hacking.

Then, when a hacker used his skills illegally, a reporter correctly said a hacker had done it. But reporters only mentioned hackers when they'd committed crimes, so now, to the news people at least, the word means, as you said, "cyberobber." However, at least among some computer people, it retains its original meaning.

It's as though a reporter was caught lying (imagine!), and people talked about the lie by a reporter, then about lies by other reporters, until "reporter" lost its original meaning and came to mean simply, "liar."

J. A. Coffeen
Houston, Texas

You described the abbreviation "TK," indicating matter to come in a manuscript. A similar device is used in Hollywood, in early drafts of scripts, to indicate missing dialogue: "DTC" or, more hopefully, "JTC," for "joke to come," which use usually occurs after a cast read-through of a sitcom's first draft has failed to produce the looked-for yuks.

Similarly, early versions of *Star Trek* scripts use "tech" as a stand-in for some yet-to-be-imagined alien wizardry, as in "Captain, they're using some sort of (TECH) to nebulize our ion deflectors!"

Gerrit Graham
Rhinebeck, New York

You wrote that "the modern term for 'cyberobber' comes from the verb *to hack*, meaning 'to chop or cut crudely,' which led to the sense of 'to do a successful job,' as in 'That fellow can really hack it.' Computer *hackers* are good at what they do until they get caught, while foreign correspondent *hacks* are ejected from totalitarian states when they are doing a good job."

The line is clever, but incorrect. The locution was originally used in recognition of computer programming wizardry—with connotations of ingenuity and elegance, not simple brute force. The term is still used in that way by many in the high-tech community.

In writing the book *Hackers,* which chronicles the origins of the technology tribe, Steven Levy traced this usage to the Massachusetts Institute of Technology's Tech Model Railroad Club. The model railroaders there used the term "hacking" to refer to their elaborate work or the electronics underneath the "board" that held the impressive train layout. When the TMRC students obtained access to a computer in the late fifties, they transferred the term to their pioneering explorations in interactive programming, and called themselves hackers. From this, the term spread.

Although no one seems to know when the railroaders first used the term, it seems certain that besides (or instead of) the oft-repeated "to improve with an ax" derivation, the usage owes to a particular use of the word at MIT. For decades, the work "hack" was synonomous with the Institute's famously flamboyant student pranks, such as covering the Institute's signature dome on Massachusetts Avenue with tinfoil.

Certainly the word "hackers" has acquired darker connotations over the years. But its origins are brighter, and better, and deserve to be noted and preserved.

John Schwartz, Steven Levy, and Mike Godwin
The Washington Post
Washington, D.C.

Of Mainstreams and Movements

"This is a race between the *mainstream* and the extreme," declared Senator Bob Dole, drawing the battle lines after his New Hampshire defeat by Pat Buchanan. That choice of words has reverberated through recent political history.

At the 1964 Republican convention in San Francisco's Cow Palace, the outnumbered and humiliated Rockefeller-Scranton "moderates" hauled a 30-foot banner emblazoned with "Stay in the Mainstream" across the floor, to the derision of the Goldwater delegates. When the nominee, Barry Goldwater,*

---

*Barry Goldwater died on May 29, 1998.

cried, "Extremism in the defense of liberty is no vice!" he stimulated a roar of enthusiastic approval from what was being called "the Goldwater movement." But observing from a box, the neutral Richard Nixon sat on his hands, telling friends later that Goldwater's choice of words guaranteed the landslide victory of Lyndon Johnson, which led to the Democrats' Great Society.

At the time, I thought that the political use of *mainstream* was a Rockefeller coinage. In fact, President Kennedy had told the Irish Parliament in 1963 that "Ireland is moving in the *mainstream* of current world events"; a month later, a Rockefeller speech writer, Hugh Morrow, fashioned a blast at "vociferous and well-drilled extremist elements boring within the party" that were "wholly alien to the broad middle course that accommodates the *mainstream* of Republican principle."

After the GOP paradise was lost, it turned out that the actual coiner was John Milton: "The neather Flood," he wrote about the fall of the angels in his 1667 poem, ". . . now divided into four *main Streames.*" Thomas Carlyle picked up the term in 1831, holding that "the Didactic Tendency . . . still forms the *main stream,*" and in 1865 the critic Matthew Arnold hailed Byron and Shelley for their "Titanic effort to flow in the *main stream* of modern literature." A century later, the word was popularized by jazz writers: "Humph"—a bandleader known by a single name—"is authentic *mainstreamer,*" wrote *The New Left Review* in 1961. "He's been influenced by everything in jazz up to the moment."

Mainstream gained a positive connotation in politics after the Goldwater debacle, though *moderate,* a seeming synonym, was considered by many to be a euphemism for "liberal." *Extremism* became pejorative again (despite its ringing defense by the Rev. Dr. Martin Luther King Jr.), and was embraced by President Bill Clinton to hammer at newly elected Republican Representatives in Congress who wanted a balanced budget on terms other than his.

Because of this use by Democrats, and notwithstanding the rhyming endings of *mainstream* and *extreme,* the Dole attack on Buchanan using that Goldwater-blessed word drew a tut-tut from Ralph Reed of the Christian Coalition: "It is strategically unwise and politically shortsighted to label Buchanan or his supporters as, *ipso facto,* extremists or intolerant," he said. "That is the language of the left." (*Ipso facto* is the language of Latin and means literally "by the fact itself," its extended meaning "as an inevitable result.") Dole then turned to derogating Buchanan as a *fringe candidate,* one that could be defined as "on the margin," but that evokes memories of Theodore Roosevelt's classic 1913 pop at ardent reformers as a *lunatic fringe.*

Mr. Buchanan's political language has ranged from the subtle to the mysterious. One use is, at least to me, obscure: when the candidate Steve Forbes complained of attacks by opponents he had long been lambasting in TV commercials, Buchanan said, "What's happened is the little rich kid, who's been sitting on his estate throwing rocks at all the cars passing by, finally had someone get out of the car and clock him one." *Clock him one?* This may be a variant of *bop him one* or a reference to *clean his clock.*

In the past, I have heard my former colleague in the speech dodge refer to himself as a *movement conservative,* meaning the Goldwater "movement" in contrast to traditional conservatives or neoconservatives. Lately, he has applied this word to his followers: "Listen, we have a great movement here. And if you bring Pat Buchanan's movement together with the Republican Party, we have a majority." That suggests his movement is separate from, and addable to or subtractable from, the GOP, holding out the threat of a bolt (a horseracing term).

It also offers an example of the vogue of third-person reference now gripping the Republican field. Nobody says *I* or *me* anymore; candidates call themselves by their proper names. Walter Bingham of Truro, Mass., wrote the *New York Times* about third-personalities: "Imagine if our country's leaders over the years had done the same: 'Give Patrick Henry liberty or give Patrick Henry death.' Or 'Douglas MacArthur shall return.' "

The most subtle use of a Nixon-era phrase was Buchanan's "Watch what we do"; this is taken from the comment of John Mitchell, Nixon's Attorney General, who answered a question about integration policy with "Watch what we do, not what we say." This was taken at the time to be evidence of hypocrisy, but later was understood as shorthand for strictly enforcing integration while publicly expressing sympathy for those opposing it.

Meanwhile, Lamar Alexander, who rejected "the Buchanan movement" and labeled its philosophy of "the wrong ideas" *Buchananism* (evoking *McCarthyism*), turned derisive fire on the best-financed candidate: he described Steve Forbes's proposal for a flat, or nonprogressive, tax as "a *nutty* idea."

"*Nutty* it's not," editorialized the *Wall Street Journal.* Milton Friedman, the Nobel-winning economist, said, "Far from being a *nutty* idea, the flat tax has a long pedigree—back to tithing for the church." Prof. David Bradford of Princeton weighed in with "*Nutty* is the word to apply to the existing income tax." Paul Craig Roberts insisted, "It is a *nutty* idea only to people opposed to American success." But the dismal scientists are not running for office; many political realists agreed with Alexander's use.

The human head is shaped like, and is hard as, a nut. "She meets with a spoony that's *nutty,*" went an English ballad collected in 1799; the meaning was "crazy with love." A century later, according to Jesse Sheidlower, formerly of Random House, the spooniness gave way to plain looniness in a book about New York's Chinatown: "He was either *nutty* or 'off his feed.' " In the mid-1930s, the simile *nutty as a fruitcake* appeared, and was used by a visitor to Al Capone in prison to sadly describe the gangster's mental decline.

Today, *nutty* is not as wild as "crazy," not as condemnatory as "foolish," not as formal or limited to the wealthy as "eccentric." Its precise synonym, which threatened to replace it until the word was rescued by anti-flat-taxers, is *wacky*.

Wonderful! I should have guessed that "mainstream," as we use it, was not more than thirty-forty years old. And here is the famous Republican, Matthew Arnold, rejoicing that Byron and Shelley "flow in the main stream (two words, I see—still) of modern literature."

I'm sorry you want more "ly"s, and I less. I shall go on wincing when a waiter asks—"Did you, sir, order the softly scrambled eggs?" No, no, no.

"Humph"—a bandleader "known by a single name." Not so. A familiar nickname to his friends. But even his concerts were advertised—"Humphrey Lyttelton and His Band." A nice chap but much deplored—on account of his profession—by his father, the George Lyttelton (Eton master and favorite correspondent of Rupert Hart-Davis—you surely have all six volumes of their Letters. If not, acquire and absorb!)

Alistair [Cooke]
New York, New York

Of Nutsiness and Madness

"An offensive *nutsy* streak" was attributed to a House historian by Barney Frank, a Representative from Massachusetts. A few days later, Speaker Newt Gingrich, taking back a proposal he had made for a laptop computer tax break, derogated his own brainchild as "a *nutsy* idea."

Mark Migotti, a lecturer in philosophy at Texas A & M University, notes, "Representative Frank's use makes nutsiness something sinister and troubling, while Speaker Gingrich's is clearly meant to render his self-criticism innocuous rather than harsh." The philosopher seeks current usage, etymology and relative popularity of *nutsy* and *nutty*.

One of the many meanings of *nut* is "head," of similar shape; to be "off one's nut" was used in 1891 to mean "to be out of one's mind." *Nutty* first appeared in an 1898 *Cosmopolitan* short story by Stephen Crane; *nutsy* made its debut in 1923, in a song lyric by Billy Rose and Mort Dixon, "*Nutsey* Fagan"; the *e* was soon dropped and now *nutsy*, the variant, is making a bid to replace *nutty*, at least among members of Congress.

How harsh is it? Note that Representative Frank needed a modifier, "offensive," to give *nutsy* a mean streak. In the 1930s, an associate of Al Capone visited the mentally deteriorating gangster in a Federal prison and reported, "Al's as *nutty* as a fruitcake"; a certain breeziness or sassiness attaches to the word, making it less severe than *insane* or *deranged.*

Which brings us to a serious point: in an age when sensitivity to slurs has been heightened, triggering a reaction parodying the sensitivity (bald people are *follically challenged*), should we think twice before using such terms as *nutty* and *loony bin* (from *lunatic*) and *wacko* (from *wack on the head,* via *wacky*)? Is *funny farm* funny to the funny farmers?

Kay Redfield Jamison, a world authority on manic depression, addresses that delicate subject in the memoir *An Unquiet Mind: A Memoir of Moods and Madness.* In the most emotionally moving book I've ever read about the emotions, one that deserves its best-sellerdom, the Johns Hopkins professor of psychiatry reveals her own genetic inheritance of the disease, as well as how she copes with it and is able to treat patients and teach other scientists.

One chapter is titled "Speaking of Madness." Professor Jamison poses the question: "Should expressive, often humorous, language—phrases such as *taking the fast trip to Squirrel City,* being a *few apples short of a picnic, off the wall, around the bend* or *losing the bubble* (a British submariner's term for madness)—be held hostage to the fads and fashions of 'correct' or 'acceptable' language?"

I would add such phrases imputing daftness, or daffiness, as *out to lunch, not all there* and one whose *oars are not both in the water* and whose *belt does not go through all the loops.*

"The pain of hearing these words, in the wrong context or the wrong tone," writes Professor Jamison, "is sharp; the memory of insensitivity and prejudice lasts for a long time. . . . On the other hand, the assumption that rigidly rejecting words and phrases that have existed for centuries will have much impact on public attitudes is rather dubious."

Context as well as emphasis is the key; Dr. Jamison notes "the powerful role of wit and irony as positive agents of self-notion and social change. Clearly there is a need for freedom, diversity, wit and directness of language about abnormal mental states and behavior."

It's cruel to call a mental patient a *nut,* but it's crackbrained to try to ban words like *nuttiness* from everyday discourse. And just as the well adjusted should refrain from directing dysphemisms toward the ill, professionals should avoid euphemisms in talking to all of us. The authoritative *Diagnostic and Statistical Manual* now uses *bipolar disorder* instead of *manic depression.*

"I find the word *bipolar* strangely and powerfully offensive," writes this remarkable patient-professor. "The description *manic-depressive* seems to me to capture both the nature and the seriousness of the disease I have, rather than attempting to paper over the reality of the condition."

Anent earlier use of "nutsy," my first recollection of it dates from the 1930s. It was used by the comedy team of Olsen and Johnson, which appeared on radio (and no doubt in vaudeville), in their theme song "Nutsy Olsen, Nutsy Johnson"—which I have enclosed with as much of the text as I can recall.

> Nut- sy Ol- sen, nut- sy John-son, They're the ones for me,
> Nut-sy Ol- sen, nut- sy John-son, Live up in a tree,
> Nut-sy Ol-sen, nut- sy John-son, They're the ones for me!

Carl Bowman
New York, New York

I would like to bring to your attention a couple of other humorous phrases I've heard to describe a person who is off their nut:

> "He's out there where the buses don't run."
> "The cheese fell off his cracker a long time ago."

Nina Garfinkel
New York, New York

OFL Truth: At This Point in Time Line

"Time Line for State Dinner" is the title on the fax transmittal cover sheet from the Office of the First Lady. (You did not know there was such an office? You thought it was still the East Wing? Regards to Rip Van Winkle.)

The next page to come whistling through was headed "The following is a tentative time line/schedule of press coverage for the White House State Dinner."

Time out. What is a *time line*? How does it compare to a *time frame*? How is it different from a *schedule*?

I shot these questions over to Michael McCurry, the President's press secretary, who—in fine bureaucratic fashion—solicited a response from an aide at OFL (you now know what office that is), perpetrator of the new term.

"Subject: Derivation of Timeline," OFL reported. "The First Lady's press office began using the term *timeline* in 1993, after the first state dinner hosted by the

Clinton Administration. The timeline is released for press planning purposes so that media organizations know what time to anticipate certain events."

That tells us that the term is to be written as a single word, *timeline*, and not two words as used in OFL press transmissions. Now to the difference between this new term and the old *schedule*, from the Greek *schida*, "split piece of wood" on which notes could be made, used in English with its modern sense and spelling in a 1560 letter by Queen Elizabeth: "We will that you shall from time to time address several Schedules."

OFL denotes: "The *timeline* refers to the sequence of events preceding and during a state dinner. A *schedule* refers to the activities of the principals (i.e., Potus, Flotus, etc.)." (*Potus* is the acronym for the initials of President of the United States; *Flotus* is for First Lady of the United States. The names of the individuals are too sacred to be used by reverent staff aides. The letters *i.e.* stand for the Latin *id est*, "that is (to say)"; what the press aide intended was *e.g.*, Latin for *exempli gratia*, "for example.")

In passing this along to me, Mr. McCurry—anticipating incoming flak— mused, "Reserving *schedule* for principals seems a little discriminatory maybe?" The word I would have chosen is *pompous*. Taking the edge off the lurch toward royalism, he said with suitable self-deprecation, "I'll worry about that on my own timeline since I can't keep a schedule anyhow."

New words find a welcome in this space, *e.g.*, the term *time frame*, which is more specific than "period." But words created by bureaucrats to raise their "principals" a cut above the ordinary folk are unnecessary and, worse, invite ridicule. Do the people in OFL (there's an acronym I'd take pains to avoid) understand the antidemocratic thrust of their coinage? For that matter, did anybody think of the meaning of *offal* when titling the Office of the First Lady?

The last time anything like that happened was in the transition to the Carter Administration. In the Nixon-Ford era, studies by the National Security Council staff were called National Security Study Memorandums, or NSSM, pronounced "nissem." To show a difference, the new staff under Zbigniew Brzezinski changed the nomenclature to Presidential Study Memorandums for about 10 minutes, until somebody pronounced the acronym, at which point another formulation was found.

Your column regarding "OFL" and its hazardous pronunciations brought to mind a story told to me by Forrest Pogue, George Marshall's biographer, about the need to choose code names carefully.

When General Pershing first landed in France in 1917, the initial code name for his headquarters was MASTERBASE. It did not take long for everyone to appreciate the need for a different name.

Mark M. Lowenthal
Washington, D.C.

The *etc.* in *(i.e., Potus, Flotus, etc.)* matters. Without it, *i.e.* should be *e.g.* as you say. But when the list ends with *etc.*, the list is complete. 'Potus, Flotus and the rest' seems correctly to call for *i.e.*

Lawrence Brown
Boulder, Colorado

Unlike a *schedule*, a *timeline* shows a sequence of events when many of the events are taking place simultaneously. The only reason it is used for "ordinary folk" is that, being a multitude, only they can be attending many events simultaneously—some at this event, some at that.

Writers recognize, and utilize, the difference between the *timeline* of events and the *schedule* of the principals. For example, on the jacket of Rod Paschall's book, *Witness to War: Korea,* published in 1995, the publisher says the book "provides the story of the war in the words of those who fought it"; at the same time, it provides "a *timeline* of events." The *timeline* here is an ongoing series of announcements the author uses at the foots of his pages. The announcement tells us what the public was hearing in Korean War news while the text above it tells us what the principal characters were doing at that time.

David Forrest Weinstein
Hicksville, NY

On Bull

In a *New Yorker* interview with Henry Louis Gates Jr., a Harvard professor and leading black intellectual, the author and erstwhile Presidential candidate Colin Powell noted that "Safire drives me to distraction." The reason was the suggestion in my political column, a suggestion repeated for years, that air power could have a decisive effect on stopping Serbian aggression in Bosnia. Just before NATO bombers did have such an effect, General Powell was characterizing my suggestion to Professor Gates with what is usually described as a "barnyard epithet."

The New Yorker, which has adopted more permissive standards on the use of obscenity and scatology than are used in the *New York Times,* quoted General Powell's use of the term forthrightly. The word, formally defined as "the excrement of a male bovine animal," is familiar to every American, and is more often used in playgrounds than in barnyards. Though not spoken in "polite company," and not acceptable on broadcast television, the compound noun has lost much of its shock value. Why?

One reason is that the first part of the word, *bull,* is stressed; in most uses, the scatological part is de-emphasized. A more important reason for its nonacceptable acceptability is that the literal meaning of the term has been superseded by its figurative meaning, "outrageously untrue." The literal meaning is lost in the current sense of "balderdash"; it is the emphatic synonym of "baloney."

The etymology available to date suggests the expletive is relatively recent. (An *expletive* is an interjected oath or obscenity, as in "every damn time." An *epithet,* which once was a compliment used to modify or replace a name— "Richard the Lion-Hearted"—is now a disparaging word, as in "Joe the Chicken-Hearted." A *barnyard epithet* is "I felt like a horse's [expletive].")

Although *bulling* was used to mean "idly chatting" as far back as 1850 (and *bull sessions,* in that sense, was used in a letter by the novelist Thomas Wolfe in 1920), the first use that can be found of the specific term used by General Powell to characterize my Bosnia suggestion as nonsense was in a 1914 letter from the poet Ezra Pound to the novelist James Joyce: "I enclose a prize sample of [the subject of this item]." Another eminent poet, e.e. cummings, defined the word in a 1918 letter as "a forte and accurate expression-du-peuple." According to the *Random House Historical Dictionary of American Slang,* edited by J. E. Lighter, this literary lions' term was also used in a 1935 letter from Ernest Hemingway, who had an interest in bullfights and all that was left in the arena.

In Jim Lehrer's novel *The Last Debate,* a Presidency hinges on a somewhat more severe obscenity uttered during the course of a televised debate. This raises the issue: Can candidates get away with the public use of words that so many of us use in private so often? Not easily, I think, and especially not during espousal of family values.

Even as barriers fall and the use of profanities and obscenities in films and magazines abounds, the bar is being raised to public saltiness in political figures. Richard Nixon made a point of not cussing in public, a position of near-prissiness that was made to seem hypocritical by the publication of transcripts of his private profanity. The expectation of privacy was further eroded when George Bush was overheard by microphone and gleefully reported to have used "kick a little ass" after a debate. Presumably General Powell was being jocular and spoke in the expectation that his epithet would not be quoted; he knows better now, and is unlikely to use such a term when speaking on the record or near an open microphone.

I vote for a tolerance of saltiness in private and for an adherence to rhetorical rectitude in public. A remark made among friends is not to be judged by the same linguistic standard as a quotation from an interview or a speech. Bess Truman, in a story perhaps apocryphal, was asked by a shocked reporter how she felt about her husband Harry's use of the term "horse manure" to characterize his opponents' views; she was reported to have replied, "You don't know how many years it took me to tone it down to that!"

Your little *essay* on *bull* reminded me of my own researches in the 70s. What is most remarkable about *bullshit* is that is used more often, I suspect, to admire than to disapprove. When some speech or writing strikes us as utter nonsense or incompetence, we tend to call it *horseshit*. In contrast, *bullshit* refers to examples of cunning deception: bluffs, skillful equivocations, spin . . . There are *bullshit* artists, but no *horseshit* artists. Indeed, once a client offered me a substantial sum to "add about ten pages of bullshit" to a proposal he was writing.

In the minds of many people, *bullshit* is precisely that mixture of exaggeration, trickery, and audience-flattery that Plato characterized as "rhetoric" in the *Gorgias* dialogue. Indeed, those of us to who teach writing and speaking often encounter the expectation that good business communication is lying with impunity—*bullshit*. (We do what we can to revise that expectation.)

Edmond H. Weiss, Ph.D.
Cherry Hill, New Jersey

On Purpose

In an altercation between the White House and the independent counsel about obtaining lawyers' notes, David Kendall, a lawyer for President Clinton, said that the prosecutor had "*purposefully* manufactured" the battle.

Did he mean *purposefully*, which means "determinedly; with unmistakable intent," frequently spoken admiringly? Or did he mean *purposely*, which has a slightly different meaning, "by design, intentionally," often spoken in criticism?

The two similar words have meanings that sometimes overlap; Mr. Kendall, writing in 1994 in the *Toronto Sun*, quoted a tax official saying, "We will insure the majority of Canadians don't suffer because of those who *purposefully* evade and cheat." But there is this nice nuance: *Purposely* means "*with* purpose," and is often used to describe a stride; *purposefully* means "*on purpose*," and often criticizes an action that cannot be excused as an accident.

Did the President's lawyer, who is known to be a careful user of words, inadvertently praise his adversary? We have a lot to learn about this case.

"I am not prepared to see the party I care for laid out on the rack like this any longer," said former British Prime Minister John Major, using a metaphor of torture to describe the internecine warfare going on in the Conservative Party. "In short, it is time to *put up or shut up*."

Only a few days before, Christopher Darden, a prosecutor in the O. J. Simpson trial, issued a challenge to the defense's lead attorney, Johnnie Cochran Jr.: "You've been mouthing off for the past 12 months. . . . Now is the time to *put up or shut up*."

Five years before that, the *Sunday Times of London* reported tension within the Conservative Party in these terms: "Michael Heseltine, stung by Thatcherite taunts that he should '*put up or shut up*,' appears ready to emulate Thatcher's gamble when she challenged Edward Heath in 1975."

This is a phrase that rings through the English-speaking world. In French, *Je n'y comperais pas trop!* challenges, "I wouldn't bet on it!" Spanish uses *Apuesto lo que quieras!* for "I'll bet you anything you like!" Yiddish ends up being the most forceful with *tokhes afn tish*, meaning "buttocks on the table!" Sol Steinmetz, retired from Random House, explains, "That figurative saying derives from card players' usage. The approximate equivalent of 'put up or shut up' in Yiddish is *riba fish, gelt afn tish* (meaning literally '*riba* means fish, money on the table!'), obviously a phrase coined in such a way that it would rhyme. The vulgar variant of the preceding is *riba fish, tokhes afn tish!* (literally, '*riba* means fish, bottom on the table!')."

Mr. Major may be the popularizer of *put up or shut up*, but the not-quite-rhyming phrase is closely associated with him this year. (*Put* is not pronounced *putt*, to rhyme with *shut*; instead, *put* and *shut* are an example of "eye rhyme," an 1871 term from poetry for words that look as if they should rhyme based on their spelling, like *tough* and *cough*. Since these verbs do not rhyme but start with different consonant sounds, "put up or shut up" has consonance—repeated consonant sounds—not alliteration.)

"Yeltsin responded to all complaints," wrote *Newsweek* a few weeks ago, "with what might be called the John Major gambit: like the embattled British Prime Minister, he told his critics to *put up or shut up*." (A *gambit* is an opening move in chess; the word the news magazine had in mind was *ploy*, a stratagem or trick.)

Put up has a rich variety of meanings. A swordsman with second thoughts can *put up*, or sheathe, his sword; contrariwise, a street fighter can *put up* his dukes, or fists; a frugal or inspired cook can *put up* a great jar of marmalade; a hunter can *put up*, or start, game for cover, and you can *put up* a building, a struggle, a candidate or a prize, or fall prey to a *put-up* job.

Mark Twain used it in a gambling sense in 1865: "And so the feller . . . *put* up his forty dollars along with Smiley's." Apparently that phrase was soon matched with an exclamatory imperative—*shut up*—which had come into the langauge in 1814, and both were initialized: "'P.U. or S.U.' means *put up or shut up*, doesn't it?" wrote Fred H. Hart in his 1878 *Sazerac Lying Club: A Nevada Book.* In his 1889 *Connecticut Yankee in King Arthur's Court,* Twain picked it up: "This was a plain case of *'put up, or shut up.'"*

The etymological mystery is this: What is being put up? "If it's fighting, it's fists," responds Fred Cassidy, chief editor of the *Dictionary of American Regional English (DARE).* "If it's card playing, it's money for the bet."

The poker origins were recalled in a 1981 usage by the fight promoter Don King, who held a press conference in Las Vegas to warn a challenger against delaying a date with the heavyweight champion: "It can't go no farther than this week. They've got to *put up or shut up.* Call or pass."

"Put 'em up" is a frequent invitation to fisticuffs. "In any case," says Professor Cassidy, "a bluff is being called: some tangible evidence must be shown that the challenge or charge is serious. Despite omission from the *Dictionary of Americanisms,* it seems clearly to be an Americanism."

I say it's most likely from cards, putting up money (not fists) in response to a bluff in a poker game. If you disagree and have a citation to back up your view, your course is clear.

One puts up one's "dukes" when challenged to fisticuffs. "Dukes" derives from ducat, a medieval European gold or silver coin frequently wagered on the outcome of hand-to-hand combative events: "Put up your ducats" soon became "put up your dukes . . ." But surely I joust.

Shakespeare is instructive: one is challenged to put up one's sword or dagger in at least seven plays (i.e., Antonio in *Twelfth Night,* III.iv; Benvolio in *Romeo and Juliet,* I.i; Casca in *Julius Caesar,* I.iii; Lady Anne in *Richard III,* I.ii; Hostess in *Henry V,* II.i; Mistress Quickly in 2 *Henry IV,* II.iv [put up your naked weapons]; and Bastard in *King John,* IV.iii).

Yet Timon of Athens advises Alcibiades to "put up thy gold" at IV,iii; Gloucester asks Edmund in *King Lear* "why so earnestly seek you to put up that letter?"; Lady MacDuff inquires (of no one in particular) "do I put up that womanly defence to say that I have done no harm?" (*Macbeth,* IV.ii); and Cardinal Beaufort accuses cousin Gloucester of cheating in 2 *Henry VI* (II.iv): "Had not your man put up the fowl so suddenly, we had had more sport."

Put up's line of origin between fighting and gambling is ultimately blurred by the Bard in Henry V (II.i):

> Hostess: Good Corporal Nym, show thy valour, and put up thy sword.
>
> Bardolph: Corporal Nym, an thou wilt be friends, an thou wilt not, why then, be enemies with me too. Prithee, put up.
>
> Nym: I shall have my eight shillings I won of you at betting.
> I think it best I now shut up.

Edward R. Curtin
New York, New York

Don King and you have a tin ear for poker terminology and logic. The phrase should be: ". . . put up or shut up. Call or fold." Not "call or pass." Once another player has bet, you can only call or raise or fold, not pass. When there is not another bet in, you can bid or pass. You can never "call or pass."

Thomas R. Moore
New York, New York

Palindromedaries

A palindrome, as word mavens know, is a word or phrase that runs the same backward; our hero is the late Burmese statesman U Nu. The key to *palindrome* is in the Greek root *dromos*, "running"; a *dromedary* is a "running camel" with a single hump. With *dromos* married to *palin*, "again, back," the word means "running back and forth," like a *palindrome*.

Every year, somebody comes out with a collection of them that hooks me. This year's is by Craig Hansen, from Plume Books, titled *Ana, Nab a Banana*, where the *taco cat* pursues *sleek eels*.

In the world of palindromes, dieters are known as *dessert stressed*, and a sharp-tongued offspring points out that *Ma is acidic, as I am*. While one cowboy sits in the rain and eats *wet stew*, another loses his hat and has *no Stetson*. A blank page at the center of Mr. Hansen's book is, appropriately enough, labeled *page gap*.

My favorites include this admonition from a man in a tank explaining military injustice to a man armed only with a knife: *Now, sir, a war is never even. Sir, a war is won*.

Even better is the sign on the wall of a law firm willing to take on the most formidable adversary: *Sue Zeus*.

I call my horse, "Palindrome," because while the other horses are running forward, he looks as if he is running backward.

Arthur J. Morgan
New York, New York

Pants, Knickers, and Plus Fours

The sainted dialectician Stuart Berg Flexner liked to show us how men and women often use different words to describe the same things. Men say *dishes* and women say *china;* men say *visitors* and women say *house guests;* men say *pants* and women say *trousers.* ("I'll sing to him," sang the female lead in the Rodgers and Hart musical *Pal Joey,* adding, "and worship the *trousers* that cling to him.")

In a recent political harangue, I fussed at the impertinence of Nixonic neophytes who—during the years that I toiled in a political wilderness—were "still in *knee pants.*" A youthful colleague promptly wondered if *knee pants* was a creased, archaic term for *Bermuda shorts,* which first took that name in 1951. Julius Ozick, a dentist from New Rochelle, N.Y., writes: "My father, a pharmacist who ran the proverbial corner drugstore for over 50 years, used the term *knee pants* in a pejorative context. In my practice I have some elderly Jewish patients well past 80. Your mention of *knee pants* evoked a host of memories about the term."

We have here a word that is preserved as if in amber by a phrase. Nobody wears *knee pants* anymore; we wear *shorts,* sometimes *long shorts* (the uniform of guest hosts) of the Bermuda variety. But we remember the old term by the current use of "when you were in *knee pants,*" and occasionally "when you were in *three-cornered pants,*" a fast-disappearing reference to cloth diapers in the age before Pampers and Huggies and Luvs enshrined disposability.

Welcome to the lexicon of leg coverings. Early in the third century, a Christian doctor who courageously ministered to the poor was condemned to death by the Romans; miraculously, he survived six execution attempts before his head rolled. Canonized as Saint Pantaleone—"all lion," a salute to his courage—he became a patron saint of physicians, and many boys were baptized in his honor.

Eleven centuries later, according to Robert Hendrickson's 1987 *Facts on File Encyclopedia of Word and Phrase Origins,* because it was considered comical to call a foolish character "all lion," the commedia dell'arte dubbed a buffoon *Pantaloon* and dressed him in skintight *breeches* that bloused out above the knee. When the word was introduced to the United States in the early 18th century, the early Sams found the *pantaloons* too long and by 1840 clipped the term to *pants.*

The English agreed to the clip but refused to go along with the sense; to them, *pants* refers to underwear, specifically "underpants," and is not a synonym for *trousers.* That word preferred by Brits comes from the Gaelic *triub-*

has, originally a leg covering meeting a stocking at the knee, later extended down to the ankle, bell-bottom style, by makers of naval uniforms.

In American use, a woman's undergarment became *panties,* construed as plural even though it was a singular item that did not extend down two legs (except in the early 1950s expression *panty raid,* which was easier for college sophomores in a more sexist age to say than *panties raid*).

Meanwhile, the British—rejecting *panties*—adopted *knickers* as a synonym for "women's drawers," to mean "women's garment worn around the loins beneath the skirt." However, the British *knickers* is a 19th-century borrowing from the American author Washington Irving (whose name has been abused as the answer to "Who was the father of our country, Sidney?"). His character was Diedrich Knickerbocker, signifying a descendant of Dutch settlers of New Amsterdam, later New York, and in 1881 the name was shortened to *knickers* to describe "Dutch-style *breeches* gathered and banded just below the knee."

In America, the *knickers* remained an outer garment, sometimes called *leggings,* as the word was adopted for underwear across the ocean.

"Why is it," asks A. Sock of New York, "that if you order a pair of chairs, you get two of them, but if you order a pair of *pants,* you only get one of them?"

Answer: Both *pants* and *trousers* are construed as a pair, like the legs they fit around, and "a *pair* of," like "a *couple* of," uses a collective noun usually treated as plural. (A couple of guys *are* here to buy pants; the pants *are* for sale.) The *s* on the end of *pants* and *trousers* and *britches* (an 1880s variant of *breeches*) also tugs us toward treating them as plural. (Don't start up with *grits* and *scissors.*)

Though first spotted in 1893, the singularization of *pants* has increased in recent years; *pants* now often drops its *s.* Why has "a pair of *pants*" sometimes become "the *pant*"? Because of the women's *pants suit.* A man's suit consists of a jacket and a pair of pants, while a women's suit used to be a jacket and skirt of the same material. With the popularity of women's *slacks,* a retronym was coined: the *pants suit,* to differentiate from the skirted suit. But try to pronounce "pants suit"; you cannot separate the *s* sounds—which is why we have the *pantsuit.*

Lest the reader get an ant in his *pant* (nope—the singular remains an oddism), let us tee off on that leg covering of fashionable golfers, *plus fours.* These baggy *knickerbockers,* with four extra inches of material, were popularized by the Prince of Wales in the 1920s. The British magazine *Isis* looked with disdain at "the desuetude of the traditional grey flannel 'bags' of the undergraduate" and announced that "*plus fours* have succeeded them." (Note the plural *have.*)

"When introduced," explains Charlotte Mankey Calasibetta in *Fairchild's Dictionary of Fashion,* "these *knickers* were four inches longer than the usual length." The deliberately baggy *pants,* gathered well below the knee, are worn to show off patterned wool socks and stout shoes that Scottish Highlanders called *brogues*. That word shares a root with *breeches* and, like *socks, stockings, garters* and other coverings of our two legs and feet, takes a plural verb.

Well that's answered.
Now, if tailors left more room in the seat would old men be less crotchety?

A. *Sock*
[Arthur Ochs Sulzberger]
New York, New York

Paramount

"The approaching death of Deng Xiaoping, the *paramount* leader. . . ." That's how Patrick E. Tyler, Beijing correspondent of the *New York Times*, like just about everybody else writing about the nonagenarian Communist, identifies the man who abandoned his title but not his power.

Fox Butterfield of the *Times*, writing in 1980 from what was then transliterated as Peking, may have been the first to choose *paramount* over *foremost* or *pre-eminent* in identifying Deng; the adjective stuck, becoming a bogus title in itself.

It's an old French word—"le chef seigneur *paramont*" is first cited in 1339—picked up in English as the *Lord Paramount*, or King, to whom other lords were vassals.

Abraham Lincoln used the word in its adjectival function in 1862 when replying to the *New York Tribune* editor Horace Greeley's long editorial demanding emancipation of the slaves.

"My paramount object in this struggle," wrote Lincoln, "*is* to save the Union, and is *not* either to save or to destroy slavery," notwithstanding his "oft-expressed *personal* wish that all men every where could be free." (Italics signify Lincoln's underlining.)

The one-volume biography of Lincoln for this generation will be David Herbert Donald's. (*Long-awaited* is the cliché beloved by blurbers; in the case of Donald's Lincoln, it's true.) Those of us who have written about emancipation in detail have long puzzled over Lincoln's widely publicized letter answering Greeley's "Prayer of Twenty Millions": because Lincoln seemed to argue that freeing the slaves was not his purpose—at a time he had a draft of the Emancipation Proclamation in his pocket, awaiting a Union military victory—the President's answer to Greeley seems deliberately deceptive.

Professor Donald interprets this seeming misdirection as a step taken to prepare Northern public opinion for the drastic move. "Like most Republicans," he writes, "he had long held the belief that if slavery could be contained it would inevitably die. . . . For this reason, saving the Union was his 'paramount object.'"

The historian suggests evidence for that is in the word *paramount:* "But readers aware that Lincoln always chose his words carefully should have recognized that *paramount* meant 'foremost' or 'principal'—not 'sole.'"

Pass the Password

Hackers are reading my mind.

No, I am not about to don a sandwich board and claim that Martians and the CIA have implanted a control device in my brain causing a biweekly explosion of right-wing imprecations. My assertion is that the growing requirement for remembering passwords and identification numbers has led me to adopt mnemonics and other memory devices that all too often do not work for me but are child's play for cyber-robbers to penetrate.

Passwords can be dangerous. The first recorded use of an identifying word was in ancient Israel, when the Gileadites used the word *shibboleth,* meaning "flooding stream," to distinguish their kinsmen from the Ephraimites, who pronounced the word as *sibboleth.* As a result, some 42,000 fleeing Ephraimites who had a hard time with the *sh* sound were slain. (Today *shibboleth* means "a word or phrase characteristic of a group," like *compassion* for Democrats or *balanced budget* for Republicans. Use the wrong word in the wrong group and you risk the Ephraimite treatment.)

Although the use of such terms is ancient, the noun *password* came into English only as recently as the early 19th century. The Scottish poet James Hogg used it first in an 1817 sketch: "The other retaliated the blame on the wounded youth, for his temerity in coming without the *pass-word.*" The earlier noun was *watch-word,* first used around 1400 with the modern sense of *password;* Shakespeare uses "give the *watch-word*" in his 1594 poem *The Rape of Lucrece*. Much more recent is the 1884 *code word*, followed by *code name* in World War I.

Like most Americans, I possess, or am possessed by, about 10 identifying code words or numbers. Social Security, passport and the personal identification number (PIN) to open my account at the nighttime window at the bank have all been nicely learned by rote, along with my Army serial number, which I no longer need but cannot delete from the program in my brain. After those comes trouble.

What numbers do I use to get into my house or my car without setting off an alarm that turns out increasingly surly state troopers? What set of numbers or letters should I use to "enable" my computer at home, and at the office, and on my lap on the road?

I was born on Dec. 17. How about the number 1217? That choice would be stupid; every hacker knows that the first number used in his target person's code is the birthday. Same with anniversary and mother's maiden name. So I use a second-order mnemonic: Dec. 17 was the day the Wright Brothers flew for the first time at Kitty Hawk, so I use one of their first names. And in another year it was the day the German pocket battleship *Graf Spee* was scuttled off Montevideo, so I use *Graf* or *Spee*. Then, two days later, I ask myself: Was it Orville or Wilbur? Or—was it the *Graf Spee* or the *Bismarck*? Or the *Royal Oak*? The password disappears into the wild blue yonder or the deep water of my memory.

Why didn't I write it down? Because I would lose the paper and be shut out of everything—bank, home, car, computer, the works—or snooping cleaning people would find my list of top secrets and copy it and make me their slave. The whole idea is to come up with words or numbers that you remember no matter what.

A perfect password was given me years ago by the first computer guru at the *New York Times*. It was *Capek*. I wondered: why did he assign me that name? Then it clicked: I was a language maven, with etymology my schtick, and I almost alone would know that the word *robot* came from a 1920 play titled *R.U.R.*, which stood for "Rossum's Universal Robots," by Karel Capek. That was such an apt choice of password that I had to write about it, blowing its confidentiality, and besides I could not sign on to my computer because I misspelled the man's last name with a K.

What to do? Mary Ann Scherr, the renowned North Carolina metalsmith who incorporates numerology in some of her jewelry designs, suggests adding up all the numbers in a date—12/17/1929 equals 32—and then you can throw in the spouse's and kids' dates, if they come to mind. At least you can rebuild the number when you forget it.

Nicholas Negroponte, director of the M.I.T. media lab, directed me to Robert Lucky, vice president for research at Bellcore in New Jersey and an authority on computer networks.

"They are a big pain," Dr. Lucky says of passwords. "People's names, birth dates and addresses are the most popular passwords, but hackers arc good at attacking them. The famous 'Internet worm' incorporated a password-cracking algorithm. First it checked to see if the user name or some variation of the name and/or account number was the password. Then it checked against a list of 432 favorite passwords. I remember seeing such a list, and it had a lot of girls' names on it." Does he recommend a sophisticated encryption algorithm to bury the worms? "I try to outwit the computer by using some dumb, easy-to-guess password." (This is on the theory of Edgar Allan Poe's purloined letter.)

Dr. Frank Connolly, professor of computer science at American University, suggests an algorithm (a vogue word for recipe, formula or set of instructions), oversimplified to make it easy to grasp: "Use pieces of words that you can remember, and each time you develop a password, add one character that would not appear in a dictionary. You might begin with your initials and that of your employer, separated by an asterisk: WS*NYT. Then reverse them and change the separator: SW & TYN. Then SW + TYN." The idea is to pick something personal and then follow a pattern that you can repeat. "Just be sure to use something less obvious," says Dr. Connolly, who's got algorithm, "than your initials and the place where you work."

I'll give it a shot, using the name of one of my Bernese mountain dogs. But I can just see myself late one night out in the rain, grimly punching a key pad next to my back door, with the dog barking wildly inside, going BEN + JAMIN, then BEN & JY, then NEB * JAMIN, then BIBI, then . . .

You get yourself a bit twisted up with the name of the Czech writer who is said to have invented the word "robot." You give this as "Capek."

You state that originally you "misspelled the man's last name with a K." But you're still misspelling the name, because language maven though you are, you disregard the háček which appears over the first letter of the writer's name, thus:

Čapek.

This is the form in which this name appears in, among other authorities, *The American Heritage Dictionary of the English Language,* 3d edition, p. 283, and *Benet's Reader's Encyclopedia* (I'm sure that the *Times,* too, has the diacritic in its font).

With the háček over the "C," the letter is pronounced "ch," as in "chug," and the name is pronounced, as it should be, "chapek." A possible mispronunciation on your part may have led to your original misspelling, and I am sorry to see that you still have a problem. It's a shame not to get the author's name right.

Stuart Marks
Salisbury, Connecticut

The Perfect Paragraph

The Greek Orator Demosthenes owes me a favor.

His oration "On the Crown," ripping into one of his detractors in an early example of negative campaigning, is rated by many classicists and students of rhetoric as the greatest speech by the greatest public speaker of antiquity. However, in the translations I've seen, he goes on and on in massive blocks of type with no paragraphs.

Sensing that the poor guy needed a break, I broke the speech of Demosthenes into paragraphs when editing an anthology of great speeches. The oration is no great shakes in modern terms—just as the Wright Brothers' plane was not much compared to jetliners—but the broken-up version of his diatribe against that "accursed scribbler" Aeschines is now a lot easier to read.

That's the purpose of paragraphing: to give the reader a breather by sensibly breaking up the prose. A paragraph is to a writer what a quick intake of breath is to a singer—a little interruption that makes possible refreshed continuation.

Barbara Weber sends in this pertinent question from an air base overseas: "Where on earth do you start a new paragraph? I know the official rule is 'when there's a change of scene or subject,' but that's an awfully broad statement. I kind of have an idea about where to start and stop paragraphs, but (a Gallic shrug of the shoulders and hands) I have looked through several grammar books, and the best I could find is that vague definition. Can you help?"

Her note was like a message across the ages from Demosthenes. The first aid I can supply is to caution against the redundancy *shrug the shoulders*. A *shrug* is a hunching forward of the shoulders; only the shoulders can be shrugged; you don't shrug your knees or eyebrows or anything else. Period. Graph.

"Nobody talks in paragraphs," notes Bill Kretzschmar, at work on the *Linguistic Atlas* Project at the University of Georgia. (The indentation before the quotation marks signifies a paragraph, called for there because a useful prose-writing convention is to start all quotations of each person in dialogue with such an indentation, and I am creating the illusion of having a conversation with an expert on paragraphs.) "The paragraph is purely something written (throughout its history, beginning with little 'pointing hands' next to significant bits of the text in medieval manuscripts), and the tired, old saws about using paragraphs for completed ideas and about making paragraphs complete by including a beginning (topic), middle (evidence, argument) and end (conclusion, transition) seem to me to be good advice."

The trouble with that advice is the narrowness of most newspaper columns. If a reporter were to write a classic unitary paragraph, with its lede, meat and snapper, the prose—cramped into a column width of just over 12 picas, using the front page of the *New York Times*, for example—would stretch down the page in an uninviting way. Copy editors exist only to make reverse-P signs in the middle of such well-constructed units, introducing that little bit of white space at the start and end of every sentence or two that tempts the reader to keep going. It is like feeding a baby tiny spoonfuls of mashed banana, building an appetite between insertions of the spoon in the ready-to-squawl mouth. That bit-by-bit philosophy is at the heart of modern newspaper layout and accounts for the new ailment of hyperparagraphication. In the paragraph you are reading, you were grabbed by a topic sentence ("The trouble with that advice . . ."), given the argumentation to support it (why some copy editors exist, then a symbol of prose-breaking as spoon-feeding) and presented with a conclusion ended by a heart-stopping neologism, "hyperparagraphication." Now pretend you have not yet read this paragraph; hold the newspaper a little farther away, and look at this article as a whole. Would you read this paragraph? Of course not; it seems never to end, which would cause you to ask: Why should any cautious reader plunge into a block of type from which he may never emerge? On the other hand, if you are into logomasochism, then at this point you are undergoing the lung-bursting sensation of a swimmer who cannot quite make it up to the surface. To save you from the need for page-to-page resuscitation, the copy editor would first break this paragraph at the sentence beginning "Copy editors," and again at "Now pretend."

Why in those particular places? One reason is what linguists call *the life-guard factor,* expressed by summer camp counselors as "O.K., you kids, everybody out of the water, you're all turning blue." In the same way, copy editors say, "A couple of inches is more than enough." Grammarians who find this arbitrary and capricious are directed to John F. Kennedy's "Life is unfair."

A second reason (an enumeration is always a good place to hit the graph key) is *the zag component:* any deviation from the march of argument is a good place to take a break. Thus, the sentence beginning "Copy editors exist" (recalling the Cartesian proofreader's "I edit, therefore I am")—with its slight delinkage from the previous thought—is a natural place for the medieval finger symbol. A third reason—excuse me. . . .

Thirdly, *the bank substitute.* Fast-leafing readers are being stopped and their attention snatched by "banks" of large type embedded in columns of small type. In that way, a provocative sentence is almost headlined, forcing the dis-intermediated reader to squint at the small type and search to see if that outrageous line could be true in context. Writers who do not trust the copy desk to jerk the right sentence out of context use the instant-paragraph device to set up their own mini-bank. The lead sentence of this piece, about some Greek character assassin's owing me a favor, is a topic sentence that should properly be followed within the same paragraph by the next two sentences. However, I have this lust to have it stand out, like a bank, and so I make it a paragraph by itself.

Finally (sentence adverbs are excellent graphing spots), there is the *not-so-fast element.* See that "However, I have this lust" sentence ending the previous paragraph? Any contrasting or contrary thought; a careful reservation beginning with *but;* a detour that acknowledges the opposing argument set up with the smarmy *to be sure*—all these are legitimate break points.

How to avoid hyperparagraphication? Consider the lowly dingbat. If you want to set off items in a list, a range of typographical devices is available. "If you mean to write a paragraph," Professor Kretzschmar observes, "follow the handbooks; if you just want to emphasize something, you can add some additional sign, such as a dash (—) or bullet mark of some kind (e.g., •, > or ■), so nobody mistakes your purpose."

Philadelphia Lawyers

A politically active group of legal eagles called themselves *trial lawyers;* advocates of tort reform prefer to derogate them as *the contingency-fee crowd.* Others, stopping short of the mean-spirited *shyster* (rooted in German scatology), blow them off as *Philadelphia lawyers.*

"The other day I used the phrase 'Philadelphia lawyer' in a conversation," writes Larry Altman, the medical columnist of the *New York Times,* "and was unable to explain it. I consulted various dictionaries; none helped me out. So, what was it about Philadelphia that made its lawyers so sharp that gave rise to the expression? Philadelphia has good medicine, but I have never heard the phrase 'Philadelphia doctor.' "

I depend on Dr. Altman to get to the bottom of the health of our Presidents and am happy to return the favor.

The first use of the phrase in print came in April 1788, in *Universal Asylum and Columbian Magazine,* published in Philadelphia. "They have a proverb here," wrote a Yankee visiting London to his Pennsylvania friend, "which I do not know how to account for;—in speaking of a difficult point, they say, *it would puzzle a Philadelphia lawyer."*

As the context indicates, the phrase meant "a lawyer of great perspicacity" or "an especially learned advocate." At the time, Philadelphia—seat of the new American Government—was the center of legal acumen in the United States. Its fame had begun to spread a half-century earlier in the libel trial—in New York City—of John Peter Zenger, publisher of the *New York Weekly Journal.* Zenger had hired the two most eminent local lawyers, but because they were among the men writing the articles that the Crown considered libelous, Zenger was forced to seek counsel out of town. The man he chose was Andrew Hamilton of Philadelphia, who proceeded to startle the judge and jury with an unheard-of argument: that truth was a defense against libel.

Taking the bold step to admit that his client was "guilty" of telling the truth about William Cosby, the wily Colonial Governor, Hamilton declared, "There is heresy in law as well as religion." Hamilton's "bad" British law— his commonsense argument—found support among Zenger's peers.

To the Crown's dismay, the jury found Zenger not guilty, and freedom of the press was given a tremendous boost. Hamilton was "the first to give great honor, admiration and the highest of professionalism to the appellation 'Philadelphia lawyer,'" writes Robert R. Bell in his 1992 book, *The Philadelphia Lawyer: A History, 1735–1945.*

That's what lawyers in the city of brotherly love like to think is the meaning, but over the centuries it has gained a pejorative sense elsewhere: "The new violation ticket will be in quadruplicate," wrote the *Chicago Times* in 1947, "and traffic officials say it takes a 'Philadelphia lawyer' to fix it." The sense has moved to "one expert in the exploitation of technicalities to get around the law," and if you're not happy with that, sue me—truth is my defense, not to mention an absence of malice.

While I'm at it, Larry, *quack* is a shortening of *quacksalver,* a phony doctor who quacked (hawked or hard-sold, sounding as abrasive as a duck's quack) salves (ointments to cure whatever ailed you).

And Philadelphians have not been singled out in the geographic derogation sweepstakes. A deck of cards is called a *California prayer book;* a roll of singles with a $100 bill on the outside is a *Michigan wad,* and a length of hose used to siphon gas out of someone else's tank is a *Georgia credit card.*

You are correct that the first reference to the Philadelphia lawyer was about Andrew Hamilton of Philadelphia who came to New York to defend John Peter Zenger, when, legend says, the lawyers at the New York Bar were afraid to represent him, as the basic argument that had to be made to defend Zenger successfully required one that the Crown did not like. As a result, the phrase, Philadelphia lawyer, in the early life of this nation meant a lawyer who was skillful and courageous and would make any reasonable argument which would help his client, even if the government thought the argument threatened the government's existence or that of its high public officials.

The other expression of the term, Philadelphia lawyer, grew out of the railroad situation in the early 30s. The Pennsylvania Railroad and the Baltimore-Ohio Railroad, like many railroads, went bankrupt. Such railroads nevertheless needed to buy heavy equipment such as passenger rail cars and freight cars. As you may or may not know, the law is generally that if a bankrupt purchased such property and took title to it, the property would become part of the bankrupt's estate and thus would be subject to the claims of all creditors, even those who existed before the purchase and acquisition of the new equipment. Obviously, in those circumstances, no manufacturer would sell to the Pennsylvania Railroad or the Baltimore-Ohio Railroad and no bank would lend money to buy the new equipment.

The Philadelphia lawyers then devised an instrument which was known as a bailment lease, which meant that the manufacturer or the bank which lent the money was the owner of the new passenger rail cars or freight cars, and the manufacturers or banks would lease them to the railroad with the provision that, if the loan for the new cars wasn't paid or the bankrupt estate attempted to include such property in the bankruptcy, the bank or the manufacturer, as the owner of the property, would simply say that the lease had been terminated and would get the property back. In the event that the railroad did pay off the debt on the cars, there was a provision that by paying an additional dollar the railroads could take possession and ownership of such cars.

Thus, the term, Philadelphia lawyer, derived an additional meaning, i.e., Philadelphia lawyers had the ability, by clearly understanding the concepts of the common law, to make transaction which, until that time, the New York and other Bars had not thought about.

William T. Coleman, Jr.
Washington, D.C.

Pinprick

A *pinprick,* coined in 1862, is a petty annoyance, like the jab of a pin that draws no blood. Today, only secretaries of defense suffer from pinpricks; the word has emerged in the 1990s in a new sense: as the primary derogation of inadequate military action.

T. E. Lawrence, in his 1926 autobiography *The Seven Pillars of Wisdom,* led the way: "The tribesmen," he wrote of the Arabian nomads, ". . . hindered and distracted the Turks by their *pin-prick* raids." Occasional military use followed, as in a 1977 *Newsweek* dispatch quoting a Thai Air Force colonel about Cambodian "shooting incidents, *pinprick* attacks, probes against our defenses."

Accused of dithering in the face of Serbian attacks on Sarajevo in 1994, the United Nations launched a couple of feeble air sorties; the strategist Zbigniew Brzezinski denounced these as *pinprick bombing,* a nice play on the World War II term for precision air attacks, *pinpoint bombing.* Since that time, data bases show a fivefold increase in the military sense of *pinprick,* which is now losing its hyphen.

Thus, as President Clinton responded to the move of Iraqi tanks into Allied-protected Kurdish areas with two volleys of Tomahawk cruise missiles, hawks who felt the response weak took up their favorite word: to answer "a tyrant's temper tantrum," wrote Mark Yost in the *Wall Street Journal,* "it will take a lot more than a few *pinprick* missile strikes."

Please Pass the Plural Pease

Today it's strictly eat-your-peas, with no going off on parenthetical tangents. (*Peas,* which we now take to be the plural of *pea,* was originally *pease,* a dishful of the vegetable; when somebody in the 17th century stuck his fingers in a dish of pease and picked out an individual component, he said, "I'll call this a *pea,* without the *s,* because it's only one." That creation of the singular from the plural is a form of "back-formation." Most people think that language is orderly, and that one *pea* led to a plateful of *peas,* a good reason not to listen to most people.)

The reason for this grim determination to stick to the point and eschew topical digressions (great verb, *eschew,* "to avoid as unwise," akin to the Old High German *sciuhen,* "to frighten off"; pronounced like a sneeze) is that the Gotcha! Gang has been after me on subject-verb agreement.

"When you write," notes Richard Valeriani of Sherman, Conn., "that 'the manufacture and distribution of cash is by far the Federal Government's biggest profit-making operation,' are you sure they is?"

We have here a compound subject: "manufacture and distribution." The writer thinks of the two functions as a single profit-making unit (could be mistaken, but I wrote it and know what I thought); therefore, that twinned entity properly takes a singular verb, *is.* Here's a line from Dee Dee Myers, a

CNBC host, in *People* magazine: "I think drinking and driving is a really bad thing." She construes *drinking* and *driving* in this usage as a combination; only together are the two functions a bad thing. Therefore, the compound subject, *drinking and driving*, takes the singular *is*.

Now consider this line from the *Washington Post:* "There is prestige and value in supporting the national museums." Prestige is one thing, value another; the two call for a plural verb. Turn it around a little, and see it as meaning "There are two reasons to support national museums, and they *are* prestige and value." That's why I would write, "There *are* prestige and value." (Sounds a little funny, though; I'd recast the sentence.)

It comes down to "notional agreement": is the notion in the head of the writer of a compound subject singular or plural? Agreement depends on whether your pairing is intended to be seen as two separate items or a single entity. A collective idea in a subject calls for a singular verb; the race, we are told in Ecclesiastes, is not to the swift, "but time and chance happeneth to them all." (The *eth* is the archaic, or lisping, form of *s* that now ends third-person singular verbs, like *happens*.) The world-weary author lumped together "time and chance." In the same way, in his 1979 novel, *Loon Lake*, E. L. Doctorow, with the precision of a Bronx High School of Science graduate, wrote, "The name and address of the grocery was painted on the slats"—taking *name and address* as a collective idea, as most of us do, calling for *was*, not *were*.

In a *New York Times Magazine* article in 1994 about the Chiat/Day ad agency, Herbert Muschamp wrote, "Half the staff *seem* to be out there treading the airwaves." A pair of lawyers wrote me about that from Chicago. Elan Chambers contended that the word *half* modified the singular collective noun *staff* and should take the singular verb *seems*. In opposition, James Damron held that *half the staff* referred to individuals composing that half and properly took the plural *seem*.

I ran this past John Algeo, a longtime professor of English at the University of Georgia and a linguistic heavy hitter: how did he construe *half the staff*? "In this case, half of the staff are probably not getting out of their chairs in unison," he replied, "and marching out the door lock-step. So we are talking about a number of persons doing the same thing, not together as a unit, but individually. My own preference would be strongly for the plural verb, 'Half of the staff *seem* to be leaving.'"

An army marches on its stomach; an army of individual dogfaces march on their stomachs. "A substantial number of Americans . . . *are* indeed alienated by a two-party system that tends to present only two options," wrote Michael Lind in this magazine two months ago, adding, "but the growing number of disaffected voters *do* not form a cohesive bloc." Prof. Diane Sharon of Fordham University in New York circles in despair the *are* and the *do*, both plural, following *number*.

One right, one wrong. Most of us construe *the* number as singular, *a* number as plural. It's correct to write, "*A* substantial number of Americans *are*"— it should be plural, not *is*. And it's incorrect to write, "*The* growing number of disaffected voters *do*"; it should be *does*.

I will not return to this subject again (and the *again* is redundant, but I use it for emphasis). Eat your pease—it's good for you. Or as we now say, eat your peas—*they*'re good for you.

Poetic Allusion Watch (PAW)

"Under the hill's new gift rules," went the subheadline in the *Washington Post*, "the question is, 'Do I dare to eat a lunch?'"

The commentary by Robert F. Bauer had to do with the ethics rules adopted by the House of Representatives restricting the taking of a meal or even a good stiff drink from anyone other than an old Army buddy or a life-long sweetheart. But the *Post* headline was an allusion to T. S. Eliot's 1917 poem "The Love Song of J. Alfred Prufrock," in which the timorous narrator asks: "Shall I part my hair behind? Do I dare to eat a peach?"

A poetic allusion can be a way of saying, "Lookame, I read poetry, I ain't no redneck Philistine" (a slur on residents of today's American South and yester-year's Israel). Or, less pretentiously, it can be a way of saying, "Anybody else out there get the same feeling I get from this memory?" Or the poetic alluder can be subtly asserting a consciousness of the continuum of civilization: Eliot, two lines later, has his narrator say, "I have heard the mermaids singing, each to each," which reached back to the 1600's and John Donne's "Song," which begins, "Go, and catch a falling star," and asks, "Teach me to hear mermaids singing."

Or it can be an unconscious evocation of poetry by someone who may not know the source in poetry or folklore but is familiar with the echoing phrase. "Records disappear," wrote the columnist Richard Cohen in wonderment at happenings in the White House residence, "appear, move and all but go bump in the night." The last five words are from a Scottish or Cornish prayer deep in Mr. Cohen's folk memory, perhaps not at the conscious level: "From ghoulies and ghosties and long-leggety beasties/And things that go bump in the night, Good Lord, deliver us!"

In the same way, when President Clinton told a news conference that some budget controversies would have to wait until election time for settlement but that others could be handled much before November, he observed, "We should not make the perfect the enemy of the good." That was a literary, not a poetic, allusion, probably drawn from the vague memory of Voltaire's comment about dramatic art in his Philosophical Dictionary of 1764: *"Le mieux est l'ennemi du bien,"* "The best [literally, the better] is the enemy of the good."

Members of PAW, the Poetic Allusion Watch, are careful not to go overboard in attributing any use of a poetic word to a deliberate allusion. "Despite the *snarky* put-downs and the fever for electronic communiqués," wrote Gerri Hirshey last summer in the *New York Times Magazine,* "we're buying more prefab passions than ever." Jim Kilker of Iselin, N.J., noted: "I have used *snarky* all my life. When my children would act up, I'd say, 'Now don't get *snarky,*' meaning 'Calm down and behave yourself.' But that doesn't seem to be the meaning in this context."

PAW is reluctant to attribute the growing use of this word to Lewis Carroll's "Hunting of the Snark." That 1876 poem was an early derogation of lawyers: "He dreamed that he stood in a shadowy Court,/Where the Snark, with a glass in its eye,/Dressed in gown, bands, and wig, was defending a pig/On the charge of deserting its sty."

Carroll had a predilection for onomatopoeic words beginning with *sn*—as in "Jabberwocky," with "The vorpal blade went snicker-snack"—but 10 years before Carroll wrote his poem, the British *Notes and Queries* used the term in 1866 about "a certain kind of *snarking* or gnashing," and John Jamieson's *Scottish Dictionary* in 1882 defined the verb *to snark* as "to fret, grumble or find fault." In his 1976 diaries, Richard Crossman, a Cabinet minister, used the word to describe a journalistic tone in the sense that *snarky* is currently used in the White House to deal with some of us who observe the passing political scene: "The stream of anti-government propaganda, smearing, *snarky,* derisive, which comes out of Fleet Street."

The champion source of PAW is still Shakespeare. The *Washington Post* headline writer of "Nongovernment Types Declare a Pox on Both Their Houses" was calling up the dying Mercutio's curse on the houses of Montague and Capulet: "A plague a' both your houses!" And the *New York Times* headline "Goals Met, Pataki Reveals a Method to His Mildness" is a play on Polonius's analysis of Hamlet's display of craziness: "Though this be madness, yet there is method in't."

Remembering My Good Friends is the title of George Weidenfeld's recent autobiography. In *Richard II,* when Henry Percy offers Bullingbrook (sometimes spelled Bolingbroke), later Henry IV, his support in the struggle to depose King Richard, Bullingbrook replies, "I thank thee, gentle Percy, and be sure/I count myself in nothing else so happy/As in a soul rememb'ring my good friends." (When first staged, Shakespeare's inflammatory deposition scene is said to have been cut, lest supporters of Essex get ideas about ousting Queen Elizabeth.)

What's that you say, falconer? Do some poetic allusions deserve to have their numbers retired for a few years because of overuse?

"How can the center hold?" asked Senator William S. Cohen of Maine in announcing his retirement, to near-universal dismay, from the world's greatest deliberative body. "Won't the system fall apart? It is not a case, to continue with Yeats's words that"—this was not Cohen's allusion, but his direct reference—"'the best lack all conviction while the worst are full of passionate intensity.' Such a poetic construct presumes too much."

Cohen ought to know; he is the only sitting Senator publishing poetry of his own. His reference, unnecessarily specific, was to William Butler Yeats's "Second Coming," a 1920 poem about the crumbling of our civilization and its replacement by some irrational tyranny. The poem states, "Things fall apart; the center cannot hold." It is constantly cited by centrists who are losing to liberals or conservatives.

Like the fashion arbiters who raise some eminent lady above the annual best-dressed lists, PAW is retiring that poem's number, along with Robert Frost's "Road Not Taken" and "Mending Fences" (in which the narrator's neighbor repeats, "Good fences make good neighbors") and Eliot's "Wasteland," to make room for allusions on roads less traveled. Something there is that doesn't love the trite and true; it would be nice to see some rough headline writer slouching toward a modern poet.

Tut, tut. Your article refers to T.S. Eliot's "Wasteland." There is no such poem. The title of Eliot's great work is "The Waste Land"—three words.

Go, and sin no more.

Roberts W. French
Santa Fe, New Mexico

You blundered into referring to the second-most famous poem of America's second-most famous poet not as "Mending Wall," but "Mending Fences." This gaffe on the part of someone who combines a love of letters with politics is pretty understandable.

Hannah Stein
Davis, California

You translate Voltaire's "Le mieux est l'ennemi du bien" as "The best [literally, the better] is the enemy of the good." Actually, "Le mieux" does not mean "the better," literally or otherwise.

The word *"mieux"* is an *adverb* meaning "better," as in "You write better than I do": *(Vous écrivez mieux que moi.)* The *adjective* "better" is *"meilleur"*: "You are a better writer" *(Vous êtes un meilleur écrivain.)*

Voltaire's aphorism has the meaning "The best [thing] is the enemy of the good [thing]." So if Voltaire were saying literally "The better [thing]," he would have to have used *"meilleur,"* not *"mieux."* But how could the cultured Voltaire have made such a mistake? Answer: he didn't.

French, unlike English, does not have a single word that means "best." Instead, it uses two words. "Le meilleur" means "best," or "the best"; it does not mean "the better." But, no doubt to confuse perfidious Albion by making stolen diplomatic documents more difficult to comprehend, the French also have *another* pair of words which, taken together, mean "best": *"Le mieux"!* Thus, Voltaire was right all along, which I guess we knew to begin with.

J. R. McCrory
Stone Mountain, Georgia

Political Figures of Speech

Of the recorded words of Ulysses S. Grant—from "I propose to fight it out on this line, if it takes all summer" to "Let us have peace"—the most unexpected and revealing are these, in a July 1885 letter to his physician, John H. Douglas, shortly before his death: "I am a verb."

That poetic self-description says the general and President thought of himself as a conveyor of action: a verb's function is to express an act, occurrence or existence, and its place is often at the heart of a predicate, the part of a sentence that moves a story along. Grant's use of the metaphor suggests his mind was more introspective and poetic than his countrymen suspected.

If Grant was a verb, what figures of speech or symbols of punctuation apply to other political figures? I think of Eisenhower as a noun, Nixon an adverb, Millard Fillmore as a mixed metaphor; others think of different politicians as past participles, attributive nouns, parentheses, dashes, commas, reflexive verbs, combining forms, etc.

William Jefferson Clinton is an adjective. He describes, modifies and delimits a noun. The noun *change,* for instance, is the name of a thing; Clinton is adept at denoting its quality and quantity, and drawing its distinction from something else, like retrogression. This is not a criticism; it's a metaphoric description, the parallel I see. Readers are invited to submit their own comparisons of famous people and grammatical terms.

What triggered this was a remark by President Clinton sure to be included in all his biographies. When he was reminded that the center of action appeared to be more on Capitol Hill than in the White House, and that some were calling him irrelevant, he responded with the most defensive declarative sentence spoken by a President since Nixon's "I am not a crook." The Clinton assertion: "The President is relevant."

"Relevance, Shmelevance" was the ringing title of a *Washington Post* editorial. (Duplicating a word, with the sound "shm" substituted for the first letter, is a Yiddishism gaining in use in American speech to denote hearty derision.) "It is ludicrous," the editorialist wrote, "to be debating the matter of whether a President of the United States is or is not 'relevant.' . . . A President of the United States is by definition always relevant. For openers, he's got the bomb."

What caused this explosion at the *Post* was not only the President's misconception of the criticism of him, but also his unwary acceptance of a word freighted with hidden meanings. *Relevant* is an adjective that reverberates. With its sidekick synonym, *meaningful,* academics made it one of the great clichés of the '60s.

Describing the demands for change in curriculum on the nation's campuses in 1970, *Time* magazine wrote, "The impetus came largely from student demands for 'relevance,' especially for the overdue admission of more minority-group students." The catchword for the rejection of a liberal arts education centered on Western civilization—scorned as "dead white males"—was *relevance,* and under its banner, many courses were substituted that students could "relate to," featuring women's and minority group heroes and interests, usually titled "studies."

Before the word became a cliché, it served another purpose: to denote practicality or timeliness in the midst of the ephemeral. Mark Twain in 1895 wrote that "Conversations consisted mainly of irrelevancies, with here and there a relevancy, a relevancy with an embarrassed look, as not being able to explain how it got there."

Relevant—like *relieve,* rooted in the Latin for "raising up," or lifting pressure—means "focused on the matter at hand." If you mean that and don't want to get in a cliché fight, use *pertinent;* if you like a legal flavor, try *germane* or *material.* Not one of these synonyms, however (nor *apposite, applicable, apropos*), has the lingering connotations that *relevant* has: to some, "sensitively close," to others "sloppily obsequious."

If you mean "You bet a President counts," ignore adjectives completely: use Grant style.

You say that "shm" is "substituted for the first letter" in expressions such as "Relevance, shmelevance." What it is substituted for is not a unit of writing (a letter) but a phonological unit, namely the "onset" of the first syllable, which can be a consonant cluster and thus correspond to more than what would be written with a single letter: "Kleptocrat, shmeptocrat," not "shmleptocrat."

Professor James D. McCawley
Department of Linguistics
University of Chicago
Chicago, Illinois

You seem to have missed the point. "Grant" *is* a verb. It means "to bestow," as in, "the government granted certain people the right to be on the dole."

"Dole" is also a verb. It means "to distribute as charity," as in, "The Defense Department doles out government grants."

"Byrd" is a noun. It is a beast which feathers its own nest.

"Bush" is an adjective. It means not quite good enough for the major leagues.

"Gore" is a pleat in a skirt, whatever that means, and "Gramm" may be a Cracker.

Gary D. Jensen
Lake Jackson, Texas

Benjamin Harrison (interregnum of Grover Cleveland's presidency) is a *parenthetical phrase.*

Madonna, the slut, is an *epithet.*

Michael Jordan! An *exclamation!*

And you, my dear sir, who regularly interrupts the political and linguistic action with commentary, you are an *interjection.*

Greg Otis
Brooklyn, New York

The Political Who

Trust is hot. At an April 15 rally outside Philadelphia, Bob Dole put it this way: "If something happened along the route and you had to leave your children with Bob Dole or Bill Clinton, I think you'd probably leave your children with Bob Dole. . . . It all boils down to, *Who* do you trust?"

In his riposte, Bill Clinton told a dinner of White House correspondents in May: "Let's say that you were going on vacation for a couple of weeks—*who* do you trust to water your plants—Bob Dole or Bill Clinton? . . . You go home tonight, and you decide to order a pizza—*who* do you trust to select the toppings?"

Because the nonpartisan rigor of this language column is a wonder to behold, no position is here taken on the puissance of the original Dole thrust or the quality of derision in the Clinton counterthrust. This is my *biennial* (that's every second year; *biannual* is twice a year) item about the persnickety *who/whom*.

Is it *who* do you trust or *whom* do you trust?

That's easy: because *who* is nominative and *whom* is objective, and the sentence parses as you/trust/the object, then it should be you/trust/him, or *whom,* not he or *who.* Thus the correct question should be "*Whom* do you trust?"

Say wha'? That's the sort of advice you get from a person whose icy secretary says, "*Whom* should I say is calling?" We are faced here with what grammarians as renowned as Henry Fowler and Otto Jespersen discussed as "the hypercorrect *whom.*"

Whom has its place in current usage. As the object of a preposition, *whom* not only is right but also feels right, as in *For Whom the Bell Tolls.* Similarly, "To *Whom* It May Concern" is natural; "To *Who*" would be anathema to a native speaker. *Whom* also feels right in "the one *whom* we feared," not "the one *who* we fear" (unless more is added: "He is the one *who* we feared would win the election").

But at the beginning of a sentence, *whom* comes across as an affectation. In politics, formality went out with neckties, and what is comfortable to the listener's ear is to be preferred in address. *Whoever* the coming election favors will begin his sentences with *who*—despite the correctness of *whomever* in that instance—and he will thank *whomever* he wants for pointing this out.

Therefore, the time has come to provide a corollary to Safire's Law, which is "Whenever *whom* is correct, recast the sentence." The corollary is "*Who* begins a sentence with *whom* will never be elected President of anything." (In that sentence, *who* is nominative, or substantive, or subjective—pick one; they all mean the same—and is right in its own right, not just because it comes at the beginning.)

Who do you trust? On this, trust me, than *whom* there is none more contemptuous of pandering.

Presumptives and Presumptions

The *Financial Times* and just about every other news publication refer to Senator Bob Dole as "the *presumptive* Republican Presidential nominee." *Likely* and *probable* (not certain enough) and *all-but-certain* (too many words) have fallen by the wayside of campaign coverage. "*Presumptive* nominee" has assumed the status of bogus title, appearing before, rather than after, the person's name.

But why *presumptive?* Presumably, it is based on the legal and royal phrase *heir presumptive,* which means "one whose right to inheritance will be lost if someone more closely related to the ancestor is born before the ancestor dies." That *heir presumptive* is in line to get the orb and scepter (or in ordinary wills, the estate) unless replaced by an *heir apparent.* That closer heir's right to the ermine cannot be denied, in the case of royal succession, or the property cannot be diverted unless the ancestor has willed it elsewhere.

Right now in Britain, Prince Charles is the *heir apparent* because he is Queen Elizabeth's oldest son; succession is a sure thing, assuming he wants it, at which point his older son, Prince William, would become *heir apparent.* But if that prince ultimately had a daughter, she would be *heir presumptive,* destined to become Queen unless he later had a son, who would become *heir apparent,* and the daughter would be out of luck, a mere princess for the rest of her days. (Grumble about sexism, but that's the way it works today; tomorrow, who knows?)

Thus, *presumptive* is weaker than *apparent.* On that analogy, if you really think Dole has it in the bag, you should use "the *apparent* nominee." But if you want to hedge your bet, you would use "the *presumptive* nominee." Logical, yes?

No; usage has little to do with logic. In most people's minds, *apparent* is wishy-washy, imputing uncertainty (as *perceived* does, though not going so far into suspicion as *supposed*), while the bumptious *presumptive* has the ring of near certainty. Makes no etymological sense, but as lexicographers say to usagists, "Go figure."

For another form of the same word, there's the past participle *presumed*. If you are hooked on the *-ive* construction and like unfamiliar words, you may be disposed to choose as dispositive *putative*, from the Latin *putare*, "to set in order," now meaning "generally considered as such" as well as "reputed." (*Compute* also marches in this orderly procession.)

While on the subject of adjectives in politics, how do we deal with Taiwan?

"Most newspapers describe Taiwan in one of eight ways," writes Robert Makolot of New York. "They say that China's Communist rulers regard Taiwan as a *renegade, breakaway, estranged, errant, splinter, runaway, wayward* or *separatist* province."

All those adjectives except *estranged* are pejorative, and should be attributed to the opinions of leaders on the Chinese mainland. But how to describe the semisovereign status of the Government that meets so many of the criteria for statehood without going all the way to *independent*, a degree of separation that its newly elected President is careful not to claim?

The "Republic of China," Taiwan's official name, is too easily confused with "People's Republic of China," whose capital is Beijing. Most of us solve the problem by calling Taiwan "Taiwan," and note that many of its Chinese residents consider themselves "part of China"; this avoids the noun *province*, which denotes a section of a nation, and does away with the need for any of the eight aforementioned loaded adjectives.

Less easy to finesse is the proposed renaming of the territory administered by Israel since the 1967 war. The area named by Jordan in 1948 "the *West Bank*" (of the Jordan River) has been called *Judea* and *Samaria*, its ancient biblical names, by the members of Israel's Likud bloc, who wanted to settle the land; other Israelis aligned with Labor accepted *West Bank*. There was no difference of opinion about the name of the *Gaza Strip*, a strip of land along the Mediterranean coast that included the city of Gaza, where the blind Samson pulled down the temple on his captors and himself. The word *strip* was chosen by Egypt in 1949, as it administered the area for most of the years until 1967 without offering citizenship to its stateless residents.

But the names are now in play. "From now on we will start saying the *District of Gaza* instead of the *Gaza Strip*," announced Talal Aukal of the Palestinian Ministry of Information, "and the *Northern Counties of Palestine* instead of the *West Bank*." This was similar to the attempt by Likudniks to identify the area by its biblical names, usage that most of the press considered a presumption. President Yasir Arafat of the Palestinian Authority explained that he wanted "to remove all signs of the past that have been used by Israel over the past 28 years."

Will the world's media adopt the new Palestinian nomenclature? Will Taiwan be described as a *renegade* province? Are these good questions to toss at any *presumptive* nominee?

Proximity Talks

"The idea is to get the parties together at one locale out of the public eye," said Alexander Vershbow, the foreign service officer who speaks for the National Security Council, "where our team can then shuttle between the delegations in a more efficient fashion than they have been able to do by having to fly."

"That's what *proximity talks* means?" he was asked by a reporter following the negotiations among Serbs, Bosnian Muslims and Croats.

"Yes," Vershbow replied, *"proximity talks*—that's the buzzword for this notion of shuttling, but within one site."

Proximity means "nearness," from the Latin *proximus,* "nearest"; it's the noun form of the interchangeable adjectives *proximate* and *approximate,* which mean "close enough for Government work."

Where did this new diplomatic phrase originate? I called Peter Rodman, at the Nixon Center in Washington, who was Henry Kissinger's longtime alter ego. "The technique, not the phrase, was pioneered by Ralph Bunche on the island of Rhodes in 1948 and '49, negotiating one of the ceasefires in Israel's war for independence," Rodman recalled.

"He brought people who would not talk directly into the same building, and he would go back and forth. The phrase itself? First I heard it was also in the Middle East, early '70s, maybe around the time of the interim agreement on the Suez Canal. Try Joe Sisco."

Joseph Sisco, the veteran diplomat, does crisis evaluation for companies doing business around the world. Reached him in Germany, and—bingo! (That's a term of delight that even anti-gambling activists can use.)

"I was the one who coined *proximity talks,"* he stated without equivocation. "It was in 1970 or '71, the time of the meetings between Israelis and Egyptians. Indirect talks had not worked, and direct talks were not then feasible. So we used the 'Rhodes formula': they stayed in separate hotel suites in the Waldorf-Astoria in New York, and the Americans would shuttle back and forth."

How was the phrase coined?

"The Israelis were calling it 'bellhop diplomacy,' and I didn't think that would do. So I called it *proximity talks.*"

Why the word *proximity?* Why not *nearness talks,* for example?

"Look, I had a Ph.D. and was very proud of it. *Nearness* would have been much too understandable."

The earliest citation from the lexicographer Robert K. Barnhart is a 1972 usage of *proximity discussions* in *Time* magazine: "Arab states refuse to deal directly with Israel, but Egypt is amenable to *proximity discussions,* in which representatives of the two nations would closet themselves in separate hotel suites while U.S. Assistant Secretary of State Joseph Sisco shuttles between them." In 1973, *Time* also carried the earliest print citation of *proximity talks.*

While he was at it, Mr. Sisco also claimed coinage of a related phrase: "On the first trip that Henry Kissinger took to the Middle East after the Yom Kippur War, I remember saying to Marvin Kalb and Ted Koppel, 'Welcome to *shuttle diplomacy!*'"

A *shuttle* is a device in weaving that carries the thread of the woof between the threads of the warp; the metaphor was adopted for the subway in New York that runs between Times Square and Grand Central Station, was picked up by Eastern Airlines to denote its New York to Washington run and was a natural for a description of diplomats flying back and forth between capitals. *Diplomacy* is a traditional phrase-combining form, from *dollar diplomacy* to *gunboat diplomacy* to *quiet diplomacy.*

Reached for verification of Sisco's recollection at Harvard's Joan Shorenstein Center on the Press, Politics and Public Policy, Kalb, the former correspondent, remembered the phrase being in the air at the time and generously did not dispute Sisco's claim.

You stated that Ralph Bunch pioneered this technique in Rhodes during 1948–49.

Sorry, but it was previously practiced to great effect by Henry Wickham Steed during the palace drafting discussions preceding the signing of the Versailles Treaty in 1919. At that time he was the editor of the *Times.* During his long career at the *Times* as a foreign correspondent and then foreign editor, and finally editor, he came to know and be known by everyone in Europe, from kings and presidents to obscure civil servants and academics. He was fluent in French and German, as well as various Central European languages. He was drawn into the Versailles discussions because he was trusted to go between the various groups that could not actually meet.

Martin Hugh-Jones
Baton Rouge, Louisiana

"Who coined the actual phrase 'shuttle diplomacy'? The answer is lost somewhere among the shifting sands of the Middle East. The first known reference appeared in the *New York Times* under the byline of Bernard Gwertzman, who wrote on January 11, 1974, about an 'unorthodox bit of shuttle diplomacy.' Barry Schweid of the AP wrote after the first round trip that Kissinger was 'shuttling' back and forth. That same day, Assistant Secretary of State Joseph Sisco came to the back section of the plane a few minutes before taking off from Aswan and said in a loud voice, 'Welcome aboard the Egyptian-Israeli shuttle!' Sisco, who had formerly been involved in UN affairs, was thinking about the Eastern Airlines shuttle between New York and Washington."

That's from *Travels With Henry*.

Richard Valeriani
Sherman, Connecticut

Proximate and *approximate* are not interchangeable. It is true that *proximate* has a dictionary definition that includes *one sense* in which it is synonymous with *approximate*, it also has a sense in which it is synonymous with *close*, in all its senses rather than the mere senses in which *approximate* is. For example, Times Square and Duffy Square are proximate; they are not approximate. The firing on Fort Sumpter was the proximate cause of the Civil War, not the approximate cause. In fact, in "π is 3.14159265 . . . or 3 1/7," the first figure is the proximate one (being physically near to the π) while the second figure is approximate (not exact). In fact even though the first figure is closer to the real value of π, it is not more approximate (though it is more proximate). The more proximate something is the closer it is. The more approximate, the farther it is from exactness.

Charles Kluepfel
Bloomfield, New Jersey

You note that the term "shuttle" was adopted as a metaphor for "the subway in New York that runs between Times Square and Grand Central Station. . . ."

Surely you mean Grand Central Terminal. There is a Grand Central Station, but it's the branch of the Post office that is located on Lexington Avenue several blocks north of the train depot.

Frank McNeirney
Bethesda, Maryland

Punmeister

"I could never watch *The Wizard of Oz in toto*," writes Gary Muldoon of Rochester to the would-be global punmeister, adding an apologetic post-script: "*Sari.*"

This is a multilingual pun, and instead of eliciting the usual unilingual groan, it sails off into the ether, unappreciated except by the most ardent of language lovers. If you need an explanation about Toto being Dorothy's dog, and *in toto* being the Latin for "in the whole," or the sound of "sorry" matching the Sanskrit word for a garment made by wrapping a long cloth around the body, this is not the subject for you. Turn directly to the crossword and pull up your shorts.

French-speaking paronomasiacs often say, "Choose your *poisson*," playing the word for "fish" against the English word *poison*. Carl Silverman of Madison, Wisconsin, enjoys his "breakfast of champignons," and Edward Weingart of Pittsburgh notes the sad ending of a bicultural affair when the gal said, "*Je t'adore,*" and the guy heard, "Shut da door."

Linda Amster of the *New York Times* has a more creative *jeu de mots,* which translates as "play on words." A Parisian fan of old Glenn Miller recordings, who called his youthful companion *mon petit chouchou* ("my little cabbage"), ordered his inamorata a case of wine. When it appeared among some other cases, he asked the wine merchant, "Pardon me, boy, is that the Châteauneuf-du-Chouchou?"

One egg like that is un oeuf; mais oui move on? (Look at that "S-car" go.)

Enough Americans have German roots to recognize the name of the forged-steel prying instrument made by the Stanley Tool Company, the Wonder Bar. The *New York Times* could not resist headlining a piece about Chancellor Helmut Kohl's epicurean enthusiasms "With Hopes for the Wurst." German bartenders, when asked for "dry martini," serve up three cocktails.

Punmeisters on their way to India to take lunch at a new deli had despaired of getting a contribution from Spanish until Marshall Bernstein of Roslyn, L.I., chipped in with Gertrude Stein's recipe for Spanish rice: "*Arroz is arroz is arroz.*"

Globe-circling translingual puns include a Japanese chinaware brush with Spanish: *"Mikasa es su casa."* A combination of Yiddish-English mixed with the sound, though not the fact, of Japanese is the teahouse, frequented by lawyers, named "Sosume." And Representative David Dreier of California titled his case for free trade with Japan "Open Sashimi."

The final entry—by James W. Fesler of Hamden, Conn., and in Latin to Japanese—requires some setting up. The Roman orator Cicero, launching his attack on the politician he suspected of plotting an assassination, expressed his revulsion at the degeneration of high principle in his era with *O tempora! O mores!* ("O, the times! O, the bad new principles!") With this as background comes the cry of the Latin-trained Japanese chef deep-frying an eel: "O tempura! O morays!"

The purpose of this compundium is to push the envelope of multilingualism, thereby displaying a lexicographer's adherence to the wok ethic.

I am so addicted to Yiddish puns that my wife calls me a jew de mot.

> Bern Marcowitz
> New York, New York

The French employ a playful kind of Franglais most of us never see.

Take the number seven, or *sept.* A CD is a CD even in France but a cassette, in an ad or in any record shop window, will appear as a *K-7. K,* of course is pronounced *kah.*

A sign outside a printing shop in a Paris suburb reads: OFF-7.

A tanning salon in Lyons, open seven days a week, displayed a sign reading: Sun—7 Sur 7.

In a *New Yorker* story many years ago, Peter DeVries (remember him?) had a soignée New Canaan matron complimenting her plumber on his new truck.

"Oh," he replied, "just a simple van ordinaire."

> Frank Prial
> New York, New York

It is said that Sigmund Freud once asked his colleague Carl Jung (who at the time was actually no longer really Jung but had grown Adler) the following poser. "What," asked papa F, "comes between sex and fear." Jung's immediate and penetrating insight provided an answer and he replied, *"fünf."* For the many psychohistorians who dispute this response, I say line up and take a number.

> David Rapkin
> New York, New York

I offer this one to add to your collection. Brutus: "Caesar, have you tried the prune danish?" Caesar: "Et tu, Brutus."

Abner M. Beder
Rockville Centre, New York

Would you accept word play on a foreign name? "Verlaine was always chasing Rimbaud."—Dorothy Parker

Warren Boroson
Glen Rock, New Jersey

An interlingual pun (my coinage): *Mise en Scene* = Ah's pregnant . . .

Gerald Wexler
New York, New York

For the sheer joy of it, I offer the following to the Punmeister:

1. The preferred Mexican cartoon character is Porque Pig.
2. On Asian dairy farms it is important to give Kurds their whey.
3. The Bolshoi Ballet is Gudenov for me.
4. Meet me in New Orleans and I'll bayou a drink.
5. He played behind the plate for the Braves but was afraid of injury, that's why they called him Chicken Catcher Torre.

Vincent P.A. Benedict
Collegeville, Pennsylvania

I hope that your next international pundemonium column will not Passover my reference to Shakespeare's "Matzodo About Nothing."

Henry R. Nusbaum
Danbury, Connecticut

Proposed ad for French telephone company to enhance afternoon usage: *L'Après-midi d'un PHONE.*

Tad Szulc
Washington, D.C.

Three cats in Montreal whose names were Un, Deux, and Trois were walking across a frozen pond, but it was spring and the ice was melting rapidly and Un, Deux, Trois quatre cinq.

Francis X. Hogan
Potomac, Maryland

Push Has Come to Shove

The moment of *moment of truth* has passed. Ernest Hemingway's coinage in his 1932 book *Death in the Afternoon* was "The whole end of the bullfight was the final sword thrust, the actual encounter between the man and the animal, what the Spanish call the *moment of truth.*" In truth, the Spanish call it *la hora de la verdad*, "the hour of truth," but Hemingway's translation was an improvement on the Spanish phrase. (Although his famously spare prose could have spared the "whole" in "the whole end.")

The *moment's* moment was pushed, perhaps even shoved, aside by the now-familiar but much unappreciated Americanism *when push comes to shove*. Its definition is given in the *Oxford English Dictionary* as "when action must back up threats." That sense of "deeds replacing words" continues, but the meaning now also embraces "now or never" and "the critical moment." A few years ago, the voguish *at the end of the day* had its time in the sun, but its meaning was closer to "when all is said and done" than "moment of truth." Today, *when push comes to shove* is undisputed king of the critical-moment hill.

Deservedly so; W.P.C.T.S., as the Phrasedick Brigade refers to it, is one of the most vividly evocative Americanisms. First compare the etymologies of its verb components: *push*, from the Latin *pulsare*, "to beat," came to mean "to exert force against"; *shove*, from Germanic roots, became the Old English *scūfan*, used in *Beowulf*, and means "to push aside roughly or violently."

Note the shading of synonymy to give the phrase its impact: W.P.C.T.S. draws a distinction between the steady exertion of force in *push* and the roughness and forcefulness in *shove*. The focus is on the point at which the *pushing* reaches a critical mass and *shoving*, with its severity, takes over.

What is the provenance of this folk poetry? The *OED's* earliest citation is 1958, in *Cast the First Stone*, a book about prostitution in New York, by John Martin Murtagh and Sara Harris: "Some judges . . . talk nice and polite. . . . Then, *when push comes to shove*, they say, 'Six months in the workhouse.'"

A couple of my correspondents dispute the American origin; one recollects, without citation, usage in the north of England in the mid-'30s. But slanguist Jesse Sheidlower, formerly of Random House reference division, notes that "we've collected two other pre-1960 examples from black authors. I'd say that a black-English origin for the phrase is pretty likely."

He's right. Peter Tamony, the one-man data base of San Francisco who left his thousands of slang clippings to the University of Missouri at Columbia, clipped an even earlier usage from page 148 of Bernard Wolfe's *The Late Risers*, a 1954 novel about the inhabitants of Insomnia Alley, or Times Square. In a conversation, a black man says: "If *push comes to shove* I might pull my old lady's coat. Could be she know some freakish mumbling man."

Note the way the *s* is clipped off both *come* and *know*, a rejection of subject-verb agreement characteristic of the African-American dialect. Amid the condemnations that "ebonics" is a denigrating substitute for Standard English, dialectologists can point to the contribution to the language of *W.P.C.T.S.*, with all its subtle synonymy.

Ol' Pete was long one of my best slang sources; I salute Randy Roberts, senior manuscript specialist at the Peter Tamony Collection, for tracking this earliest citation. Other evidence there of the phrase's black origin is a recollection from Norman Pierce of Jack's Record Cellar in San Francisco of *Shove Day*, or *Bump Day*, the traditional Thursday off for domestic servants in the 1920s, "on which blacks 'accidentally' jostled whites in public places, railways, streetcars, etc."

Rock music picked up the phrase with "When Push Comes to Shove," a song by the Shoes in 1984, remade by the Grateful Dead three years later. "If Push Comes to Shove" was the title of another song, recorded by Delbert McClinton. (It's surprising, in light of the black-English etymology, that no early blues use has been found.) Obviously this is a phrase whose origin cries out for further scholarly digging and the help, with citations, of Lexicographic Irregulars.

Push is making it big in American English. *Pushing the envelope* comes from 19th-century mathematics, in which curves were said to be "enveloped" by each other; in 1944 *envelope condition* was applied to lighter-than-air aircraft, and in 1979 the writer Tom Wolfe popularized the phrase being used by astronauts in *The Right Stuff*. "The 'envelope' was a flight-test term referring to the limits of a particular aircraft's performance," he wrote. " '*Pushing the envelope*,' probing the outer limits of the envelope, seemed to be the great challenge and satisfaction of flight tests."

But *push* has its dark side. *Push poll* became controversial when the technique surfaced in politics in 1994. Peter Black wrote in the *Rocky Mountain News* that Mike Bird, a Colorado gubernatorial candidate, "continues to be outraged by a '*push poll*' . . . designed to alert voters to Bird's alleged political failures."

A *push poll* is more a trick of persuasion than a legitimate polling technique.

The caller, posing as a scientific pollster, presents negative information about a candidate and asks the potential voter's opinion of it—in effect, *pushing* the voter into a decision. ("Would you vote for So-and-so if you knew he was once arrested for mopery?") The June 1996 *Washington Monthly,* making an analogy to telemarketing, denounced the sneaky polling as "tele-mudslinging." Its practitioners matched this dysphemism with their own euphemism: "advocacy calling."

And then there's *push technology.* This popped up in an interview in the Jan. 2, 1995, issue of *Computerworld* magazine. Asked about the Internet, the director of the M.I.T. Medialab, Nicholas Negroponte, said: "The way to think about the 'net is to compare it with the technologies of '*push*' as we know them today in newspapers, magazines and television. The 'net will be the technology of 'pull' tomorrow, where people reach into it or have their intelligent agents do so on their behalf."

Mr. Negroponte's phrase—using *push* to describe salesmen hawking products or services—was rearranged into *push technology* by others who thought such pushiness to be akin to godliness; in March 1996, Brad Chase, a marketing vice president of Microsoft, was quoted in *M2 Presswire,* an on-line business-newsletter service, saying, "By working with innovative '*push*' technology vendors" his firm was able to provide "personalized delivery of information."

When this *push* appeared on the covers of *Business Week* and *Wired* and on the front page of the *Wall Street Journal,* James Gleick wrote in the *New York Times Magazine:* "The idea behind this huge four-letter word goes something like this: the Internet is a vast and confusing junkyard. You should not have to click your way aimlessly hither and yon. Companies with the information you need should *Push* it to you."

To lovers of the independent spirit (sometimes called apostles of anarchy), the wave of the future is *pull,* where the self-controlling individual fishes for what he or she likes; to them, *push technology* are dirty words, almost as sinister as *pusher* is to a narcotics cop. "*Push* implies interruption and salesmanship," wrote my colleague in columny. "*Pull* implies choice."

To many others in the news business and the advertising industry, *push technology* is key to future free enterprise, capital formation and the American Way. If a showdown is imminent, it won't be when pull comes to yank.

Years before rock music picked up on *when push comes to shove,* a ballet by Twyla Tharp, called "Push Comes to Shove," was premiered by American Ballet Theatre, on January 9, 1976. Among the principal dancers were Mikhail Baryshnikov and Martine van Hamel. The score was a beguiling mix of Franz Joseph Haydn's Symphony No. 82 in C, and ragtime music by Joseph Lamb. The choreography featured a playful contrast between ballet and show biz dancing, embodied in the antics of Mr. Baryshnikov and a derby hat. I suppose the title was suggestive of the tension between old and new, although what Ms. Tharp had in mind by it, precisely, I can't say. "Push Comes to Shove" was an audience favorite and provided Mr. Baryshnikov with one of his signature roles.

Lou D'Angelo
New York, New York

I am prompted to write to you by your parenthetical remark about Hemingway's, "famously spare prose [which] could have spared the 'whole' in 'the whole end.'" You were alluding to his novel, *Death in the Afternoon*.

Had he written, "The end of the bullfight was the final sword thrust . . ." he would have been giving a simple, factual bit of information about that part of the event. But his interest was not merely to inform about, say, the chronological order of the stages of the bullfight. With the word "whole" where it is, I think, he adds a sense of drama building up in the bullfight and now reaching its critical mass just at that moment, which becomes the fulcrum for the decisive thrust with the sword. With the sword comes the moment of death for the bull, and that is the "whole" point of the bullfight.

Oscar Zambrano
Philadelphia, Pennsylvania

If Hemingway had omitted "whole," it would have sounded as if he meant that the kill was the *conclusion* of the corrida. "Whole" shows he meant "end" as purpose, aim—perhaps final cause.

Judith S. Stix
St. Louis, Missouri

Queuing Up

"Amid the quotidian trials of suburban life," wrote *Newsweek* in appreciation of Erma Bombeck, "she found a way to make us laugh."

Paradoxically, *quotidian* is just the sort of word that the late humorist would never use. She dispensed simple wisdom in plain style: "Never go to a doctor whose office plants have died." Highfalutin language was not in her.

Quotidian is a highbrow word for "ordinary, humdrum, routine." The best synonym for that Sunday word is "everyday," but many writers shy away from such a commonplace word. The Latin roots of *quotidian* are *quotus*, "of what number," and *dies*, "day." Other words from the Latin *quotus* include *quote*, *quotient* and the infamous *quota*.

Shakespeare's Rosalind, evading her admirer in *As You Like It,* uses the word as an attributive in the phrase *quotidian fever,* a chronic condition. She observes, "I would give him some good counsel, for he seems to have the *quotidian* of love upon him."

"School uniforms, the evils of tobacco and the mindless dreck on television," wrote Michael Elliott in the *Washington Post,* are the *"quotidian* issues" engaging so many of us today. (*Dreck,* first cited in print by James Joyce in *Ulysses,* is a Yiddish word that today is euphemized as "rubbish, nonsense, junk.")

Reviewing a performance called "Timepiece," Don Shirley in the *Los Angeles Times* observed how "the piece explored both cosmic and *quotidian* time." Karen Matthews of the Associated Press wrote of a comic-strip character created by Ben Katchor, Julius Knipl, who "inhabits a world forever caught between the *quotidian* and the surreal." In the *New York Times,* Trip Gabriel noted that Bill Gates of Microsoft foresees a future in which people equipped with pocket P.C.'s will no longer need *"quotidian* encumbrances" like money, identification or a watch.

The word is hot, and when a word beginning with *qu* gets hot, ordinary readers—*quotidian* types—need to brace for it.

Just look at the rise of *quantum.* That word, from the Latin for "how much," was legalese for "amount" in English law courts for centuries. Then along came Max Planck and Albert Einstein with a theory of matter and energy that later became *quantum* mechanics and *quantum field theory,* about the uncertain way atoms and molecules work.

When did *quantum* begin leaping and jumping? More to the point, when did *quantum* gain the metaphorical sense showing a "sudden, significant increase"? On Dec. 3, 1970: "The ability of marine technology," wrote Tony Loftas, the marine correspondent for *New Scientist* magazine of London, "to take *quantum* leaps in innovation means that a laissez-faire approach to ocean mineral resources can no longer be tolerated."

Every time I use *quantum jump* to mean "giant step" or "radical increase," nuclear physicists wearily write to point out how illogical the phrase is—that in their teeny-tiny atomic universe, the change is so small as to be hardly observable. But what do physicists know from semantics? The phrase means what laymen take it to mean, and we think of it as one whopping lurch into a new order of magnitude.

When Prof. Alan Sokal of New York University parodied literary theorists in an unsuspecting academic journal, he subtitled his spoof "Toward a Transformative Hermeneutics of *Quantum* Gravity," illustrating the vague voguishness of *quantum.* And when the *Wall Street Journal* reported recently on the disappointing record of the financier George Soros's *Quantum* Fund, the headline chosen was the punning *"Quantum* Fund: No Leap."

We're not out of the Q Soup yet. "The Museo Archeologico is a gem of a collection," wrote Glenn Collins of the *New York Times*, "housed in a building that is a copy of a *quondam* temple." Is a *quondam* temple the latest place for a campaign fund raiser? No; the word comes from the Latin *quom*, "when," and means "former, previous, onetime, erstwhile." (My personal favorite in this nexus of nostalgia, "whilom," is archaic.)

Some years back, Milton Lewis, a former colleague of mine at the old *New York Herald Tribune*, expressed his irk at my too-frequent use of the verb *aver* in one of these columns, and identified himself under his signature as "Quondam, *N.Y. Herald Tribune.*" When his note was included in a collection of these language columns, and came out signed "Milton Lewis, Quondam, N.Y.," he wrote again to ask, "As a *quondam* New Yorker, can you please tell me where 'Quondam, N.Y.' might be?" Ain't no such place, except in a former life.

In the queuing-up sweepstakes, there is a final entry, though the *qu* sound is spelled more logically. The *New York Times*'s Maureen Dowd, a *quondam* reporter who is now anything but a *quotidian* columnist, took a *quantum* jump into political sociology with an article justifying the return of debutante cotillions among the White Anglo-Saxon Protestant community: "If there is Kwanzaa, why not cotillions?"

Kwanzaa, according to an Internet site specializing in the subject, is a seven-day, post-Christmas, post-Hanukkah, nonreligious African-American holiday "formulated, devised, developed and initiated by Dr. Maulana Ron Karenga on Dec. 26, 1966" to celebrate the black cultural heritage and spirituality in the black family.

In Clarence Major's 1994 dictionary of African-American slang, *Juba to Jive,* *Kwanzaa* is defined as a Swahili word meaning "first fruit." Another Swahili word with the *qu* sound used by celebrants is *kwaheri,* a farewell expressed with the expectancy of meeting again, a happy note on which to conclude today's column.

As a WWII serviceman, I worked in a quondam hut called a Quonset.

Leonard Kian
Grand Rapids, Michigan

Neither the popular usage of "quantum leap" to mean a huge increase nor the physicists' grounds for objection to that usage has any validity. Arguing about the *size* of the leap is simply beside the point. It is its *suddenness* that is relevant.

In the submicroscopic world, particle energies can change from one specific magnitude to another with infinite suddenness—literally, in no time flat. In other words, the amount of energy changes from this quantity to that without spending any time whatsoever in between. (In fact, in-between values are impossible, but that's another lecture.) "Quantum leap" can be accurately used, then, to mean an exceptionally sudden leap or jump or, in your word, a lurch, but not necessarily a giant, radical, or whopping one. Or a tiny one, for that matter.

But a metaphor for zero-time suddenness isn't very useful in the real (macroscopic) world. So, ever in search of the most impressive superlative, speakers and writers have adopted "quantum jump" as a mark of their erudition. They miss that mark, of course, but since usage diffuses like a drop of ink in water, the mark has moved to accommodate them.

Robert L. Wolke
Pittsburgh, Pennsylvania

Quo Lingua?

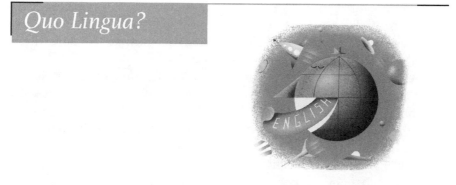

A century hence, our 69th President (assuming nobody will get re-elected) will take the inaugural oath and begin his address, "Fellow countrymen and women . . ."

Downloading that transmission directly into his brain through the receiver in his tooth, some way-post-modern literary critic in Ulan Bator will say, "The use of 'fellow' in that salutation is redundant." Half a world away, a refrigerator demonstrator in Antarctica's leading shopping center will reply, "And he has to use 'and women' after 'countrymen' to avoid sexism, leading to an awkward prolixity." Intruding into their discussion via the Interthink, an Australian aborigine checking seat belts on the moon shuttle will pile on with "Why doesn't he just say 'fellow citizens'?"

I believe that discussion among people of different cultures will be in English because English will be the world's first second language in A.D. 2100. (Note the placement of "A.D." On the plaque left on the moon in 1969, under the "Here men from planet Earth" copy, is the date "July 1969, A.D." I helped write that copy, and to sneak in a mention of God, I used the initials for *anno Domini*, "in the year of our Lord." But I didn't know at the time that "A.D." should come before, not after, the date. That plaque has got to be fixed.)

On what can such a prediction be based? Bilingualism, for one thing. A billion or so people already speak English as a second language, which no other one of the more than 3,000 languages now being spoken can claim. More people speak dialects of Chinese, but not as a second language; by 2100, people will use one language to speak to family and neighbors, and will need another to deal with the world. With all its grammatical irregularity and illogical pronunciation, English is best suited to be that bridge tongue. Why? One reason is that it's the most welcoming, absorbent, easily adaptable language in the world.

We borrow words from everywhere and forget to return them. Loanwords abound; even *loanword* is borrowed, from the German *Lehnwort*. Sometimes we shade the meaning a little—the French *crayon*, "pencil," in our borrowing means "a writing instrument of colored wax"—but we call our footwear a "shoe," related to the German *Schuh*, though the British prefer "boot," from early French.

Some of our loanwords are recognizably foreign: *honcho*, Japanese for "squad leader," was recently absorbed to mean "boss" (a word we picked up from Dutch and from South Africa's Afrikaans' *baas*), and we further turned *honcho* into a verb meaning "to oversee." A Hindi word like *guru* is obviously "Indian," but not all English speakers realize the Hindi origin of *dungaree, thug* and *pundit*. ("Elite media pundit" mixes French, Latin and Hindi.)

Spanish words enliven our vocabulary. Not just the obvious borrowings like *bronco, fiesta* and *siesta*, but takings that aficionados recognize like *stampede, chocolate, tomato* and the word George Washington noted in his 1751 diary, *avocado*. Jeff Flannery, at the Library of Congress, supplies the diary entry from Washington's visit to Barbados, where he enjoyed "the Pine Apple," as well as "the *Avagado* pair." (The father of our country was a lousy speller.)

We have shlepped words from Yiddish (some say that "phooey!" comes from *pfui*), from Philippine Tagalog *(boondocks)*, from Africa *(jazz, yam, gumbo, voodoo)*, as well as from aboriginal Americans: the Algonquian *naiack*, "point or corner," led to our "neck of the woods," and though we found *cawcauwassoughes*, "tribal leader," hard to pronounce, we simplified it to *caucus*, meaning "private meeting of leaders," or so the elite media pundits *kowtowing* (Chinese) to them say.

Not every language is so open-mouthed. The French have a Government body, the *Conseil Supérieur de la Langue*, looking with horror at *le weekend* (insisting on *la fin de semaine*). This ossification bureau issues *diktats* (German) and *ukases* (Russian) against *le software*, demanding *logiciel*. Americans hoot at this foolish tongue-depression as we freely lift a few words to tell the French to relax on a *chaise longue*, belt down a *cognac* or go to a *matinee*.

Because of that melting-pot openness, English is equipped to strengthen and extend its second-language lead in the coming century. What holes in its vocabulary need filling? To help English along, let us select from the *smorgasbord* (Swedish) of world languages some of the terms likely to fill those holes.

We have already gleaned *Schadenfreude*, "the guilty pleasure one takes from the misfortune of others," from the German; I would add *Finger-spitzengefühl*, "a sandpapered-fingertip sensitivity and savviness," to English's repertory. To counter pedantic language mavens, the Germans offer *Schlimmbesserung*, "making a mistake in correcting." (The English neologism *incorrection* does not have the fierce denunciatory sound of "That, Sir, is a *Schlimmbesserung!*")

In return for giving *sunaku* to Japanese (it's a "snack bar"), we can happily appropriate *higamu*, a word of enriched meaning that goes beyond the English *moping* to encapsulate "feeling sorry for yourself for being burdened with some misfortune you did not deserve." Prof. Leo Hanami of George Washington University also suggests we lift a subtle Japanese word for a form of demurral that is pronounced like "endeero" and means "the act of pretending not to want something even when you do, out of respect for someone in authority."

From the Hindi or Arabic—there's some argument about origin—we could appropriate *khabar*, "news or information." Tired of the endlessly repeated *Information Age?* No *khabar* is good *khabar*, but be sure to get the throat-clearing sound of the *kh*.

From China, where we got *gung ho*, English could take *tiu lien*, pronounced twe-leen, which carries the important concept of "losing face," or being unacceptably derogated and shamed. (When the journalist missed the *khabar* and was *tweleened*, he made a little *endeero*.) Davis Lee and Richard Yin, also of George Washington University, suggest a term that to me sounds like *chutong sunyi*, which stands for "seeking common ground while resolving differences," but which could come a-cropper when discussing *zhishi chan quan*, "intellectual property rights."

Along about 2050, the French, including the most chauvinist, will have incorporated the Cajun and Parisian word *canaille* into their second-language English. This useful term (from the Italian *cane*, "dog") is often used to denote "a curiously endearing corrupt politician." This is more specific than "amiable rogue" and, as democracy spreads across the globe, will be a widely used noun. An especially loyal, endearing crooked pol is a "yellow-dog *canaille*," though that will get resistance from the antiredundancy Squad Squad. (The French are good with words drawn on animal images. I'm betting on *chatoyant*, "glittering like a cat's eyes in the darkness.")

The competition among world languages will be keen to replace the English *no big deal*, in the sense of "never mind, don't bother," which is already showing signs of weakening. The German *mach nichts*, Anglicized by a generation of

American G.I.'s to *mox nix,* is in the running, but Samia Montasser, an instructor in Arabic at Johns Hopkins School of Advanced International Studies, says that *maalish,* pronounced mah-LISH, is a worthy entry. Another Arabic word, for people tired of "wow-ee" and "hoo-boy," is *yasalaam,* which might meld into the Americanism *yessiree.*

Spanish, spoken so much in the United States, will undoubtedly give future English an *abrazo.* This is usually translated as an "embrace," but it misses the hug's formality as well as its enthusiasm. A "man on horseback," or figure of military authority, is a *caudillo,* and there is no reason for that not to develop into *caudilla,* for a woman in charge, and not riding sidesaddle, either. Cynthia McClintock, a scholar of Latin American life, offers a delicious word likely to be picked up in English: *coyuntura,* "the will of the electorate"; unlike the German *Zeitgeist,* now part of the English language, meaning "spirit of the age," *coyuntura* is directly concerned with the era's political spirit. Watch for this one; it won't just be used by *Latinos* or by *mestizos,* "people of mixed Latin American Indian and Caucasian parentage."

If I am right about all this—if, a century from now, a deliciously peppered English is the first language of a third of the world and the second language of the rest of the world—my *chatoyant* descendants will have a right to *sismek.* That's a Turkish verb meaning "to swell, to puff up with pride."

Arigato and good night.

The term for "losing face" is "diu lian" in Chinese current Romanization; "twee-leen" must be a dialect aberration. "Tiu" in the old-fashioned Wade-Giles system was in fact pronounced "diu" or "deeoh," and "t'iu" was actually pronounced "teeoh" in the old system.

"Qiu Tong Cun Yi" definitely means what they say it means. The PRC uses it constantly, but in practice it often turns out to mean: "what is mine is mine and what is yours is negotiable."

"Zhishi Chan Quan" is phonetically correct. "Zhishi Fenzi" in Mao's time was however a pejorative term. "Zhishi" means "intellectual" and "fenzi" means "faction."

Ambassador James R. Lilley
Director of Asian Studies
Resident Fellow
American Enterprise Institute for Public
Policy Research
Washington, D.C.

In the Chinese national language (kuoyu) the compound you cited which expresses the concept of "losing face" does not sound much like the "twe leen" you suggested.

The sound of "tiu lien" (as it stands, a reasonable kuoyu romanization), is perhaps better represented by "dee-o lee-en." The "t" is unaspirated.

As to gaps in English which could use some remedy, the "he/she" conundrum is neatly solved by the gender-neutral Chinese "ta" ("t" aspirated this time), which is used interchangeably for he, she, or it. That's one we desperately need!

A. J. Poppen
Oakland, New Jersey

I must dispute your categorization of "chocolate" and "tomato" as of Spanish origin. We have received the name of these two excellent foods from the Náhuatl-speaking ancestors of contemporary Mexicans. The names of the two plants were respectively: *chocólatl,* and *tómatl* (referring only to the green kind). A red tomato before Cortés was known as a *xictómatl,* in contemporary Spanish *jitomate,* a red tomato. The Spaniards had difficulties with the Náhuatl "*tl*" ending, and changed it to "*te*" *(chocolate, tomate).*

However it is not surprising that General Washington had trouble with his avocadoes. The proper Nahuatl word for this delightful vegetable is *ahuácatl,* which the Spanish wisely turned into *aguacate.* However, somewhere along the line (perhaps only in the British colonies) *aguacate* later became "avocado," a word which the *Real Academia Española* does not recognize as being in the Spanish language.

No wonder President Washington had difficulties with this vegetable! By the time he visited the Barbados, the English colonists there must have decided that the Spanish word *aguacate* was unpronounceable, and therefore changed it to "avocado," influenced—perhaps—by (lawyer), since the intervocalic "v" and "b" are interchangeable at least in Latin America. Why must avocados remind us of lawyers?

John Foster Leich
Cornwall Bridge, Connecticut

Perhaps it would have been more accurate to have credited Mexico and the Nahuatl language for tomato and chocolate in your article last Sunday. The Spanish language is just about a pass-through, especially for tomato.

The Nahuatl words *tomatl* and *xocoatl* are cited by *Webster's Third New International Dictionary.* I was told by my linguist father that the "X" in Mexican is pronounced "sh" but maybe it is closer to "ch," which would explain both chocolate and Chicano. Spanish changed the "x" to "j" in Mexico (Mejico).

Mary Laird Flanagan
Nantucket, Massachusetts

Was it just coincidence that you closed your piece on loanwords with *arigato?*

This is probably the only instance of the Japanese taking a word from Portuguese. The original is *obrigado*—The Spanish *obligado* altered by the typical Portuguese l–r consonant shift.

I learned this from a tour guide in Portugal. If his story is unreliable then I may be guilty of *schlimmbesserung.*

Norman Brust
New York, New York

P.S. Your *"mach nichts"* should be *"macht nichts."* Oh, well—mox nix.

The Rage Rage

The Angry American, an especially timely book by the political scientist Susan J. Tolchin, is subtitled *How Voter Rage Is Changing the Nation.*

The word *rage* (from the Latin *rabia,* "madness," from which comes *rabid*) is coming at us with a roar. Psychologists took up *suppressed rage* as the source of violent acts, and in its outwardly directed word from (although *outrage* comes from the French *outre,* "beyond," not from *rage*), it was attacked by Bob Dole in his acceptance speech: "A society that cannot defend itself from *outrage* does not deserve to survive."

Beyond *voter rage,* which merely throws incumbents out of office, is *road rage,* which forces autos off the highway. In 1988, the *St. Petersburg Times* reported, "A fit of 'road rage' has landed a man in jail, accused of shooting a woman passenger whose car had 'cut him off' on the highway." After flirting with *driver's rage* and *motorist's rage,* writers have settled on the alliterative form. It is viewed with opprobrium; an Irish newspaper noted that a publication in Uganda criticized Britain as a land "beset by hooliganism, illegitimate births . . . necrophilia and even road rage."

Beware of voters unwilling to take it anymore driving to the polls; *rage* is all the rage.

Rescinderella

When Brit Hume, the intrepid ABC White House correspondent, tried to pin down the press secretary about his interpretation of the meaning of *rescission,* Michael McCurry admitted, "That's what a rescissions bill is—cutting spending that's already been appropriated by Congress."

The official transcript spelled the word with three *s*'s. Mr. Hume then called me to say that a controversy was developing over this: Was it spelled *rescission* or *recision?* Was there not a fine shade of difference in meaning when the three *s*'s were used?

Perceptive question. The extra *s*'s make a difference, as Mr. Hume suspected; these are different words with overlapping meanings. (William Lee of New York reports seeing a third spelling, *recission,* on an ABC News on-screen caption.)

The *Oxford English Dictionary* argues that *rescission,* with an *s* before the *c,* means "a pruning, a cutting back"; that's what *scissors* do, using the Latin root of *rescindere.* The similar Latin word *recidere* has the more severe meaning of "to cut off, annul."

Thus, a *recision* is a cutting off, while a *rescission* is merely a cutting back. Put another way in a different metaphor, a *recision* is an annulment, a *rescission* a divorce.

We are really splitting hairs here; is it worth it? I turned to Elizabeth S. Girsch, associate editor of the *Middle English Dictionary,* the much-needed language project now going on at the University of Michigan. (They're already up to *W;* keep going, fellas—the end is in sight! Or as they would say in Middle English, the ende time aprocheth.) After giving me a close reading of the incorporation of the two roots into the Middle French and English languages, the *MED* scholar predicts a merger:

"Because of the long-standing semantic overlap and orthographic similarity between the two words," Ms. Girsch observes, "and because languages resist excessive homonymy [different words that sound the same], it's hardly surprising that *recision* and *rescission* have been, and are being, confused, conflated and probably ultimately merged in the lexicons of some speakers of English. Under the circumstances, the simpler form has the edge."

Logic is on her side. But in the meantime, fine-tuning writers will use *rescission* to mean "cutback, sharp reduction," and *recision* to mean "cancellation, annulment, chopping off without a nickel."

When discussing budget cuts, the *New York Times* prefers the spelling *rescission* though the word is thought to carry the stilted feeling of Government jargon and its routine use is frowned on.

To keep the two spellings straight, the mnemonic is "use scissors to prune the *s* out of *rescind* when the decision is a cruel, all-out *recision.*"

Television reporters, however, are home free: the related words are pronounced the same.

The term is a matter of law, the Congressional Budget and Impoundment Control Act of 1974, where it is spelled out [rescission] and defined [at section 1011 (3)]. Thus, other spellings cannot give nuanced meanings, but only inaccurate ones.

A rescission is a technical, legal submission of a proposal to cancel [rescind] previously enacted legal authority to spend money. The budget act provides a process for considering those rescissions.

I was amused—and appalled—to notice just a few weeks ago that Congress's hometown newspaper, the *Washington Post,* misspelled the word in its lead front-page headline as well as in the text of several articles over several days. It finally ran an explanation [which it refused to call a correction] that henceforth there would be only one allowed spelling, rescission. Even the venerable *New York Times* at the same period ran more than one article with the term misspelled—but no correction.

Charles Stevenson
Washington, D.C.

Retronym Tops Oxymoron

"White House 'Volunteers' Were Paid by D.N.C." was the *Washington Post* headline. The word *volunteers* (coined around 1600 to describe those who enlist for military service of their own free will, coming to mean those who perform services without pay in 1638) was surrounded by quotation marks because the workers were paid by the Democratic National Committee under the guise of being unpaid White House helpers.

Such aides have been known as *paid volunteers* for several years, at least since the Clinton Administration proposed its Americorps program; in that activity, unconnected to the recent White House use, members receive a $7,500-per-year stipend, health-care benefits and a $4,725 one-time bonus toward college costs for doing local community work described as *volunteer activity.* The phrase *paid volunteers* is an oxymoron (like "thunderous silence"), since it joins words that are in seeming contradiction.

When a White House spokesman, Barry Toiv, was asked what one of the *paid volunteers* did before she took her White House job, he replied that she had worked in the same office without pay. To describe that work, the creative spokesman then coined a term known as a retronym, or a phrase minted to modify what had not needed modification before.

His retronymic coinage of a person really, no foolin', working without any remuneration in this world of recompensed good Samaritans: *"volunteer volunteer."*

A *retronym* is a word or phrase created to redefine a word overtaken by events, like "day baseball" and—as a *Times* colleague, Barth Healy, notes—"postal letters" (not E-mail).

Remember eggs? The makers of artificial eggs—Egg Beaters and Better'n Eggs—refer to their rival product (shot through with cholesterol and nourishment) not as mere *eggs*, but as *shell eggs*. Wandering through a supermarket looking for a grapefruit juice "not from concentrate," I came across Mott's *unfrozen concentrate*, which separates itself from the old-fashioned *frozen concentrate*.

Frank Mankiewicz, the retronym maven, sends in a clipping from the travel section of the *Washington Post* that hails a restaurant "nestled on a tiny piazza in the heart of the *Jewish ghetto*." Says Frank, "I cannot think of a more classic retronym."

He's right. *Ghetto* is the Italian word for "foundry," from the Latin jactare, "to cast"; it was the quarter in Venice occupied by Jews that had been the site of a cannon foundry. Later, the word was used to mean the Jewish quarter of any city, gaining a connotation of the place to which they were restricted. In the past generation, the word's meaning was broadened to cover any "quarter" or poor neighborhood, as in *urban ghetto*. That's how *Jewish ghetto*, recently a redundancy, became a retronym.

According to my copy of *The Oxford Universal Dictionary* (1955 edition), "ghetto" is an abbreviation of the Italian word *borghetto*, the diminutive form of *borgho*, or "borough." It refers to the section of a city where, chiefly in Italy, Jews were required to live.

John Boyce
Bethany, Connecticut

"Did you receive my *hard fax?*"

If yours is a lightning-like mind, equipped with a Dixium chip (32 times as fast as the snaily Pentium now in computers), a phased array of synapses will fire off in your brain to place in context and figure out what a *hard fax* is.

Opposite of an easy fax? No; no such thing as an easy fax. Must be a retronym.

A retronym is a noun phrase created to denote things that have been overtaken by events. Among early examples of retronyms was *day baseball*, created after *night baseball* became the norm, back when major league baseball was played at any time. *Acoustic guitar* was formed when most loud twanging was produced by *electric guitars*, and the old-fashioned guitar needed a special designation to assert its identity.

Do you remember *non-junk mail*—the collective term for those charming little personal letters, often written by hand, with colorful stamps on them delivered by the postal carrier, formerly the mailman? With the advent of *voice mail* and *E-mail*, we needed a new term for the old post; many electronic communicators use the term *snail mail*, but that derogation pains the carriers, and we seem to be settling on *hard mail*.

You won't find this in most dictionaries yet, but *hard* has a new sense of "written" or at least "on paper." Thus, a *hard fax* is—like *hard mail*—something you can hold in your hand, on the analogy of *hard copy*, "material written on a paper page that can be clenched and thrown into a basket by an irate editor."

The retronym was needed because a plain *fax* is being replaced by faxes received electronically, shown on a computer screen and not printed out. As these phantom faxes began to take hold, the fax printed on the antique fax machine instantly became a *hard fax*.

All this has happened in *real time*, a retronym necessitated by the emergence of *virtual time*. Frank Mankiewicz of Washington, who is the world's leading collector of these coinages, recently reported "one of my colleagues today told me she had enjoyed a weekend of *snow skiing*." (There are water skiers who have never seen the white stuff.) This came on top of Dr. Richard Franklin's report from Jersey City that he had spotted *caffeinated coffee*, drunk by those who hate *decaf* but cannot be sure what they will get if they ask only for coffee. (With *real cream*, a retronym necessitated by *half-and-half* or a *nondairy creamer*.)

These late flashes from the retronym front are being brought to you in *print journalism*, which used to be "the newspaper business" plus news magazines before *electronic journalism* forced the need to specify the ink that stains us rich wretches.

David Freedman, professor of history at the University of California at San Diego, reports this wild extension of a retronym on radio station KFSD. "I could hardly believe my ears," he writes, "but I heard a woman prefacing her music announcement with 'This is Christmas Eve day morning.'"

Robert Heinbein, in his 1959 book *Starship Troopers*, refers to two of his futuristic soldiers hitting the chow line for "half a dozen shell eggs." This is probably to distinguish them from that bare of military cuisine, the dried egg. Heinbein served in the Army in WWII and probably picked up the term there, though this is surmise. Anyway, the retronym preceded the existence of artificial eggs.

David B. Pittaway
New York, New York

The origin of the term *real time* has to do with the analog computer, a type of computer in which physical processes represented by mathematical equations were simulated physically through the interconnection of electro-mechanical devices. (These computers were popular through the 1950s and were used through the 1960s, but are rarely used any more. They have been replaced by digital computers, which are now just called computers.)

Often, the physical processes simulated on analog computers had time as the independent variable, and might represent, for example, the operation of an airplane wing in response to the stresses of acceleration and wind resistance, or the movement of continental land masses grinding against each other.

An equation could be simulated with time speeded up, so that very slow processes could be carried out more conveniently, or simulated with time slowed down so that very rapid processes could be better observed. If a physical process were simulated in the time in which it would be expected to occur naturally, it would be said that the process was carried out in *real time.* I do not recall that the term *virtual time* was used in connection with a non-real-time simulation.

Roy G. Saltman
Columbia, Maryland

"Real time" is a phrase that has been around for about thirty years, or since electronic logic elements were reduced to high-speed silicon chips. Therefore, "real time" is not a retronym for the recently-coined "virtual time."

As opposed to a non-real time operation such as the updating of a bank's accounts on the night after business, a computer program operating in real time is activated by external stimuli *as they happen,* and responds in some logical, timely manner to manipulate the forces behind the stimuli. Thus, the computer is temporally interposed into some immediately controllable environment, and is said to operate in "real time."

In electronic warfare, for example, the airborne computer provides real timeliness in interpreting radar tracking signals emanating from enemy SAM sites, and then instituting appropriate jamming against such radars in order to deny lock-on to the foe. However, because the jamming also obliterates the aircraft's interception of the ominous radar, jamming is turned off from time to time in accordance with a sophisticated algorithm that allows just enough unprotected time to take a peek at how effective the jamming has been so far; the computer program then re-evaluates and reinstitutes jamming.

Allan Silver
New York, New York

With sadness and nostalgia, I note the increasing use of: "Gin Martini."

David C. Green
Pittsburgh, Pennsylvania

Further to *snow skiing:* the distinction depends on which word you stress in speaking. Stress *snow,* and you distinguish the activity from water skiing. But stress *skiing,* and you distinguish it from snowboarding.

Lawrence Brown
Boulder, Colorado

Regarding your discussion of retronyms, we do a lot of translation for computer companies. The other day, a gentleman called from California to say he wanted menus translated and I told him we in fact had done such things for a number of computer companies and was certain we could assist him as well. It took a little explaining before I understood that what he wanted translated was menus, as used in restaurants, and that the items to be translated were names of foods!

Lee Chadeayne
Acton, Massachusetts

The term *real time* long precedes the concept of *virtual time.* It was coined by musicians, classical and popular, who create pieces and performances in the studio by accretion, by generating sounds, by overdubbing, mixing and editing. Afterwards they have to figure out how to perform the studio-created music live and *in real time.*

The analogy would be between movies which are shot in separate bits and pieces and edited together and theater performances which, of course, must also be played *in real time.*

Even better than *acoustic guitar* is *acoustic piano.* Van Cliburn, for example, is an acoustic pianist.

Eric Salzman
Brooklyn, New York

You point out that hard fax and hard mail imply "on paper." From my vantage point as a computer professional, I realized that the term hard has evolved as an opposite to "soft," soft being derived from "software." With the advent of electronic mail and other methods of electronic communication, computer users have needed a way to distinguish between a paper copy and an electronic or "soft" copy. I often ask colleagues for a soft copy of a particular document or memo. This means that I want an electronic copy and either do not want to be bothered with paper or I need to modify the contents of the document or memo. The soft copy can take the form either of a floppy disk, or, as is increasingly the case, of an e-mail file.

Once we (computer professionals) started using the term soft copy, it was only a matter of time that the word "hard" would begin to be "retronym"-ed to other forms of communication, as you point out, such as hard fax, hard memo, hard mail, etc. And it was also just a matter of time before this term made its way into more general usage (that is beyond the computer profession.)

Christopher S. Riello
Hamden, Connecticut

Riffraff

After Bob Dole ruminated aloud that he had been chosen as President Ford's 1976 running mate because his name, like Ford's, had only four letters, Katharine Q. Seelye of the *New York Times* wrote, "His aides worry that these idle *riffs* will continue until he feels secure that he has won the nomination."

Next day, the newspaper editorialized about what it called Senator Dole's "laundry list *riff*" about what the campaign was likely to address in coming months.

Only a week before, Alessandra Stanley, co-chief of the *Times*'s Moscow bureau, described a Muscovite's grumblings as "a *riff* about high consumer prices and the black market."

Use it, don't abuse it; what is a *riff*, that all our scribes commend it? In one sense, it is a frequently repeated phrase or passage inserted, like boilerplate, in conversation or oratory. In another sense, it is an improvised "line," put out to create a favorable impression. In yet another meaning, a *riff* is a "play on" or "take-off on" a more serious subject: the writer and director Gregory Weiden called one of his recent movies "a theological thriller about angels gone bad. It's a *riff* on Milton's Paradise Lost."

The origin is in jazz. "If you listen enough, and dig him enough," wrote a critic in the Sept. 20, 1935, issue of *Hot News*, "you will realize that that . . . *riff* is the high spot of the record." In 1950, in his biography of Jelly Roll Morton, Alan Lomax observed, "No jazz piano player can really play good jazz unless they try to give an imitation of a band, that is, by providing a basis of *riffs*." In the 1991 *Oxford Companion to Popular Music*, Peter Gammond defined the noun as "the repetition of a short distinctive phrase behind either a soloist or section and often used as a melodic feature. The device came early into jazz but was a special characteristic of the big-band era of the 1930s."

A *riff* can be an ostinato phrase—that is, a musical figure repeated at the same pitch throughout a composition. *Merriam-Webster's 10th Collegiate Dictionary* defines *riff* as "an ostinato phrase (as in jazz) typically supporting a solo improvisation" and then, right on top of current usage, gives an extended meaning of "a short succinct usually witty comment; also, bit, routine." That extension of meaning to "a repeated phrase" began about 1970, when *The New Yorker* wrote of a comedian, "He has an opportunity for some lovely comic *riffs.*" (Use it; don't abuse it.)

Controversy surrounds the etymology. *The Oxford English Dictionary* suggests a clip of *riffle*, based on the Old French *riffler*, "to graze, scratch, plunder," coming to mean "rubbing" in English. By 1894, *riffle* meant the special massage given playing cards by a cardsharp (now "card shark"); this fast shuffling led to the meaning of "a quick skim," as in *riffling* the pages of a book.

Cut the deck and deal over. Other lexicographers hold that *riff* is a shortening and alteration of the French musical noun *refrain*, "a repeated phrase or verse." (As Cole Porter wrote, "Let's skip the old verse and sing the refrain.") This theory strikes me as more likely because of the musical connection and the sense of repetition in a *riff*.

No, there's no connection with the *Riffs*, a Berber people living in the Rif, a mountainous region of Morocco, nor probably with *riffraff*, a third-order reduplication meaning "rabble" or "the great unwashed." That was originally *rif and raf*, meaning "every single one," from the French *rifler*, "to scratch," and *raffe*, "the act of sweeping."

Use it, don't abuse it. That's a wrap on a *riff*.

"Let's skip the old verse and sing the refrain"? Well did you evah? Could it be you? Between you and me, Cole Porter wrote "I'll skip the darn thing and sing the refrain."

Ronald Ley
Albany, New York

Rig That Jury, Jerry

Today we are going to straighten out, once and for all, *jury-rigged, jerry-built* and the confusing blend, *jerry-rigged*.

"They [the Iraqis] are trying to *jury-rig* SAM's," a Pentagon official was quoted about the replacement of surface-to-air missiles damaged by U.S. attacks, ". . . with radars to make them operational."

Steve Johnson of MSNBC's on-line service writes: "I'm assuming he meant that they were being fixed on a temporary or emergency basis. But he could have meant that the SAM's were rebuilt in a cheap manner, for which the phrase would be *jerry-built*. Are the two phrases of common origin?"

Old salts know that a *jury mast* is hastily put up to replace a mast that has been broken or swept away. The origin of this phrase, first used in print by Capt. John Smith in 1616, is obscure; logic suggests a clip of *injury*, but no citation support can be found.

In Herman Melville's 1851 novel *Moby Dick*, Captain Peleg describes what he and Ahab did when their ship lost three masts in a typhoon: "Life was what Captain Ahab and I was thinking of; and how to save all hands—how to rig *jury-masts*." The meaning is clearly "makeshift," a temporary contrivance for use in an emergency.

Jerry-built, first spotted in 1869, may be a corruption of *jury*, or a reference to Jeremiah or Jericho. When panning a musical in 1994, the *New York Times* critic David Richards wrote, "The *jerry-built* book by Mr. King and Mr. Masterson is just a series of stillborn sketches." The meaning is "slapped together, rickety," same as *jury-rigged*, but while the *jury-rigging* is admirable in a storm, the *jerry-building* is always pejorative.

Nice difference in meaning, no? If you agree, avoid *jerry-rigged*, which has been popping up lately, and *jury-built*, which has not yet appeared but will soon. They fuzz the distinction between the shipshape *jury-rigged* and the shoddy *jerry-built*. (And if you're complaining about a verdict, say the jury was *tampered with* rather than *rigged*, if only to keep things clear.)

Robusting Out All Over

Foggy Bottom is a good place to plumb for vogue words. I called Richard Holbrooke, former Assistant Secretary of State for Europe and Whatever Else Strobe Talbott Was Too Busy For (a long title, but descriptive), and asked what locution was hot.

"The word du jour is *robust*," Holbrooke replied without hesitation. "It is usually used in diplomacy when the opposite is meant. 'To put out a *robust* statement' means 'don't do anything but be noisy about it.' I was talking to Ambassador Bill Crowe in London, and he used it, then caught himself and said, 'I hate that word *robust*—what I mean is *vigorous*.'"

Dutifully, I ran an Infobank search and found the usage of this word—from the Latin *robustus,* "oaken," hence "strong"—busting out all over.

"This move by Beijing," said Robin Munro, Hong Kong director of Human Rights Watch about the arrest of a United States citizen, Harry Wu, "calls for the most *robust* and sternest response from Washington." (Meaning: "powerful, potent, puissant, vigorous, spirited.")

"This isn't a dessert wine," said a New Jersey vintner about his oak-aged raspberry wine. "It goes with *robust* steak and with spaghetti with lots of garlic." (Meaning: "hearty, hardy, sturdy.")

"We believe our competitive position will continue to improve," said an oracular C.E.O., "due to a *robust* product cycle." (Meaning: confused. Sales and earnings can be "robust," in the sense of "healthy," but a cycle cannot be. Maybe he meant "on the upswing.")

Scientists and mathematicians have been using the strong term in a specialized sense: a result that is approximately correct despite the falsity of the assumptions on which it is based is *robust*—"right for the wrong reasons."

A few years ago, I referred to the attorney Floyd Abrams, a First Amendment specialist, as being in the law firm of "Uninhibited, *Robust* & Wide-open." This was an allusion to the 1964 Supreme Court decision of *Times v. Sullivan,* in which the old word was newly popularized in a sentence that every journalist should memorize:

"We consider this case against the background of a profound national commitment to the principle that debate on public issues should be uninhibited, *robust* and wide open," wrote Justice William J. Brennan Jr. for the Court, "and that it may well include vehement, caustic and sometimes unpleasantly sharp attacks on government and public officials."

That's when *robust* was robust, "muscular" and "ruddy with health." Now the word is all too often used as a rhetorical cover for moves better described as "anemic."

You say that "robust" may be applied to sales or earnings, but not to a "product cycle," presumably because a cycle has both low and high points and ends up where it began. However, in business jargon, "product cycle" refers to the sales of a product—low when it is introduced, increasing as it becomes popular, and decreasing as becomes obsolete or passé. The product cycle is properly described as robust where the product quickly becomes popular and sales stay high for a long time.

Also, in the scientific and mathematical senses, "robust" refers not to a result that is "right for the wrong reasons" but rather a process that gives valid results even with imprecise input. Garbage in, pearls out.

Kenneth R. Shaw
Brooklyn, New York

Run to Daylight

Jerry Kramer, Hall of Fame lineman for the Green Bay Packers in the 60s, wrote an Op-Ed column during Super Bowl month about Coach Vince Lombardi that included this sentence: "A series of Nike commercials portray him as a gruff but lovable old coot."

Question: Should it be "series of commercials *portray*" or *"portrays"?*

Answer to this subject-verb agreement conundrum: depends on the writer's "notional concord." If you think of the subject "series" as plural, and especially if you have the plural "commercials" up tight against the verb, then you use the plural *portray*, but if you think of the subject as singular, as primarily a group or collective, then go for the singular *portrays*, as you would with "The World Series is. . . ." (I know that leaves the moorings-hungry unsatisfied, but grammatical life is hard.)

Kramer, behind whom the quarterback Bart Starr loved to sneak, went on to quote Lombardi: "You don't do things right once in a while, you do them right all the time."

Time! Question: Should that be a comma or a semicolon after "while"?

I say that sentence contains two independent clauses requiring a semicolon; as it stands, the sentence is joined into a "comma splice," grammar's equivalent of a goal-line fumble.

Sol Steinmetz, the Hall of Fame lexicographer, disagrees: "Because the emphasis here is on 'once in a while,' a semicolon doesn't fit because it would separate a continuous thought into two ideas. The sentence is punctuated correctly with a comma because there is a parallel between the two independent clauses."

That's what makes linguistic ball games. Go with my call if somebody gives you 14 points.

Run to Saving Daylight

Today, as you have been reminded by people irritated at having been kept waiting an hour, marks the onset of Daylight Saving Time.

Not Daylight Savings Time. As an adjective, *saving*—without the *s*—has the sense of "rescuing" (a *game-saving* catch), "redeeming" (a *saving* grace) and "economical" (a *saving* housekeeper). As a noun, a *saving* is something that is saved.

"Daylight saving" moves the clock forward an hour—the mnemonic is "Spring forward, fall back" (the first *m* in *mnemonic* is silent; how do you remember that?)—to gain extra daylight at the end of the day. The British prefer "Summer Time," first used in 1916, although their season stretches from the end of March to October. Before the official adoption of "Summer Time," a 1908 "Daylight Saving Bill" had been introduced in England "to promote the earlier use of daylight in the summer."

Congress adopted "Daylight Saving Time" in 1918 to save electricity and coal during World War I, but farmers forced its repeal in 1919, making it subject to local legislation. According to Stuart Berg Flexner in *Listening to America,* the bill passed again in 1966 as the Uniform Time Act over the protests of farmers, because "there were fewer of them to protest: America had become an urban nation since 1919."

In using the gerund, here's the hard part: when does a *saving* become *savings?* Answer: When it is the sum of acts of saving. You deny yourself and make a saving here, you find a bargain and make a saving there, and all of a sudden you have a pile of *savings,* which you take to a bankrupt Savings and Loan Association, or open a *savings account* in a *savings bank.*

The advertiser who touts "great savings throughout the store" is correct, because the reductions are plural; the hawker of "pre-owned vehicles" who raves about "a huge savings on this baby" is acting as if one saving were more than one, and thereby gives used-car selling a bad name. One purchase at a lowered price is a *saving;* it takes two to add up to *savings.* (People who like to pluralize singulars love to verbify nouns.)

Saving space, the *saving* in "daylight saving time" is often dropped when a time zone appears: on the East Coast, the term is expressed as "Eastern daylight time," abbreviated "E.D.T." Federal law marks daylight time, in areas that do not exempt themselves, from 2 A.M. on the first Sunday of April until 2 A.M. on the last Sunday of October.

In talking about the kind of time we have in the summer, we use a compound—*daylight saving*—and a case could be made for hyphenating it (as The Associated Press does), or running it together as one word, but I am not about to take on that battle today, because I am an hour late already.

Yes, the initial "m" in *mnemonic* is silent; I don't say it *out loud.* But I hum it to myself. (That's how I'll remember how to spell it.)

I also hum the first "M" in *Mnemosyne,* one of Zeus's more memorable girl friends. Having slept with the main god one time, as far as we know, she gave birth to all the nine muses: Calliope, Clio, Erato, Euterpe, Melpomene, Polyhymnia, Terpsichore, Thalia, and Urania.

Remember them and their respective arts, if you can.

Arthur J. Morgan
New York, New York

Salami in a Spoon

At the annual conclave of executive heavies, political powers, scientific Nobelniks and media biggies known as the World Economic Forum in Davos, Switzerland, words have historic resonance and metaphors fly. This was the year of the "network society," plugging a plugged-in world, and the netties found it easy to get hooked.

Benjamin Netanyahu, Israel's erstwhile Prime Minister, held a breakfast for diplomatic reporters and foreign-policy sages. He used a word that he knew would reverberate among the hypercognoscenti.

"This will come as a shock," he told the assembled power pack, "but in the case of Europe, Israel hopes for an *evenhanded* policy."

Netties nodded knowledgeably. *Evenhanded* has long been a code word in America's Middle East diplomacy. From the '50s through the '70s, State Department "Arabists" (some of us apply that term as a derogation, to mean "striped-pants pro-Arab cookie pushers," but it is borne by many diplomats with pride, to mean "those experienced in Middle Eastern affairs") felt with suave fervor that United States policy in that region was unduly influenced by political leaders eager to curry favor with American supporters of Israel.

The Arabists called for an *evenhanded* policy, imputing fairness and impartiality. Pro-Israel advocates, citing America's moral commitment to an island of democracy that was also a reliable strategic partner, retorted that "what Israel needs is not a broker but an ally"; to this group, *evenhandedness* was a code word made famous by the U.S. fact finder William Scranton in the late '60s for helping the rest of the world press Israel for concessions.

The adjective was coined by Shakespeare in *Macbeth* and carried an ironic overtone: "This *even-handed* justice/Commends the ingredients of our poison'd chalice/To our own lips." In Netanyahu's use, it meant "Israel is prepared to settle for a fair shake from nations usually on the side of the Arabs." (*Fair shake,* an 1830 Americanism, may be a metaphoric extension of the even hand.)

Emboldened by the ready reception of this allusion, the Prime Minister— educated in the United States and familiar with the nuances of the American political vernacular—went overboard. Speaking of the way the previous Government had made concessions little by little, he charged that the Israeli public had been *"spoon-fed* with *salami slices."* The press gasped at the audacity of the mangled metaphor, and Netanyahu responded, "Do something with that, Safire."

Right on. The compound verb *spoon-feed* began in 1615 to describe a means of feeding the infantile or feeble. By metaphoric extension, to *spoon-feed* means "to explain or persuade in small, understandable portions; to make easy to swallow and digest information."

Salami—from the Italian salame, "salted pork"—led to a more overtly political phrase, *salami tactics.* Coinage is attributed to Matyas Rakosi of Hungary's Communist Party in 1945; he described the way he overcame his opposition by getting it to slice off its right wing, then repudiate its centrists, until only those left in power were Communist collaborators. The specific Rakosi citation has not been found, but the phrase's popularizers were surely the columnists Joseph and Stewart Alsop, who much preferred the striking image to the bloodless "gradualism." In 1971, Stewart wrote prophetically in his *Newsweek* column about Czech politics: "Alexander Dubček will certainly not be the last of the liberals to fall victim to the *salami knife.*"

Both the feeding by spoon and the slicing with a *salami knife* are delicious figures of speech, but both in the same sentence, as the Prime Minister belatedly realized, are a lot to swallow.

You stated: "The specific Rakosi citation has not been found . . ." Well, now you can say you have found it.

"Salami Tactics" were described in a 1952 speech by Rakosi. The text can be found in *Társadalmi Szemle* (Budapest) February/March 1952.

You can find a description of the speech in my book, *The Soviet Union and the Occupation of Austria.*

William Lloyd Stearman
North Bethesda, Maryland

The Scheme Plan

Democratic campaigners adopted a two-track approach: Vice President Gore employed a railroad track in "It would knock our economy off track," and then switched to a hunting trope in deriding the Government shutdown: "President Clinton stopped them dead in their tracks."

Bob Dole tried to sidetrack the deft Democratic response to the Dole tax package. Mr. Clinton called his own proposal a "targeted *plan,*" while characterizing the Dole proposal as a "risky *scheme.*"

His use of *scheme* riled Dole. "I'm a little offended by this word *scheme,*" he said in their second joint appearance. "Last time, you talked about a 'risky *scheme,*' and then Vice President Gore repeated it about 10 times."

Is the noun *scheme* pejorative, as the verb *to scheme* is? Fred Mish at *Merriam-Webster* says it is, and Prof. Randolph Quirk of University College in London agrees: "Used to designate a plan," says Quirk, "*scheme* has a negative connotation." But David Crystal, editor of *The Cambridge Encyclopedia of Language,* differs: "The noun has come down to us as a neutral term. I think of its connotation as quite positive." (He probably benefits from his insurance *scheme.*)

My judgment is that the noun *scheme* in British usage can be either positive or negative, but in American usage, the word is always negative. Here, a *plan* is a "design," which is good, while a *scheme* is more of a "plot," which is bad. A man with a plan is to be admired, but a schemer is to be distrusted. No wonder Dole took offense.

Onetime GOP Vice Presidential candidate Jack Kemp used a football metaphor skillfully: "We cannot just *run the clock out* on the 20th century." However, he missed the extra point on the classics with "Clearly, the *Gordian knot* needs to be broken in *one fell swoop.*"

The difficult knot was tied by Gordius, king of Phrygia, who decreed that it would be untied only by the future ruler of all Asia; Alexander the Great crossed him up by cutting the knot with his sword. Thus, a *Gordian knot* can be untied or cut, but not—as Kemp suggested—broken, even in *one fell swoop* (in which *fell* means "fierce, cruel," evoking the image of a hawk dropping suddenly on its prey, and has the same root as *felon*).

You opine that the noun *scheme* "is always negative" in American usage. However, I've never encountered an interior designer whose *color scheme* was worked out to deliberately induce depression. On the other hand, Mother Nature's *scheme of things* is a double-edged example of both positive (oxygen, food, water) and negative (earthquakes, poisons, faltering body parts) usage.

If we must follow the maxim of never say *never,* can we ever say *always?*

Donald Garvelmann
New York, New York

Scramble 'Em Soft

"I have just come back from Boston," writes Alistair Cooke of the BBC, "where—at the Ritz-Carlton—I called room service and ordered 'soft scrambled eggs.' The nice kitchen girl 'repeated,' with meticulous articulation, 'softly scrambled eggs.'"

The educated ear of Cooke caught the insertion of the adverbial suffix *-ly.* He goes on: "And—not an hour ago—one of the news anchors at CNN said, 'The news came in fast and furious-*ly.*' I expect any minute to hear the ultimate gaffe of this ilk—perhaps by an editor telling her staff to 'stand up straight-*ly*.' "

Are people adding an unnecessary -*ly* to modifiers? The culinary worker (formerly kitchen girl) gently correcting her customer was using *softly*, the adverb, to modify the verb *scramble*, her attention directed to the action of cooking the eggs, while Mr. Cooke was using the adjective *soft* to modify the noun phrase "scrambled eggs," firmly fixing his eye and mouth on how the eggs would turn out. Both uses are considered correct, illustrating the differing emphases available by making a choice between adjective and adverb. In the same way, when Dylan Thomas wrote, "Do not go gentle into that good night," he chose the adjective *gentle* to focus attention on the condition of the unstated "you," rather than the adverb *gently* to modify the verb *go*.

So who cares about these delicious subtleties? I do, because my worry has been the opposite of Alistair's: that we are mindlessly clipping the -*ly* off too many adverbs. Also, it's time to make a fast pass at grasping the power of syntax.

I sleep naked. That only seems like, but is not, another illustration of rampant -*ly* clipping. (In reality, I sleep in a T-shirt emblazoned with "Because I'm the Maven, That's Why.") I use *naked* here as an adjective to modify the unclothed state of the subject (who is me), and not as an adverb to modify the action of the verb "to sleep," as I go gentle, etc.

But consider the loss of these -*ly*'s: *Drive Slow*, adjures a sign in my neighborhood. *Get Rich Quick*, offers the mutual-fund pitchman. *Party hearty*, advises the enthusiastic hedonist. He was *hurt bad*, boasts the vituperator. *Run Silent, Run Deep*, titles the World War II novelist Edward L. Beach. "It *works perfect*," says the mechanic, over the cacophonous pinging, wheezing and rattling of the engine. Do all these -*ly* clips signify a trend? Concerned sign painters wonder: Is *Drive Slow* correct?

The University of Chicago superlinguist James D. McCawley believes the distinction between adjective and adverb remains alive and well; the professor tells me that much depends on where the word is placed in the sentence. "In syntactic positions where adjectives otherwise don't occur," he says, quickly supplying the needed f'rinstance, "(for example, as modifiers preceding a verb or adjective), adverbs don't get replaced by adjectives: 'He quickly recovered his composure' (not 'quick'), 'He was badly hurt' (not 'bad'), 'Recently it's been pretty cold' (not 'recent')." If it's up front, it hangs on to its adverbial -*ly*.

"Interestingly, it is not only adjectives that are excluded in that position," notes McCawley, happily living in syntax, "but even adverbs that are homophonous with"—sound the same as—"adjectives. Even *fast* never occurs in 'He _____ recovered his composure' (as opposed to 'He recovered his composure _____,' where *fast, quickly* and *quick* all occur."

Now here comes the power of syntax, that instinctive organization of words that is the wonder of language: "English syntax provides frames that have to be filled by an adverb," says this deeply structured correspondent, "and to my knowledge, no native speaker of English ever puts adjectives in those frames. You thus have no grounds for worrying that adverbs might disappear from English, at least not in the next couple of centuries."

Until then, drive slowly, do justly and walk humbly with thy God.

Sighted Verb Sank Same

In an Associated Press story about the Senate's decision not to raise cigarette taxes to finance a Hatch-Kennedy children's-health-care proposal, Paul Reilly used an interesting verb: "The White House and Senate Majority Leader Trent Lott had warned the proposal could *submarine* the balanced budget agreement."

June LeBell of WQXR-FM in New York ripped Mr. Reilly's words off the ticker (no, we don't have tickers to rip off anymore, just a computer printer) and sent them along with "Is this Beltway Speak? Well, full speed ahead."

What is the meaning of *submarine* as a verb? "I was thinking of the use of 'submarine' as a verb in football, when a lineman cuts the legs out from under the player he's blocking," said Mr. Reilly. In basketball, knocking the legs from under an opponent in the air is also called a *submarine* as well as a *lowbridge* and *undercut,* and is a personal foul. In baseball, a pitcher *submarines* a ball when his arm describes a low arc below waist level.

I ran into Tom Young, Mr. Reilly's editor at the A.P. in Washington. He said: "I've been thinking about that *submarine* verb, and maybe *torpedo* would have been better. The notion is that it would sink the agreement."

Simpsoniana

"This case is about a *rush to judgment,*" the defense counsel, Johnnie L. Cochran Jr., told the jury in the O. J. Simpson trial, and repeated the phrase twice to drive it home.

The term was the title of a 1966 book by Mark Lane, among the first to suggest a conspiracy in the Kennedy assassination, and has been used ever since to describe hasty assumptions. Fred Shapiro of the Yale Law School library checked the Westlaw data base, which covers court cases back to the 1700s, and found no earlier legal use of the term. "If Mark Lane didn't coin the term," Fred says, "at least he popularized it."

Mr. Lane, a Washington lawyer, recalls: "When I wrote the book back in '64, I was looking for a title that would have some historic resonance. I came upon the phrase I needed in a speech by Lord Chancellor Thomas Erskine, back when he was defending James Hadfield around 1800. Hadfield was charged, appropriately enough for my purposes, with the attempted assassination of George III.

"Erskine spoke these words in defense of Hadfield: 'An attack upon the king is considered to be parricide [murder of a close relative] against the state, and the jury and the witnesses, and even the judges, are the children. It is fit, on that account, that there should be a solemn pause before we rush to judgement.'

"The British spelling of *judgement,* of course, has an extra *e* in it."

It may be rushing to judgment on the language used at the trial transfixing so many viewers, but there seems to be a widespread use of the fuzzy *kinda-sorta.* "These opening statements are normally given by attorneys," said Judge Lance Ito, "to *sort of* give you an overall view of the evidence." Describing some guest housing units, the prosecutor, Marcia Clark, said, "It's *kind of* like one long building." Ronald Shipp, a former police officer, reported that Simpson *"kind of* jokingly said, '. . . I've had some dreams of killing her.' "

Kind of and *sort of* are adverbials. The great British grammarian Sir Randolph Quirk has identified these terms, in informal speech, as "downtoners for adjectives and adverbs," ways to tone down the force of the words that follow. "The informality of expressions used on both sides of the bar," the lexicographer Anne Soukhanov adds, "not to mention pervasive use of the non-standard adverb *like,* simply points up the stress factors inherent in a trial."

About the kind-of-jokingly described dream noted by Mr. Shipp, Ms. Clark told the jury: "I think Walt Disney said it best, in—what was it?—*Sleeping Beauty:* 'A dream is a wish your heart makes.' " The use of *I think* is also a fuzzifier—I think I write "I think it was" or "what was it?" when I'm too lazy to call a source or look up a fact—and sure enough, the prosecution was only half right; the Walt Disney movie was *Cinderella.* (When I err that way in this column, it takes two wicked stepsisters to haul in the mail.) To be evenhanded, I should point out a similar error by the defense: "He's the man who received the Nobel Peace Prize for this invention," Mr. Cochran said of a DNA expert, Kary Mullis, who shared the 1993 Nobel Prize in Chemistry. The Peace Prize, however, is in a separate category, not awarded for scientific breakthroughs.

Mr. Shipp also testified that he turned down financial offers for his story: "I personally thought it was blood money that I didn't want any part of." The term *blood money* dates to 1535 and has at least two senses: "funds paid for a wrongful death" and the more familiar "payment gained from another's death."

This phrase comes from the 30 pieces of silver paid to Judas for the betrayal of Jesus before the Crucifixion. In 1535, the Coverdale translation of the New Testament used the term; in Matthew 27:6, when Judas tried to return the silver pieces to the treasury, the officials said, "It is not laufall to put them in to the Gods cheste for it is *bloudmoney*."

When the trial started, Judge Ito explained to the jury about frequent trial interruptions: "If we have to take an unscheduled break, *that's life in the big city!*" His expression builds on *that's life,* a 1924 acceptance of reality based on a 1796 expression of resignation, *such is life.* The use of *big city* is an Americanism introduced in 1909 by William Sydney Porter, writing under his pseudonym, O. Henry: "The *big city* is like a mother's knee to many who have strayed far and found the roads rough beneath their uncertain feet." That comforting simile has turned around, with *that's life in the big city* as a metaphor for anticipating disturbance, interruption or discomfort.

The judge also warned jurors about not discussing trial events among themselves, adding, "You're not to discuss what goes on at *sidebar.*" Before the Simpson case, that term was more familiar in journalism than law; a *sidebar,* since the 1940s, has referred to any short piece that accompanies the main news article, like a profile of the judge or a feature on Mezzaluna (that Los Angeles restaurant where Ronald Goldman worked takes its name from the Italian for "half-moon").

As the legal term for a discussion area near the judge's bench, *sidebar* was first used in the early 1700s for a bar in the Outer Parliament House in Edinburgh. In 1795, Edmund Burke explained the purpose of this spreading courtroom term: "The criminal will climb from the dock to the *side-bar,* and take his place . . . with the counsel."

Christopher Darden, assisting in the prosecution, complained of the technology used in court. When a videotape of Mr. Simpson and his in-laws was shown, Mr. Darden looked at the equipment and marveled, "All this stuff is space-age stuff, and no slo-mo!" As an adjective for "modern, up-to-the-minute," *space-age* marks its 50th anniversary next year. More recent is *slo-mo,* a reduplication formed by clipping "slow motion," for the button that allows a videotape to be advanced at a slower speed. The clipped form first appeared in the *Washington Post* in 1978: "I realize that a videotape *slo-mo* replay is to our advantage."

Pronunciation has also proved trying. The prosecution stumbled over *integral* as in-TEG-ral, but that adjective should be stressed on the first syllable,

IN-te-gral, not the second. On the other side, a lawyer used *lambasted* in complaining of how the defense has been lam-BAS-ted; that verb should take a long *a*, lam-BAY-sted.

On the final page of his instant best seller, ghosted by Lawrence Schiller, Mr. Simpson comes up with a simple error and a skilled allusion in one: "I have been totally unjudgmental of people all my life." The word *judgmental*, usually dismissed in dictionaries as merely the adjectival form of *judgment*, has gained a meaning all its own: "severely critical, censorious, unforgiving," with an overtone of "not objective." In 1952, it gained a prefix: *non-*, not *un-*, as Mr. Simpson wrote. To be *nonjudgmental* is to be "neutral, dispassionate, impartial," with a connotation of "forgiving." That sense probably stems from Matthew 7:1: "Judge not, that ye be not judged," a point that the Simpson defense would surely like to make.

Re: *blood money*, shouldn't you have traced the term to Numbers 35:31–33? That would precede 1535 by close to 3 millennia, rather impressive.

Especially noteworthy when, in Hebrew, the words for *blood* and *value* are tantalizingly twinned!

Rabbi Shlomo Kahn
New York, New York

You say the pronunciation should be "lam-BAY-sted," but *Merriam-Webster's Collegiate Dictionary, Tenth Edition (1993)*, accepts *both* pronunciations!
I have always used the short-"a" lam-BAS-ted myself.

Fiona Bayly
New York, New York

Sing for Scupper

"Prime Minister Blair proposes a needless white paper on a freedom of information measure," noted a *New York Times* editorial about Tony Blair's fast start in office. "This step only invites long delay and bureaucratic *scuppering.*"

Shrug off the misplaced *only* and consider the unfamiliar *scuppering*. The noun *scupper*, from the Latin *exspuere*, "spit out," is, as old salts know, an opening on a ship's side to let water and refuse run out. In the mid–20th century, *scupper* became British underworld slang for "prostitute."

Blind alley. Try the verb, which first appeared in 1885 to describe the massacre by the Sudanese Mahdi of British and Egyptian expeditions led by Gen. George Gordon. The *Pall Mall Gazette* wrote of "the fierce warriors who *scupper* Tommy Atkins within the lines of Suakin." A decade later, Kipling wrote of brave men being *"scuppered* and left in the lurch."

From that horrific meaning of "surprised and destroyed," *scupper* cooled down to "defeat, ruin," and in 1957 *The Economist* wrote of "secret rejoicing in Whitehall if the French Assembly had *scuppered* the common market."

Thus, the *Times*'s use of "bureaucratic *scuppering,*" which might have come from a ship's waste chute, is more likely derived from the killing of "Chinese" Gordon (named for crushing the Taiping rebellion of 1863–64) and his compatriots. Historic color abounds when we stop to examine an unfamiliar word.

Snowy Thinking

I owe Steven Pinker an apology. He's the M.I.T. cognitive neuroscientist who makes sense to the layman out of the linguist Noam Chomsky's theory that language is rooted in the deep structures of the human brain. In a column last month, just in passing, I ascribed to Pinker the notion that Eskimo languages "have 27 different words for snow."

In fact, in a recent book he argues the opposite, quoting from Geoffrey Pullum's "Great Eskimo Vocabulary Hoax," treating as a myth and a canard the assertion that any Arctic language contained so many synonyms for the cold white stuff. This argument was used to put down the "linguistic determinism" of Edward Sapir of Yale and his disciple Benjamin Lee Whorf, dominant language theorists of the recent past. Chomskians like Pinker deride the anthropologists' theory that words enter language because of usage, say that "anthropological anecdotes are bunk" and estimate that Eskimos have about a dozen words for types of snow, the same as speakers of English. *(Sleet, slush, hardpack, powder, dusting, blizzard, avalanche, flurry* and the latest from pompous weather persons, *freezing precipitation activity.)*

No less an authority than Prof. James McCawley of the University of Chicago zaps me for this hurtful misattribution, which is important to academics, as is the longtime tug-of-war between those who emphasize environment or heredity. I don't want to be unfair to the deep-structure crowd and lose Big Jim as a source.

However, Mark Halpern of Oakland, California (a fellow alumnus of the Bronx High School of Science), sent me a scholarly paper arguing that professional linguists are not always to be trusted on language usage. The paper included this letter sent to *New York* magazine in 1994 by Elise Sereni Patkotak of Barrow, Alaska: "I have spent the past 22 years living in an Inupiat Eskimo community. According to the North Slope Borough's Inupiat History, Language and Culture Division, the Inupiats have more than 30 words for snow, and more than 70 for ice. In the Arctic, the specific conditions of snow and ice are critical to hunting and survival; two or three words would hardly cover our needs."

In discussing figures of speech and similes, you inadvertently (?) raised a related point. Eskimos and terminology for snow led you to write of the "many synonyms for the cold white stuff."

Suddenly, my mind said, "elongated yellow fruit writing." Someone long ago hung that definition on the device you exhibit here, and your predecessor at the *Times*, the lamented Ted Bernstein, wrote of it this way in his classic, *Watch Your Language*:

> A monologophobe (don't try to look it up) is a guy who would rather walk naked in front of Saks Fifth Avenue than be caught using the same word more than once in three lines of type. What he suffers from is synonymomania (don't look that one up, either), which is a compulsion to distract and, if possible, puzzle the reader by calling a spade successively a garden implement and an earth-turning tool . . .
>
> "Elegant variation" is the term applied by Fowler to this practice of mechanically inserting synonyms to avoid repetition of words.

Your "white stuff" is also favored by TV weatherfolk, as is "precipitation" (five syllables stating what "rain or snow" would do in three; even adding "sleet" would only make it four). Economists love "the yellow metal," and sportscasters flailing for varieties of "defeated" (beat, crushed, downed, edged, etc.) are with us daily (not "on a daily basis," *please*, if, in closing, I may raise yet another bugaboo, along with my hackles).

Emerson Stone
Greenwich, Connecticut

Snubbed Nose

The most misguided judicial decision of the year—the one by a judge in Ohio to impose prior restraint on a publication, in contravention of the First Amendment—was accompanied by the mixed metaphor of the year.

"I cannot permit *Business Week*," ruled Federal Judge John Feikens, "to *snub its nose* at court orders."

A *snub nose* is one short and upturned at the tip, stumpy, sometimes called "pug." Akin to the Old Norse *snubba*—"to cut short or make stumpy"—its verb took on that cut-short sense of "rebuke, scorn, insult, mortify."

You may *snub* a person, even a *snub-nosed* person, but—unless you are a plastic surgeon skilled in rhinoplasty—you cannot *snub* that person's nose.

You can, however—if you choose to introduce a somewhat coarse idiom to Federal jurisprudence—*thumb your nose* at anyone or, if you are prepared to risk contempt of court, at a court order. As George Stoddard of New York notes, *thumbing one's nose* is an Americanism meaning "putting the thumb to the tip of the nose and wiggling the fingers in a gesture of defiance and contempt." The gesture may once have had a specific meaning, but it is lost in the mists of frontier antiquity.

Business Week has the right to appeal to the Supreme Court on more grounds than one.

Snub Guidance

In what was called here "the most misguided judicial decision of the year"— United States District Court Judge John Feikens's order restraining *Business Week* magazine from publishing an article about a lawsuit—I noted the judge's metaphorical error in writing, "I cannot permit *Business Week* to *snub its nose* at court orders."

What the judge meant to write, I assumed, was not *snub*, but *thumb*. To *thumb one's nose* is to place the tip of the thumb against the tip of the nose and wiggle the fingers, long symbolizing an invitation to make an obeisance to the nose-thumber's posterior. He confused a *snub nose* (one with a pug, turned-up tip), which has no connotation of arrogance, with a *thumbed nose*, which is overtly contemptuous.

Judge Feikens writes me that "on reflection, I think I should have used '*thumb its nose* at court orders,'" but argues that "your statement 'the most misguided judicial decision of the year' may also be open to question. In *Webster's New International Dictionary,* Second Edition, Unabridged, I read these definitions for *misguide:* 'to guide wrongly; to cause (oneself) to do wrong; to misbehave; to mismanage; misgovern; abuse; spoil.' I can assure you that I knew what I was doing, that I was not guided wrongly by following legal precedent (*Seattle Times v. Rhinehart,* 467 U.S. 20, 1984). I do not believe that I misbehaved."

First of all, Judge, retire your second edition of the *NID*; it's a valuable old collector's item, but Merriam-Webster has had the third edition out since

1963. Citing an old unabridged dictionary is a good way to find cover for just about anything, but *misguide* no longer has anything to do with most of the synonyms you cited, and certainly not "misbehave."

In today's language, *misguide* (to use *Merriam-Webster's 10th*) means "to lead astray"; *misguided* means "led or prompted by wrong or inappropriate motives or ideals," which is precisely what I meant. Forget all those other historical *mis-es.*

It's not for me to argue the First Amendment case against prior restraint before the Sixth Circuit Court of Appeals, which I hope will step up to a decision on this and not duck by declaring the case moot. (*Business Week* has since seen fit to publish the article.) Nor do I knock a correspondent willing to engage: "In any event," concludes Judge Feikens, "what you might have meant to say is 'the most disagreed-with by the media judicial decision of the year.'" No argument there.

Judge John Feikens may have caved in too soon in agreeing that he ought not have used "to *snub its nose* at court orders," in his ill-advised order restraining *Business Week* from publishing a piece about Procter & Gamble.

Many years ago, I began a print journalism career on the *Ironton Tribune.* At that time, any resident of the Ohio Valley would have known that the Judge meant he would not permit *Business Week* to ignore his court order. Or, if you prefer, to turn up its nose at his court order.

I agree that persons with turned-up noses (snub) are not necessarily arrogant. But a person who "turns up his or her nose" is something else again—perhaps even arrogant.

In Ohio Valley idiom, "to snub its nose" was (and may still be) used as a less inflammatory phrase than "to thumb its nose."

G. Richard Schreiber
Lake Bluff, Illinois

Judge Feikens's conclusion still was a little inapt/inept: "... is the most disagreed-with by the media judicial decision of the year." The phrase "by the media" is badly jammed into the sentence. I would rewrite it thus: "the most disagreed-with (by the media) judicial decision of the year."

Gary Muldoon
Rochester, New York

Soccer Moms

As the presidential campaign of 1996 enters its final week, its most powerful catch phrase has just been determined. Neither candidate coined it. No commentator had a hand in it. The phrase is to this campaign what *gender gap* was to the Bush-Clinton coverage in 1992 and the catch phrases *angry white male* and *Contract With America* were to the 1994 Congressional contest.

The envelope, please. And the winner is: *soccer mom!*

The columnist Ellen Goodman of the *Boston Globe* calls 1996 "the Year of the *Soccer Mom.*" The British correspondent Hugh Davies, writing in the *Daily Telegraph of London,* notes: "The *soccer moms* of America are being pursued for their votes. . . . They run around in four-wheel-drive 'recreational vehicles' and need to be reassured that someone in Washington is thinking of them."

Who is this *soccer mom?* Does she play soccer? No. Is she the mother of a soccer player? Yes. "She is someone who brings children to practice and to games," says Kit Simeone, of the United States Youth Soccer Association, the fastest-growing unit of the National Soccer Federation. "Kids' soccer teams consist of 14 players, so there are usually six of these moms per team. Figuring that there are five million kids under 19 who play soccer, I estimate there are at least a million *soccer moms.*"

What characterizes such a parent? She often drives a sports-utility vehicle or a minivan, carries snacks and orange juice for the kids, sometimes takes along extra lawn chairs. She can be a full-time homemaker or can also work outside the home. (Nobody's going to trap me on *working mother* again; all mothers work—even lazy ones.) The *soccer mom* is an enthusiast: "Every Saturday," says Cathy Mayne, who helped lead the effort to introduce major-league soccer to Columbus, Ohio, "I'm up in time to bring my 7-year-old and a neighbor's son to an 8 A.M. game, and there's a lot of camaraderie among the parents on the sidelines."

The earliest citation in print I can find is from a 1982 Associated Press dispatch from Palmer, Mass., and hardly augured well for the sport or its female enthusiasts: "A judge has found a husband guilty of looting $3,150 from the treasury of the *Soccer Moms* booster club in Ludlow headed by his wife."

That suggests coinage years earlier, and Pat Harrison, a GOP political activist from Arlington, Virginia, recalls the approximate time: "The phrase started in 1976, when women were first starting to enter the work force in droves and had to sacrifice to participate in their children's extracurricular activities. There are typically three practices per week, games are played on Saturdays and meets are held during the Thanksgiving holidays."

But what gave the phrase its political coloration, and when? "As an identifiable group with shared values and opinions," says Harrison, "we were first distinguishable in the mid-80s. And we were usually uncommitted politically; that's why all Presidential candidates started seeking the *'soccer mom* vote.'"

In the Nixon years, working-class men—especially union members in the construction trades—were known as *hard hats,* and affected elections as they switched political allegiance from Democrat to Republican. In the 1980s they became "Reagan Democrats"; in the '90s, many unions have sought to woo them back to the Democratic fold. (*Soccer dad* is not a phrase in use, perhaps because of the recent coinage of *deadbeat dad.*)

But *soccer moms* are not exclusively working class—many are upper-middle-class suburbanites—and they tend to be hardheaded rather than hard-hatted: "This is a year of pragmatic politics when people are looking for answers," in the columnist Goodman's formulation.

Other analysts think of this mom as being in her 30s, harried, family-oriented, carpool-pallored, ethnically diverse, with her vote up for grabs. And as the *soccer mom* goes, so goes the election, if she's not too tired to get to the polls.

Sorry, Pal

In the midst of suspicions of *hush money* and revelations of fund-raising excesses, some political activists were dismayed by a spelling mistake rich in irony included in papers released by the White House from the trove taken home by the former Deputy Chief of Staff Harold Ickes.

An anonymous White House aide sent a memo in 1994 to Martha Phipps, then working at the Democratic National Committee. It began, "In order to reach our very aggressive goal of $40 million this year" and then listed 10 Presidential uses, from "Two seats on Air Force One" to "White House residence visits and overnight stays," concluding with "Photo opportunities with principles."

A Democratic partisan in New York circled the misspelled last word and sent it to me with the sad notation "not too many of these."

The Spinner Spun

The Brooklyn pitcher "Candy" Cummings, who flummoxed the Harvard base-ball varsity by inventing the curveball just after the Civil War, has been ill served.

In an *Esquire* article on "The Age of Spin," Randall Rothenberg noted how the slang meaning of *spin* changed from the pejorative "deceive" in the 1950s to a mockingly admiring "polish the truth" today.

The author had called me, as a former legerdemainliner, for my definition. Instead of looking it up in my own political dictionary, which has it right, I spun off as follows: "*Spin* is what a pitcher does when he throws a curveball. The English on the ball causes it to appear to be going in a slightly different direction than it actually is."

Not only is that sentence awkwardly constructed (in writing, you get a chance to fix what you say, a benefit denied to talking heads as we mouth off), but also the notion that a curveball appears to curve, but does not, comes strictly out of left field—that is to say, it's wrong. The correction comes from Michael McCurry of Washington, press secretary to the President, whose assortment of sinkers, sliders and illegal spitballs during the recent political campaign left his reputation for credibility, according to the heavy-hitting editorialist of the *New York Times*, in "tatters."

"When a pitcher tosses a curveball," writes Mr. McCurry, who denies being on a post-election charm offensive, "he affects the physics of the motion so that the ball actually 'breaks.' It does more than 'appear' to go in a slightly different direction—unless, of course, the curve 'hangs' like tortured *spin* falling on deaf ears."

The Clintonian Newtonian then proceeds to slam the metaphor out of the park: "The spinner's 'English' on a story is designed to move the story in a more favorable direction. That said, the pitch had better cross the plate. Too many wild *spins*, and someone sooner or later sends you to the showers." McCurry then steps back in the box and swings for the bleachers: "In America's pastime, the *spin* on a curve is for real—even if it's a Cuban or Japanese doing the throwing."

Spin in this sports sense began in cricket. "The more *spin* you give the ball," wrote James Pycroft in his 1851 book on the British sport that antedated American baseball, "the better the delivery; because then the ball will twist, rise quickly, or cut variously, the instant it touches the ground."

English—the twist, not the language—came into use through billiards, first recorded by Mark Twain in 1869, its origin obscure. In 1906, as *body English*, it was applied to the unconscious wriggling of a player seeming to try to affect the course of a rolling ball. That was the precursor to *body language*, the move-

ments people and other animals make—often unconsciously, sometimes with
sly political intent—that communicate emotions.

Spookspeak in Deutchland

Neither the NIO for warning nor any of the SIBlings knew that this article was
being prepared for publication. Transmitted outside the WASHFAX, it has not
appeared in the latest SNIE and was done with no knowledge in Deutchland.

"Deutchland" is what the surly set at the Central Intelligence Agency calls
the mole-shocked agency in its post-Ames era.* John Deutch, the new D.C.I.
(Director of Central Intelligence), is a hearty fellow from M.I.T. and the Pentagon, given to hugging and back-rubbing insecure case officers, who suspi-
ciously refer to such physical reassurance as "the hug of death."

As the agency staggers from being penetrated by the K.G.B. to being rigor-
ously examined by CODELS (Congressional Delegations), one element of its
culture remains sacrosanct: spookspeak. In the land of acronyms, we now
have FUSS (Fleet Undersea Surveillance System) and FORMICA (not the counter-
top material, but Foreign Military Intelligence Collection Activity). But initialese—without the creative acronymic word-formation—is rampant.

Take it from the top: within the NIC, or National Intelligence Council, there
are NIO's, or National Intelligence Officers: the guy who tries to keep the Government from any blind-siding by the competition or the media is the NIO for
warning. He is in close touch with members of the Strategic Intelligence
Board, or SIB, whose brothers under the skin are SIBlings, and they all share
SNIE's—Special National Intelligence Estimates.

A WASHFAX is a secure, encrypted telephone fax line that nobody in the intelligence community trusts. If the communication was until recently labeled
WNINTEL/ORCON/PROPIN, the spooks felt better hand-carrying it over. WNINTEL
meant that remote sensing technology—like a long-distance bug—was used
to gather the information. ORCON meant "originator controlled," with the
writer to be consulted about future clearances. PROPIN meant "contains proprietary information," like the formula for Coca-Cola syrup or the sketches
for a French designer's collection.

The INT, for "intelligence," is a standard acronym-former: HUMINT is "human

---

*This column originally ran on November 19, 1995.

intelligence," SIGINT "signal intelligence," which includes "KEYHOLE," the code word for data derived from an imagery satellite, and MASINT, "measurement and signature intelligence," the telltale clues to identity picked up by acoustic, nuclear and seismic sensors, hand-carried over (not the WASHFAX, stupid) to the A.S.D. (C31) who is Assistant Secretary of Defense for Command, Control, Communications and Intelligence, who was hugged by Deutch and survived. An unofficial usage is RUMINT—for "rumor intelligence," the gossip and scuttlebutt that often proved more reliable than the HUMINT sent in by one of the K.G.B. or Stasi double agents who the D.D.O. (Deputy Director for Operations) thought was working for us. (A House Intelligence staff member has pledged to review the C.I.A. "INT by INT.")

The word from DODIPP (the Department of Defense Intelligence Production Program) is that PROPIN is no longer used. The intelligence community's sort-of-secret budget ($28 billion and change) will depend on how well it does on the economic stuff; because its plan is to set up more "front" companies to run agents abroad, future phony corporate entities like the Deutchland Seismic Sensor and Escort Service will be sourced in agency documents with a word that does not indicate anything to do with "proprietary." I do not include the new code word here because I am not eager to help French counterintelligence.

The key element in many intel estimates is probability. Within the community, the word used for the lowest probability is *conceivably*. A less-than-50 percent chance draws a *possibly*, and just over 50 percent a *probably*. In the 60 to 70 percent range, spooks use *likely*, and in the 80s it gets to *almost certainly*. An estimated sure thing is *no doubt*, a rarity.

One member of the community, not in the Defense Intelligence Agency, defines *conceivably* this way: "Nobody but D.I.A. believes this, but if we didn't put it in, they wouldn't coordinate, and we figured it wasn't worth the fight because no sane reader would take it seriously."

Squish-Squash, Chinky Chose

"Time Warner is three times as big as Rupert's company," said the cable tycoon Ted Turner, joshing his rival Rupert Murdoch before an audience of media moguls. "I'm looking forward to *squishing* Rupert like a bug."

In reporting this jejune jocularity, Reuters, *Variety,* and the *New York Daily News* spelled the key verb *squash,* with an *a.* In Atlanta, Gareth Fenley compared these accounts with this report from the Associated Press: "Ted Turner says he would *squash* media magnate Rupert Murdoch 'like a bug,'" wrote an AP television writer, Lynn Elber, but in transmitting the direct quote, she used *squish.* Notes Mr. Fenley, who works for one of the Turner companies: "I found the pertinent sound bite on videotape, and an accurate transcript of it in our tape log. Mr. Turner definitely did not say *squashing,* although his pronunciation of *squishing* might conceivably be rendered as *squooshing.*" He wonders why print journalism felt the need to conform the spoken *squish* to the written *squash.*

Before we can address that, to the more basic question: What do you do to a bug when you step on it?

Squash, formed from the Vulgar Latin *exquassare*—*ex-* ("out") and *quassare* ("to shake")—was first on the scene in 1565, meaning "to press into a flat mass," and it gained an extended meaning of "to suppress." (Yes, the name of the racquet game comes from the sound of a ball being momentarily mashed, flattened or squashed by a racquet. No, the vegetable that Martha Stewart grows in her window box comes from a shortening of the Narragansett word *askutasquash.*)

Only a century later, *squish* appeared both as an alternative to *squash* and with special reference to the soft, damp sound made by the act of pressing a boot into mud. Other variants of this onomatopoeic verb are *squush,* more recently spelled *squoosh,* and *smoosh,* as in "You can try jamming your garment bag into that overhead bin, Buster, but you better not *smoosh* down my fur hat."

The use of the *i* instead of the *a* is widespread: in 1970, Vice President Spiro T. Agnew derided radical liberals as *squishy-soft,* and a few years ago, a

telephonic friend of Princess Diana used *Squidgy* as a term of endearment.*
(Perhaps that is rooted in *squeeze,* as is the window-cleaning instrument
squeegee, and is beyond the purview of *squash-squish* analysis, because the
Princess did not say she preferred "Squadgy.")

Which is correct, *squish* or *squash?* Wrong question, because in words imi-
tating sounds, latitude is given to variants. The Standard English word for the
sound made by crushing a bug is *squash;* legitimate dialectal variants are
squish and *squoosh.* To give this seemingly minor subject universal relevance,
let us issue a stylistic diktat: When a reporter quotes someone using the variant, the quotation should use the spelling that most closely follows the sound
of the variant usage; on second reference, or even in the lead if outside of
quotes, the standard form should be introduced. Thus: "'I'll *squish* you!' he
cried. Smiling at the joking threat to *squash,* he replied. . . .'"

By-passing the "ex-" of your Latin *Exquassare,* the root, *quassare* gives rise to the legal lingo
relative of "squash," "quash," which means "to annul or make void" a law, decision, writ, etc.

However unlike its cousin squash, which can be squish or squoosh, quash is always
quash, and never quish or quoosh.

Arthur J. Morgan,
New York, New York

Stacking the Ringers

Paul Simon of Illinois took a Parthian shot before retiring from the Senate.
(Not a *parting* shot—the ancient Parthians liked to take pops at opponents
over their shoulders while running away.) The bow-tied Senator Simon voiced
concern that politicians may be appointing "pro-gambling *ringers*" to the new
National Gambling Impact Study Commission, an examination he had long
supported of a multibillion-dollar industry, and that such appointments
might *"stack the deck"* in favor of gambling.

Nice use of a slang metaphor. In gambling, the noun *stack* is a column of
chips, but as a verb, *to stack a deck* is to arrange a pack of cards in a sequence
to give the dealer an advantage over the poor sucker who is being dealt a losing hand.

---

*Diana, Princess of Wales, died on August 31, 1997.

A *ringer* has meant "look-alike" since the early 19th century, perhaps based on the 1812 British slang term *ring in*, meaning "to exchange or substitute fraudulently." When emphasis is desired, the phrase is *dead ringer*, coined in 1891, using *dead* in its curious sense of "exact," as in *dead center* or in horse racing's *dead heat*. A century ago, *ringer* made its appearance in turf slang, as "a horse fraudulently slipped in under another's name." A 1914 slang dictionary soon gave purpose to the practice: "a name applied to a man or a horse dishonestly entered in an event with others far below his class."

When Simon says *ringer*, he means "an appointment made of an ostensibly objective person who is actually on the side of the gamblers."

Politics loves horse-racing terms. Beyond mere bargaining is *horse trading;* a candidate of unknown potential is a *dark horse*, coined in an 1831 novel by Benjamin Disraeli; professional pols wonder if an amateur will *bolt* the party, or who is the choice of the *front runner* (one who *shows early foot*) for his *running mate*.

A less familiar horse-racing term picked up by politics is *shoo-in*, for "sure winner." *Shoo!* is a colloquial imperative meaning "run along," a form of gently urging on a child or animal. In olden times, among corrupt jockeys, a long shot was selected to beat the faster horses, and the pre-selected winner was "shooed in" by the others.

Metaphor mixing of sports and gambling terms is permitted because racing and gambling have long been linked. If a few *ringers* on the commission add up to a *stacked deck*, according to the Simon formulation, one would expect a pro-gambling report to be a *shoo-in*.

Stakeholders Naff? I'm Chuffed

Tony Blair, Britain's Prime Minister, came to the colonies to get acquainted with Wall Street movers and shakers, visit his political role model, President Clinton, and—most important by far—lunch with America's media bigfeet.

Host of the session was Roone Arledge, who chose the John Hay room of Washington's Hay-Adams hotel for the introduction of the head of the Labor Party to the journarati. (Nice touch: Hay was United States Ambassador to the Court of St. James's in the McKinley Administration.) In that moment of canapés, light conversation and forced good cheer before sitting down to serious questioning, I asked Mr. Blair about his frequent use of the word *stakeholder* in his speeches. He uses it to mean any group that has an interest, or stake, in a company's actions—not merely owners (who are often called *share-holders*).

"That's from an American expression, I think," the bright, slight British politician said. "From your frontier days."

True; when Western land was made available to those who would work and live on it, a *stake* became a section of land marked off by stakes and claimed by the farmer. By extension, a *grub stake* was money advanced for food, or grub, as an investment or loan. *Stakeholder*, in the sense of one who holds the stake of a bet or wager, dates back to 1708; an article in *Sporting* magazine in 1815 mentions "a Bank of England note, which was lodged in the hands of a *stake-holder*, as a deposit." (Since then, the compound noun has lost its hyphen.)

A new sense of *stakeholder* was invented recently on the analogy of *share-holder*. Cynthia Barnhart of Barnhart Books has a citation from 1964, in an article about Cyprus by Ralph Allen in *Macleans* magazine: "The three main *stakeholders* in the sorry little island, Britain, Greece and Turkey, decided they'd had enough." At Merriam-Webster, the editor Fred Mish found a 1975 citation in a *Handbook for Managers*, a British book by P. Croon and W. A. C. Whitlau, with the current sense: "The needs of our '*stakeholders*'—i.e., the persons and groups having a direct stake in our organization: the owners, employees, . . . customers, suppliers, financiers, managers, the area in which the organization is established, etc." A decade older is this citation from H. I. Ansoff's textbook, *Corporate Strategy*, quoted in the *Oxford English Dictionary*: "The objectives of top management can and frequently do come in conflict with objectives of other *stakeholders* in the firm."

Blair uses the word much as former Secretary of Labor Robert Reich does, suggesting that corporations have social responsibilities beyond those of making profits for owners. Vituperative right-wing columnists see this as a "New Socialist" plot to use companies as surrogates for welfarism that voters will not pay for directly.

The novelist and commentator Sally Quinn, listening to the etymology and political usage of *stakeholder*, put in: "But what about *naff*? That's the British word taking hold here. I hear it all the time."

Mr. Blair—prepared to discuss NATO enlargement, the troubles in Ireland and other weighty subjects—turned to the adjective *naff* and said it was a widely used dialect word for "not very tasteful." Ms Quinn defined it with greater brio as "tatty, tacky," and in French, *gauche*, which Mr. Blair did not dispute.

The term's origin, however, has long been in dispute. The most common explanation is that it comes from Naafi, the Navy, Army and Air Force Institute, which operated canteens for members of the armed forces, similar to the American Post Exchanges. If an item was *naff*, it was not fashionable. *Naffing* was an R.A.F. euphemism for an adjective-verb-gerund originally denoting copulation. *Naff off* was popularized by Princess Anne in 1984, when she was reported to have told harassing journalists at the Badminton Horse Trials, "Why don't you just *naff off?*"

People magazine, in a 1990 survey of British slang, defined *naff* as "undesirable, tasteless." In 1993, *The Independent* wrote about types of souvenirs: "*Kitsch* is as self-conscious as *tat* is simple-minded. *Kitsch* is camp. *Tat* is *naff.*" A British tennis player, Chris Mabire, told the *Daily Telegraph* last year: "I'll do whatever it takes to become a champion if a sponsor can be found. There is plenty of room on my shirt sleeves for advertising logos. At present all I've got is my Boy Scout house orderly badge and, to be honest, it looks a bit *naff.*"

In Paul Beale's 1984 edition of Eric Partridge's great *Dictionary of Slang and Unconventional English,* another origin is offered: backslang for *fan,* or *fanny,* which Partridge refers to as the "female pudenda." Before I could bring this etymological dispute up in the pre-luncheon small talk—which would have been a bit *naff*—the verb *chuff* came up.

Chuff, familiar to the British but not to most Americans, is used mostly in the form of its past participle: "to be *chuffed*" is to be irritated, disgruntled, more than a mite displeased. Curiously, it is a Janus-esque word that also has the opposite meaning: "delighted, flattered." (A third meaning, to make a noise like the regular puffing of an engine, is expressed by the American *chug.*)

"Annoyed" and "put off" were the synonyms of the dialect term given by Mr. Blair, who was able to pinpoint the localities to which the term was native. He added, "But be careful how you use it." I took this as a signal that, in addition to the opposite senses, there might be other meanings, and sure enough, in Partridge there is a noun form equivalent to *duff,* from American slang.

Then we had to break it up and go in for the heavy stuff. All the other bigfeet had to take notes and pull their chins, but my work was done. British lingo gets to you; I'll see what else we can gin up in future.

Stakeholders and naff you are right about; chuff hardly ever means "irritated, disgruntled, more than a mite displeased" anymore, even though the big OED does give that as a second meaning for the past participle chuffed. Yes, there are other meanings for chuff—a plumped out cheek, a buttock, and there is a bird. But you will be quite safe in this country if you say you are "always chuffed to be taken up on a small point," meaning that you are pleased. As I hope you are.

Elizabeth Young
London, United Kingdom

Your remarks about the word "chuff" reminded me of a similar word used by old New Hampshire residents. During my sixteen-year residence in the central part of that state, I heard on several occasions old timers in the region refer to junk or useless, piled-up items as "chuffy," as in, "Someday, I'm going to have to clean all this chuffy out of my desk"; or, "There's so much chuffy in my garage that I can hardly get in the door."

Richard E. Crockford
Holliston, Massachusetts

I was amazed to read in your column that "chuff" or "to be chuffed" is to be annoyed or put off.

I am a 77-year-old Yorkshire woman living in exile in sunny California, but go home every couple of years or so, and am in constant correspondence with friends and relatives.

I can assure you that in the Dales to be "chuff" or "chuffed" is to be pleased and happy. It is a dialect word I have used all my life but I think it only came into general use during Hitler's War. Those effete Southerners are quite capable of turning black into white, good into bad, and a good, honest Yorkshire saying into a nonsense.

Laura Chenoweth
San Leandro, California

Starr Quality

We are quietly building a dictionary of Whitewater usages; entries run the gamut from Richard Ben-Veniste's *shenanigans* to Carolyn Huber's *knickknacks*. Under "historic allusions," a new category of Whitewaterese, we have this subtle usage by David Maraniss in the *Washington Post*, reporting on Hillary Rodham Clinton's appearance before the grand jury, after she was subpoenaed by Kenneth Starr, the independent counsel: "The First Lady's appointment in Mr. Starr's chamber began at 2 P.M."

That was a play on the *Star Chamber*, the inquisitorial court that sat without a jury in England until abolished by the Long Parliament in 1641. Famed for its harsh judgments and punishment by pillorying, the Court of the *Star Chamber* was so named because of the stars gilded on its ceiling. *Star-chamber proceeding* is used today to characterize an unfair, secret judicial action.

The origin of the expression "Starr [or Star] Chamber" has never been conclusively determined. The *OED* approvingly cites the 16th-century conjecture of T. Smith that it was so called "because at the first all the roofe thereof was decked with images of starres gilted"—but there is no documentary or architectural evidence to support this notion.

Other readers may already have informed you of the view first expressed by William Black-stone (and supported by Maitland and others down to the present time) that the locution may derive from a chamber in which the Jewish starrs were brought together from the provinces after the expulsion of 1290.

Norman Golb
Chicago, Illinois

Starr Turn

As a service to headline writers in the year to come, here are some uses of the name of the independent counsel Kenneth Starr.

Readers have already been blessed with *Starr Chamber,* a *Washington Post* coinage (based on the inquisitorial English court with stars on its ceiling, known for its secrecy) that was praised in this space under the title *Starr Quality.*

Time magazine headed an article about Whitewater investigators *Starr Power,* and the *Wall Street Journal* editorialized about the possibility of a con-frontation between the President and the independent counsel under the heading of *Starr Wars.*

For an article on a person indicted by the independent counsel's grand jury (note that the jury, not the counsel, does the indicting, and the indictment is always handed up, not down), a probable headline will be *Starr Struck.* Specu-lation about possible prosecution will be *Starr Gazing,* and travel to Little Rock courtrooms will be dubbed *Starr Trekking.*

As all Washington becomes known as *Starrdom,* the decimated White House staff will be said to be *Starr-studded,* as bemused readers become *Starry-eyed.* A *Starr-shaped* probe may cause the President to rerun the "Saturday Night Mas-sacre," in which a *Starr-crossed* Clinton orders his firing, a dire eventuality headline writers anticipate will be dubbed *the Starry Night* (after a painting by Vincent Van Gogh).

A courthouse pennant held aloft for photographers by the independent counsel will be the *Starr Spangled Banner,* while accounts of the prison life of any he convicts will be headed either *Starrs and Stripes* or *Starrs and Bars.*

After his self-imposed silence ends, *Super-Starr* will be known to literary agents as *the Starr of stage, screen and television*—unless, of course, he fails to uncover scandal, in which case he will be characterized as *falling Starr,* his investigation mere *Starrdust.*

Will a review of his prosecutorial methods be called the *Starr system?* If so, I can guarantee one of its authors will be *Starr Sapphire.*

I enjoyed your piece on words or phrases growing out of Kenneth Starr's investigations. Here's two others you might want to consider: "starrlings"—small fry (or in this case, small birds) caught in Starr's web; and "starrlets"—those exonerated by Starr. This latter term also could be used to describe those working closely with Starr, his supporting cast.

John J. Di Clemente
Tinley Park, Illinois

I've been trying to figure out where I stand in the Starr game. It could be said that I was once a Rising Starr. It might be said now, after thirty years as the Senior Editor of the Newhouse newspapers, that I'm a Fading Starr.

David Starr
Springfield, Massachusetts

Supining Away

I pronounce *supine* soo-PINE; most younger people, and most modern American dictionaries, prefer SOO-pine. That shift of emphasis from the back of the word to the front is an example of "recessive accent," the tendency of English (and German) speakers to stress the first part of a multisyllabic word. We take French words like *menu, charlatan* and *souvenir* and switch 'em around.

Same thing happens when compound verbs like *hand over* and *take over* are squeezed together into one-word nouns; the accent moves from the *o* in *over* to the *hand* and the *take*. ("Hand OHver that island, Brits." "O.K.; the HAND-over will take place July 1.")

Pronunciation fans have objected to my recent diktat about *seminal*, which I wrote is pronounced "SEE-men-ul, contrary to what you hear from bowdlerizing academics."

"Despite what the sperm banker would assert," writes Charles Harrington Elster of San Diego, "there is no SEE in *seminal*, nor in *disseminate, seminary* and *seminar*, all of which sprang from the same seed (Latin *semen*), pronounced with a short *e*: SEM-un-ul."

No doubt I'm in a minority; *Merriam-Webster's Third International* gives my way as a less-common alternative, and only old British pronunciation guides say SEE-mun-ul. "The SEE was a deviation," Edmund Weiner, deputy chief editor of the *OED*, informs me, "used by people who wanted to emphasize the connection (hardly more than etymological now) with *semen.*" With that point made, I will now adopt SEM-un-ul, though it makes me seem SOO-pine.

Surveille

"I've noticed the emergence of a strange new verb," Christopher Valdina of Newton Centre, Mass., writes, "often in the context of the Oklahoma City bombing. *Surveille,* pronounced sur-VAIL, the verb form of *surveillance*—as in 'The F.B.I. must *surveille* any individual or group that advocates violence.' It seems to fill a linguistic niche, but it's an odd duck of a word."

It does and it is. *Surveille* (sometimes *surveil*) is a 1949 back-formation from *surveillance.* The French *sur* means "over," and the verb *veiller* means "to watch"; thus, to *surveille* is "to keep watch over." The temptation to pronounce the Englished word in French as sur-vei-yuh should be resisted; it's sur-VAIL, with the French spelling retained for etymological purposes.

In an age of snooping, the word fills a void in the language. In an interview at Federal Security Service headquarters on Moscow's Lubyanka Square, Aleksandr Mikhailov, the press agent for the former KGB, used the Russian word *razvedka,* pronounced rahz-VHYED-ka, which was at first interpreted as *reconnaissance,* but on second thought was translated as *surveillance* and *intelligence-gathering.*

The synonymy of snoopery: the general *snooping on* or *spying on* is always pejorative; *tailing* or *shadowing* is police slang for "following," but does not include *wiretapping* or *bugging,* which keeps an electronic eye or ear on the watched-over person; *stalking* has gained a sense of intentional harassment; *observing* has more of a medical connotation and is less intense than *surveilling,* which is the only word we have for "close observation of a subject or place, as by a detective or intelligence agent." We do not yet have a term for "decrypting and monitoring data transmission," but the language has a way of catching up.

Surveying Maskirovka

In *Betrayal: The Story of Aldrich Ames, an American Spy,* three of my *New York Times* colleagues in Washington explore the tangled-web world of deception. Quoting the Civil War General Thomas (Stonewall) Jackson's strategic advice to "mystify, mislead and surprise," the authors—Tim Weiner, David Johnston and Neil A. Lewis—note that the craft of misleading "was deeply respected within the KGB, which had an entire branch devoted to *maskirovka,* or deception techniques."

What a beautiful word, pronounced mas-kir-OAF-ka. The United States Army's 1955 *Glossary of Soviet Military Terminology* defines *maskirovka* as "camouflage; concealment; disguise." Leo Carl's 1990 *International Dictionary of Intelligence* agrees that it was a World War II term for camouflage, but takes it into the modern intelligence era by defining it as "Soviet GRU jargon for deception," and notes that the *Soviet Military Encyclopedia* divides *maskirovka* into "strategic, operational and tactical deception."

That's the broad term, used by the GRU, the military intelligence service; the more specialized word, preferred by the KGB (now the Federal Security Service—the name changes every few months), is *dezinformatsiya,* "disinformation," the section referred to by the *Times* Ames trio. (*Dis*information should not be confused with *mis*information, which is simply mistaken or false data; the *dis-* prefix denotes intent to mislead, a knowing attempt to deceive.)

Anatoly Golitsyn, the longtime Soviet defector whose mole warnings were taken to heart by the late CIA counterspymaster James Jesus Angleton, turns out a newsletter in the United States, Soviet Analyst, and I'm on his mailing list. Still clinging grimly to the theory that the China-Soviet split was a huge deception, Golitsyn or one of his acolytes writes, "A report in the *New York Times* . . . carried the following *maskirovka* fantasy for public consumption in the West . . ." and derides the story's Beijing source as "disoriented by Soviet *dezinformatsiya.*" (Nice use, in the Chinese context, of *disorient.*) In his usage, *maskirovka* is the general fantasy, *dezinformatsiya* the specific deception.

"*Maskirovka* means 'disguise,'" reports Viktor Klimenko, an interpreter in the *Times*'s Moscow bureau who accompanies me on visits to KGB headquarters in the old Lubyanka prison. "One sense is 'camouflage,' like covering a tank with branches, and the other is generally 'concealment.' A spy given diplomatic status is an example, although that form of *maskirovka* is usually expressed by the Russian word *krysha* for 'cover.'" (That noun, which also means "roof," is pronounced KREE-sha.)

Irena Ustinova, a visiting scholar at the Maxwell School of Citizenship at Syracuse University, recalls that the adjective form of *maskirovka* was used to describe the white uniforms worn by Russian troops in snow during their invasion of Finland in World War II. Before that, "it was used for a children's game like hide-and-seek. But now, when a spy is good at changing his image, at pretending to be somebody other than who he really is, he is said to 'use good *maskirovka.*' The Russian word is rooted in the English *mask.*"

Which has its roots in the Middle French *masque,* which was taken from the Italian *maschera,* which may have jumped the Mediterranean from the Arabic *maskhara,* "buffoon, clown," who disguised the face with makeup. That's also how we get *mascara,* which every Mata Hari knows.

The art of deception was of course "deeply respected" not only within the KGB. The art of deception was one of the cornerstones of the Communist regime in the Soviet Union from the very beginning. It was its birthmark. Without *maskirovka* totalitarian rule in my country would not have lasted so long. The same applies to what is known as *dezinformatsiya*. De facto *dezinformatsiya* always existed in the Soviet Union. But in the Orwellian language it was called *informatsiya*. But, interestingly enough, in one particular instance our regime introduced *dezinformatisiya* as such and even institutionalized it.

During the war against Hitler's Germany there was created a special Department of Dezinformation under the auspices of the Sovinformbureau. The best and the brightest of Soviet journalists were recruited to disseminate the dezinformatsiya in order to weaken Germany's fighting spirit. We called it *pustit dezu*—to fly *dezinformatsiya*. *Deza* was, so to speak, the pet name of *dezinformatsiya*, its hypocoristic suffix. I still remember one of the most effective *dezas* concocted by the Department of Dezinformation. It was a leaflet which our planes dropped over the front. Its content was very simple but devastating. Soldiers, it read, while you are fighting against us, selected impregnators from the SS are living with your wives and girlfriends in coupling houses especially erected for this purpose by Gestapo to breed pure Aryans (now you understand why this *deza* was so penetrating!) The author of this particular *deza* was one of our leading political commentators, David Monin. Colleagues were making fun of him: David, while you are making up new *dezas*, the N.K.W.D. bulls are sleeping with your wife to breed pure Russians! (David was a Jew).

After the war, the Department of Dezinformation was disbanded but *dezinformatsiya* continued, and our political vocabulary was further enriched by the expression *pustit dezu*—fly dezinformation.

Melor Sturua
Political Columnist for *Izvestia*
Professor and Senior Fellow
Humphrey Institute of Public Affairs
University of Minnesota
Minneapolis, Minnesota

Sweet and Sour Revenge

Eating Well Is the Best Revenge is the title of a cookbook by Marian Burros, the *New York Times* food columnist, and the subtitle is a meal in itself: *Everyday Strategies for Delicious, Healthful Food in 30 Minutes or Less.*

I went down the hall here at the Washington bureau to see if there was still time to change the subtitle to "30 Minutes or Fewer," but it occurred to me that *30 minutes* is so synonymous with *half-hour* that the use of *less*—properly reserved for amount, not number—has become an idiom in this case. (I would, however, stick with "29 minutes or fewer.")

Instead, I flashed a gros point pillow that a kind correspondent sent me reading "Writing Well Is the Best Revenge," and asked Marian who was the source of these one-ups on vengeance.

"George Herbert, the English metaphysical poet, in the 17th century," she replied, after looking it up in 10 minutes or fewer: "Living Well Is the Best Revenge.'"

I remember Herbert for his canine coinages: "His bark is worse than his bite" was his, as well as "He that lies with the dogs, riseth with fleas." (Quoting well is the best, etc.)

Polenta—in this case a Hungarian concoction of chicken with peppers, tomatoes and yogurt, 510 calories and 10 grams of fat—is described by Ms. Burros as a *"cross-culinary* dish."

The use of *cross-* as a combining form is proliferating. It has a long tradition—*crossbow, crossbreed, cross-index, cross-stitch* and, a century ago, lawyers spoke of *cross-action* suits within the same lawsuit—but Marian derived her usage from *cross-cultural,* involving two or more ethnic or racial groups; *cross-dressing* is wearing clothes usually associated with the opposite sex.

Crossover, in show business, is a star in two media whose audiences do not usually strongly overlap; Whitney Houston, recording star and movie actress, is an example. It can also be a single-medium phenomenon, as occurred when Linda Ronstadt, rock star, recorded albums of golden oldies that reached an audience usually entranced by Karen Akers. In politics, a *crossover voter* is one registered in one party who votes in the opposing party's primary election.

Rooted in ancient words for "spine" or "ridge," *cross-* has a relatively modern meaning of "opposed"; from that we get the sense of "irritable." That is at cross-purposes from the aim of Ms. Burros's cross-culinary Hungarian-American polenta.

Your objection to "30 minutes or less" is baseless. What that locution refers to in the title you cite is the amount of time, not the number of units of time, and *or less* here is combined with the whole amount expression, not with the numeral that is part of it (as in "30 or fewer minutes"). The fact that 30 minutes is equivalent to "half an hour" is beside the point: 29 works the same way as 30 (29 minutes or less; 29 or fewer minutes). *Fewer* would sound absolutely bizarre in a sentence such as "He can run a mile in 4 minutes or fewer": there, where what's at issue is the amount of time and not the count of minutes, only "4 minutes or less" sounds normal.

Finally, I suspect a malapropism in your reference to a Hungarian dish supposedly called "polenta." My Hungarian dictionaries (admittedly, not very good ones) list no such word, and the Italian dish of that name is of course a cornmeal porridge, not a chicken dish. (Polenta is of course an appropriate accompaniment for many chicken dishes.)

James D. McCawley
University of Chicago
Chicago, Illinois

It jolted me to have you describe "a crossover voter is one registered in one party who votes in the opposing party's primary election."

I'm sure a word maven such as you knows that voters don't register but enroll in a political party in order to be eligible to vote in a primary election. A crossover voter is, therefore, one, who though enrolled in one party and having registered to vote, votes for an opposing party's candidate in a general election.

Warren M. Anderson
Binghamton, New York

In my dictionary (as well as in my local gourmet shop, and in numerous *Italian* restaurants) polenta is *corn meal mush,* often prepared with Parmesan cheese and a red sauce. (No doubt Hungarians also use this excellent ingredient—it has great *cross-culinary* potential.)

Lynn Wasnak
Cincinnati, Ohio

Please tell us that your quibble about "30 Minutes or Less" was some kind of subtle self-parody. That usage is most certainly correct. For example, in *Modern American Usage: A Guide,* Wilson Follett (or perhaps his editor or one of his numerous collaborators) writes,

"We take *a million dollars* as a sum of money, not as a number of units; *fifty feet* as a measure of distance, not as one foot added to forty-nine other feet; *thirty minutes* as a stretch of time, exactly like *half an hour.* With these expressions a singular verb is appropriate (*A million dollars is more easily accumulated than it used to be*/*Fifty feet is too short a distance),* and the quantitative *less* is therefore correct in comparisons; *fewer* would sound absurd."

Surely 29 minutes is as much a stretch of time as is 30 minutes, and demands the same usage. I really don't see that you have a semantic leg to stand on here. Are you in the habit of telling the fellow who invites you to join him for a drink that you'll be ready in "a minute or fewer"? Tsk.

Paul N. Hilfinger
Berkeley, California

Nerds and *dorks* and *doofuses* may come and go, but *jerks* lurch resolutely on.

To learn how that word is used in the American dialect—and where it began—we are now blessed with Volume Three (*I* to *O*) of the *Dictionary of American Regional English (DARE)*, edited by America's lexicographical giant, Fred Cassidy, with Joan Houston Hall.

In 1805, a student of superstition and religion, Herbert Mayo, back-formed the noun from the old verb to apply to the vigorous movement of the heads of those manifesting religious ecstasy: "I have seen all denominations of religion exercised by the *jerks.*"

Railroaders, especially in Pennsylvania, also used the verb to coin *jerkwater town,* from the scooping of water from the track pan (a trough between the tracks) in a town too small for a train stop. Southwesterners came up with *beef jerky,* strips of dried beef, based on a Spanish-American word, *charqui,* for jerked meat. In 1883, the humorist George Peck in *Peck's Bad Boy* gave the verb a meaning of "serve, draw, dispense," with "I must go down to the sweetened wind factory, and *jerk* soda." ("86 on the houseboat, 99—I'll shoot one and stretch it" means "We're all out of banana split, chief soda *jerk,* so I'll draw a medium Coke.")

Indian, now under attack by those who prefer "Native American," has a history of forming many phrases. *Indian corn* is a cereal grass used for food, but *Indian bread* is corn bread made from real corn. An *Indian burn* is inflicted by "grasping a person's arm with both hands and twisting in opposite directions simultaneously." (In the Bronx, that's called a *noogie.*)

No wonder some aboriginal Americans resent at least some of these usages; as an attributive noun in *Indian corn, Indian burn* and especially *Indian summer* and *Indian giver,* the word means "false." The *Indian sign* is a hex, and the *Indian side* is the wrong side of the horse for mounting. A *squaw winter* is unseasonably cold.

About *squaw:* Ron Libertus, a member of the Ojibwa tribe who teaches at the University of Minnesota Twin Cities, holds that the word does not mean "woman" or "female mate" in Algonquian and Iroquois languages, but means "vagina" and should therefore be considered a slur. When a couple of feminists demanded that the offensive word be dropped from all state names, legislators complied unanimously, the Governor signed the bill and the word was banned.

In Lake County, however—where *Squaw Bay* and *Squaw Creek* had a historic flavor that never bothered anybody—the corrections sent in to comply with the new law by County Commissioner Sharon Hahn were "Politically Correct Bay" and "Politically Correct Creek."

Glen Yakel, of the Minnesota Department of Natural Resources, does not find that funny and expects a more suitable new name. Commissioner Hahn is holding her ground. Reached in Two Harbors, Minn., Ms Hahn tells me: "I grew up next to an Indian reservation, and have lots of friends there. We've talked about it, and they don't take offense. I believe we in Lake County should have the right to do what our community wants to do."

I'm with her. When in New York City, and my destination is J.F.K. International Airport, I still throw my bag in the cab and say, "Take me to Idlewild." The cabby thinks I'm crazy.

It is regrettable that you have joined the revisionists who project into the past the attitudes of the present. Let me suggest some alternatives to the origins of expressions pertaining to the American Indian that you and your correspondents regard as pejorative.

Indian corn. Corn meant "grain" among the English settlers. They called maize *Indian corn* simply to distinguish it from the wheat that had been more familiar to them.

Indian summer. The origin of this expression for a beautiful time of the year is debated. But in 1832, the *Boston Transcript* plausibly suggested that the name arose from the lull in weather that occurred at the time "Indians break up their village communities and go to the interior to prepare for their hunting." An alternative theory traces it to the similarity of autumn haze to the smoke of Indian fires.

Indian giver. This term arose from the custom among a number of Indian groups to seal a friendship or an agreement with an exchange of gifts. In 1764, the term appeared in a history of Massachusetts: "An Indian gift is a proverbial expression, signifying a present for which an equivalent return is expected."

Squaw. This term, so offensive now, had no pejorative implication in early colonial days. Every standard dictionary traces the word to Massachusett *squa*, meaning "woman" or "young woman." The settlers of Massachusetts had to deal with two people they called "squa sachems"—leaders they regarded with due respect.

Charles L. Cutler*
Rockfall, Connecticut

*Charles L. Cutler died on October 12, 1999.

My father and a number of my uncles were railroad men in Minnesota and Washington State from the turn of the century until after World War II. When they referred to a jerkwater town they meant a small community, sometimes without even a station, that had a railroad water tank with a spout held vertical against the wall of the tank by a weight on a pulley. When a steam engine pulled up, the fireman would grab a rope hanging from the end of the spout and "jerk" it down to an opening atop the engine. The water would then run in by the force of gravity until the fireman released the rope.

These jerkwater tanks were in small towns all over the country, and also gave rise to the other derogatory term "tank town."

Don Mullen
Huntington, New York

The Noogie Rebellion

You have to watch those parenthetical asides. I toss them in occasionally, drawing on memory rather than research, and I get burned every time. In a column celebrating the new volume of the *Dictionary of American Regional English,* I wrote about the adjectival use of *Indian:* "An *Indian burn* is inflicted by 'grasping a person's arm with both hands and twisting in opposite directions simultaneously.'" So far, so good; there are those who call this reddening of the skin a *snakebite* or even an *arm hickey,* but *Indian burn* is the most widely used term. Then I added, "(In the Bronx, that's called a *noogie.*)"

"Doze gize in da Bronnix dunno nuthin' 'bout giving no *noogies,*" writes Peter Rossi ("formerly of Brooklyn and don't you forget it"). He defines *noogie,* hard *g,* as "grabbing the other guy in a one-arm headlock, making a fist with one's free hand with the middle-finger knuckle raised slightly from the pack and rubbing that knuckle into the scalp of the headlockee."

"From the relative placidity of St. Paul, Minnesota," writes Amy Levine, "I recall the peer-inflicted pain of *noogies* from my Bronx childhood. However, they hurt not the skin but the skull, against which one's tormentor briefly but harshly ground his knuckles."

New Yorkers (as carpetbagging pols ask, "Where *are* the Bronx?") who became eminent doctors have also taken me to task. "In Brooklyn," writes Dr. Nicholas Christy of the College of Physicians and Surgeons of Columbia, "*noogie* means a bop on the top of the head with the knuckles; a refinement is that the knuckles are rubbed around a little to intensify the pain." Dr. Allan Gibofsky of the Hospital for Special Surgery in Manhattan notes, "A variation on this is the *noogie pop,* which is just a sharp blow to the head by another's knuckle, and was frequently administered to me by my cousin Jay (who did live in the Bronx)."

It could reflect a mock fierceness. "Administering a proper *noogie,*" adds Gene Linett of Summit, N.J., "invariably a playful gesture denoting nothing more than mild annoyance, was accurately demonstrated on more than one occasion some years ago in the 'Saturday Night Live' skits involving Lisa Loopner (Gilda Radner) and her boyfriend, Todd (Bill Murray)."

A query to the American Dialect Society's E-mail list elicited this response from Daniel Long of Tennessee at the Japanese Language Research Center in Osaka, Japan: "It's rubbing with the knuckles on the head, painful because the hair gets pulled."

Noting the hard g, making the word rhyme with *boogie-woogie*, etymologists will make the connection of *noogie* with *knuckle*, rooted in the Dutch word *knook*, "bone." That was related to the Middle Low German *knoke*, and to the Middle English *knockel*. By the 1940s, *knuckle* was also a slang word for "the head," leading to the World War II use of *knucklehead* as a jocular put-down.

Further evidence that the Bronx term has roots in Holland is that the transitive verb *knuckle*, "to press or rub with the *knuckles*," is also known as giving a "Dutch rub" (causing many a victim to "*knuckle* under"). That is the only synonym to *noogie* noted in scholarly literature, though there is an unexplained 1993 Rhode Island reference to a *wedgie* that calls for further research. But a *noogie* is clearly not an *Indian burn*.

I have it on good authority (my kids) that a "wedgie" is when your underwear is scrunched up in your butt. A "wedgie" may occur one of two ways—as the result of someone pulling the back of your underwear between your legs (probably the grandchildren of those who gave "noogies"—today's children being less overtly physical) or simply from everyday activity ("I rode my bicycle twenty miles and when I finished I had a 'wedgie.'") One synonym (there are undoubtedly many) for "wedgie" is "hinder-binder" with the *i* in hinder pronounced long to rhyme with binder. A "wedgie" is not to be confused with a "swirlie." A "swirlie" is when your fraternity brothers hold you upside down and stick your head in the toilet and . . . well, you get the picture.

Cory Franklin
Chicago, Illinois

In a recent column you seemed uncertain what a wedgie was, and though others may have enlightened you by now, I'll pass along what I just (meaning "this very minute" or "the other day") learned from a rerun of *Seinfeld*: When guy 1 grabs hold of the back of guy 2's undershorts by the waistband and pulls sharply upward so that the fabric is yanked up ("wedged") deep between the buttocks, he has executed a wedgie. If guy 1 pulls hard enough (and if the garment is commodious enough) to pull the shorts all the way up over guy 2's head, he has executed an atomic wedgie. It's always guys who do this to guys. Boys will be boys.

Natalie Bowen
Providence, Rhode Island

Here in Pittsburgh, at least, the word "wedgie" applies to a maneuver whereby one approaches the victim from behind, takes hold of his pants or undershorts waistband with one or both hands, and jerks briskly upward as far as possible, crying, "Wedgie!"

I have this upon the advice of my youngest son, Alex, who suffered and inflicted many a wedgie while he was in middle school, without losing his temper or his virility. The damage is not great, except to the wedgee's dignity and possibly his clothing. When transacted between friends, it is a sort of greeting, comparable to the high five.

Oscar Shefler
Pittsburgh, Pennsylvania

The Rhode Island version may be something altogether different, but in British schools a wedgie is performed by grasping a victim's underpants at the rear, and pulling violently until the elasticated waistband (and most of the attached material) is left halfway up the victim's back. If strength of underpants and weight of victim allow, the victim may then be hung from a coat hook.

Richard Preston
London, England

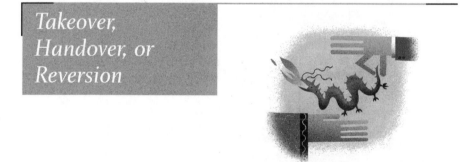

Takeover, Handover, or Reversion

"Where you stand depends on where you sit" is a political adage. In the same way, where you stand often determines the word you choose. Take the transfer of Hong Kong on July 1, 1997, after the British lease on the island territory ran out.

If you look at the change as a legal seizure by China, you tend to use the grabby noun *takeover,* with its hostile connotation based on American finance. "This is an area that views the *takeover* of Hong Kong by China," an old Asia hand told a financial reporter this month, "as the end of the Opium War started in 1850."

If you think of it as a British action, more of an old empire's giving than a new empire's taking, then you are likely to prefer *handover*. "Businessmen . . . involved in Hong Kong's *handover*," noted a *New York Times* dispatch from Shanghai, "say they must try to bridge the gap." In the *Wall Street Journal*, the British Governor urged the United States not to impose trade restrictions "after the *handover*." He also used another term: "after its *reversion* to Chinese sovereignty."

If you are eager to make obeisances to the Chinese, who want it remembered that the ancient city spent only 150 years under the British flag, then you use the word Beijing prefers: *reversion*, which means "going back to a former state."

If you want to be scrupulously neutral and are attracted to the colorless, you use *return*.

In the past year, the *New York Times* chose *return* about half the time, *takeover* a fourth, *reversion* and its variants a little less than a fourth and *handover* about 5 percent. (Zero for *relinquishment*, a word that reveals more of a pedantic affectation than a political slant.)

Tchotchkes

"In the article on 'Selling Sinatra,'" wrote Zvi Aranoff of Brooklyn in December, "please explain the history and origin of *tchotchkes*."

That was about the $2 million sale of the contents of Frank Sinatra's former house in Rancho Mirage, California: "Items, many of them gilded," went the alliterative caption in the *New York Times*, "varied from *tchotchkes* to china, posters to pianos."

A few months later, the word surfaced again, stimulating a query from Peggy Munsterberg of New Paltz, N.Y. On the Op-Ed page of the *Times*, the novelist Patricia Volk wrote of the Sotheby's auction of the estate of Jacqueline Kennedy Onassis, "In the auction of a famous person's estate, the fun is seeing close up what you were never meant to, the intimacy of a stained rug, *tchotchkes*, bedroom items, for God's sake."

According to Sol Steinmetz, author of the 1986 *Yiddish and English: A Century of Yiddish in America*, *tchotchke* is a borrowing from the Eastern Yiddish *tshatshke*, which came from the obsolete Polish *czaczko*, meaning "knickknack, trinket, toy." The current *Oxford English Dictionary* gives the origin as the Russian *tsatska*, and defines it as "a trinket or gewgaw." (But nobody says "gewgaw" anymore—it's one of those words you see in dictionaries.)

In the most current usage, however, the meaning is no longer "toy" or "bauble," and the pronunciation is no longer CHOCH-keh. A *tchotchke* today—pronounced CHOCH-key as it travels from Yiddish to English—is a derogation of a souvenir, a disdainful description of a small item to be left on a table for decoration or remembrance or because somebody gave it to you and you don't want to throw it out. (My mother called them "dust collectors.")

As I write this, I look around my roll-top desk to see a Chinese opium dealer's weight, an Indian elephant bell (the need may arise to call an elephant), a leather beanbag as a reminder of what politics is not, a boxing glove given me after the President threatened to bop my nose, a carved wooden whale and a funny-looking china bird with a long nose that I kept to remind me of somebody I forgot. All these are *tchotchkes*.

A second sense, an extension of the original "toy" or "pretty object," is "cute little girl," especially when used in the diminutive *tchotchkeleh*. A third sense, "bimbo," can be safely ignored.

Is it fanciful to suppose that there is a common origin for tshatshke, tchotchke, and czaczko and the English kickshaw (a folk mispronunciation of the French quelque chose)? All seem to have the same meaning: a trimming, or extra, usually fancy, expensive or unnecessary. Vide: my favorite diarist, James Agate:

"A tournedos which in England would cost four and sixpence" (this is 1937!) "is here" (New York) "eight pounds, without kickshaws."

Alistair [Cooke]
New York, New York

1. "Choch-key" is a terrible adulteration of the correct pronunciation, "Choch-keh" (the font of wisdom being Vilna and environs);
2. "Tchotckelach" *do*, in fact, refer to those collected items in your office, and I presume, your home. Actually, we refer to knickknack, gift, or sundry stores as "Tchotchkeh shops";
3. Lastly, and at least as importantly, that "cute little girl," or even, forgive me, that "bimbo," is actually and correctly referred to, in our Litvack (Litvesheh) circles, as a "Tsatskeh" (as in "she is some Tsatskeh!").

Saul Levine
San Diego, California

You speculated on the origins of the word, chachkas, of Yiddish usage that has crept into our general usage. The sources you credited did not include one that I always assumed as the Yiddish corruption of the Russian word for small cups, and by extension any other small china pieces that used to (and still may) clutter up a china closet.

The word is *chashechka*, or its diminutive, *chashka*. It seems to me a more likely candidate than the ones you nominated.

Victor Trasoff
New York, New York

In my husband's family vocabulary (origin Ukraine), a "tchochkeh" is an inanimate trinket or piece of junk; and a "tsotskeh" is a derogatory name for a woman, usually someone's wife.

In my family lexicon (origin Lithuania), a "tsotskeh" is a toy; and a "tsotskehleh" is a slightly pejorative term for a female. It would be more derogatory to be called a "machshayfa" and still worse to be called a "cholerya."

We both agree that none of the above would be used to describe "a cute little girl." The only term that comes to mind at present is "sheinkeit."

Gita Pearl
Outremont, Quebec, Canada

Anyone versed in the nuances of the Yiddish language would never refer to a cute little girl as a tchotchkeleh. The word is anything but flattering. It has nothing to do with looks. It is a pejorative term used to describe a "real cutie" . . . a female who is shrewd and who is constantly scheming to cook up a good deal for herself. Some people pronounce the "tch" sound as "tz" making the word "tzatzkeleh."

Hy Grober
Teaneck, New Jersey

Tea with Milk

Without fear or favor, this department will continue to correct errors of all sides in connection with (pick your slug) the campaign money scandal, or Asian Connection, or Indogate, or—as the White House prefers—necessity-driven Administration countermoves to the obscene Republican fund-raising advantage.

In an otherwise insightful thumbsucker about campaign finance, a rosy-cheeked analyst at the *New York Times* quoted Tip O'Neill, the late House Speaker, as having said, "Money is the mother's milk of politics." Error in attribution; it was another large Democratic politician, Jesse Unruh, the California State Treasurer, who uttered that immortal apothegm in the mid-'70s. Tip's aphoristic contribution to the political quotation book was "All politics is local."

In a variation on the use of *coffee* to describe a meeting at which coffee and cake were served, Marie Ridder, widow of a founder of the Knight-Ridder newspaper chain, told the *New York Times* food reporter Marian Burros of her White House visit: "I was invited to *high tea,* and the petits fours were fabulous. It was like a Viennese pastry shop."

Correction comes from Gary Glynn of New York. "I have seen three references to *high tea* recently when the speaker or writer meant *afternoon tea.*"

We all know what the food at *afternoon tea* is: pastries, round or triangular quick bread called *scones* and smoked salmon and cucumber slices on bread with the crust removed called *finger sandwiches*—not, as popularly believed, so named by cannibals. When served about 4:00 with a nice pot of tea, including a "slop bowl" nearby, the traditional if fattening repast is called *afternoon tea.*

But a special sense of the word *high*—as in the British usage *high street,* meaning "main road"—takes us to a different kettle of fish. "*High tea* is actually supper," explains Mr. Glynn, "a substantial evening meal of hot food and tea. I believe there is a working-class connotation to *high tea,* but dictionaries are too polite to mention it."

A 1981 story in the *New York Times,* quoting a person with an English accent at a Bronxville gathering, confirms this: "*High tea* means kippers, ham and eggs, treacle. It's what the working class eats instead of supper."

The error in America probably stems from considering the fine afternoon service to be "high-class tea." If, however, you're invited to the White House for *high tea,* expect to stay overnight in the Lincoln Bedroom. On second thought, that's now out; better assume they mean *afternoon tea.*

Than Me?

In a generally forgiving piece about the planned unveiling of a marble bust of former Vice President Spiro Agnew in the Capitol, I wrote, "Nobody was angrier at Agnew than me."

I knew what controversy this sentence would ignite. Sure enough, the Concerned Conjunctionites turned out in force:

"As all Bronx Science graduates should know," harrumphed Edward Silberfarb of New York, "the conjunction *than* should be followed by the nominative *I,* which is the subject of *was angry.*"

"Nobody was more surprised than I," responded Jack Rosenthal, editor of the *New York Times Magazine*. Bemoaned Harvey Fried of that city: "Whither have standards fled?"

"Never comb through your work to find flaws," wrote Gary Schuster of Bethlehem, Pa., "but couldn't help noticing *angrier . . . than me*. Always thought that, in that case, *me* was not the proper personal pronoun. As you can tell from this letter, am afraid to use the *I* word until the swami speaks. Tell about *I* versus *me*."

When it comes to *than*, I am a preppy. That is, I treat *than* as a preposition taking the object *me*, and not—as great parsings of English teachers and great squeezings of editors do—as a conjunction taking the subject *I*.

Yes, it's illogical. The meaning is "angrier than I was," which is why those hordes of careful writers hurling their missives into my "U-ofallpeople" file stick with the *I* when they chop off the *was*. You are good, rule-abiding grammarians, you Conjunctionites, and like a card-carrying empathetic, I feel your pain. But the language, it is a-changin'.

We have gone unto this breach before, dear friends, when we discussed the predicate nominative—that noun or pronoun that follows a linking verb and becomes part of the sentence's predicate, as in "It is she." It used to be *she*, when you were pointing at Jane Austen, but now it has become *her*.

Similarly, in the 1611 King James Version of the Bible, Jesus was quoted by St. Matthew as saying, "Be of good cheer; it is I." In a future translation, watch for "It is me." (Be not afraid.) The spoken language forces a change in the written language the way a glacier carves a valley through a mountain range.

The sainted usagist Henry Fowler tried to make a case for treating *than* as a conjunction (taking *I, she, he*) in the interest of clarity. Using as an example *You treat her worse than me*, he noted that the sentence could mean either "You treat her worse than you treat me" or "You treat her worse than I treat her"— confusion that would be avoided by "You treat her worse than I," which could mean only "than I do."

But Fowler knew the preppies were coming: "But the prepositional use of *than* is now so common colloquially *(He is older than me)*," he wrote, "that the bare subjective pronoun in such a position strikes the reader as pedantic."

The hard-line Conjunctionites have been fighting this battle a long time. Give them credit: they had to go up against the poet Milton's treatment of *than* as a preposition—*than whom* in "Paradise Lost"—and against Shakespeare's "a man no mightier than thyself or me" in "Julius Caesar." Bishop Robert Lowth gave in on *than whom* but held that Shakespeare made a mistake, and the grammarian's followers have been trying to hold the line against the rising tide of spoken usage ever since.

I ran this past Dennis Baron, director of rhetoric at the University of Illinois in Urbana, and author of *Guide to Home Language Repair* published there by the National Council of Teachers of English. He copped a straddle: "Like the old 'Saturday Night Live' routine, both interpretations are right: *than* is both a conjunction and a preposition; it's a floor wax and a dessert topping."

When no verb follows, I say it's a prepositional dessert topping, period. (And if you've seen one dessert topping, you've seen 'em all.) A tradition in grammar is to be treated with great respect, but dealing with the language is like the old saying about having an elephant on a string: when the elephant wants to run, better let him run. (And nobody hates to cave in more than me.)

You would be closer to reason if you had expanded that: "when no verb follows and no verb is implied or 'understood,' it's prepositional."

"Nobody was angrier at Agnew than me" is incorrect because a verb is implied: ". . . Agnew than I was." Nobody was angrier than I at Agnew.

Agnew is uglier than me. That's right. It's pure comparison. No verb or no implied verb follows. I'm older than him. (I'm older than he is old? Gibberish.)

You treat her worse than me. Meaning is obvious: you treat her worse than you treat me. No verb or implied verb follows "than."

You treat her worse than I do. Meaning is obvious; you're both abusers. She hates you both, but him just a bit more than you.

There's a great similarity in the thought processes we go through in handling "than" as in handling "like." If a subject and predicate form follows or the implication of a following subject-verb form is given, chances are you're wrong in using "like." But try to tell ex-Gov. Guy Hunt of Alabama that. He could not write a paragraph that did not contain misuse of at least one "like."

In your case, look for an *implied* verb after "than" and if it's there, watch your step. Chances are it takes the nominative.

Richard Patrick Wilson
Mobile, Alabama

May I suggest that your position might be supported by noting that in both cases the pronoun is used *disjunctively* and then contending that the form "me" is now preferred for disjunctive uses. This argument borrows from French grammar, in which language your statements would read: "*Personne n'était plus furieux contre Agnew que* moi." and "*Pas* moi."

French grammarians recognize four functions of personal pronouns: three "conjunctive" when the pronoun is conjoined with a verb as its subject, direct object or indirect object, and the fourth "disjunctive" when not so tied to any express verb. In third person plural masculine, there are even distinct pronoun forms: *ils* (subj.), *les* (dir. obj.), *leur* (ind. obj.) and *eux* (disj.). (In first person singular, the disjunctive form *moi* duplicates an object form, as in "*donnez-moi*.") See Larousse, *Grammaire du Français Contemporain* 228 (1988).

English has only two pronoun forms, called "nominative" when the subject of a verb, and "objective" when direct or indirect object of a verb. So, which form is proper when a pronoun is used disjunctively?

The objective form is standard when a pronoun follows a preposition, for which in French their disjunctive form is required: "We walk behind *them.*" (*Nous marchons derrière* eux.) This point is obscured when the pronoun is called the "object" of the preposition.

I suggest that in modern American speech, we have developed a preference for the objective form whenever a personal pronoun is used disjunctively: "*Them? No, they* are too big." (Eux? *Non,* ils *sont trop grands.*) "Who's ready? Not *me*" instead of "*I* am not ready." *(Qui est prêt? Pas* moi.—*Je ne suis pas prêt).* If my idea is valid, then your Agnew statement conforms to American usage since, as in French grammar, the completion of a comparison without repetition of the verb is a disjunctive use.

> William P. Hindman, Jr.
> Gladstone, New Jersey

The "Agnew Controversy" actually has two contentious usages. The "than me" was the central thrust of the piece, but I do believe you have double-errored by stating that "Nobody was angrier at Agnew. . . ."

Unless the language is changing quicker than I'm aging, years ago the correct usage (supported by my *Webster* and your former editor Theo. M. Bernstein with his "Do's, Don'ts and Maybes") was that "there was nobody angrier *with* Agnew."

> F. Raymond Candeletti
> Ridgefield, New Jersey

You were quite right to say, "Nobody was angrier . . . than me." But you were wrong to justify it by turning "than" into a preposition. The "me" in this case is a good example of the accusative absolute. It is akin to the French *"moi,"* as in *"l 'état c'est moi."* Imagine if Louis Quatorze had said *"l 'état c'est je"!* The whole course of history would have been changed. Or, to come closer to home, imagine American policemen, after long pursuit, finally catching sight of their quarry and shouting, "It is *he.*" They'd have to turn in their badges.

> David K. Edminster
> Washington, D.C.

Solution: No one was angrier at Agnew than *moi.*

> Gary Muldoon
> Rochester, New York

That "Certain Age"

How old is a *woman of a certain age?*

Only a Nosy Parker would try to find out. But the expression is becoming androgynous, and the age seems to be creeping upward.

Sidney Wade, a woman who lives in Gainesville, Fla., reports that she was complaining to a friend, Debora Greger, about a loss of hair: "My friend remarked that we, as *women of a certain age*, were prone to a number of peculiar developments. At first I was surprised by her use of the phrase to describe us (we are mildly ripening), remembering it from my more youthful days in France as an insulting kind of polite locution but one that remains rather wonderful and precise."

Then Ms. Wade was stunned to see a headline in the *New York Times*—"3 Explorers of a Certain Age, Scaling Mountains and More"—about three men in their 80s. "Reeling, I reported this to Debora, who supposes that the phrase itself seems to have developed a pronounced middle-aged spread. Is this so? I hope not."

The phrase, in English, can be traced back to 1754: "I could not help wishing," wrote an anonymous essayist in *Connoisseur* magazine, "that some middle term was invented between *Miss* and *Mrs.* to be adopted, *at a certain age*, by all females not inclined to matrimony." (This was two centuries pre-*Ms.*)

The *certain age* suggested spinsterhood; the poet Byron in 1817 wrote, "She was not old, nor young, nor at the years/Which certain people call a *certain age*,/Which yet the most uncertain age appears." Five years later, in a grumpier mood, he returned to the phrase: "A lady of a 'certain age,' which means Certainly aged." Charles Dickens picked it up in *Barnaby Rudge*: "A very old house, perhaps as old as it claimed to be, and perhaps older, which will sometimes happen with houses of an uncertain, as with ladies of a certain, age."

The *Oxford English Dictionary* defined that sense of *certain* as "which it is not polite or necessary further to define." That was the sense meant by William Dean Howells when he wrote of "gentlemen approaching a certain weight." The special sense reverses the literal meaning of the word *certain*, which is "fixed, definite" (much as "I could care less" means "I could not care less").

The phrase was repopularized in a 1979 book by the psychotherapist Lillian B. Rubin, *Women of a Certain Age: The Midlife Search for Self*, in which *midlife* spanned 35 to 54.

Reached in San Francisco, Dr. Rubin, whose book indicates she is now in her early 70s, was surprised to learn of the long English history of the phrase because "it has a long history in French, where it refers to women of fortyish and thereabouts who are able to initiate boys and young men into the beauties of sexual encounters. The early use in English seems to be about spinster-hood, but the French meaning has nothing to do with marriage."

In French, the phrase has erotically or sexually charged overtones. "It comes from a society where sexuality is freer," Dr. Rubin notes, "and more understood as an important part of human life."

The phrase in French is *une femme d'un certain âge*. The term, however, can apply to either sex. Without the *certain*, the phrase *un homme d'un âge* trans-lates literally as "a man of an age" and is defined in the *Oxford-Hachette French Dictionary* as "a man of advanced years."

And now to the point: is that certain age getting older?

"When I wrote the book in 1979," Dr. Rubin says, "the 'women of a certain age' were in their late 30s and early 40s. I think that has changed with the baby boomers and the lengthening of the life span. I'd say the 'certain age' has now moved to the age of 50 or 55."

Look at it this way: the time of late 30s or early 40s is no longer that "cer-tain age"; it's moved up a decade. The good news is that 40 is still young, at least linguistically. That's how it seems to a language maven of a certain weight and getting long in the tooth.

Which brings us to *long in the tooth*, which I used in a political column in an unkind reference to vigorous Senator Bob Dole. (The first user was William Makepeace Thackeray in an 1852 novel: "She was lean, and yellow, and long in the tooth; all the red and white in all the toyshops of London could not make a beauty of her.") In my piece, I was impelled by word-mavenhood to give the derivation of the expression: "As horses age, their gums recede, mak-ing their teeth appear longer." My source was the *Oxford English Dictionary*: "displaying the roots of the teeth owing to the recession of the gums with increasing age; hence *gen.*, old."

This folk wisdom about the illusion of tooth-lengthening was promptly challenged by Michael Brisbane McCrary, former Hong Kong polo player and now a squire in Hunter, N.Y.: "Horses actually *do* get 'long in the tooth.' It is not receding gums; their teeth continue to grow out (like beavers, and there is a word for it beginning with 'ex-') throughout their lives until the teeth actually fall out."

Mr. McCrary continues: "The growth of the horses' teeth is required because they would wear down in the process of eating in a natural setting. As the teeth grow out, lines show; this is how one usually tells the age of a horse. And this is the background to the phrase 'Don't look a gift horse in the mouth'; i.e., if it is a gift, don't ask how old it is."

That moved me to call the National Zoo. I don't call the Bronx Zoo any-more; any zoo that calls itself a "wildlife center" cannot be trusted. (A spokesman at our national zoological park, Mike Morgan, remembered me as the one who revealed the reason that pandas have reduplicating names like

Ling-Ling and Hsing-Hsing: they can't hear well and zoo keepers have to call them twice.)

It seems that Mr. McCrary could be right and all of us lexicographers could be wrong. "As horses age," noted Dr. Richard Montali, one of the National Zoo's veterinarians, "their teeth actually do continue to grow for some time. The incisors appear to look longer, but it's mainly because the angle of the teeth changes. Instead of perpendicular growth, the teeth angle out as they grow and wear."

Maybe the gums recede a little as the growing teeth angle out; that's why horses' teeth reveal their age. As a result of receiving this new information, and with deference to animal rights groups, I will no longer refer to old horses as being *long in the tooth*. They are *horses of a certain age*.

The *Oxford-Hachette Dictionary* is a bit off: *un certain âge* is not "advanced years," but midway to that point. The proper rendering is "no longer young."

Jacques [Barzun]
San Antonio, Texas

That "Oi" Sound

Can a speech writer, in a single stroke, remake a politician's image?

Louis Lefkowitz, the beloved New York Attorney General who died in 1996 at 91, lost a race for mayor in 1961. That hapless Republican campaign is remembered best for its exquisite ethnic balance, with sound trucks driving through Harlem blaring the Spanish rendition of a ditty about the ticket: "Lefkowitz, Gilhooley and Fino."

On election eve, Louis was scheduled to address the city's voters on the new medium of television. Some image expert had made him self-conscious about his Jewish accent—especially the pronunciation of *er* as *oi*, changing *girl* to *goil*—and Louis asked me, as his speech writer, if anything could be done about it.

I drafted a 10-minute address in which it was impossible to make that *er/oi* mistake. The biggest challenge was his current title: "Attorney General" (an office to which he kept getting re-elected, and nobody ever complained about his accent), which was kind of hard to avoid. To slip past having him say, "Attoiney General," I wrote, "This is Louis Lefkowitz, the chief law officer of New York State." And for every word sure to be mispronounced (like "word"), a synonym was found (like "expression"). We told him to stick to the text like glue.

Louis went on the tube and, to those of us in the control room, sounded almost like a WASP. Gaining confidence as he spoke, he came to the last line, about the need for a mayor to be right there in person, on the streets, among the people. He looked up from his text, raised a finger and ad-libbed an emphasizer—"by *voitue* of his presence"—and blew the whole thing.

Louis is remembered as an extraordinarily warm politician, with a hello for every passerby, a man whose neighbors and colleagues were made more civil by *voitue* of his presence.

There, There

"There's millions of elderly Americans who live on Social Security, who depend on Medicare," said the House minority leader, Richard Gephardt of Missouri, making a not unpopular observation, but treating all us geezers as singular.

"There's the talkers," said President Clinton, "and there's the doers."

There is millions? There is talkers? If these two adept public speakers square off in the primaries, what will become of subject-verb agreement?

We stand now, in linguistic awe, before the mysterious word *there*. It can be an adverb ("There you go again"), a noun ("Let Newt take it from there"), an interjection ("There, there, our day will come") and a pronoun replacing a name ("Hi, there").

Today we examine the use of *there* as a "dummy subject," with no derogation intended of the gentlemen whose usages I cited.

There are two kinds of dummy *theres*. One is the existential there, as in "There are two kinds, etc." It is always indefinite and unstressed, perhaps because it is not the true subject of the sentence, which is "two kinds" in a sentence that means "two kinds exist." The other dummy there is locative, and usually definite and stressed: "Right there is the money" tells you where the money is, even as "the money" remains the true subject of the sentence.

Why do so many people use *there is* or *there's*, construing their dummy subject as singular when the true subject that follows the linking verb is plural? Otto Jespersen, the great Danish grammarian, took a guess: people sometimes begin speaking before they know what their true subject will be.

Shakespeare, unvexed by our modern rules of agreement, was all over the lot on this issue. In *King Lear*, Gloucester warns his bastard son (no, wait—his illegitimate son. No, wait—his out-of-wedlock son), "There is strange things toward, Edmund; pray you be careful." But in *Julius Caesar,* his dummy subject took a singular verb that matched the true subject's number: "There is a tide in the affairs of men."

Gertude Stein, however, beloved in Oakland, Calif., for her "There is no there there" in a 1937 autobiography, used a dummy *there* to stand for a real *there,* and chose the proper singular verb. (Had she wanted to derogate Oakland's suburbs, she would have written, "There are no *theres* there.")

We can do as well as Stein and better than Shakespeare. If we agree that subject-verb agreement counts, then we should agree that the verb following the dummy *there* should agree with the real subject that dribbles out after the verb. Even when the result is slightly awkward, like "There're talkers and there're doers."

That's being prescriptive, I know. To shore up my confidence before getting on my ukase, I turned to one of the great grammarians, James D. McCawley, the linguistics professor at the University of Chicago. Did he agree with me that such usage as "there's millions" should be condemned?

"The only sorts of usage that I condemn," he responds, "are those that obscure useful distinctions and thus force others to do extra work when they want to draw the distinction. *Here's the orders* and the like clearly does not fit that description. But if it'll make you feel better to condemn it, I won't try to take away the (in this case) innocuous pleasure that it would give you. (I likewise think it's O.K. for you to get drunk, as long as you aren't going to be driving.)

"Unlike many of the usages that prescriptive grammarians condemn," says the only man in linguistics whose reputation challenges Noam Chomsky's, "which contribute to clarity and efficiency (the so-called split infinitive, for example), this one doesn't buy any advantage that I know of, and so you probably wouldn't do any harm by discouraging people from using it."

Through the Wronger

"It is wrong," I wrote in medium dudgeon (as opposed to high dudgeon, in which I would have written, "It is morally corrupt"—a *dudgen* or *dudgeon* is an archaic word for a wood-handled dagger, and nobody knows how it came to mean "a fit of indignation," with its first citation in 1573), and what kind of tangent am I off on? Begin again.

"It is wrong to use tax-exempt money to support political activity," wrote the moralizing vituperator. "It is *wronger* for a lawyer paid by the people to use the claim of 'executive privilege.'"

"Say it ain't so!" writes Kenneth Palmer of Kannapolis, N.C. "Our search of the *American Heritage Dictionary* failed to turn up such a word. . . . One of us is *wrong.*"

The question is: Should it be *more wrong* or *wronger*? In his *Syntactic Phenomena of English,* which I carry around in my pocket, Prof. James McCawley of the University of Chicago department of linguistics writes that comparatives are formed with "long adjectives and adverbs generally demanding *more* and short ones demanding *-er,* subject to some exceptions such as *more right* and *more wrong* that are preferred to *righter* and *wronger.*" Robert Burchfield's edition of *Fowler's Modern English Usage* agrees.

Gee. Even E. Ward Gilman, editor of *Merriam-Webster's Dictionary of English Usage,* who is no prescriptivist, holds that "although such writers as George Bernard Shaw used *wronger,* it is an infrequent use of the comparative of *wrong.*" He has on file a *New York Times* headline from 1987—"Longer and Wronger"—but that was apparently chosen because of the rhyme.

The *Oxford English Dictionary* offers me no succor; the only use of *wronger* is as a noun, "one who *wrongs* another," its first use in 1449 as "Defenders agens *wrongers* and diffamers of the . . . wickid world," now a self-description of the White House special counsel Lanny Davis.

I could claim that *more wrong,* to my ear, is not as strong a comparative as *wronger,* but as Richard Nixon never said, that would be *wronger.* I erred, Mr. Palmer, and would now rather be more right than President.

Time, Supposin'

"Will he run?" asked *Time* magazine on its cover. "If Colin Powell has the nerve, he could change America."

To grammarians, the question was: Does the conditional protasis fit the suppository apodosis? In other words, does the *has* in the iffy clause go with the *could* in the dreamy clause?

Some would put it, "If he *had* the nerve, he could change America"; others would say, "If he *has* the nerve, he *can* change America." *Time*'s construction sounds awkward; is it correct? I ran it past great grammarians on both sides of the Atlantic.

"It's O.K.," says Randolph Quirk, professor of English at University College, London, using an Americanism. "If the headline writer had put it, 'If Powell *had* the nerve,' it would be rejecting the possibility as unreal; the writer would be saying, 'I know he has not.' But by using *has* rather than *had,* the writer leaves it neutral or open.

"It is certainly odd that it goes on, 'he *could* change America,'" says Professor Quirk, picking up the uneasy feeling of many native speakers at this construction, "but it still is a perfectly good hypothesis. If he *has* the nerve, then it would be in his power to change America, so it makes Powell's choice open: he can but he needn't; he could if he wanted. The writer concedes that it is possible he has the power. Certainly it's irregular, as you note, but it is rhetorically, in my view, perfectly good."

Prof. James D. McCawley, original syntactician at the University of Chicago, responds: "Presumably *Time* didn't want to insult Powell by presupposing that he doesn't have the nerve, so *has* is the appropriate form of that verb, not *had.* The difference between *can* and *could* in this context is more subtle."

Let us brace ourselves for the subtlety. "I think *Time* got that verb right, too," says McCawley. "*Can* would suggest that Powell is already in a position to make the changes, while *could* suggests just that he can get into such a position, say, by getting elected President. Similarly, I'd say, 'The White Sox *could* win the World Series this year,' not *can,* since they first need to win the American League pennant."

Lesson: Not everything that sounds funny or looks out of whack is wrong. (Will Powell run? Sorry, this is my language column.)

The distinctions between *has* and *had* and *could* and *can* in the *Time* comment on Colin Powell misses the most obvious and grammatically consistent (and correct) explanation of the usage(s) chosen by the original writer. As used, *has* is a future subjunctive (I think), as is more apparent in an expansion of the original quote such as, "If he *has* the nerve, when the time comes, he might run, and if he runs it might happen that he would change the world." It is not idiomatic English to say, "If he will have the nerve," but that is what the writer meant and what the clause means. *Could* is the only proper counterpart of *has* in the succeeding independent clause, given what the writer is trying to say.

John Strother
Princeton, New Jersey

To Be Sure . . .

Want to anticipate a rebuttal? Want to show how profoundly you understand your opponent's arguments before demolishing them? Then play the popular rhetorical game of *to be sure . . . but.*

This has nothing to do with the earliest meaning of the phrase, which is "to be certain." Nor is it synonymous with "of course," as in a 1657 discourse on the Book of Common Prayer: "Morning and Evening, to be sure, God expects from us . . . a publick worship." By 1795, a new sense emerged, of offering a concession before countering it: "The wind is contrary, *to be sure, but* it is far from a storm." The current, heavy use of the phrase in the prose of persuasion has that seemingly reasonable purpose, but it conceals the real goal: to pull the teeth of targets before they can bite back.

In op-ed-ese, *admittedly* is as outdated as *true enough. Concededly* is too likely to be confused with *conceitedly. Stipulated* is too legalistic, almost as billable to clients as *arguendo.* About the only other introduction to a grudging concession used these days is *granted,* but that, like *admittedly,* lacks the sonorous seriousness of the most voguish fang-extractor.

"*To be sure,* Mr. Gingrich has a right under House ethics rules to write a legitimately financed book and make money from it," goes a *New York Times* editorial. "*But* he cannot expect . . ."

"*To be sure,* the next afternoon things were marginally better . . . ," Jonathan Yardley writes, coining his cliché in the *Washington Post.* "*Still* . . ."

"*To be sure,* there will be no opportunity for cooperation in the middle," writes Norman J. Ornstein of the American Enterprise Institute, pulling back his rubber band further for counterargument with "*Indeed,* the GOP has maintained a strikingly high level of party unity," before snapping back soon with "*But* moving to the majority makes a difference."

The straw-man modifier, *to be sure,* is sometimes intended to lull the opponent into thinking a valuable point has been conceded; more often, it treats as minor a portion of the opposing argument while setting up an assertion of what the to-be-surer wants to be considered more important. The telltale clue in detecting the construction of the straw-man modifier is the contrarian conjunction: *but, still, nonetheless.*

In the ranks of the practitioners of this *there-are-those-who-will-point-out* school of rhetoric, however, nobody comes close to our former Deputy Secretary of State, Strobe Talbott. Perhaps because he used to be a pundit for *Time* magazine, he is extraordinarily sensitive to the need to anticipate and tolerantly acknowledge counterargument.

"*To be sure,* elections are neither a panacea for social ills nor a guarantee of enlightened government," he lectured his audience at Oxford, adding, "*Nonetheless* . . ." Then, "*To be sure,* the United States still has disputes with Russia and with China . . . *but* there is, for the first time, no defining polarization."

For variety, the adept concessionarian slipped the phrase into the middle of a sentence: "The central issue . . . did, *to be sure,* involve land and power. . . . *But* the cold war was not just about land and power." Then back to the old-fashioned way: "*To be sure,* there are still a few countries that continue to decorate their flags with red stars . . . *but* these holdout communist states, too, offer reason for what might be called strategic optimism."

Sometimes it takes an explosion of uses in a single place to shock us into taking the anti-cliché pledge. Because Mr. Talbott is the only professional writer at the high levels of the Administration, it is fair to thank him for his pyrotechnic display of to-be-surety. Granted, he didn't know he was doing it. . . .

I'm belatedly catching up with my four paragraphs of fame in your lingo column. I am, to be sure, mortified at having been caught cliché-mongering, and I have indeed now, duly chastened, taken the anti-cliché pledge. But I'm also surely glad that you read the speech.

> *Strobe Talbott*
> Deputy Secretary of State
> Washington, D.C.

"To" vs. "With"

"To" is from Mars; "with" is from Venus.

"I have noticed a telephone locution lately that is beginning to drive me nuts," interoffices Philip Gefter, my colleague who works in *Business Day*. (You don't like *interoffice* as a verb? You've got a better verb for such communication?) "It's 'I'll get back *with* you.' I've always said, 'I'll get back *to* you.' Style police—help!"

When prepositions like *with* and *to* are used to shade direction, they are also known as particles, and are as important to the subtle writer as they are to high-energy physicists.

For example, *speak to* implies dictation, or at least a one-way direction of words, while *speak with* suggests conversation or communication between at least two speakers.

Contrast *compare to* with *compare with* (or, if you're feeling squishy, compare *compare to* with *compare with*).

The *Washington Post* broke its pick on this in an article about the House Republicans' blueprint to balance the Federal budget: "The plan calls for . . . $1.4 trillion in savings over seven years . . . *compared to with* $960 billion in savings proposed by the Senate GOP a day earlier. Here are the proposed savings and costs over seven years *compared with* the Senate plan." Apparently a copy editor was changing *to* to *with* and inadvertently left one *to* in.

The most Talmudic usagists say *compare to* seeks to show similarity between *un*like things: "Shall I compare thee to a summer's day?" or "Can the human brain be compared to a computer?" *Compare with* examines differences among *like* things: price tags in discount stores urge customers to "compare with T-shirts selling at $4."

Most practical usagists, including me (preferable to *myself included*), draw a simpler distinction: *compare to* sharply discerns similarities, while *compare with* somewhat more fuzzily examines both differences and similarities. But my purpose here is to note the way the particles act: *to* seems tough and decisive, *with* soft and ruminative.

Now to getting *back to you* or *back with you.* "Variation in usage of prepositional particles," says William A. Kretzschmar Jr., who runs the Linguistic Atlas Project at the University of Georgia, "such as *back to/back with,* arises because speakers are looking for a particular shade of meaning: *back with* might seem more familiar, or conspiratorial, than *back to.*"

He's touched the essence of the difference with "conspiratorial": *with* warmly or sneakily hooks in the other person, while *to* coolly leaves him the recipient with no reply. "I'll get back *to* you" means "Give me a little while and I'll tell you what I've decided"; on the other hand, "I'll get back *with* you" means "Just ahead is this warmly participative discussion between the two of us."

In the *Post* example, based on this principle, it should be "$1.4 trillion in savings . . . compared *with* $960 billion" and "savings and costs over seven years compared *with* the Senate plan" because both similarities and differences were being examined; if the likenesses were being played up, then *to* would be used. And if the editors wanted to stress the differences, they had available *in contrast to.*

Feel free to differ; I'll get back *to* you.

Tohubohu

Decrying the current state of poetry, in which there is "no common ground on which poets, critics, scholars, students or even readers (are there any left?) can share assumptions," the poet David R. Slavitt wrote in the *New York Times Book Review.* "To suggest this tohubohu in a manner that may be unfair but is quick, efficient and vivid, let me cite . . ."

Tohubohu? Off to the unabridged dictionaries to find that it means "confusion, disorder" and even "chaos." It's a word that starts at the near beginning, from the Hebrew *tohu wa-bhohu* in the second verse of Genesis, translated in the King James Version in 1611 as "And the earth was without form, and void."

Earlier, Rabelais brought the Hebrew word into French as *thohu et bohu,* and by 1776 Voltaire changed the spelling to *tohu-bohu,* the form now used for the word in English.

Where does an American poet get it from? Perhaps from Robert Browning, who wrote in 1883, "How from this *tohu-bohu*—hopes which dive,/And fears which soar." Or maybe he was reading the Bible in the original, to find a common ground on which to share assumptions with poetry readers, of which there are some left. (I like my *whiches* better than Browning's, which in this century should be written as *thats.*)

Tohubohu—unhyphenated, pronounced TOH-hoo BOH-hoo—is similar to *brouhaha,* "confused uproar," which some etymologists say is a corruption of the Hebrew *barukh habba,* "blessed be the one who comes"; some trace *brouhaha* to noisy stage entrances in early French farce. That's speculative; *tohubohu's* derivation is certain.

Poets and pundits like to throw in an obscure word now and then. I tried *kak-handed,* a dialect term used by my English father-in-law to mean "clumsy, fumbling," and may be related to "dirty" or the Greek-rooted "bad," as in *kakistocracy,* "government by the worst people." But most readers assumed it was a typographical garble of *backhanded.*

The word *tohu-bohu* occurs in Rimbaud's *"Le Bateau ivre."* It's in the third stanza; the lines are:

> . . . *Et les Péninsules démarrées*
> *N'ont pas subi tohus-bohus plus triomphants.*

I would imagine that a fair number of Anglophone readers learned the word from this poem.

Alan Cook
Austin, Texas

Too Close to Call

If one phrase dominated the headlines and the newscasts on the day after the election in Israel, it was *too close to call.*

When did we start using that phrase, now ubiquitous whenever journalists and pollsters are nervous about projecting the results?

The root phrase is *close call:* "My! but that was a *close call"* can be found in an 1881 *Harper's Magazine* article, followed a year later by another use in "a *close call* for Sunday." (Fifty years before that, the favored phrase for a narrow escape was a *close shave*—the writer Charles A. Davis reported in an 1834 letter that "I did not so much as get my feet wet when the bridge fell, though it was a *close shave*"—but that phrase has all but disappeared in our time as stainless-steel blades have made all shaves close.) The alliterative phrase is still current: after encountering a tornado in the 1996 film *Twister*, the storm-chaser hero reassures his girlfriend that it was "just a *close call*."

Too close to call, as best I can tell, comes from political broadcasting. Since 1647, a *call* has meant a judgment, and it was popularized after the 1860s by baseball. (A strike is *called* by an umpire, who also *calls* a sliding runner out or safe and *calls* a game on account of rain.) Daniel Schorr of National Public Radio remembers the phrase from the early days of television, and directed me to Martin Plissner of CBS, a pioneer of electronic election coverage.

"That phrase was invented at CBS between 1962 and 1964," says Plissner with the confidence never shared by lexicographers. "During that period, instead of using the exit polling we have today, we used a model we had devised for predicting or *calling* elections based on certain reported-precinct results. That gave us a sample to which we could apply mathematical formulae to determine a *call*. When we had a situation in which all the votes were reported but there was no clear winner, we called that election *too close to call*."

Plissner, a strict constructionist, thinks the phrase is today being stretched past its original meaning: "The phrase should not be used to describe pre-election polling. It should be used only after voting has taken place. The election in Israel fit the meaning perfectly: when the margin of victory is 2 percent or under, an election is *too close to call* until all the results are in."

The pundit who predicted a *dead heat* took his metaphor from racing. A *heat*, first used in this sense in 1577, was a run given a race horse to warm him up; it then defined a single course in a race of two or more trials, and was used by the poet John Dryden in 1685 in a way that idealists could apply to political races today: "Feigned Zeal, you saw, set out the speedier pace;/But the last *heat*, Plain Dealing won the race." The modifier *dead*, in the sense of "even, equal," appeared in 1635, and the phrase appeared in *Sporting Magazine* in 1796: "The whole race was run head and head, terminating in a *dead heat*." (With a hyphen, *dead-heat* is used as a verb, meaning "to end a race in a *dead heat*.") Today, all nearly *dead heats* in racing are decided by a camera taking the *photo finish*.

We don't have the first use for *cliffhanger*, but *American Speech* first defined it in 1937 as a "type of serial melodrama." The origin was certainly the movies: Pearl White, who starred in the 1914 silent film *The Perils of Pauline*, was later known as "Queen of the *Cliffhangers*." (She also did her bit for alliteration, with *The Exploits of Elaine* as well as *Perils of Paris*.) The compound noun quickly back-formed a verb, *to cliffhang*, used by *Time* magazine in a 1938 article about a villain "who often threatened cinema death to the daring, *cliff-hanging* heroine White." The picture of the heroine hanging by her fingernails from the edge of a cliff in the final reel of an episode, with "to be continued" superimposed, lent itself by metaphoric extension to the suspense of election night.

When an election can be looked back on as having been *too close to call*, ending in a *dead heat* or a *cliffhanger*, the assessment can be made by historians that it was a *squeaker*.

In British criminal slang, that word defined an informer through most of the 20th century; American crooks called the one who helped the police a *stool pigeon*, or in onomatopoeic similarity to British usage, a *squealer*.

But how did *squeaker* develop a sense of a "close election" (a phrase defined in Noah Webster's 1828 dictionary as "an election in which the votes for the different candidates are nearly equal")? It began as a "bare chance" in the early 18th century—a 1737 English writer pleaded with readers "to give me a *Squeak* for my Life (as the Saying is)"—and narrowly escaped to America to emerge in the 1930s as meaning a "tight race." *The Oxford English Dictionary* defers to Merriam-Webster for a 1961 citation, but Fred Mish of Noah Webster's old outfit has come up with one from 10 years earlier. "It was used to mean a 'close contest' in a *Newsweek* article dated Dec. 3, 1951," says Dr. Mish. "The context was the 1951 Rose Bowl playoffs, and the sentence read, 'Illinois clinched the W.C. [Western Conference] title and a Rose Bowl ride in a 3–0 *squeaker* against Northwestern.' The allusion is to the sound of a squeak, calling up two images: one is of a mouse squeezing through a small hole, and the other is the sound of elements coming so close to each other that there is an audible indication of their proximity—for example, the sound of fingernails on a blackboard."

From this use we can deduce that *squeaker* is rooted in the 1930s verb phrase *to squeak through*. Appropriately enough, the *OED* cites one usage from a *Time* magazine article in 1977 on the late Prime Minister Yitzhak Rabin, who "only *squeaked* through by sweeping the votes allotted to Israel's conservative kibbutzim."

Then and now, as the Duke of Wellington is supposed to have said about the Battle of Waterloo, "It was a damned *close-run thing.*"

In your discussion of *close call*, I enjoyed the abundance of synonymous phrases and their history, but I wondered why you stopped short and ignored *near thing* and *near miss*. And by the way, wasn't the first of these what Wellington said of Waterloo? Rhetorical question, but I think I could find three or four instances of this wording in books on my shelves.

Jacques [Barzun]
San Antonio, Texas

Tortious Interference

A colleague came by the other day to ask if I'd heard of *tortious interference*. The term is kicking about in journalistic circles, and we may be hearing more of it soon; I figured it was time to look it up to be ready to amaze my legal-eagle friends.

A *tort* is a wrong. The word is rooted in the Latin *tortus*, "crooked, dubious, twisted," from *torquere*, "to twist." (The *torque* of an engine is its rotating power; that's a good twist.) In English, a *tort* is not a crime; it is a civil wrong like "alienating the affection of a spouse" or "misuse of trade secrets," which can be subject to lawsuits.

The adjective form is *tortious*, and should not be confused with *tortuous*, from the same Latin root, which means "winding, twisting," and must not be confused with *torturous*, "painful," as when your arm is twisted. (A winding road is *tortuous* and only *torturous* if the traveler is being arm-twisted on the way. I think I'm lost.)

Tortious, as well as *tortious interference*, is defined heavily in the big, fat second edition of the *Dictionary of Modern Legal Usage*, by Bryan A. Garner. *Tortious interference*, his book explains, is "the tort of intentionally persuading or inducing someone to breach a contract made with a third party." I called Mr. Garner in Texas and had it explained in layman's terms: "Say you had a contract with Joe Blow, and I for some reason tried to get you to break that contract. Or say that Pepsi has an exclusive contract with a hotel chain to carry Pepsi products, and Coke tries to get the hotel to carry Coke despite that contract. That's *tortious interference*."

In pro football, the penalty is an automatic first down from the point of the tort.

Fear or Favor?

Readers puzzled at the unasked-for explanation in this space of *tortious interference* ("wrongly inducing the breaking of a contract with a third party") were soon rewarded by finding themselves nicely ahead of the news curve. The unfamiliar legal phrase came up in the story about the dismaying decision of "60 Minutes" not to broadcast an interview with a tobacco company whistle-blower on the advice of CBS lawyers, lest that company be sued for inducing the whistler to break his secrecy agreement with the Brown & Williamson Tobacco Corporation.

In a personal note at the end of the broadcast revealing the decision to suppress, Mike Wallace assured viewers, "We'll be able to continue the '60 Minutes' tradition of reporting such pieces in the future, *without fear or favor.*"

The veteran broadcaster used an alliterative phrase that resonated in the world of journalism, especially at the *New York Times,* which promptly published an editorial critical of CBS's excess of caution.

In the lobby of the *Times* building on 43d Street in Manhattan is Vincenzo Miserendino's bust of Adolph S. Ochs, who purchased the newspaper 99 years ago, a fact to be celebrated by his descendants and their colleagues with appropriate hoo-ha next year. With the bust is this excerpt from his credo, expressed in his opening issue in 1896: "To give the news impartially, *without fear or favor,* regardless of any party, sect or interest involved."

Rudyard Kipling, 10 years after the Ochs usage, popularized the phrase in a poem: "That we, with Thee, may walk uncowed/By *fear or favor* of the crowd." Before Ochs, a Judge McCaleb told a Federal grand jury in 1846, "The wise, human and salutary enactments of Congress must be respected and enforced *without fear or favor.*" Fred R. Shapiro of the Yale law library, who is editor of the *Oxford Dictionary of American Legal Quotations,* finds an even earlier citation in a legal data base: "The tenure of their offices," a legislative committee of the Commonwealth of Virginia declared in 1810, referring to United States Supreme Court justices, "enables them to pronounce the sound and correct opinions they may have formed, without *fear, favor* or partiality."

This research has led to a couple of other items from the credo of Adolph Ochs that I can use. The great-grandfather of the current publisher also directed that the news be written "in language that is parliamentary in good society." He was using *parliamentary* in a sense now obsolete, to be found in the *Oxford English Dictionary,* of "such as is permitted to be used in Parliament; hence allusively, admissible in polite conversation or discussion; civil, courteous."

As one of his paper's resident language mavenim, I'll buy that, and I cannot resist also passing along Ochs's declared "advocacy of the lowest tax consistent with good government, and no more government than is absolutely necessary to protect society, maintain individual vested rights and assure the free exercise of a sound conscience."

There it was, in a prominent box in the *New York Times,* a direct quotation from a dignified and well-brought-up woman now serving as Governor of the great state of New Jersey (and a person often cited by the Great Mentioner as a potential President of the United States) about requiring candidates to appear personally in attack ads:

"I happen to think that if you are looking in a camera," said Gov. Christine Todd Whitman, "saying so-and-so is a complete *schmuck,* I think that you are going to have to phrase it a little differently."

A year before, Roger Rosenblatt, in the *New York Times Magazine,* quoted the publishing executive Dick Snyder's demurral: "I don't want to sound like some new-age *schmuck.* "

The Associated Press has also disseminated the word widely, and the *Santa Fe New Mexican* this year reported, "The Mayor had warned Councilor Peso Chavez that she was prepared to sue him for slander and called him a *'schmuck.'* "

The Councilor could not have sued the Mayor back, because the current meaning of *schmuck* in that context is clearly "thoroughgoing jerk, absolute fool, unmitigated ass," none of which is slanderous. Why, then, do I wince when I hear that word spoken on television or see it in family newspapers?

Because I was brought up to believe *schmuck* was rooted in "penis." Am I hypersensitive and prudish?

"The word came into Yiddish from the old Polish word *smok,* " says Sol Steinmetz, former head of Random House reference, "meaning 'snake.' The spelling *schmuck* came about in English through the influence of the German *schmuck,* meaning 'ornament, jewelry.' But the standard Yiddish transcription is *shmok.* "

Come on, Sol—where did I get the idea it meant the male member? "Since Yiddish lacked a common word for *penis,* " says the lexicographer in his scholarly way, "it borrowed the Polish word for 'snake' in the 1600s for the more vulgar term."

In his *Joys of Yinglish* (1990), Leo Rosten deals with *shmuck* forthrightly (and spells it without the Germanic *c*). In the sense of "penis," it was considered obscene, and generated the euphemism *shmo.* In the more general sense—of "bumbler"—it is "widely used by males, and with gusto; few impolite words express comparable contempt."

The similar shape of both referents is the basis of the Yiddish borrowing from the Polish. But if the German meaning is "jewel," and Yiddish is so close to German, what caused the semantic leap from "jewel" to "penis"? Rosten speculates: "By mothers bathing or drying their baby sons. What better word for the 'member' than 'little jewel' . . . 'ornament' . . . 'cute pendant.'" He associates this with the use of "family jewels" to mean "genitals," and adds usefully that the diminutive of *shmuck* is *shmekel*.

Would I use *shmuck* (spelled without the first *c*—we're not talking jewelry here) in public or in front of impressionable little *shmekels?* I would not; the slang term, though onomatopoeically satisfying, still has a vulgar connotation.

If the sound really grabs you—and few imprecations have the ring of "What a dumb *shmuck!*"—consider the euphemism *shmo,* or try the related, if not entirely synonymous, *shmegegge* or *shlemiel.*

Sol Steinmetz's etymology of the Yiddish word for penis, *shmok,* is off the mark. What negates his assertion is his mistranslation of the Polish word *smok.* The word does not mean "snake." It has for centuries meant *dragon,* as in the legend of St. George.

I support my contention by recalling an old Polish legend about a dragon that lived in a cave under the hill where the Wawel castle stands in the city of Kraków (in English Cracow), the ancient capital of Poland. In this legend, the cave is known as "Smocza Jama," where "Smocza" means "dragon's" and "Jama" means "cave." Again for what it is worth, I know of no historic or logical connection between *dragon* and *penis* in any European language I speak (Yiddish, Polish, Ukrainian, Russian, German and English).

The above notwithstanding, there is a connection between another Yiddish slang word for penis and the word for snake in a language other than Polish. The German word for snake, *Schlanger,* became, in Yiddish, *shlang* or *shlong,* which, beside its literal meaning, is also used as another euphemism for penis. In this case it is not derogatory, but rather a left-handed compliment, because it defines a penis of a prodigious size.

Alexander Zwillich
Pittsburgh, Pennsylvania

On the authority of Sol Steinmetz you state that *schmuck* derives from the Polish word for snake, *smok.* Assuming that Mr. Steinmetz is correct about the influence of Polish on Yiddish in the 17th century, the Jewish imagination was much more flamboyant, since *smok* in Polish has only one meaning—*dragon.* The word for snake is *wąż,* pronounced *vonzh.* There is still a different word for a poisonous snake, a viper.

The primary meaning of the word *shmok* in Yiddish was, as far as I remember, penis. A derivative meaning was that of a male gender person that behaved like a penis. Both American English and colloquial Hebrew incorporated the latter meaning with a somewhat blurred definition. *Shmegegge* and *shmo* are attenuated variations. *Shlemiel* is completely unrelated and simply describes a clumsy or inept individual.

Mordecai Shelef
Bloomfield Village, Michigan

Dear Mr. Shelef:

William Safire forwarded your letter concerning the provenance of the word *schmuck*.

Though I like your suggestion that the Jewish imagination was extraordinarily flamboyant in former times, I'm afraid I must challenge the notion that Yiddish *shmok* was borrowed from the Polish word meaning "dragon."

Since Mr. Safire writes a language column intended for the general public, a certain amount of simplification of rather complex facts can be expected. In this particular case, a couple of facts were omitted, perhaps inadvertently by me, of the full account of the origin of the Yiddish word.

Here are the facts: In the 16th century (not 17th), there appeared to be no common word in Yiddish for penis. The word used euphemistically was the Hebrew-origin *eyver*, literally, "limb" (this is still used in some formal contexts). For the common, literal word Yiddish speakers borrowed the Polish word *smok* in the sense, now obsolete, of "(grass) snake." An obvious parallel is Yiddish *shlang* (in English slang often spelled *shlong*), meaning "penis" and, literally, "snake." It was about that time that the German sh- sound started to be spelled with an s (as in German *stadt*, pronounced *shtat*), causing Yiddish speakers to pronounce *smok* with the sh- sound. In present-day romanization of Yiddish, since a similar-sounding German word, spelled *Schmuck* ("ornament") already existed, this spelling was adopted for the Yiddish word that should be spelled *shmok*.

The above is a rough outline of the history of this word. Needless to say, I did not invent it. A well-known Yiddish linguist, David L. Gold, has written extensively about this as well as many other English words borrowed from Yiddish. Many of his writings have appeared in the organ (no pun intended) of the American Dialect Society, *American Speech*. Mr. Rosten is a wonderful popularizer of Yiddishisms and a very funny man. But in all truth (and he will be the first to admit it), he is not a scholar. What he told Mr. Safire about the origin of *schmuck* is pure and simple conjecture.

I have probably told you more than you wanted to know. I would just like to add that Stanislawski's Polish-English Dictionary, which you give as evidence and which we at Random House distribute, is a rather small book and does not cover the semantic history of most of the words it lists, including that of the word *smok*.

In any case, I hope I have answered the question you raised. And of course, you're quite right about those other great Yiddishisms, *shmegege, shmo,* and *shlemiel*.

Sol Steinmetz
Editorial Director
Random House Reference &
Information Publishing
New York, New York

Tweaking

"U.N. Secretary-General Boutros Boutros-Ghali *tweaked* those who feel the United Nations has too much power," wrote Betsy Pisik in the *Washington Times*. The global official's *tweaking* consisted of a mocking statement of how it was "fun to be at work here blocking reforms, . . . imposing global taxes, demoralizing my staff." The reporter used the verb *tweak* in the sense of "take a dig at" or "tease."

Eleanor Cary of Dover, Mass., demands: "Will you tweak *tweak?* It is everywhere. What gives? And why did I always think that *tweaking* had something to do with one's fingers snapping another's nose?"

Occasionally an offbeat word gets hot and pops up seemingly everywhere, stretching its meaning in the days of its voguishness.

In a piece about cosmetic surgery, *New York* magazine observed that "most patients are okay-looking people interested in a few *tweaks*," using the noun to mean "twist" in the sense of "minor adjustment." That's the meaning of what auto makers call "freshening," which Marshall Schuon of the *New York Times* describes as "*tweaks* in the design of the grille, side moldings and trunk lid."

A *Times* sportswriter, looking at a veteran quarterback, wrote last month of "the *tweaks* of age," suggesting another sense: the pinched look of the skin after it has been *tweaked* by Father Time. Another sportswriter reported in August that an athlete's "knee gave him a little *tweak*," meaning "twinge."

This is a word that is being tugged and twisted too much. Its central meaning—"pinch"—has been around for four centuries. *The Oxford English Dictionary* extracts it from Philemon Holland's 1601 translation of *Pliny's Historie of the World, Commonly Called the Natural Historie*, in which Holland wrote, "These Spiders hunt also after the young Lizards: . . . they catch hold and *tweake* both their lips together, and so bite and pinch them."

If you mean "slip a zinger or zotz to," try *needle, goad* or *prod*. As for Eleanor Cary's hazily recollected association, it is from *Hamlet*: "Who calls me villain, . . . *tweaks* me by the nose, gives me the lie i' th' throat as deep as to the lungs?"

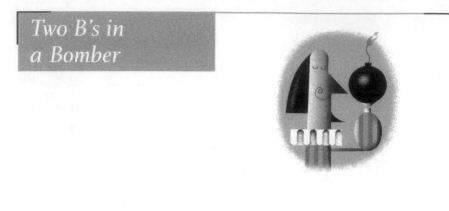

Two B's in a Bomber

Pronunciation rules spelling. Not always, of course—the *ou* in *rough, cough* and *drought* has three different sounds, but a front-page murder case illustrates the power that pronunciation exerts on the way we spell words.

"The Hunt for the Unabomer" was headlined on the cover of *Newsweek* in 1995, and a year later, when a suspect was apprehended, the headline read, "The Unabomer Saga." In the *New York Times*, text sometimes referred to "the Unabom case," while a photo caption read, "The first Unabomb book"—with two *b*'s, as in *bomb*. As Lou D'Angelo of New York writes, "To 'b' or not to 'b': that is my question."

The confusion began as the FBI Agents on the case, who are allowed to give a case file an informal name, created an acronym: *UNA* stood for *Universities and Airlines,* where bombs were received in the mail over nearly two decades, and *BOM* stood for *bomb.* Nobody at the bureau is willing to take responsibility for dropping the second *b.* Reporters picked up the FBI usage and wrote of "the Unabom case." (In *New York Times* style, if an acronym contains more than four letters, the first letter of that acronym is capitalized and the rest is lowercased.)

The problem came with the addition of the *-er* to denote the perpetrator. In *Unabomer,* the *e* signals the pronunciation of the previous vowel as a long *o:* "bome," rhyming with "home." But the perp is a bomber, not a "bomer"; without the second *b,* the word looks as if it should rhyme with "Homer." After considerable internal anguish (once a word has been spelled one way on two covers, editors feel committed to that spelling), *Newsweek* bowed to the pressure of readers and other publications and put in the second *b.* At the *New York Times,* the policy decision was *Unabomber* from the start; all the cases of dropped *b*'s were typos or errors by journalists who didn't get the word.

But a more basic question arises: Why are there two *b*'s in *bomb,* which is pronounced "bom"? The second *b* is silent; who needs it? Blame the Latin *bombus,* leading to *bombo,* "a humming noise," picked up in Spanish as *bomba de fuego,* "ball of wild fire," leading to the English *bomb,* probably related to *boom.* The first use in English—a 1588 description of war in China—was "many bomes of fire, full of olde iron," omitting the last *b*, and is remembered with great fondness at *Newsweek*.

The suspect's name is Theodore Kaczynski. The way to pronounce it is to forget the name has a *z*. In Polish, *cz* is pronounced *ch*; no matter what you hear on television, the name is ka-CHIN-ski.

Correct usage of a much-abused proverb first recorded in the 16th century has become evidence. In paragraph 185 of his 35,000-word "manifesto," published under duress by the *Washington Post* and the *New York Times*, the Unabomber wrote, "As for the negative consequences of eliminating industrial society—well, you can't eat your cake and have it too—to gain one thing you have to sacrifice another." In a letter discovered in Kaczynski's mother's home—a letter that inexplicably found its way into the media—the same proverb appears in the same words, with the same lack of a comma before the "too."

In both instances, the having and the eating were in correct order. Many people err in saying, "You can't have your cake and eat it, too," because you can—first you have it, and then you eat it. The impossible is the other way around; to "eat your cake and have it" is the absurdity that makes the point. Both the Unabomber's creed and the Kaczynski letter had it right, which is more than can be said for half the quoters of the proverb.

Unwelcome News

Used to be, when somebody said, "Thank you," the other person replied, "You're welcome"—automatically, as the night the day, as *bitte* followed *danke*.

Along came *no problem*. Somebody politely said, "Thanks"; the other guy said, *"No problem,"* or in idiomatic Russian, *"Nyet problema."*

When the *no problem* response faded away, did *you're welcome* come back? No; it's been expunged from the lexicon of courtesy. Now, all you hear in answer to "Thank you" is "Thank *you*." After billions of usages across centuries of parlance, *You're welcome* is now unwelcome.

The time for exchanging gifts is upon us, but our natural response to largesse has been belittled. I'm afraid to say it aloud, but if you want to express your appreciation for my pointing this out, you know what you are.

Has anyone else noticed the other response to "Thank you" I hear more than any other—"*You* welcome"?

Anne Mullen
Brookline, Massachusetts

Your discussion of the demise of "you're welcome" struck a chord, but I was surprised that you failed to mention the most common substitute I've encountered—not a perky "thank you," as you suggest, but an utterly laconic "uh-huh." It seems to have started with black usage and spread.

Karen Wilkin
New York, New York

As usual, you are right. "You're welcome" is no more. Or hardly any more.

I noticed it first when I had occasion, some years ago, to make a number of phone calls to companies below the Mason-Dixon Line, (Lat. 39°43′26.3″ N.)

When the operator said, "If you'll hold just a minute, I'll put Mr. Blasingame on," I said, "Thank you." She said, "Uh-huh," which threw me.

But I was only surprised the first time; I got used to that response as it spread like a miasma or a plague across the benighted land.

Arthur J. Morgan
New York, New York

Upside the Head

Right from the get-go, we're going to knock ourselves out by tracing the origin of *upside the head.*

Heath Shuler was the high-priced young quarterback for the Washington Redskins. "He is now in the National Football League," David Aldridge wrote in the *Washington Post* in 1995, "and soon will have all types of men just waiting to crack a forearm upside his $19.25 million head."

Bob Levey, a columnist in the same newspaper, did a piece that showed how the use of Black English sometimes harmed its users in mostly white workplaces. An African-American lawyer from Richmond called him to say her "noticeably black turns of phrase" made her the butt of jokes.

"I asked the woman whether she pronounces 'ask' as if it were 'ax.' She said she does. I asked whether she sometimes says 'be' when she correctly should say 'am.' She says she does. I asked whether she uses colloquialisms like 'hit him *upside the head.*' She said she uses them all the time."

Like all slang, Black English has its place, which is not always the workplace; however, some of its lively locutions cross over into general use. One such is *upside the head,* adopted by Southerners of all races, and spreading by sports usage throughout the population.

The word *upside* began as *up so* in a phrase that in the 16th century became *upside down.* In 1927, reports *Merriam-Webster's 10th Collegiate,* it became a noun meaning "upward trend" or "positive aspect," as in "Even being President or Speaker has an upside." Then, in 1929, another meaning emerged, as a preposition, in works by or about blacks: "on, up against, alongside, or against the side of." Lonnie Johnson, the blues singer, wrote, "Layin' in this death cell,/Writin' my time *upside* the wall," and Robert MacKenzie, a TV critic, wrote, "If they wish to knock a thug *upside the head,* they do so."

By the 1970s, the knock on—or slap against—the noggin crossed into general usage. *The New Yorker* wrote in 1976, "There is a further penalty of a hit *upside the head* for stiffing the toll collector." Two years later, the crime novelist Joseph Wambaugh was more graphic: "When I busted her old man that time he went *upside her head* with a meat mallet."

In a related development, a semantic change has overtaken a familiar phrase. "What does *knock yourself out* mean these days?" Laura L. Gugenheim of New York asks. "For example: 'I'm off for a walk on the beach.' 'Knock yourself out.' Or 'May I have the pruner?' [a garden tool]. 'Sure [handing it to me], knock yourself out.' "

A generation ago, *to knock oneself out* was to strain for effect, to make a great effort; as the *OED* defined it, "to apply oneself energetically (to the point of exhaustion)." Its contrary version, *Don't knock yourself out,* meant "Don't try too hard" or "Don't bother if it's difficult." That meaning still exists, though it is sometimes expressed as *knock yourself loose.*

However, the predominant sense in sitcomese today is "enjoy yourself" or "get your kicks on this." On "Dave's World," a CBS sitcom based on the humorist Dave Barry's life, a baby-sitter hands Barry's younger son a bowl of chocolate cake mix and says, "Here, Will, knock yourself out." On "Roseanne," when Darlene, the teen-age daughter in a rebellious phase, buys a wardrobe of all black clothes, she hands her mother her choices with a sighed "Knock yourself out."

Returning to the contributions of Black English, we have this letter from David H. Mortimer of the American Assembly at Columbia University: "A peculiar word has thrust itself at me in three business meetings, in Sam Shepard's *Simpatico* and Charles Busch's *You Should Be So Lucky.* The word is *get-go.* "

The *Dictionary of American Regional English* lists this, with its variant spelling *git-go,* as "especially frequent among black speakers." In Clarence Major's 1970 *Dictionary of Afro-American Slang,* it is defined as "the beginning," and the *Random House Historical Dictionary of American Slang* has a 1966 citation.

The slanguist Robert L. Chapman (who, as a Funk and Wagnalls editor, coined *quasquicentennial* for "125th anniversary" and suggests *terquasquicentennial* for 175) thinks its origin in Black English was the verb phrase *get going,* and notes that Black English delights in alliteration and rhyme.

From the get-go is now used in the whitest-shoe law offices, and any Pecksniffian derogator of it deserves a figurative slap upside the head.

Vulgar? Moi?

The same euphemistic technique—this time in reverse, from noun to verb—was employed by United Nations diplomats to soften a controversial word. Madeleine K. Albright said in a closed meeting of the Security Council that a proposal by Secretary General Boutros Boutros-Ghali to draw American forces into Eastern Slavonia would be "misguided and counterproductive."

Those words would be taken as polite conversation in most political discourse, but diplomats accustomed to soft words found them at the outer edge of diplomatese. The Secretary General, speaking in French, said he was "shocked by the statement of the American spokesman and shocked by its vulgarity." (He must have just come from a showing of *Casablanca*.)

Albright slammed right back with "to use a word like *vulgar* is unacceptable." Seeking a diplomatic way out, the translator suggested that it may not have been the noun *vulgarité*, but could have been the verb *vulgariser*, which means "to disseminate to the public," from the Latin *vulgus*, "common people."

Again, few bought the reinterpretation—this time from offensive noun to inoffensive verb—but many admired the creative twist. A French diplomat smoothed it over further with "We don't think *vulgarity* was the most precise translation of what the Secretary General said. We think the term he had in mind was 'tastelessness.'" Nice try, but *counterproductive* does not strike most nondiplomats as tasteless.

Waiting On

Larry King, the television interviewer known for his aliveness, put the question squarely to Vice President Al Gore: "Would you serve again if asked?"

After shyly expressing thanks for "a privilege to have this learning experience," Mr. Gore had to hedge: "We're *waiting on* any formal announcements."

Waiting on is a dialectical locution on the rise and splitting its meaning. In the past, it has meant "serving"; it's what a waiter does for a living. (Sorry, *waitperson* and *waitron* never made it; women who waited did not feel put down by *waitress*.) Customers in slow-service restaurants sit around steaming, waiting to be *waited on*.

The other sense, and the one used by the Vice President, is synonymous with *wait for*. A man holding packages and looking lost explains to a helpful clerk, "I'm *waiting on* my wife." A dynamic drill sergeant barks at a recruit, "Whut you *waitin' on*?"

Jean M. Peck writes from Ohio: "We've lived in Cincinnati for 18 years where I first heard the expression *waiting on* in place of *waiting for*. Everyone here says it and I mean everyone."

Across the Atlantic, the Rolling Stones picked it up for their 1981 rock hit, *"Waiting On a Friend."*

When last we visited this subject with Fred Cassidy, editor of the *Dictionary of American Regional English*, he reported it to be a Southernism (much as *standing on line* rather than *in line* is a Northernism). But the second sense of *waiting on* is spreading, and resistance to it, says the man from *DARE*, is "mostly a Northern prejudice with no real basis in usage."

I detect a nuance of impatience or exasperation in the use of the *on*, while the *for* is neutral. In some cases, the two senses of *wait on*—to serve, and to hang around in anticipation—merge, as in the King James Version use of *"Wait on* the Lord, and he shall save thee." For now, *wait on* for *wait for* is still considered dialect, but better not correct anybody who uses it.

You state, *"Waiting on* is a dialectical locution on the rise."

It is best to preserve a distinction between *dialectical* and *dialectal*. The former should be reserved for logical disputation (dialectics) and the latter for regional speech (dialect). See Fowler and Follett, among others. When one can avoid confusion, one should do so.

Caldwell Titcomb
Auburndale, Massachusetts

I haven't written for some time but your recent column on *wait for* and *wait on* stirs me.

Used to be, in the schools, every child was made to learn "by-heart" Milton's sonnet on his blindness. Eager to do his duty to his Maker, but disabled, he consoles himself with the thought that "they also *serve* who only stand and *wait.*"

The service of a waiter includes standing till he gets his orders. Same for waitresses. Whether he/she waits *on* or *for* in the USA today is a matter of geography. Milton probably *thought* in the biblical words you quoted, waiting on the Lord. (But not at the *table* of the twenty-third psalm, "before mine enemies.")

DARE III is now in nearly final galleys, going to press. With luck it should be out by the end of next summer. The financial crunch has not been relieved though there is some hope of relief. I'm still "looking for Maecenas."

Best wishes—

Frederic G. Cassidy
Chief Editor, DARE
Madison, Wisconsin

Wankers Wonk

"Who are these unreconstructed *wankers?*" demanded Tony Blair, Britain's Prime Minister. In an unguarded moment after getting a rough time from left-ist journalists interviewing him in Scotland, Blair expressed his irritation by using a slang noun not widely understood in America.

In a commentary headed "Mind Your Language, Mr. Blair," Magnus Link-later of the *Times of London* recalled how Prime Minister John Major's use of the expletive "Bastards!" to describe some of his own right wingers had endeared the conservative leader to millions. "Whether *wankers* will do the same for Tony Blair is more doubtful; indeed, I'm not certain whether the edi-tor of the *Times* will permit its use in these columns at all."

The editor did, as editors here do on occasion, because the use of a vulgar-ism by a prominent and respectable political figure—rather than by an enter-tainer or other celebrity—invites reporting (perhaps with secret glee) on the fact of its use in the most august publications.

The supplement to the *Oxford English Dictionary* defines *wanking*, a late-1940s word, as "of a male: (an act of) masturbation," with an extended sense for *wanker* of "an objectionable or contemptible person or thing." The supple-ment warns, "This word and its derivatives are not in polite use."

The most insightful *OED* citation is a bit of dialogue from the 1978 novel *Jake's Thing*, by Kingsley Amis: "'Damon, what's a *wanker?*' . . . 'These days a waster, a shirker, someone who's fixed himself a soft job or an exalted position by means of an undeserved reputation on which he now coasts.' 'Oh. Nothing to do with tossing off then?' 'Well, connected with it, yes, but more metaphor-ical than literal.'"

Americans interested in British elections should not confuse the British slang verb *wank*, frequently associated with *off*, with the American slang noun *wonk*. The latter may be rooted in the Chinese *huang gou*, "yellow dog," noted in Herbert Allen Giles's 1900 glossary of Far East terms, perhaps picked up by sailors; *wonk* is defined in Frank Charles Bowen's 1929 *Sea Slang* as "a use-less hand" and in a later naval slang work as a "midshipman." In current use as a "nerdish grind," *wonk* is a disparagement of excessive studiousness or con-cern with minutiae, as in *policy wonk* (which Tories could accuse Mr. Blair, in the Clinton mold, of being).

Unremarked in the linguistic furor over Mr. Blair's nonethnic slur was his deft use of *unreconstructed*. This is an Americanism dating back to just after our Civil War, in the period Northerners called Reconstruction. The doubly prefixed *unreconstructed* was applied to Confederates who refused to accept the conditions for reinstatement in the Union. Tony Blair's choice of an adjective to describe Old Laborites refusing to accept newly centrist Labor positions was more apt than his choice of a noun.

Wanna Cracker?

My last name rhymes with *satire*, and as same-sex marriage came up as an issue, I put my irony in the fire with a modest proposal on behalf of *polyandry*, the marriage of a woman to more than one husband. I contrasted this with *polygamy*, which I incorrectly defined as the marriage of a man to more than one woman, and condemned as sexist.

"While *polyandry* is the state or practice of a woman having more than one husband or male mate at one time," writes N. Menachem Feder of New York, "*polygamy* is a marriage in which a spouse of *either* sex may have more than one mate at the same time; it is anything but sexist; it is, in fact, sex-neutral. The state or practice of a man having more than one wife or female mate at one time is *polygyny*."

Mr. Feder admonishes me not to confuse *polygyny*, the word I meant, with *polygeny*, the descent of humankind from two or more pairs of ancestors.

We can't all be polymaths.

Dear Mr. Blowout:

> My reason for writing
> Is not all ire (only half ire)
> Regarding what rhymes
> With Mr. William Safire.

> Either retract your statement
> That it rhymes with satire,
> Or change your name
> To Mr. William Flat-Tire.

Let me quote from the introduction to *Wood's Rhyming Dictionary*: "Rhyme is the repetition of an identical accented vowel sound, as well as of all the consonantal and vowel sounds following; with a difference in the consonantal sounds immediately preceding this accented vowel sound."

Safire and satire would rhyme only if they were both accented on the second syllable. Since Safire is accented on the first syllable, a rhyme must repeat the "a" vowel sound and all that follows (including the "f" consonantal sound) and differ from the "s" sound that precedes it.

I know that forty years of rock lyrics have left all our ears blunted, but I expect more rigor from you.

Michael Mooney
New York, New York

You're in danger of having your poetic license revoked because, as you will undoubtedly be hearing from other poets, rhymesters, and devotees of doggerel, the word "satire" is, at best, a faux rhyme for "Safire." It's comparable to rhyming such look-alikes as "drifting" and "dripping." In words of more than one syllable, when the final syllables are identical in each of the pair rhymed, the *penultimate* syllable determines the rhyme. If I may hasten to chasten in a demonstrative quatrain:

> Your fired-up attempt at a rhyme-match with "Safire"
> Turns out to be less than a watered-down *half*-fire.
> Though it punctures your pride, I must tell you that "satire"
> When rhymed with your name, sir, is strictly a *flat*-tire!

Eugene Gramm
Forest Hills, New York

What Nature Abhors

A part of speech can be the basis for a series of angry speeches.

After the Senate Whitewater committee wrested a memo from the White House with the threat of a court suit, attention focused on one word of one line in the memo written by the associate White House counsel, William Kennedy 3d: "*Vacuum* Rose Law Firm files."

Republicans read *vacuum* as a verb, meaning "clean out; sanitize; empty." The verb was formed to describe the action of a vacuum cleaner, invented in 1903, which uses a partial vacuum to suck particles of dust into a bag.

The White House counsel, Mark Fabiani, in charge of rebuttals of Whitewater accusations, was able to present a different interpretation of the note by changing the verb to a noun. Thus, *vacuum* was treated as a short form of "information vacuum," or a regrettable lack of copies of documents in the Rose Law Firm files. Changing from verb to noun changed the meaning from suspicious act to innocent fact. This creative deconstruction of the line was widely hooted at by journalists, but sometimes a stretch is better than no explanation at all.

Both noun and verb come from the Latin *vacuus*, "empty"; the adjective *vacuous* means "empty-headed, stupid."

I was surprised to find your statement that the vacuum cleaner was invented in 1903. Enclosed is a copy of U.S. patent No. 91,145 on a manually operated vacuum cleaner that was issued to Ives McGaffy in 1869.

Gordon K. Lister
Williamsburg, Virginia

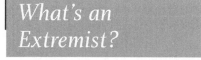

What's an Extremist?

"Not a day goes by," wrote the *Wall Street Journal* editorialist, "without some Clinton official using the word *extremist* to describe something in Washington."

That was surely the word of the year for President Clinton. "If the Congress gives in to *extremist* pressure," one statement began; a radio broadcast included, "We can't let welfare reform die at the hands of ideological *extremism*"; a farewell to a rejected nominee began, "By choosing to side with *extremists* who would do anything to block a woman's right to choose," and in a philosophical moment, he observed, "Ideological purity is for partisan *extremists.*"

What "economic royalists" were for F.D.R., and "the do-nothing 80th Congress" was for Truman, *extremists* are for Bill Clinton: the villain, unnamed but clearly labeled, and you know who you are.

The noun was apparently coined in the magazine the *Eclectic Review* during the Polk Administration, was noted in Joseph Worcester's 1846 dictionary and was popularized in 1850 by Senator Daniel Webster in connection with views about slavery and its abolition: "The *extremists* of both parts of the country are violent."

An earlier term, *extremite*, did not catch on: in 1546, Bishop Stephen Gardiner, criticizing a Protestant leader, noted, "Following the newe scoole of *extremities*, he denied all degrees of grace." Another form of the noun was used in an English proverb cited in 1639: "*Extremity* of right is wrong."

But *extremist* triumphed, and as night follows day, the *-ist* led to the *-ism*. The *Daily Telegraph of London* wrote in 1865 of "these days of extravagance and *extremeism*," trying it out with an *e* before the *-ism*.

In our time, when the label was tagged on Senator Barry Goldwater by supporters of moderate Republican Nelson Rockefeller, he blasted back at the

1964 GOP convention with a contrapuntal line submitted by the speech writer Karl Hess: "I would remind you that *extremism* in the defense of liberty is no vice." A roar went up from his partisans as he continued: "And let me remind you also that moderation in the pursuit of justice is no virtue!"

That only defense of the word in its history led to political disaster for its user. I was there in the Cow Palace of San Francisco, vainly pulling along a banner reading "Stay in the Mainstream," and looked over at Richard Nixon's box: in the pandemonium, Nixon was sitting on his hands, shaking his head; he knew that Goldwater lost all chance of winning with that refusal to move toward uniting the party. A few weeks later, Nixon pointed out to the GOP standard-bearer that his applause line was being construed as an endorsement of extremism, and Goldwater responded he should have said that "wholehearted devotion to liberty is unassailable and that half-hearted devotion to justice is indefensible." But it was too late to rewrite the speech.

The Clinton use of *extremist* was encouraged by his public-opinion adviser, Richard Morris, as part of a plan to "triangulate"—to rise above party and to place Mr. Clinton as a man of moderation between the liberal left and the true-believer right. (This Washington vogue term was bottomed on the Nixonian strategy of exploiting the break between Russia and China; "playing the China card" was in that era synonymous with *triangulation*.) That led to the adoption of *extremist* as a regular part of Clintonite rhetoric, its effectiveness endangered only by possible overuse.

True believers of the right are searching for a word to serve as a rhetorical riposte to *extremist*. It is hardly effective to counteraccuse the labeler of being a *moderate* or *centrist*, words that are losing their pejorative connotations as the position becomes more popular than *leftist;* more pointed is *compromiser,* or *waffler,* or—if an extreme reaction is wanted—*unprincipled sellout artist.*

You referred to Barry Goldwater's famous remarks on extremism as "the only defense of the word in its history." But Martin Luther King, Jr., also defended the term in his "Letter from Birmingham Jail," when he wrote:

. . . though I was initially disappointed at being categorized as an extremist, as I continued to think about the matter I gradually gained a measure of satisfaction from the label. Was not Jesus an extremist for love: "Love your enemies, bless them that curse you, do good to them that hate you, and pray for them which despitefully use you, and persecute you." Was not Amos an extremist for justice: "Let justice roll down like waters and righteousness like an ever-flowing stream." . . . Was not Martin Luther an extremist: "Here I stand; I cannot do otherwise, so help me God." And John Bunyan: "I will stay in jail to the end of my days before I make a butchery of my conscience." And Abraham Lincoln: "This nation cannot survive half slave and half free." And Thomas Jefferson: "We hold these truths to be self-evident, that all men are created equal. . . ." So the question is not whether we will be extremists, but what kind of extremists we will be. Will we be extremists for hate or for love? Will we be extremists for the preservation of injustice or for the extension of justice? . . . Perhaps the South, the nation and the world are in dire need of creative extremists."

Laraine Fergenson
Bronx Community College, CUNY
Bronx, New York

When a Justice Needs a Friend

There are two kinds of legal kibitzers: those who pronounce *amicus* uh-MEE-kuss and those who pronounce it AM-uh-kuss. Each submits a brief as an outsider, ostensibly not with an interest in the outcome of a case but as a "friend of the court"—in Latin, *amicus curiae.*

Tony Mauro, who watches the Supreme Court with a legal-eagle eye for *Legal Times*, noted that Justice Stephen Breyer has his own pronunciation. "During arguments Jan. 15 in Lambrix v. Singletary," wrote Mauro, "Breyer said 'a-MY-cus' so many times that the hapless lawyer before him, solo practitioner Matthew Lawry, adopted the same, clearly incorrect pronunciation just to be accommodating."

The reporter checked with Prof. William McCarthy of the Greek and Latin department of Catholic University, who agreed that Breyer's pronunciation was, to say the least, nonstandard; the professor preferred "AH-me-kous."

Is Breyer a pronunciational extremist? I cannot fault the solo practitioner before him for going along with the a-MY-cuses from the bench. He probably said to himself: "I'll pronounce it any cockamamie way Breyer likes, as long as he comes down for Lambrix." In the long history of that honorable Court, it is unlikely that any lawyer has corrected a Justice's pronunciation.

That's for the gutsy Mauro to do, and for me as language maven to adjudicate. Because my *bona fides* in Latin are nonexistent (that's "bone-uh FEE-days"), I turn to a friend of the column—*amicus columnae*—as expert witness.

Bryan A. Garner is editor of the *Dictionary of Modern Legal Usage* and was chosen to edit the seventh edition of *Black's Law Dictionary*. Credentials he's got.

"If I'd been in the Supreme Court's chamber to hear Justice Breyer say the phrase," he confesses, "I'd have thought it a gross lapse. But I'd have been wrong."

Aha! You looked it up in the *Oxford English Dictionary*, huh? Where it says ăməi•kŏs kiŭ•riī. In easier-to-understand form, that sounds like uh-MY-kuss kyoor-ee-eye.

Yes, says Garner the lexicographer, and Breyer also has support from William Henry P. Phyfe's 1937 *20,000 Words Often Mispronounced,* as well as two modern dictionaries of pronunciation.

"Justice Breyer has adopted an Anglo-Latin pronunciation," Garner explains. "It will make any Latin teacher apoplectic. But it has English and American history behind it, and that, in the end, matters more than how Cicero might have mouthed the phrase."

That's it. Let Scalia dissent. Object to Breyer at the Supreme Court, not to me; its ZIP code is 20543. I take refuge in Francis Bacon's 1612 comment, "Those that ingage Courts in quarrels of Jurisdiction are not truly *Amici Curiae,* but *Parasiti Curiae.*"

You misread the notoriously abstruse and minute diacritics of *amicus curiae* in the *OED.* They don't transliterate into your "uh-MY-kuss kyoor-ee-eye" but rather into uh-MY-kus KYOO-ri-ee, with the final syllable (*ae*) pronounced like a long *e* and not like *eye.* Moreover, you miscite the orthoepist W. H. P. Phyfe. My 1926 edition of his *18,000 Words Often Mispronounced* (with a supplement of 2,000 words) echoes the *OED,* with no *eye* in sight.

As *Webster 2* (1941 ed.) explains in its "Table of Latin Pronunciation" (page *liv* in the front matter), in the so-called Roman or classical method preferred by scholars and Latin teachers, the digraph *ae* (or ligature *æ*) is pronounced like the *i* in *ice;* in the Anglo-Latin or English system traditionally employed in the profession of law, it is pronounced like a long *e,* as in *aegis.*

Thus, the Roman or classical pronunciation of *amicus curiae* puts *e* before *i:* uh-MEE-kus KYUR-ee-eye. The Anglo-Latin or English puts *i* before *e:* uh-MY-kus KYUR-ee-ee (or, as the *OED* prefers, KYOO-ri-ee, with a long *u* and short medial *i*).

The pronunciation you recommend, which employs I before EYE (*my* in *amicus* and *eye* in *curiae*), is half English and half Latin, neither fish nor fowl. It does not appear, to my knowledge, in any dictionary or pronunciation guide. If this hybrid uh-MY-kus KYUR-ee-eye was in fact Justice Breyer's pronunciation of the entire locution, then lawyers and Latin teachers alike have good cause to become apoplectic.

Charles Harrington Elster
San Diego, California

Where's My Umbrella?

In a political diatribe about the United Nations abandonment of Bosnia, I zapped the British general in charge, Sir Michael Rose, as the reincarnation of the British Prime Minister Neville Chamberlain, who sold another small country down the river in Munich in 1938.

In a visit to America, General Rose took note of this criticism and handled it in as deft a put-down as I have experienced in years.

"One of the early facts I shall put straight," Sir Michael said, "came from a columnist writing in a very, very distinguished newspaper, a very distinguished gentleman with whom I have absolutely no quarrel at all.

"But he accused me of being the arch-appeaser and the reincarnation of Chamberlain. I would just like to put the record straight and say that, even if one did believe in reincarnation, this would not be physically possible, because Chamberlain died after I was born."

Reincarnation, rooted in the Latin *carn-*, "flesh," is the doctrine that the soul reappears after death, in another bodily form. I could have asked Shirley MacLaine, a current popularizer of the doctrine, but I can't get there from here.

Who's John Doe?

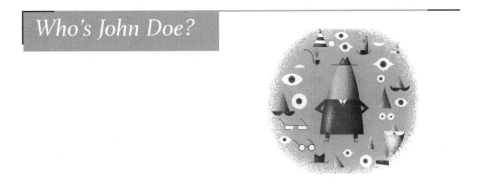

Searching for the perpetrators of the Oklahoma City bombing, the FBI issued warrants for *"John Doe* No. 1" and *"John Doe* No. 2." After the quick identification and accusation of Timothy McVeigh, a second *John Doe* remained at large.

Why do we call him that? Why not "Mr. X" or "Suspect Unknown"? The answer is in the deep recesses of English legal tradition.

Under the Magna Charta in 1215, two witnesses were needed for legal action; to protect their identities, substitute names were often placed on documents. Two of the most often-used names appeared in landlord-tenant disputes: the plaintiff protesting eviction, or "ejectment," was called *John Doe* and the defendant landlord was listed as *Richard Roe*. "The security here spoken of," Blackstone commented in 1768, ". . . is at present become a mere form: and John Doe and Richard Roe are always returned as the standing pledges for this purpose."

By the 19th century, the legal-form name had become a symbol of the ordinary citizen. It was used in an 1825 book, *The O'Hara Family*, which included "Tales, Containing . . . John Doe." The name traveled to America as the average man, or Everyman; a 1941 Frank Capra film starring Gary Cooper was *Meet John Doe*. The name still appears in this sense as signatory on checks in advertisements.

But a difference exists between "a person unknown" and "the average person." Ordinary guys include *Joe Doakes, John Smith, Joe Blow, Joe Zilch* and *John Q. Public;* when describing a signature, *John Henry,* and more recently, when wearing an undershirt and a construction helmet, *Joe Sixpack*. All these are male names, following the tradition of *Everyman,* and were once construed as embracing the female, just as *mankind* did before *humankind* was insisted upon. The "average woman" substitutes *Jane* for *Joe* or *John,* but we do not yet have an androgynous name for "the average person." (*Leslie Doakes* doesn't exactly sing.)

So much for the "average" sense; for the "unknown" sense—needed by judges to issue warrants for the arrest of someone to be identified later—we have *John Doe,* and his female counterpart, *Jane Doe*. It's easy to see why *John, Richard* and *Jane* were chosen—those have always been among the most common English first names—but why *Doe* and *Roe,* which don't cram the phone directories nearly so much as *Smith* or *Jones?*

A *doe* is a female deer; *roe,* a less-familiar term for deer, is also a name for fish eggs. Venison and fish were and are favorite English foods. "It could be," Stuart Berg Flexner speculated in his *Listening to America* in 1982, "that *Doe* and *Roe* were what landowners called men who poached deer and fish, and who would be just the kind of men willing to witness legal documents against the landowners and their landed rights."

A nice guess, though that could as easily have led to John Buck and Richard Fish. It's unlikely that the origin is in a real person named John Doe, but the source remains a mystery—which is apt, since the idea was and is to disguise an identity.

The British have come up with a typically cryptic pseudonym of their own for the unnamed. When an unidentified corpse turns up in a British hospital, it's given the name "A. N. Other." Another. Two peoples separated by a common language.

Michael Moran
London, England

What's the Spanish equivalent of John Doe? It's Fulano de Tal, or "Fulano or similar."

We also have the unspecific everybody or anybody, "Tom, Dick and Harry." And Hispanic speakers have something similar: "Fulano, Zutano y Mengano."

Fulano may be used alone, but Zutano and Mengano may only be used in combination. Fulano or Fulán is also used in Portuguese, but neither of the other two.

"Fulana de Tal" is also permissible for Jane Doe.

Arthur J. Morgan
New York, New York

I thought the term for a signature was "John Hancock" for the patriot who made his signature on the Declaration of Independence very large so that "King George could read it without his spectacles," not "John Henry," who died trying to prove that a man could out perform a machine.

Thomas R. Moore
New York, New York

Why Do They Shoot Horses?

Alain Juppé, the politician Jacques Chirac chose to be Prime Minister of France, has long come across as a bit of a stiff. With his popularity plunging to a new nadir, the brusque technocrat, to dispel his image of intellectual arrogance, has decided to let all his hidden passion and repressed angst hang out in a new book titled *Between Ourselves.*

When Roger Cohen of the *New York Times* asked Juppé if such personal confessions as those in the book might make matters worse, the Prime Minister answered in a curious way: "Perhaps. *They shoot horses, don't they?"*

What is the origin and meaning of this phrase, expressed by Juppé in French as *On achève bien les chevaux?*

A former bouncer in a marathon dance hall, Horace McCoy, titled his first novel, published in 1935, *They Shoot Horses, Don't They?* Its theme was defeatism in life's long dance, its style hard-boiled; its plot centered on the killing of a marathon dancer, a hopeless derelict, by her partner, out of what the murderer insisted was kindness, as "the only way to put her out of her misery."

Like James M. Cain, another hard-boiled novelist of the period, McCoy was popular in France; his publisher, Random House, blurbed that McCoy was "hailed by the critics of France as the peer of Hemingway and Steinbeck." The phrase was reinforced in France at about the time Juppé was growing up by the 1969 release of the Sidney Pollack film of that title, starring Jane Fonda, in which Gig Young won an Oscar in a supporting role as the unctuous contest promoter.

The meaning in France as well as America, in light of the misery-ending plot, is clear: "Sometimes you have to be cruel to be kind." But considering the possibility that his book might make matters worse, Premier Juppé's use of the phrase is ambiguous; it could mean "So maybe I shot myself in the foot," or "With this personal revelation, I could be ending my career and putting myself out of my misery."

Was the phrase original with the hard-boiled McCoy, who died in 1955? *Bartlett's Quotations* as well as the *Oxford Dictionary of Quotations* cites him as the source. The French use horses in sayings: *Il n'est si bon cheval qui ne bronche* means "The best horse may stumble," and *Il est aisé d'aller à pied quand on tient son cheval par la bride,* "It's easy to step down from high position when that position can be resumed at will." (*Écoutez-vous,* Newt?) But our misery-loves-dispatching adage cannot be found among French proverbial sayings; until otherwise refuted, it's the real McCoy.

A cascade of E-mail (only my snail mail gets a terse postcard reply) can be expected about the misuse of the reflexive in *Between Ourselves*. A reflexive pronoun should refer to a subject that precedes it, and there is no referent for *ourselves* in Juppé's title. Same problem with the somewhat more proper "Among Ourselves"; nothing to hook onto. Better use "Between You and Me" or, if searching for a larger book sale than one, "Between Us." (They shoot grammarians, don't they?) The German idiom is more vividly confidential: *Unter vier Augen,* "in the presence of only four eyes." Chinese intelligence officials in Beijing say, *Qing bu rang biede ren kan,* literally "Please don't let other people see this."

Final note: in the *Times's* headline, Prime Minister Juppé is referred to as "Premier." For decades, the *Times* used *Prime Minister* for heads of government in British-influenced countries and *Premier* for all others, but as Allan M. Siegal, an assistant managing editor, recalls, "That could drive you crazy, and we stopped." Now the preferred term in text is *Prime Minister,* with the shorter *Premier* O.K. for headlines.

Wimpmush

"The President today announced," read the White House news release, "his intention to nominate Ray L. Caldwell . . . Deputy Assistant Secretary of State for Burdensharing."

As a single word, *burdensharing* is not in dictionaries or stylebooks. Ordinarily, that means the phrase is written as two words; as the use becomes more frequent, the two are treated as a compound and separated by a hyphen. But in this case, the Clinton Administration has put the title on the fastest track, whizzing past slow stylists at the Government Printing Office.

Rule 6.8 of the GPO's style manual covers solid compounds. "Print solid two nouns that form a third when the compound has only one primary accent," the Fed arbiters say, "especially when the prefixed noun consists of only one syllable or when one of the elements loses its original accent." You can break your head over that for a month, but the rule comes into focus with these examples: *bathroom, bookseller, fishmonger, locksmith.*

You ask: When a fishmonger and a bookseller find themselves trapped in a bathroom and send for a locksmith, are they engaged in highly stressful *burdensharing,* one word? Answer: Unfortunately, under Rule 6.8, only if the word is pronounced BUR-densharing, and not, as the barge-toters say, BUR-den-SHARE-ing.

Some of us remember the great moment of editorial sabotage during the Carter Administration, when a prankster at the *Boston Globe* removed a headline that read "All Must Share the Burden" and replaced it with a headline that was somewhat more colorful and probably more accurate: "Mush From the Wimp."

Following GPO Rule 6.8, that would produce *wimpmush,* pronounced WIMP-mush, but two stressed syllables make impossible the State Department's furtive attempt to stretch the rule to fuse the nouns *burden* and *sharing.*

Ambassador Caldwell is groaning under quite a load, and I'd like to help him, but in my personal stylebook he is Deputy Assistant Secretary of State for *Burden-Sharing.*

You say that "You can break your head over that for a month." This is the first time I've seen the Germanic *"Darüber kann man sich einen Monat lang den Kopf zerbrechen"* in English. Has it been there long or did you introduce it?

George H. Spencer
Washington, D.C.

Word From the Great Alliterator

"A common grammatical error," writes Spiro T. Agnew, "is the use of singular subjects and verbs with plural pronouns, brought about by feminist sensitivity to 'his' to refer to both sexes."

This observation, made by many anti-permissivist readers over the years, is indisputable. In "Each to their own," for example, the singular antecedent *each* does not agree with the plural *their*. But if you use "Each to *his* own," your pronoun (or adjective of possession) seems to leave out half of mankind—or *humankind*, as we are now collectively called. One answer, of course, is to say, "Each to *his or her* own," but that is labored, takes forever to say and sounds pedantic. We have in the disagreeing pronoun the most awkward result of the desire to eradicate sexism in language (or, put another way, to assert the feminist prerogative). Is there a way out?

My correspondent offers one: "My suggestion would be for the authorities of English to make a forthright declaration that *their* is a correct alternative to be used with a singular human subject."

Abandon pronoun-antecedent agreement? Cave in to the radio-lib forces of usage permissiveness? Not me; that would scatter those members of the word-maven constituency seeking moorings.

Here comes the voice of Self-Anointed Authority: until the need passes to reject the idea of the male gender's embracing the female, or until a unisex pronoun takes root *(s/he?)*, use this alternative: recast the sentence as "All to our own."

On a related matter, Ted Agnew makes an unassailable point: "I rebel and my skin crawls," he notes, "when I see an advertisement stating that Sears is having *their* anniversary sale or hear an announcer inform me that inanimate Green Bay has the ball on *their* 20-yard line. Who could be offended by the use of *its?*"

The former Vice President is right. If an advertiser wants to be warm and human, if a copywriter is eager to shed the neutral, impersonal *its*—then let him *(them?* Then recast to "if advertisers want") use a little extra space with "the people of Sears" or "the players of Green Bay." In that case, as Gertrude Stein would put it, there's a *their* there.

You discuss alternatives to "Each to his own," which many today perceive as excluding half the human population. I sympathize with your reluctance to promote the disagreeable "Each to their own" and the awkward "Each to his or her own." However, I find a problem with your authorization of "All to their own": It seems to reverse the sense of the original. That is, the collective "All to their own" might be (mis)understood as suggesting a unanimity, or at least a consensus, whereas the singular "Each to his own" has a strong sense of individualism of view or action.

How about "Each to one's own"?

Joel S. Berson
Arlington, Massachusetts

Each to one's own.

Brian Graifman
New York, New York

I think you were too quick to dismiss the former V-P's suggestion that the pronoun *their* be used with a singular antecedent in order to avoid an awkward *his or her*. This usage is admittedly ungrammatical, but it has an excellent pedigree and can be found in the work of leading nineteenth-century novelists, e.g.:

". . . she never willingly suffered *anyone* to depart from her house without enquiring as much as possible into *their* names, families and fortunes." —*Tom Jones*, by Henry Fielding, Penguin edition, 1966, page 371.

". . . if we are to be peering into *everybody's* private life, speculating upon *their* income." — *Vanity Fair*, by William Makepeace Thackeray, Penguin edition, 1968, page 592.

"*Every body* [sic—two words] likes to go *their* own way." —*Mansfield Park*, by Jane Austen, Penguin edition, 1966, page 115.

Louis Jay Herman
New York, New York

Your pal from Maryland (odd he should have the same name as the non-contesting Governor) is wrong about about what we used to call collective plurals. "The government are intending . . ." is the regular and proper British usage. It was so in these 'ere colonies until—when? Perpend!—

"If it be said that the legislative body are themselves the constitutional judges of their own powers. . . ."
The Federalist, LXXVIII (Hamilton)

Fowler deplored the weakness of English in this respect. Give ear!—

"*They, them, their, theirs* are often used in referring back to singular pronominals (as *each, one, anybody, everybody*) or to singular nouns or phrases (as *a parent, neither Jack nor Jill*) of which the doubtful or double gender causes awkwardness. It is a real deficiency in English that we have no pronouns, like the French *soi, son*, to stand for *him-or-her, his-or-her* (for *he or she* French is no better off than English)."

Que faire?
Avec mes sentiments les plus profonds (comme d'habitude)

Alistair [Cooke]
New York, New York

Please understand that I am with you in opposing a cave-in to those who ignore pronoun-antecedent agreement. What I think should be done is to reconstitute the pronoun "their" to make it grammatically correct with both singular and plural subjects and verbs. Frankly, I prefer the British way of treating an inanimate subject as plural at all times, as in: "Worcester have the ball behind their own goal." However, it is hopeless that we Americans could ever adopt this usage.

[Spiro] Ted [Agnew]
Rancho Mirage, California

The Word That Brought Down the House

"The House erupted into partisan shouting," wrote Adam Clymer in the *Sunday Week in Review* section of the *New York Times,* "after Representative John L. Mica said of Mr. Clinton and his shifting views on budget balancing, 'We're here to nail the little *bugger* down.'"

The Florida Republican was ruled out of order for his choice of a word, and was permitted to resume speaking only after the House voted to let him; then he apologized.

Certainly the word was disrespectful. But in the newspaper account written the same day by Mr. Clymer, the offending word had been edited out, although other terms of disrespect—like *twerp* or *nerd*—probably would not have been. Evidently there was some concern on the news desk about obscenity, which was resolved a short time later.

Broadcast journalists had the same feeling about using the word. On CNN, Larry King asked Bill Plante of CBS, "Representative John Mica today called Clinton a 'little *bugger*'—what do you make of that?" Plante said, "There's something wrong with that word, and you don't want to get into it on this broadcast, I think, but in England it means something very specific and not very nice." King swerved off the subject.

Is *bugger* fit to print, or to use in polite company or on the air? This space is the place we face up to these decisions without fear or favor.

"What a cheeky *bugger*," wrote the *Daily Telegraph* in Britain about a sports photographer, Dennis Taylor, last month. At the same time, The *Bangor Daily News* in Maine reported on a costly attempt to stop beavers from damming a small town's culverts, quoting Candy Roy, the town manager: "I think they're winning. You can clear them out, but they're persistent little *buggers*." The *International Herald Tribune* ran a piece by Steve Vogel out of Washington quoting a Himalayan guide as seeming "well suited to solo travel, having been described as a 'grumpy *bugger*' by a colleague."

None of these usages is obscene. ("None *are*" would be obscene to purists.) The *Oxford English Dictionary* Supplement categorizes the word as "coarse slang," but not a vulgarism; the *Random House Historical Dictionary of American Slang* shows four senses: "a despicable person," "a fellow; person," "a thing" and "an undertaking that is difficult," and adds, "The Standard English sense 'sodomite' is no longer commonly understood in the U.S."

In the same way, the slang verb *bugger off* means only "beat it," or "get out of here," or their extension, "don't give me that stuff." James Joyce used the term in that imperative-departure sense in his novel *Ulysses:* "Here *bugger off*, Harry. There's the cops!" This is predominantly a British usage, as is *bugger-all,* meaning "nothing."

As a verb, however, *to bugger* is now, and has been since its coinage from a 1555 noun, plainly obscene. It means "to engage in anal copulation." No ifs or ands. A second sense of the verb is not obscene, with its past participle meaning "cursed, damned," as in "I'll be *buggered.*" A third sense, often combined with *up*, means "confuse, discombobulate." This is as acceptable as *screw up*, which followed the same metaphoric trail from verbal obscenity. (You can say *all screwed up* on American television or *all buggered up* on British television without raising eyebrows.)

It would help if the noun *bugger* were applied only to small objects, and the slang term for "sodomite" were limited to *buggerer,* but such orderliness cannot be imposed on language.

Both noun and verb could be attacked on grounds of ethnic slur: the French *bougre* comes from *Bulgarian,* a name for a sect considered heretic in the 11th century, to whom various abominations were ascribed. The good citizens of modern Bulgaria have a right to complain, but life is unfair.

To come to the point, it was disrespectful to call the President a "little *bug-ger*," or even a big *bugger* or a canny *bugger*, but it was not intended to be, or widely taken to be, obscene; a family newspaper or broadcaster was proper to report the noun as spoken. Just be careful about using it as a verb.

I found your comments about "bugger" interesting. In Brazilian Portuguese, *bugre* (per-haps taken from the French, who fought the Portuguese for control of Brazil during the 16th century) means "Indian, savage, aborigine." The figurative meanings of the word are "brute . . . treacherous, untrustworthy person."

Related words (*bugia*, she-ape, and *bugiar*, to ape or mimic) refer to monkeys or monkey-like behavior. It's surely not coincidental that the names of several indigenous groups in Brazil, such as the Kayapo, mean "monkey" in the languages of their hostile neighbors. (The Kayapo call themselves *Mebengokre*, "The People from between the Waters.")

When I've asked Brazilians about the origin of *bugre*, they've told me that the Portuguese called the Indians by this insulting name because they believed that indigenous people were homosexuals. But homosexuality seems to be rare (or at least rarely reported) among Brazil-ian indigenous groups. So the use of *bugre* as an expletive may have something to do with the common human habit of characterizing "The Other" as quasi- or subhuman.

This etymology for *bugre* may call into question the standard explanation of the origin of the French *bougre* as a corruption of "Bulgarian." Portuguese words such as *bugalho* (gall-nut or eyeball) and *bugalhudo* (goggle-eyed) probably come from the same Indo-European root as the English words "bug-eyed," "butt" and "bulge," all of which refer to rounded or swollen shape. I'm no linguist, so this is just a guess, but perhaps "bugger" and its Romance mates refer to the rounded protuberances so dear to the buggerer. That would relieve the Bul-garians, wouldn't it?

Linda Rabben, Ph.D.
Takoma Park, Maryland

Surely when you reminded us that as a verb "to bugger" means "to engage in anal copu-lation," adding "no ifs or ands," you were tempted to assert (no pun intended) "or butts."

Jerome Agel

In his play for voices, *Under Milk Wood*, Dylan Thomas named his fictive Welsh village LLareggub. Looks like a proper proper noun. But read it backwards.

R. Lasson

Did you ever question: How does *"ands"* fit in with *"ifs"* and *buts"*? Answer: It doesn't. It was never: "No ifs, *ands,* or buts." It was always: "No ifs, *ans,* or buts."

"An" is an archaic English word meaning "if." *That* fits, as in: "No ifs, *ifs*, or buts." Look it up; tho interestingly, I have found the old word absent in at least one large "unabridged" dictionary.

Abraham Azulay
Dix Hills, New York

Wordplay

Just as sex therapists believe that foreplay is a necessary stimulant, language therapists argue that wordplay arouses interest in the way we communicate.

(You didn't know I had hung out a shingle as a *language therapist?* If you can get a rubdown from a massage therapist, you can get a dressing-down from a language therapist. Job descriptions these days fit into two categories: therapists and providers. Grocers are split between *nutrition therapists* and *provision providers.* Writers who resist being called *content providers* are promptly dubbed *language therapists.*)

The example of parenthetical pyrotechnics in the paragraph above is a form of wordplay. Happily, such linguistic lollygagging is on the increase; we are surrounded by paronomaniacs, also known as punsters.

In punning, the homophonic trick is to use one sound to carry two meanings. Shakespeare begins *Richard III* with a play on *son/sun:* "Now is the winter of our discontent/Made glorious summer by this son of York." (Richard's father was the Duke of York, and his brother is Edward IV, whose badge depicts the sun.) The object of a pun is not to elicit gales of laughter; a silent internal smile will do, or even a small groan to pretend the wordplay is outrageous while the one who gets the point acknowledges its presence.

Puns probably began with plays on people's names. The most famous does not play in English: Jesus, in Matthew 16:18, renames Simon with "Thou art *Peter*"—in Greek, *Petros*—"and upon this *rock*"—in Greek, *petra*—"I will build my church." Two millennia later, plays on people's names are doing much better. The three closest aides to Prime Minister Shimon Peres of Israel, Hy Grober of Teaneck, N.J., was the first to note, are called the *Peres troika.* Excruciating subtlety, verging on obscurantism, was demonstrated by a word maven (now language therapist) who asked rhetorically, "How can I be Saussure?"—an arcane reference to the great Swiss linguist Ferdinand de Saussure. This was the same punster who headed an article about the highhanded tactics of Sheik Ahmed Zaki Yamani, then the Saudi oil minister, "Yamani or

Ya Life." When Stuart Ostrow, the theatrical producer, wrote an article about his mentor, Frank Loesser, for *Theater Week,* he recalled an aphorism (credited to Robert Browning and favored by Ludwig Mies van der Rohe) and sent the piece along with a note: "Loesser's more."

The *New York Times* columnist Maureen Dowd referred to President Bill Clinton's "coming-of-age saga" as a *Billdungsroman.* Bilingual puns, like Schadenfreudean slips, are delicious to catch: Dowd's addition of a second *l* used the President's first name to play on the German *Bildungsroman,* meaning "a novel of formation," like Goethe's 1795 *Wilhelm Meister's Apprenticeship,* a novel about building character. (I would have missed this myself were it not for the heads-up offered by Jerome Agel of New York, who added, "At least she didn't pun on the second syllable.")

Most puns play on common nouns and verbs rather than names. The Bible is a good producer of twists: Hilaire Belloc took a line from Isaiah 1:18— "though your sins be as scarlet, they shall be as white as snow"—and based a couplet on it, ending with a pun: "When I am dead, I hope it may be said:/'His sins were scarlet, but his books were read.'" Daniel Schorr of National Public Radio, who received the Columbia-Dupont Golden Baton Award for Lifetime Achievement, reached back to a 1549 translation of the Lord's Prayer for "Forgive us our trespasses" to tell an audience, "Forgive us our press passes." (In the 1611 King James Version, this line is translated as "Forgive us our *debts,*" which calls to mind the headline of a review, written by Frank S. Nugent of the *New York Times,* for a Clifford Odets drama: "Odets, Where Is Thy Sting?")

Amy Dalton, a publicist for a publisher that calls itself "HarperSanFrancisco" (run-ons may work for a publisher, but don't try it if you're a bank), caught my eye with a pitch for an anti-diet book, "Nothing to Lose." Her cover note began, "A waist is a terrible thing to mind." Not long ago, a publishing figure pseudonymed "A. Sock" wondered, "Could beating up on the distribution of the population in this country be characterized as an assault on the census?" And Norman Gilbert of the International Save the Pun Foundation, headquartered in Toronto, includes among his "Best Stressed Puns" this encouragement to the height-impaired: "It's better to have loved a short person and lost, than never to have loved a tall."

The rigorous practice of punning has now become de rigueur for headline writers. Some efforts are strained: The *New Republic* headed a review of a controversial movie about priests "Altar Ego." Others are more pointed: *Time* magazine headed a piece about Benedictine monks who scored a hit with their religious music "Leaving Little to Chants." Some tut-tutting is going on about the overuse of pun heads, but I think the judgment should be based on the quality of the wordplay.

Punsters permeate the White House Press Room, too. When asked if President Clinton had spoken to Congressional leaders in a conference call,

Michael McCurry, the White House press secretary, said, "No, he called them serially." A killer reporter observed, "A serial caller."

Copy editors usually don't like puns. When Michael Molyneux, who was my copy editor for years and has now escaped to the Metro section, wrote about the newly designed New York subway token, he noted that in this era of fare cards "the token itself is becoming an endangered specie." He felt the pressure to change *specie*, "coin," to *species*, "kind, class," as in the fused phrase "endangered species." He won, but it was a struggle.

One task assumed years ago by Harvey Shapiro, the poet who lends his editorial wisdom to this magazine, is to vet my copy for puns that might be construed as salacious double-entendres. After the copy editing, Harvey reads my submission with a fine-toothed comb (hyphenate the compound adjective, *fine-toothed*) and, like a goalie in the Great Game of Good Taste, blocks my most hilarious shots. He never missed. But a few weeks ago, I zipped one past him by using a device never before tried—the first stealth pun—a play on a missing word.

It was the piece on *bugger*, an innocent word as a noun, but as a verb, I wrote, "plainly obscene." And then I added, "No ifs or ands."

The copy editor missed the play on the withheld *but*. Harvey missed it. Even the Gotcha! Gang missed it, and those nit-picking readers don't miss much. But I got it, and to an inveterate punster, that's all that counts.

Inspired by your column on puns, I feel duty-bound to report that when I was covering (then British) Guiana back in the late 1950s, I was able to smuggle the following description of the local prime minister, whose parents had come from India, past the Foreign copy desk:

Dr. Cheddi Jagan, a dentist of Indian extraction, was elected today, etc. . . .

Tad Szulc
Washington, D.C.

The source for the pun "Odets, where is thy sting?" has to be not from the Lord's Prayer, but from Paul's first letter to the Corinthians, Chapter XV, verse 55: "O, death, where is thy sting. O, grave, where is thy victory?" That appears on page 330 of The Book of Common Prayer (1928) and is used in many Christian burial services.

Esther Talcott
Pittsboro, North Carolina

You, Sir, are not a language therapist; I am. I belong to a group of professionals known as "speech therapists," "language therapists," "speech and language therapists," or, more formally, "speech and language pathologists." We work in hospitals, clinics and schools. We are the ones who teach a three-year-old with autism to talk, or help a seventy-year-old, post-stroke, to regain his powers of communication.

Speech and language therapists generally do not attain great wealth or fame, and rarely are in a position, as you are, to inform or offend the powerful and obscure alike. Nevertheless, we touch the lives of individuals as surely as you do, and probably more often for the better. A language therapist you are not. That title is ours.

Lauren K. Krause
Chicago, Illinois

Some years ago my wife and I went on a Mayan archaeological tour in Mexico: seven tourists, a driver, and an archaeologist–tour guide, all in a seven-passenger VW bus. At one evening meal, we were so far back in the "boonies" that the restaurant menu wasn't in Spanish, it was in the Mayan Indian language, and we were all trying to puzzle it out. When one item turned out to be Spanish rice, I said, "Ah, well, *arroz* by any other name . . ."

Jack E. Garrett
Jamesburg, New Jersey

Many years ago the *Times* (London) reported that Albania's economy was improving, and headed the story "Tirana Boom Today." But maybe it would have no meaning for too many fortunately unacquainted with that ridiculous ditty "Ta ra ra boom dee ay" or however it goes.

Sheila Somner

The Working Reader

When a working writer tries out an unfamiliar word, a working reader feels the need to notice, and to do something about understanding it. If the writer is merely showing off erudition, or if he challenges the reader too often, he will lose his audience in a hurry; no reader is obligated to decipher a code. But on the two-way street of communication, a happy symbiosis is achieved when a writer tosses up an offbeat usage or a puzzling word and the working reader figures it out and savors it.

Recently I was reading, and disagreeing with, a *New York Times* editorial about standards for teaching history being promulgated by a panel of historians at the behest of the National Endowment for the Humanities.

"Most of what annoys conservatives can be *remediated,*" the editorial writer asserted. As a working reader, I rose to the bait: why not the simpler, more easily understood *remedied?* I looked up *remediated* in the *Random House Unabridged* and *Webster's New World,* and could find only the noun, *remediation,* which *WNW* defined as an Americanism used in education, "the act or process of remedying or overcoming learning disabilities or problems." The most familiar use of the word is in *remedial reading.*

Why did the writer choose *remediate?* According to the lexicographer Cynthia Barnhart, that verb was first back-formed in this sense in 1954 in the *Britannica Book of the Year; remediated* was defined there as "subjected to remedial education" and is now firmly fixed in education jargon. The *Times* editorial writer used it, I think, to give a classroom connotation to the fix possible for the legislative proposal.

That was nice coloration of prose; though the writer's position, to my thinking, was harebrained, the demand placed on me as a working reader by the editorial writer was legitimate, and the result of my search for meaning was satisfying. (I have not called my colleague for fear of hearing, "Yeah, the word I meant was *remedied.*")

Now put the shoe on the other foot. In a political harangue, I used the word *kak-handed* to mean "clumsy." I could not find it in any dictionary, but I felt confident in using the term, though I knew it would be unfamiliar to most readers, because it's a word in use: I can still hear the late Albert Julius of London using that snippet of dialect to describe my lack of manual dexterity. My guess was that it was related to the Greek word for "bad," as in *kakistocracy*— "government by the worst people." It might be related to *kaka* or *caca,* baby talk for dirty stuff, also found in the Latin *cacare,* "to void excrement."

Fortunately, I had a working reader. My spelling had thrown me off. "Re your *kak-handed,*" Stanley H. Brown of New York wrote, "two of my dictionaries—*American Heritage* and the *Oxford English Dictionary*—spell it *cack-handed,* and neither gives your spelling as an alternative. What is your source on this spelling? As another autodidact word-maven, I am most interested."

The self-taught Mr. Brown (that's how to subtly save a nonworking reader from guilt for failing to look up *autodidact*) steered me to the illumination of the *OED* Supplement: "*cack-handed* . . . dialect or colloquial. Also *cag-, keck-handed.* [See? That's my source] Left-handed; ham-handed, clumsy, awkward." First recorded use was 1854, and in steady use to this day. Houghton Mifflin's *American Heritage Dictionary, 3d edition* notes the word is "chiefly British," and speculates it may come from the Old Norse *keikr,* "bent backwards," akin to the Danish *keite,* "left-handed."

Before I first inflicted this word on an unwary public, an alert editor at the *New York Times* News Service, Pat Ryan, queried me about its meaning. I told her what little I knew about it at the time. To avert a deluge of "And what the hell is this supposed to mean?" from paying clients, she sent out this advisory to other editors: "Mr. Safire sometimes uses obscure words in his column to tease his readers, arouse their curiosity or get them thinking about language. He welcomes readers' inquiries and comments. We request that client papers preserve the reference and make no changes in the column."

And so we all now have a handle on a useful bit of dialect, which is what happens when writers and readers work together. Of course, it's easiest in a language column like this, with participation urged and expected, but it also takes place when any writer gets up the gumption to assume at least some readers are willing to work, and those working readers return the compliment by accepting the writer's challenge.

I wrote an editorial for American Biotechnology Laboratory which I entitled "Cacogenics" to indicate the opposite of eugenics. I was proud of having invented such an apt word, and I pointed this out with pride. By chance, I then found the very same word in my old *Funk & Wagnalls Standard College Dictionary. Sic transit gloria mundi!*

Gabor B. Levy*
Wilton, Connecticut

*Gabor B. Levy died in 1999.

Frequent use of the word "remediate" is not confined to discussions regarding education. This word is used as a noun, verb, and adjective to enliven the jargon of hazardous waste site management. Countless corporate and government document writers have employed the term to denote removal, treatment, or containment of contaminated soils, ground water, and sediments: "site remediation," "remediate the sediments," "remedial action." The simpler "remedy" occasionally appears in the turgid tomes produced by enlightened engineers.

John Cantilli, Environmental Scientist
Cranford, New Jersey

When I first started studying environmental engineering in 1990, my advisor suggested "remediation" was the goal and defining buzzword for any research proposal. Thus, I assumed that this word was one of general and long-standing usage. In the environmental context the word includes all measures taken to treat contaminated land and the detoxify the contaminants found on that land.

Intrigued by your article I took another look at the literature in my field. The use of the word "remediation" has increased greatly in the last few years. One data base had 33 papers from 1984–1991 and 106 from 1992–1994. The earliest paper in this data base that used the word "remediation" was a 1986 report from a Hazardous Waste and Hazardous Materials conference. While I can not claim to have made an exhaustive search, earlier literature prefers the words "restoration," "reclamation" or more simply "clean-up." Another parallel, but more cumbersome, word is "remedial action" and this is the term that appears in Federal legislation governing the approach to contaminated land.

In my own mind the substitution of "remediation" for "restoration" is a concession that the former goals of removing all traces of contaminating material are unrealistic. In practice the best results generally return the land to some alternative use or prevent the contamination from having effects on water supplies and adjacent properties. Remediation is not always a "remedy" in the sense of cure for the environmental problem but an amelioration of the effects of the problem.

Robert S. Ehrlich
Wilmington, Delaware

"Kakhanded" is a common colloquialism in South African English, where it is universally understood to be derived via Afrikaans from the Dutch *"kak,"* which is etymologically identical to English "kaka" without being slang or baby-talk. "Cackhanded"? No way.

Jacob Brooke
Bronx, New York

In a late collection of Mr. Campion stories by Margery Allingham there is one called, I believe, "Mr. Campion's Christmas," in which the word "cack-handed" appears. Amanda and Albert have quarreled, Albert is sitting alone at midnight when the dog begins to speak to him. Shortly after that, Amanda comes back to apologize for getting mad at him, though she specifically does not withdraw the epithet "Cack-handed." She has been drawn back by thinking poor Albert has been making up a conversation with the dog out of sadness over their fight, but the dog has just been doing what folk-wisdom says animals do at midnight Christmas, even in Britain.

I also learned the word "gormless" first from Allingham.

Paul A. Lacey
Richmond, Indiana

Worth a Thousand Words

"One picture is worth ten thousand words."

That, as we all know, is an ancient Chinese proverb. At least most of us think that's what it is. But in the *Macmillan Book of Proverbs, Maxims and Famous Phrases,* the quotations sleuth Burton Stevenson exploded that myth, attributing the saying to one Fred R. Barnard. As helpful phrasedicks do, Stevenson included the earliest citation's source, which was first in *Printer's Ink* of Dec. 8, 1921, and again in that magazine on March 10, 1927.

I stumbled over this information in writing the introduction to a book of famous news photographs that have appeared in the *New York Times*, part of the celebration of 100 years that the newspaper has been in the Ochs family. (Adolph Ochs bought the struggling daily in 1896.) That led me to the nefarious way the most famous remark about photography was coined, and it has never been told in full before.

Fred Barnard was national advertising manager of Street Railways Advertising, in the 1920s a sizable agency having offices across the nation and boasting that "the cars on our list carry more than 10,000,000,000 passengers a year," but it was derailed in 1941. Barnard took an ad in *Printer's Ink* with this headline: "One Look Is Worth a Thousand Words."

The copy block began: "So said a famous Japanese philosopher, and he was right—nearly everyone likes to 'read' pictures. 'Buttersweet is good to eat' is a very short phrase, but it will sell more goods if presented, with an appetizing picture of the product, to many people morning, noon and night, every day in the year, than a thousand-word advertisement placed before the same number of people only a limited number of times during the year."

But his slogan didn't work; a *look* does not stand in sharp contrast to a *word*. He could have said, "A look is worth a thousand descriptions," which sounds more like parallel construction, but the adman was destined to do better.

Six years later, planning another ad to attract business to his agency, Barnard changed "one look" to "one picture," which contrasted nicely with "words," and while he was at it, escalated the "one thousand" to "ten thousand." The famous Japanese philosopher (whom nobody ever heard of because he never existed) fell by the wayside. The adman hired a calligrapher to put the words into Chinese characters, and under them captioned, "Chinese Proverb: One Picture Is Worth Ten Thousand Words." We do not know why he switched from *Japanese* to *Chinese*; perhaps the artist he hired knew only Chinese, and the picture of the Chinese characters was worth more than a lot of copy. Barnard later confessed he made that attribution to an ancient Asian "so that people would take it seriously."

He was right; we do slavishly accept the primacy of pictures over prose. Although writers could readily deride the wisdom of a mere car-card salesman like Fred Barnard, we are reluctant to take on Confucius or some other venerable sage when it comes to a subject as controversial as the derogation of the written word. The lesson in all this: As Diogenes used to say, one original thought is worth a thousand mindless quotings. Make that ten thousand.

While your quote is not exactly a Chinese proverb, there is a Chinese equivalent dated approximately A.D. 100. In *Han Shu*, a book of Han Dynasty, there is a statement which can be literally translated as "Hearing a hundred times is not as good as one look." In the context of the writing, it means "Listening to a hundred sources is not as accurate as one look," and can easily be construed as "One picture is better than a hundred descriptions."

Although the adman who coined the slogan "One picture is worth ten thousand words" might not know the correct Chinese source, he could have taken liberty to dramatize something that he thought was an ancient Chinese proverb. After all, most American readers couldn't tell the difference between the Chinese characters "hundred" and "ten thousand" that appeared in the advertisement. The Chinese artist who wrote the Chinese characters for the advertisement might have known better. (By the way, until quite recently, Japanese used Chinese characters when they composed literary works, particularly poetry, and some still do.)

Tung Au
Walnut Creek, California

Fred Barnard may have been prescient. As defined in this computer age, the amount of "information" in one picture may be about the same as the amount of information in ten thousand words. It takes some sixty thousand bytes to store ten thousand words. How many bytes it takes to store a picture depends on a lot of things—the size of the picture, the degree of resolution of the image, whether it is in color or black and white, and what compression algorithm is used to hold down the number of bytes. It would take someone more expert than I to tell you just how many bytes are needed to store a particular picture—i.e., how much "information" the picture contains—but the ratio ten thousand to one for pictures and words is probably not a bad estimate.

Kenneth W. Ford
Philadelphia, PA

Would-Be Assassin

"While I don't wish to turn the shooting of a man into a mere grammatical issue," writes Richard S. Kaufman, a copy editor at the Book-of-the-Month Club in New York, "I was puzzled by a phrase in an article about former Gov. George Wallace's injuries at the hands of 'a would-be assassin.'" Mr. Kaufman points to a 1958 book, *Watch Your Language* by Theodore M. Bernstein, who was then the *New York Times*'s guardian of the language. Bernstein wrote: "An *assassin* is a person who either kills or tries to kill treacherously. Thus, for all practical purposes there is no such thing as a 'would-be assassin.'"

Bernstein based his usage judgment on the *Oxford English Dictionary*'s definition of *assassin:* "One who undertakes to put another to death by treacherous violence." *Undertakes* denotes "tries," and would make *would-be assassin* redundant.

Let's see how two of the newest dictionaries define the noun. *The Random House Webster's College Dictionary* (which has such current terms as *bad hair day, control freak, family leave, Generation X, mondegreen* and *no-brainer*) defines *assassin* as "a murderer, esp. one who kills a politically prominent person for fanatical or monetary reasons."

The Cambridge International Dictionary of English, which ranges across American, British and Australian English (and has a nice way of listing each sense separately—*bollocks,* for example, has one definition for "body part" and another for "nonsense"), similarly defines *assassin* as "a murderer, esp. one who kills a famous or important person for political reasons or in exchange for money." Again, no suggestion that the assassin is anything other than one who has completed his mission of murder.

Usage has changed in these four decades. Probably because the noun *assassination* has long meant a completed act of murder, *assassin* is now its successful perpetrator—and *would-be* and *intended* are legitimate modifiers for one who tries but fails to hit the target.

Ted Bernstein, whose 1965 *Careful Writer* is still a useful usage dictionary, is not spinning in his grave: he knew that all usage diktats are snapshots in time.

You Betcha

Is America in danger of being seized with absolutism?

Used to be, *yes* was the preferred affirmation. The military tried a variant: *affirmative.* Now all we hear is *absolutely.*

William Abbott of Westport, Conn., notes that today's vogue word for eager assent and unquestioning assurance is not only pervasive but anachronistic: "I heard Mel Gibson give an emphatic *absolutely!* at least twice in his 13th-century epic 'Braveheart.'" The adverb did not appear in the English language until the 14th century, in the sense of "certainly, positively," and not until 1597 did Shakespeare use it to mean "conclusively, finally, unreservedly."

Absolutely-watchers note what Mr. Abbott calls "a corrective to the world's insincerity" in the movie *The English Patient,* written by Anthony Minghella. The character of Almasy, played by Ralph Fiennes, is trapped with Katherine (Kristin Scott-Thomas) in their vehicle during a North African sandstorm. When she asks if they will be all right, he replies, "Yes, yes, *absolutely.*" She differentiates nicely between straight assurance and strained overassurance with "*Yes* is a comfort, *absolutely* is not."

This dramatic observation shows how the overuse of *absolutely* is weakening the word, introducing an impurity to absolution. (Yes, *absolutely* comes from the Latin *absolut*, past participle of *absolvere*, "to set free.") We in the vanguard of the anti-*absolutely* movement do not suggest that speakers go to the formal extreme of *without qualification, unequivocally, unquestionably* or the colloquially dated *yes indeedy*. But whenever one word races triumphantly through the language, are we not better off to cut it down to size? Isn't it better to live in synonym, set free from voguish convention?

You bet. Right on. Without a scintilla of doubt.

All the dialogue in *Braveheart* is "anachronistic": If the characters talked the way Scots in the 13th century actually spoke—in Middle English, or perhaps Gaelic—the film would have to be subtitled. Spotting anachronisms in the dialogue is like complaining that Claude Rains would *really* have said "Round up the usual suspects" in French.

Jim Naureckas
New York, New York

The Young Old

"Geezer strategy" was the headline of a front-page story in the *Wall Street Journal* about the attempt of CBS to woo an older audience back to the network. The lead: "The grown-ups are battling back."

Those two locutions—*geezer* and *grown-up*—run the gamut of characterizations of age. As a modifier, *grown-up* has all those good things going for it: "mature, experienced, dry behind the ears." But the last time I used *geezer* in a column—denouncing the *"geezer* power" of the most powerful lobby in Washington—a mail clerk, with a military cry of "Incoming!" dragged in a load of mail complaining of an ageist slur. These advocates of the silver set were far from T. S. Eliot's "quiet voiced elders"—one creative soul signed his blast "Gerry Atrix."

Age-ist is an awkward word, easy enough to say, harder to put on a page. The spelling *ageist*, though sanctioned by *Webster's New World Dictionary*, looks as if it should sound like a-GUYST, and when you drop the *e*, to *agist*, it seems analogous to *aginner*. The hyphen in age-ist can be used to signal the pronunciation of a hard *a* and a soft *g*, at least until the word and its *-ism* become more familiar.

Oldsters in their 60s can use *geezer* with impunity because we're ensconced in early codgerhood. The word may be rooted in *disguise:* in Scotland, the *guis-*

ers were revelers who, like mummers, dressed in ancient costumes, or *guises*, on certain holidays. (Sound farfetched? You got a better etymology, y'old coot?) With the meaning "fool," usually but not necessarily old, *coot* had its first citation in 1766; *old coot* is not redundant, while *old geezer* is; all *geezers*, no matter how sprightly, are old, just as all pups are young.

But how old is *old?* To many, it seems that the old-age clock begins to run at Social Security's 65, though the American Association of Retired Persons begins hitting you up for membership at 50. "You're as old as you feel" is a helpful adage, reminding us that age can be a state of mind.

With the general aging of the population, a differentiation is being made among the *young old* (65 to 75), the *old old* (75 to 85) and the *oldest old* (85 to 99). Beyond that is *centenarian*, a word chosen by David J. Mahoney, the philanthropist who heads the Charles H. Dana Foundation, for his seminal Rutgers commencement address, *The Centenarian Strategy*. He spoke about how the *old young*—now in their 20s, just beginning to trust anybody over 30—should plan their lives on the probability of living to 100, with worn-out organs transplanted and brain functions, especially memory, relatively unimpaired.

In the synonymy of age, *elderly*—with its comparative sense of "older than," as in "elder sister"—is the gentlest, signifying respect bordering on veneration, as in "tribal elder" and "elder statesman." As an adjective, *elderly* connotes judgment based on experience rather than only the seniority of age; as a noun, it suggests a group only approaching old age. Plain *old*, without the modifiers of *young* or *old*, deals with "advanced years" but not with degrees of physical decrepitude, first cited in this space in 1980 as "the dwindles." *Superannuated*, though fallen into linguistic desuetude, occasionally gets used to describe people pensioned or forced to retire because of arbitrary age limits. However, to be in one's *dotage*, from the Middle Low German *doten*, "to be foolish," suggests a state of near-senility, though the portmanteau pun *anecdotage* has softened that word's meaning.

Slang treats age breezily. *Granny*, from *grandam* via *grandmother*, is gaily applied in fashion's *granny glasses* and *granny dresses*, but is more poignantly applied in the abandonment of aged dependents, called *granny dumping*.

The shunning of elderly women shown by the disparaging *crone* or *hag* is to be discouraged. At the 1972 Moscow summit, Alexei Kosygin pointed to a female American reporter and asked Pat Nixon, "Who is that *bag of rocks?*" Mrs. Nixon professed not to hear. However, *no spring chicken* is acceptable, and *of a certain age* is preferred. The American equivalent of the Russian *bag of rocks* is *battle-ax*. (Spelled either *ax* or *axe*, it will get you a pocketbook in the choppers.) Wise guys who use the pejorative *gramps* are invariably called *whippersnappers*. The 1780 *fogy*, cited in 1879 as "phogey," extra military pay for long service, can be young or old, but *old fogy* is a label more derogatory of hidebound beliefs than of age.

The hypersensitive old or their unctuous caregivers are constantly plumbing the depths of the fountain of euphemism. *Senior citizen* has had its day, as have *golden years* and *sunset years*. The jocular *chronologically advanced* is a play on correctness, and *old folks* is considered patronizing.

What's good *geezer* etiquette? *Gray* is acceptable, but *silver* is the preferred adjective; forget *gold*. Those teeth in the glasses will really smile at the use of the aforesaid *grown-up*. Although *adult* has been seized by the porno crowd to describe sexy movies, that has not tarnished the adjective in the minds of what used to be known as the *Geritol set; older adult* is guaranteed to offend nobody.

The best-loved euphemism of all is *mature*. (The name of the A.A.R.P.'s publication is *Modern Maturity*, Pops, not Old-Fashioned Old Age.) In the reality-avoiding terminology of Geezerland, *mature* is to *old* what *full-figured* is to *buxom*.

When the band strikes up the Stephen Collins Foster song that begins, "Way down upon the Swanee River," substitute "Lordy" for "darkie" to bypass racism and then watch out for that last line. Ditch its reference to *old folks* and get ready for a fast fix at the end to the updated title, "Mature Adults at Home."

Zeens and Mags

Arabic has given us the word *makhazin,* meaning "storehouses." By 1596, *magazine* was applied by military men to warehouses of ordnance, and in 1731 by journalists to the superduper reading on supercalendered paper we snatch off the newsstands today.

Teen-agers who call parents *rents* call magazines *zeens* (sometimes spelled *zines,* but that triggers mispronunciation). Those of us in the media world call them *mags,* but now we stand in danger of confusion.

"When the Secret Service told me that 30,000 people had gone through the *mags,*" President Clinton told a rain-soaked crowd, "I knew you wanted to keep America on the right track."

The *New York Times* reporter on the scene, Alison Mitchell, explained to readers that *mags* were "metal detectors."

"To me, *mags* are magazines," writes Richard Weiner, who has revised the *Webster's New World Dictionary of Media and Communications,* "but in the President's case, the reference is to *magnetometers.*"

The language required a shortening of *metal detector,* because five syllables will never do. Somebody must have tried "M.D.'s," which would be confused with doctors, and "Mets," which would have recalled New York ballplayers; neither made the slangification cut. At that point, metal-detector technicians came forward with their word for the shortening, *mags,* which could only be confused with Maggs Brothers, a bibliophile's paradise on Berkeley Square in London. The Secret Service picked it up, and the clip was adopted by the President of the United States.

Some people say mag-NET-om-et-ers; many more prefer mag-na-TAH-ma-ters, but we don't need to bother our heads about that whole word, coined in 1827; it's now reissued as *mags,* setting off a loud alarm as you try to pass through with loose change in your pocket. News junkies will now have to join the teens in reading the zeens.

Dear Mr. Safire—

I have enjoyed your column for many years and I know you would not mind being set in the right direction on the word *zine* (*never* zeen). A zine is not a magazine which is big, glossy, and corporate (*Rolling Stone, Spin, Time,* etc). A zine is perceived as independant, low-rent, and usually of an extremely narrow point of view. Most zines are xeroxed and given away free, although quite a few are glossy and some zines, with enough financial backing, actually become magazines. A zine, any one can make.

This all came out of the punk culture. The first zine I recall was a xeroxed one (maybe even mimeographed at the time) called *Sniffin Glue* (circa '76). That started what was called the zine explosion.

Francis Powers
Staten Island, New York

Although you may not want to prolong the debate about the word "zine," I thought I'd put my two cents in. The word "zine" flows from fanzine, not the other way around. It originated as best I can tell in the 1940s to describe the small newsletters being produced by science fiction fans on mimeograph machines. Zine has never been short for magazine, at least not among people who produce them, and certainly not among teenagers unless they're trying too hard to be hip.

As for defining "zine," the *Wired* version works. But to me, the crucial difference between a magazine and a fanzine isn't size but motivation: A magazine is produced with other people in mind (i.e., readers and advertisers), while a zine or fanzine is produced solely for the entertainment of its creator. You're also right about the problems people have pronouncing "zine." Look no further than the *Wall Street Journal,* which recently wrote about the zine scene and gave the article the headline "Zines of the Times."

A forthcoming anthology of zine writing I've put together for Henry Holt & Co. is called *The Book of Zines.* I make a point in the introduction that zine is properly pronounced "zeen."

Here's a new word for you, in the meantime, from the zine world: magalog. That's a catalog that includes articles, i.e., both a magazine and a catalog.

Chip Rowe
Chicago, Illinois

Acknowledgments

The thankees are: Fred Cassidy, the late editor-in-chief of the *Dictionary of American Regional English*, Joan Houston Hall and Leonard Zwilling also of *DARE*, Fred Mish and Joanne Despres of Merriam-Webster, Jesse Sheidlower of Oxford North America, Margot Charlton of the *OED* on the other side of the pond, Mike Agnes of *Webster's New World*, Wendalyn Nichols of Random House, Joe Pickett and David Pritchard of *American Heritage*, and Antoinette Healey of the *Dictionary of Old English.*

OLBOM, the "On Language" Board of Octogenarian Mentors, has grown up to become, OLBONOME (rhymes with metronome): the "On Language" Board of Nonagenarian Mentors. Jacques Barzun, Alistair Cooke, and Allen Walker Read are going strong; Sol Steinmetz doesn't meet the age requirement, but I include him anyway.

Others I call upon for lexicographic or usage advice include David Barnhart of the *Barnhart Dictionary Companion;* Anne Soukhanov, editor-at-large of *Encarta Dictionary;* Connie Eble of the University of North Carolina; Allen Metcalf of the American Dialect Society; Fred Shapiro of Yale Law Library; Gerald Cohen of the University of Missouri-Rolla; Arnold Zwicky of Stanford; Ron Butters of the University of Georgia; Bryan Garner, Paul Dickson, Christine Ammer, John Algeo, David Crystal of the University of North Wales; William Kretzschmar of the *Linguistic Atlas* Project; Wayne Glowka of *American Speech;* Ron Gephart of the Library of Congress; Robert Burchfield, former editor of the *OED;* Constance Hale, Harry Newton, Laurence Urdang of *Verbatim;* and Charles Harrington Elster, the pronunciation maven.

My editors at *The New York Times Magazine* have been Rob Hoerburger, Abbott "Kit" Combes, Jaimie Epstein, Jeff Klein, Bill Ferguson, Jack Rosenthal, Adam Moss, Harvey Shapiro, and Michael Molyneaux.

My Random House group includes Pete Fornatale, Dorianne Steele, Mark McCauslin, Eli Hausknecht, and Elina Nudelman.

In addition to Jeffrey McQuain's and Kathleen Miller's language research aid, those helping me at the *Times* Washington Bureau include my assistant Anne Elise Wort, who keeps her eye out for current words, Elizabeth Phillips, my current researcher, and Todd Webb, who tries keeping up with snail mail, which I prefer to e-mail because writers devote more care to it. The Bureau's chief librarian, Barclay Walsh, and the librarians, Marjorie Goldsborough and Monica Borkowski, are always there to lend a helping hand or foot.

The saviors of my political column who keep the Gotcha! Gang at bay are Steve Pickering, Linda Cohn, and Sue Kirby.

The final thankees are the Lexicographic Irregulars, the Squad Squad, and the Gotcha! Gang. They keep me on my toes (a ballet metaphor).

Index

Edmondson, W. T., 80
effeminate, 77
effete, 77
eft, 80
egg cream, viii
egghead, 78
Eisenhower, Dwight D., 68, 237
either, 30
Elber, Lynn, 290
elderly, 368
Electronic Frontier Foundation's Guide to the Internet, 158
Elements of Style (Strunk and White), 91
Elfin, Mel, 100
Eliot, T. S., 76, 234, 236, 367
elite, 76–78
Elizabeth I, Queen, 214
Elliott, Michael, 253
emeritus, 147
Emmerich, Adam O., 20
English (spin), 287
English as world's first second language, 255–60
epanodos, 138
epistrophe, 138
epithet, 216
Erskine, Lord Chancellor Thomas, 278
eschew, 232
Eskimo words for snow, 281–82
Esquire magazine, 287
-ess suffix, 46–48
Establishment, the, 76–78
-eth suffix, 233
eupatrids, 77
eureka!, 2–3
Evans, Bergen, 170
evenhanded, 273
exclamatives, 19
exit strategy, 78–79
experiment with, 79
expletive, 216
extremism/extremist, 209, 343–45

Fabiani, Mark, 342
facially valid, 81–82
Facts on File Encyclopedia of Word and Phrase Origins, 221
Fairchild's Dictionary of Fashion, 222
Faircloth, Lauch, 175
Fairlie, Henry, 76
fair shake, 273
famously, 82–83
Farrell, James T., 147
fast-food, 139

fatwa, 161
Feikens, John, 282, 283, 284
felon, 275
Fenley, Gareth, 290
Ferguson, Sarah, 83–84
fewer and *less,* 16, 300–301, 302
Fielding, Henry, 353
fig leaf, 84, 85
Fillmore, Millard, 237
Film at 11, 158
Financial Times, 241
Finger, Bill, 122
finger sandwiches, 311
Fitzwater, Marlin, viii
fizzy water, 87
Flannery, Jeff, 256
flap/caper/scandal, 204
flaunt and *flout,* 154, 155–57, 176
Flexner, Stuart Berg, 221, 272, 348
Flinn, Kelly, 1–2
Flotus, 214
flout and *flaunt,* 154, 155–57, 176
fogy, 368
Forbes, Steve, 209, 210
Forbes magazine, 58, 100, 160
Ford, Ford Madox, 76
fore- prefix, 90
forgo, 90
for- prefix, 90
Fortune magazine, 100
$40 word, 91
Fountain, Andrew, 22
four-letter word, 91–94
Fowler, Henry W., 47, 174, 191, 240, 282, 312, 353
Fowler, Scott, 58
Fowler's Modern English Usage, 156, 191–92, 320
Frank, Barney, 211
Franken, Bob, 58
fraternization, 1–2
Freed, Alvyn M., 160
Freudian slip, 161
Friedman, Milton, 210
Friedman, Tom, 144
fringe candidate, 209
from the get-go, 337
Frost, Robert, 183, 236
fuhgeddaboutit, 94–96
Fukuyama, Francis, 144
full bore, 97
full frontal, 128–29
fund-raising, 43, 44
Fung, Dennis, 56

mull, 187–88
Mullis, Kary, 278
multiple and *many*, 74
Munro, Robin, 270
Murray, Sir James A. H., 26, 82
Murtagh, John Martin, 249
Muscatine, Lissa, 138
Muschamp, Herbert, 233
mushroom journalist, 205–6
Myers, Dee Dee, 232–33

naff, 293–94
names of people that become part of the
    language, 177–78
neck down, 189–90
neck of the woods, 256
Negro, 14
Negroponte, Nicholas, 251
Neologic Nellies, 45–46
Netanyahu, Benjamin, 76, 161, 273
Neusner, Jacob, 194
New Left Review, The, 209
New Republic, The, 53, 358
news, 55
New Scientist magazine, 253
Newsweek, 78, 100, 169, 176, 180, 203,
    218, 232, 252, 274, 327, 334
newt, 80
New Yorker, 43, 92, 155, 176, 215, 268,
    337
New York magazine, 333
New York Sun, 116
New York Times, 2, 9, 11, 32, 43, 49, 56,
    57, 67, 71, 79, 82, 90, 94, 97, 103,
    107, 112, 114, 122, 131, 145,
    151, 153, 159, 162, 184, 186,
    223, 235, 246, 253, 254, 262,
    267, 280, 287, 299, 308, 310,
    315, 322, 329, 330, 333, 334,
    354, 360, 369
  style rules, 47, 52, 58, 81, 113, 183,
    187, 261, 350
New York Times Magazine, 8, 233, 235,
    251, 330
New York Tribune, 223
New York Weekly Journal, 230
NGOs, 139
Nixon, Richard, 130, 209, 216, 237,
    344
Nobles, Charlie, 145
no ifs, ans, or buts, 355, 356–57, 359
non-junk mail, 264
noogie, 303, 305–6
Noonan, Peggy, 139
no problem, 335

Notes and Queries, 235
notional agreement, 233–34
not-so-fast element, 229
nubile, 190
Nuessel, Frank, 73, 149
nugatory, 192
Nugent, Frank S., 358
Nunn, Sam, 82
nutsy, 211–12, 213
nutty, 210–12

-o, pluralization of words ending in, 191
Ochs, Adolph, 329
O'Conner, Patricia T., 172
O'Connor, Michael, 194
of a, 202–3
offense, 62
"offense is the best defense," 62, 63
Ogden, R. M., 42
O'Hara, John, 122
oi pronunciation of *er*, 317–18
old, 368
Old Testament and *Hebrew Bible*,
    194–96
one fell swoop, 275
O'Neill, Tip, 310–11
"one picture is worth ten thousand
    words," 363–65
only and *just*, 172–73
Orlando Sentinel, 10
Ornstein, Norman J., 322
Orth, Maureen, 100
Orwell, George, 133
or what?, 149–50
Ostrogorski, Moisei, 22
Ostrom, Carol M., 169
-*out* formation, 171
outrage, 260
over, 16
over the line, 51
Oxford Companion to Popular Music,
    267
Oxford Dictionary of Quotations, 350
Oxford English Dictionary (O.E.D.), 1,
    25, 27, 28, 41, 49, 82, 97, 101,
    106, 111, 144, 145, 149–50, 153,
    162, 189, 201, 249, 261, 268,
    293, 308, 315, 316, 320, 327,
    329, 333, 337, 340, 345–46, 355,
    361, 365
Oxford English Dictionary Supplement,
    75
Oxford-Hachette French Dictionary, 316
Oxford Universal Dictionary, 263
oxymorons, 262

paid volunteers, 262
palindromes, 220
pander, 186
Pangloss, 185
panties, 222
pants, 221, 222
pantsuit, 222
paragraphing, 227–29
paramount, 223–24
Pareles, Jon, 184
parka, 135
Parker, Dorothy, 23
parliamentary, 329
Partridge, Eric, 10–11, 201, 294
password, 224–25
passwords, 224–26
pasty, 57–58
patsy, 57–58, 201
P.C., 206
peas, 232
peccadillo, 191
Peck, George, 303
penultimate, 20
People magazine, 294
Pepys, Samuel, 163
Perry, William, 109
-person suffix, 2
Philadelphia lawyer, 229–31
Phyfe, William Henry P., 346
Pierce, Norman, 250
Pinker, Steven, 281
pinprick, 231–32
Pisik, Betsy, 333
pixels, 183–84
pixilate and *pixilated,* 184–85
plan and *scheme,* 274–75
Plante, Bill, 355
Plissner, Martin, 326
plunk down, 175
plus fours, 222–23
Poe, Edgar Allan, 226
poetic allusions, 234–37
POG, 171
polenta, 301–2
political figures of speech, 237–39
Pollyanna, 185–86
polyandry/polygamy/polygyny/polygeny, 341
pooh-pooh, 53
pop, 86, 88
Popular Mechanics, 181
Porcairi, Chuck, 72
Porter, Cole, 110, 268
Porter, Eleanor Hodgman, 186
portray and *portrays,* 271

possessive of a noun or pronoun before a gerund, 183
Potus, 214
Pound, Ezra, 216
Powell, Gen. Colin, viii, 78, 82, 215
power structure, 77
Premier, 350
prequisite and *prerequisite,* 28–29
presumptive and *apparent,* 241–42
prewashed, 29
Prime Minister, 350
principles, 286
Printer's Ink, 364
problematic, 197
problemsome, 197–98
prone and *supine,* 176
pronoun-antecedent agreement, 352, 353–54
proved and *proven,* 118–19
province, 242
proximate and *approximate,* 243, 245
proximity talks, 243–44
puerile, 84
pull, 251
Pullum, Geoffrey, 281
punch in/punch on, 52
puns, 246–49, 357–60
Purdum, Todd S., 57, 114, 120
purposefully and *purposely,* 217
Purvis, Edward, 27
pushing the envelope, 250
push poll, 250–51
push technology, 251
putative, 242
put up or shut up, 218–20
Pycroft, James, 287

Qaddafi, Muammar, 162
quack, 230
quantum, 253, 254–55
quash, 291
Quayle, Dan, 76, 90
question marks, 15–16, 19
Quinn, Sally, 293
Quirk, Randolph, 33, 81, 274, 278, 320–21
quondam, 254
quotidian, 252–53

Rabelais, François, 325
rage, 260
raising and *rearing,* 139, 154
Rakosi, Matyas, 274
Randolph, R. D., 6

Stanley, Alessandra, 267
Star Chamber, 295–96
Starr, Kenneth, 295, 296–97
Steed, Henry Wickham, 244
Steele, Richard, 152
Stein, Gertrude, 319
Stein, Herbert, 62–63
Steinbeck, John, 116
Steiner, Claude, 159
Steinmetz, Sol, 106, 218, 271, 308, 330, 331, 332
Stenholm, Charles, 21
stentorian, 72
step down/step aside/stand down, 199
Stern, Howard, 172, 173
-ster suffix, 103
Stevenson, Burton, 363
Stewart, Martha, 71
Stills, Stephen, 11
Stockman, David, 8
Strom, Stephanie, 151
Strunk, William, Jr., 91
subject-verb agreement, 232–34, 318–19
submarine (verb), 277
suit, 206
Sumner, William Graham, 131
Sunday Times of London, 83, 218
superannuated, 368
supine, 297
supine and *prone,* 176
Suro, Robert, 11
surveille, 298
Sutherland, Shelley, 100–101
Swift, Jonathan, 43, 152
synod, 119
synonym use to avoid repetition of words, 282

Taiwan, 242
takeover/handover/reversion, 307–8
Talbott, Strobe, 322–23
Tamony, Peter, 250
tantrum, 140–41, 143
Tatler, 152
Tauzin, W. J. (Billy), 21
Taylor, William, 66
tchotchkes, 308–10
tea, 43, 311
temper tantrum, 140–41, 143
template, 186–87
tergiversation, 192
Thackeray, William Makepeace, 316, 353
than me and *than I,* 311–14

that's life in the big city, 279
their, 352, 353–54
there as "dummy subject," 318–19
"There is no limit to what a man can do or where he can go if he doesn't mind who gets the credit," 63–64
they shoot horses, don't they?, 349–50
thinking outside the dots or *outside the box,* 123–25
Thomas, Dylan, 276, 356
three-cornered pants, 221
through a glass, darkly, 114
thumbing one's nose, 282–83, 284
Tianen, Dave, 132
timeline/schedule/time frame, 213–15
Time magazine, 142, 169, 238, 244, 296, 320, 327, 358
Times of London, 128, 340, 360
tiu lien, 257, 258
TK, 205
to and *with,* 323–24
toast, 144–45
to be sure. . . . but, 321–23
tohubohu, 324–25
Toiv, Barry, 262
Tolchin, Susan J., 260
Toles, Tom, 60–61
tomato, 256, 259
too close to call, 325–27
Toronto Sun, 217
tortious interference, 328
tort/tortuous/torturous, 328
touchy-feely, 160
Trans Action magazine, 75
treff, 206
triangulation, 344
Trie, Charlie, 55–56
trousers, 221–22
Truman, Bess and Harry, 216–17
Tucker, Jim Guy, 6
Tucker, John, 80
Turner, Ted, 144, 290
turnout, 63
TV Guide, 178
Twain, Mark, 88–89, 114, 116, 174, 202, 204, 218–19, 238, 287
tweak, 333
Tyler, Patrick E., 131, 223
Tyson, Laura, 113

ukulele, 27
Unabomer, 334–35
unfrozen concentrate, 263
Universal Asylum and Columbian Magazine, 230

Solution to puzzle, page 124: